A BASIC
CLASSICAL and OPERATIC
RECORDINGS COLLECTION
on COMPACT DISCS
for LIBRARIES:

a buying guide

by
KENYON C. ROSENBERG

The Scarecrow Press, Inc.
Metuchen, N.J., & London
1990

British Library Cataloguing-in-Publication data available

Library of Congress Cataloging-in-Publication Data

Rosenberg, Kenyon C.
    A basic classical and operatic recordings collection on compact
discs for libraries : a buying guide / by Kenyon C. Rosenberg.
        p.   cm.
    ISBN 0-8108-2322-5 (alk. paper)
    1. Music--Compact disc catalogs.   2. Operas--Compact disc
catalogs. I. Title.
ML156.2.R73   1990
016.78'0266--dc20   90-8317

TO JANE:

FOR HER ENTHUSIASM AND ENCOURAGEMENT--
WITH LOVE,

K.C.R.

Table of Contents

Table of Contents

PREFACE

The essential reason for having written this work is exactly the same as that for which I wrote its immediate antecedent, A Basic Classical and Operatic Recordings Collection for Libraries (1987, Scarecrow Press). Taking an author's liberty to plagiarize from himself, the following quote is from the Introduction to the earlier book:

> "It is the author's hope and intention to provide school, public and academic librarians (other than those whose libraries must support the programs of music schools or conservatories) with the means for either creating or augmenting a nuclear classical and operatic recordings collection. Nuclear is here taken to mean not only the usual representative group of well-known works by easily recognized composers (e.g., the Beethoven 5th, Tchaikovsky 4th, and Brahms 1st Symphonies), but also those works of quality by, perhaps, lesser known composers which are capable of either sustaining the interests, or satisfying the curiosity of intelligent audiences. Obviously, given the constraint of space, and the expressed aim of this work, not every composer will be represented."

I apologize in advance if a favorite work, composer, or performance is not represented between these covers. The composers, works, and performances listed herein are choices made by the author. He trusts (and earnestly hopes that you will find) that these choices are judicious, and that this volume will serve both your professional and personal needs. To those who require a reference tool that is so inclusive that it reflects all their own preferences, I recommend putting this book back on the shelf, purchasing a copy of the most recent Super Schwann catalog, and choosing whatever strikes your fancy.

This book is the result of a combination of both love and madness. The love is a lifelong one for music (coupled with the irrepressible urge either to talk or write about it). The madness is evidenced by undertaking it almost immediately after finishing its predecessor.

Before beginning the current work I had written a rather extensive pair of articles in which I recommended specific compact discs (CDs) for <u>Library Journal</u> (March 1, 1987 and March 15, 1987). As a result, I received several letters inquiring into whom I thought I was to have made some of the critical statements I had written. To preclude additional such letters, I propose to introduce that portion of myself which is appropriate to my "credentials" for having written this work, and its immediate ancestor. If this kind of thing brings you to ennui easily, let me suggest that you skip directly to page xii ("Arrangement"), *subito*.

I studied percussion at the Roy Knapp Studios in Chicago, from age seven until reaching maturity at ten (the Knapp Studios produced Gene Krupa and several percussionists who perform(ed) in many major orchestras throughout the world). I then undertook trumpet studies with Ralph Killian, at the Chicago School of Music from age ten to fourteen. I also attended the School's classes in theory, harmony, and conducting. These efforts ended when my family relocated to Los Angeles (there is no truth whatever to the rumor that a member of my family was bribed by a group of neighboring music lovers to remove me from Chicago). In Los Angeles, I became a private violin student of Sascha Jacobson, onetime concertmaster of the Los Angeles Philharmonic Orchestra and, in the mid-1950s, a frequent member of an informal chamber ensemble that included Jascha Heifetz. I studied with Jacobson for about three years--my studies being terminated by our mutual agreement that my chances of becoming another Heifetz (or even another Jacobson) were about as great as my becoming the heir apparent to the throne of the Hapsburgs.

At UCLA, I audited two master classes taught by Heifetz (I have never picked up a violin since). I took courses in the psychology of music; music criticism (taught by the well known erstwhile Music Critic of the <u>Los Angeles Times</u>, Albert Goldberg); and the usual required courses in music appreciation and music history. My undergraduate major was English (minor in music) and, in my senior year, I was Editor-in-Chief of the campus literary magazine. While in graduate school at the University of Southern California, I took a course in composition taught by the relatively eminent composer, Ingolf Dahl.

I have been writing remunerated music criticism (of both live and recorded performances) since 1960 for newspapers and professional journals. I was the Classical Recordings Editor of Library Journal from 1969 to 1971, then held the same title with Previews magazine (a defunct magazine for librarians that Bowker published from 1971 through 1973--I was with them for the entire voyage).

Besides writing music criticism and reviews, I have taught courses in Music Appreciation and Music History, and a course called Reviewing the Arts for the Mass Media, in the Schools of Music and Journalism, respectively, at Kent State University. Additionally, I taught courses in the arts generally, in the Honors College, also at Kent State.

*   *   *

Arrangement

The basic arrangement of this work is alphabetical by composer's surname (spellings follow the <u>Super Schwann</u> catalog for those names that require transliteration to the Roman alphabet). Within that primary alphabet, works are alphabetical by general type (i.e., Ballet, Chamber, Choral, Concerted, Instrumental, Operatic, Orchestral, Symphonic and Vocal); then alphabetical by title, and possibly numerical by work, opus or catalog number (e.g., by the <u>Bach-Werk-Verzeichnis</u> [BWV] <"Index of Bach's Works">).

For J.S. Bach specifically, I have chosen to use the general type (e.g., Chamber, Choral, etc.), then list the works by BWV number. I have done this due to the profusion of Bach's works, and because most people can readily identify a work with only the BWV number, if necessary. I believe this should make finding individual works of this composer somewhat simpler. Where more than one performance is given, the arrangement is, again, alphabetical by performer or ensemble.

Symbols Used Herein

"*A*"	Required in every library
"*B*"	Useful in medium and large public and academic libraries
"*C*"	Recommended only for large public and academic libraries
"!"	Monophonic recording
"(TT=)"	(T)otal (T)ime per disc in minutes and seconds

"[AAD]"   Recording made from analog master,
           analog remastering, digital
           mastering for CD

"[ADD]"   Recording made from analog master,
           digital remastering, digital
           remastering for CD

"[DDD]"   Recording made from digital master,
           digital remastering, digital
           mastering for CD

A large library is here taken to mean one which serves a population of over 500,000, or an enrollment of over 15,000. A medium library is, therefore, one which serves a population of between 200,000 and 500,000, or an enrollment of between 10,000 and 15,000.

There is a Table of Contents which indicates the beginning page of each composer for whom there is an entry. Moreover, there is an Index which lists most of the included named (or nicknamed) works. The Index is arranged alphabetically on a more or less word-by-word basis. I say "more or less" because I have attempted to index only the titles, excluding the composers' names which follow the titles. In those cases of duplicate titles by different composers, the composers' surnames are then included in the indexing method. In the Index, articles (both in English and foreign languages) are dropped. Hence, Der Geist Hilft will be found under "Geist" and An American in Paris is listed under "American."

Unfortunately, not all manufacturers include total disc timings. For those discs which do not provide manufacturers' timings, I have relied on the readouts given by my CD player.

Similarly, not all manufacturers indicate how the CD material was processed (i.e., whether from analog master to analog remaster, etc.). In cases where the information was not given, I have guessed at the processes by using external evidence, to wit, the date of the original recording and whether tape hiss is very discernible. In any event, such guesses are followed by a question mark ("?"), e.g., [AAD?].

Cross references are to the "curly bracketed" numbers and lower case letters (e.g., {1}a) which precede entries and specific performances (when more than one performance is given), respectively.

Keys are given in the usual fashion, that is, lower case letters (e.g., "e") indicate minor keys while upper case letters (e.g., "E") indicate major keys.

Compact Discs: What They Are

The CD became a commercial reality in 1982. It is not in any way similar to the long playing (i.e., 33 1/3 rpm) disc (LP), which became available in 1950. The difference is most easily discerned by their relative sizes: most LPs are twelve inches in diameter, the CD is only four and seven-tenths inches in diameter (about one-sixth the area of an LP).

The long playing record (LP) was simply an extension of the older discs that were produced from 1888, having been invented by Émile Berliner (Edison's invention of ten years earlier, used cylinders, not discs). The nominal playing speed of the older discs was seventy eight rpm.

In both the seventy eight rpm and the LP, the sound to be "stored" on the disc was converted by a recording stylus to analogs of the original sound. "Analogs" are here taken to mean virtually exact replications of the sound waves flowing through the air, but miniaturized to the extent that they could fit into the small groove of the disc. Although this is an oversimplification of the process, it is accurate enough for our purpose.

The CD differs from the LP much as the analog watch (the one with hands to show the time) differs from the digital watch (where the time is displayed in discrete increments, as numbers). Several years of research and development went into the creation of the CD. Much of the refinement and standardization was done by Philips of North America and Sony. The earliest actual manufacturing was done in Japan, and, while many CDs are now manufactured in West Germany, England, and the United States, Japan still produces a very large number.

The new recordings that now come to market (both LPs and CDs) rely, essentially, on digital recording. In this process, the sound to be recorded is encoded in digital form. This sound ("signal") is fed to a computer system wherein the signal is "sampled" on average about 44,000 times a second. These "samplings" are recorded on the master tape as "data" not unlike those that a digital computer (the type we now usually use, from mainframe to micro) can "understand." In creating the CD master from the tape master, a laser burns "pits" into a disc, each pit and the space between it and the next pit representing either a binary "zero" or binary "one." In playback, a laser in the player "reads" the data on the disc. Perforce, lacking anything coming into physical contact with the surface of the CD (unlike the LP or tape, which are "read" by a stylus or magnetic "head" that are in intimate contact with the LP or tape, respectively), the CD is not degraded by repeated playing.

This master disc is replicated, in mirror image, to create what used to be called a "stamper": the disc used to create the commercial copies. The essential advantages of the CD over the LP are six:

1.   Every copy sounds exactly like the original.

2.   The devices to "read" the CDs read only the information that they should read: the recorded music and no background noise.

3.   The recording is not degraded by repeated playing. The first playing of a CD (assuming no damage, and proper storage--dust and fingerprint free and without warpage) should sound exactly like the hundredth or thousandth.

4.   The dynamic range of a digital master is much greater than that of analog recordings. At best, the dynamic range of an LP from an analog master is about thirty-five decibels. A digitally mastered CD can have a dynamic range of about ninety decibels. It must be remembered that the decibel is a logarithmic measure, hence the increase from ten to twenty decibels is not a simple doubling of loudness--it is actually an increase in loudness of one hundred times. In practical musical terms, this means that when the volume control of the receiver or amplifier is set so that a very quiet passage (e.g., "ppp") is barely audible, when a very loud passage (e.g., "fff") is encountered, the difference between the two will be one of straining to hear and then being completely overwhelmed. Very few human habitations have a decibel level below ten (because of traffic sounds, ventilation mechanisms, etc.). A decibel level of ninety-five comes close to standing near the engines of a jet aircraft. At 120 decibels, most humans experience pain and with extended exposure to such a level, permanent hearing damage can result.

5.   Overall specifications are markedly in favor of the CD. Channel separation for a CD is about ninety decibels, for an LP it is about thirty decibels. Total harmonic distortion for a CD is about five-thousandths of one percent, for an LP it is about one percent. The wow and flutter of a CD is essentially unmeasurable, for an LP it is about three-hundreths of one percent.

6.   Each CD has information encoded so that, when the CD is inserted into the player, the player's display will inform the user of the number of "cuts" (i.e., separate items, approximately equivalent

to "bands" on LPs) on the disc, plus the total playing time of the CD. Further, as each cut is played, the display can indicate the time remaining of that cut (i.e., the elapsed time for the cut). Some more sophisticated devices can display the elapsed time for the disc and for the specific cut. This is very helpful for purposes of dubbing, broadcasting, and classroom use.

Were these differences not sufficient, there are at least two more: the device in which the CD is played encloses the CD during playing, thus reducing the possibility of airborne dirt or dust landing on the CD's surface. Also, selecting a "track" on a CD is done electronically, that is, the user presses buttons to select desired tracks to be played--no longer need one worry, as with the LP, about dropping the stylus heavily onto the playing surface and damaging either or both the stylus and playing surface.

For librarians and collectors, there is one large potential drawback to the CD--its archivability. This factor is, so far, an unknown. CDs are generally presumed to have a life span of minimally five years (admittedly longer for CDs stored in ideal archival conditions). Some manufacturers project a thirty year longevity for them, but neither five nor thirty years can be accounted as being a truly archival duration. In this, as with most things (and there is some irony intended here), only time will tell.

Another drawback is the essential inability of the consumer actually to replicate a CD. One can "dub" a tape to another tape, or even an LP to a tape, and have a satisfactory copy. Dubbing a CD usually results in an inferior copy. To replicate a CD exactly, one must have the same kind of equipment that the CD manufacturer has. The only replication medium that is capable of approximating the sound quality that is available to the average consumer is the stereo videotape cassette recorder, and it does come close to the original.

Now coming onto the American market is the "digital audio tape" (DAT) in cassette form. This medium offers the potential of being able to reproduce CD dubbed tapes with the same fidelity as the original. The author has no experience with DAT, but has it from several informed sources that DAT dubbings of CDs suffer by comparison. Although not the most convenient way to archive CDs, it is possible. The author wants to make clear that he is certainly not advocating copyright infringement, just explaining the technologies.

Many CDs now being sold were originally recorded using analog means (and this includes many monophonic recordings), but have been "remastered" digitally. If the original master was fairly "clean," then the digital remastering can produce an even cleaner copy. The best sound, logically, though, is that obtained from digitally mastered recordings.

Some listeners complain that the CD has a "hard" sound. This same complaint was made when solid state devices (e.g., transistors) replaced tube-type amplifiers and preamplifiers. I think that, if good scientific research were conducted on this phenomenon, it would be found that the large majority of listeners are not used to hearing the "transparency" and clarity offered by CDs. It is this that is often confused with "hardness" of sound. Usually, a "warmer" or "softer" sound is simply a subjective description of a "fuzzy," or inferior, sound.

I should add that, as the owner of a very large collection of LPs and open reel and cassette tapes, I am not about to give them up. My personal listening is determined more by the performance than the quality of reproduction. If I have to choose between a great performance of a work that has been recorded poorly, or a mediocre performance that has been recorded splendidly, I will inevitably choose the former.

I believe this is the case with most people who are really familiar with, and care about, the music. For the newcomer to classical music, however, the sound is more often than not the means to the end of appreciating and listening to the music. I mean no disparagement to those who are impressed by technology. My feeling is that whatever brings one to listening to and appreciating any music that is worth the listening--so be it.

The CD is capable of storing up to about seventy-five minutes of sound. Those that offer only forty or less minutes of music are, to my mind, to be avoided, unless the performance is of such quality that no other recording is comparable.

Compact Discs: How to Care for Them

Because CDs are a relatively new phenomenon, the knowledge of how to care properly for them is not widely known. It is a happy fact that the CD is, for the most part, a hardier and easier medium to deal with than the LP or any magnetic tape format.

The easiest way to destroy a CD, though, is to scratch it circumferentially. A thin radial scratch, depending on the width and depth of the scratch, tends to be relatively harmless. This is so because much of the CD contains redundant musical data that is there in case small defects might be encountered that would impede the accurate "reading" of the disc.

Do not let this addition of error correction lull you into complacency. A piece of dust, a small scratch along the circumference (or a large enough radial scratch), or manufacturing imperfections can cause playback problems. Therefore, the first thing is to keep CDs clean.

The most common bane of all recording media is fingerprints. Handle the CD by its edges--just as you would an LP; and keep it free of dust. This latter is most easily accomplished by storing the disc in its container when it is not being used. Store CDs vertically. They don't warp easily, but keep them out of direct sunlight, away from heating vents, and other sources of heat.

There are several CD cleaning compounds on the market. Most of these are overpriced, and many will not do the job. Some of these are intended to remove dust and to fill in minor scratches. Try Rally cream auto wax--it's inexpensive and works well. Be sure that, whatever cleaning method you use, you employ a *very* soft and lint-free cloth in the process.

If you are in need of assistance in choosing a CD player, read the May 1987 issue of <u>Consumer Reports</u>: there is a wealth of information to be found there.

It is the author's hope that this volume will be succeeded by regular compilations which will be comprised of recommendations for classical and operatic music in all of the recorded media, including the new music video discs.

Additionally, should you have any questions with which you feel the author may be of assistance, by all means contact him through the publisher.

N.B.: The recordings whose labels bear the prefix "MHS" are available only from the Musical Heritage Society. The Society's address is: 1710 Highway 35
Ocean, NJ 07712

K. C. Rosenberg
Alexandria, Virginia

INTRODUCTION

Like every other serious critic or reviewer, I have formulated a set of precepts to which I tend to adhere when making my judgments. To understand why specific performances are (or are not) recommended herein, I will set forth my critical credo. If the following sounds similar to a philosophical tract, let the crotchets fall where they may. A caution: the word "critic" herein is synonymous with "reviewer." Similarly, by "criticism," the author intends it to stand for either "criticism" or "reviews." Any good "reviewer" ultimately writes criticism, and "critics" usually review a performance or other artwork.

I am aware that some might cavil about the distinctions to be made between "criticism" and "reviews;" and I am also aware that "criticism" denotes more in the way of theoretical and philosophical care for the subject than does the work of the reviewer. Therefore, I have defined as I have for purposes of ease and brevity: to those who wish to quibble with my non-distinctions, my exiguous regrets, gratis.

Critics serve a few basic functions, which are most easily and swiftly apprehended by simply listing them:

1.   The education of the general public by bringing to its attention performances or art works which, in the critic's mind, are worthy of notice ("worthy of notice" is construed to mean excellent, egregious, or so bland as to be a true *rara avis*). The critic must also, unfortunately, review the gamut of offerings within his or her purview, to help the public decide how best to spend its money.

2.   Having brought these items to the attention of the public, the critic serves by providing an informed judgment or opinion on the items. It is immaterial, or should be, whether the reader agrees or not with the critic; if the critic is truly informed, he or she will state the reasons for the judgment or opinion.

3.   The critic, if he or she can write sufficiently well, will express some aspect(s) of the material under consideration which the general public might feel intuitively, but not be able to express.

4.   One function of the critic which is often misunderstood, is that of provoking sufficient interest in the material under consideration. Provocation, here, is used in the sense of virtually forcing the audience to think and talk about what the value and meaning of the criticized work are.

There are few things worse than an utterly predictable and noncontroversial critic. Such a person is worse than a bore--he or she is stultified and can hold no opinions (and probably no original thoughts). This type of "critic" offers nothing about which to think, and must hold himself or herself in low esteem, indeed.

5.   A critic should always approach the work to be criticized with an open mind--this, however, doesn't mean an empty one. A good critic will prepare himself or herself as much as possible for the work under review. For musical performance, this often means a study of the score, assuming it is available, before listening to the performance. It even occasionally means following the score while listening to the performance. If the critic is not thoroughly aware of the work being performed, he or she may not notice cuts or other ostensibly logical emendations that the performers have made-- and these changes may often prove the making or undoing of a performance.

6.   A critic's open mind should extend to being willing to judge a new composition or performance by a composer or performer on its individual merits. This occurs despite previous estimations of other efforts of the composer or performer. A couple of anecdotes here may serve to illustrate the point. I had for some time believed Daniel Barenboim to be a very fine pianist (that opinion hasn't changed), but a dull conductor. My opinion of him in this regard did change, though, when, after listening several times to his performance of Tchaikovsky's <u>Romeo and Juliet</u>, I realized that what I had taken to be dullness was, in fact, exemplary tact and reticence. Barenboim explores the work with affection, but all the while avoiding the overindulgences with which many other conductors imbue this war horse.

Likewise, I had often disparaged (both in print and to myself) the dry and distant pianism of Claudio Arrau. Only after several years of exposure to this artist did I understand that Arrau is an intellectual, and not overly obvious, pianist. Although I don't always prefer his performance of a work to that of some other pianist, at least I understand that Arrau has brought a distinctive and aristocratic emotional view to the piece. Neither Barenboim nor Arrau is necessarily always for my palate; but neither are they any less than fine artists for that.

Similarly, I unashamedly admit that it took me years to understand what there was of significance in the works of Roy Harris. My estimation of him is that he was moderately talented but without compositional greatness or genius. However modest that stated estimation, it only came after repeated listening and study.

7.   Occasionally a critic will encounter a performer who really has not got the technique or the musical intelligence (sometimes neither) which allows that performer to be worth anyone's time. An honest critic will say so. It is a sad fact of life that there are people who are in lines of work in which they offer no real contribution. It is a service to the audience to inform them when this is observed.

8.   Following on the heels of number seven, above, if the benighted performer is sufficiently young, and the critic sufficiently astute, the performer may either learn something valuable or take up a more appropriate calling (those lacking musical intelligence are not welcome in the International Brotherhood of Music Critics--the musically intelligent but technically ill-equipped may enter the Novitiate, assuming they can write better than they can perform). Whatever the case, for the critic to give less than as honest an evaluation as he or she can is to dissemble, and does service neither to the performer nor the audience.

9.   The critic has the added problem of evaluating new works. This is not always a happy task since it entails putting the new offering into historical perspective. This is probably the most difficult technical function of a critic. It presupposes a relatively encyclopedic knowledge of whatever the art form is that is under review, and the

3

ability to fit this new piece into its proper area. It then requires that the critic judge the work, both on its own and in its formal and historical contexts. It is in this area that the critic is most probably made to feel like Polonius, when Hamlet persuades the poor old fool that a specific cloud is at once of several definite and different shapes.

Hearing a new work is always, in the anticipation, an unalloyed pleasure. It is the actual hearing and, worse, the subsequent evaluation, which causes many critics to have no fingernails (and very poor digestion).

The reason for this is simpler in the concrete than in the abstract. Let us assume that the American composer Roy Harris were still alive and that he had just brought forth a spanking new symphony. The first piece of critical business is of the work as a work: did it succeed in being that which it was supposed to be; was it enjoyable; did it have anything new to say; does it deserve future performances? The next consideration is that of determining (by following the score-- if one is fortunate enough to have one) how well the performers followed all the composer's wishes. And for each of these questions is the omnipresent one of "why?"

Then the hard part. How does it fit into the rest of the catalog of Mr. Harris' works? Where does it belong in the mainstream of American symphonic repertoire? What is its place in the symphonic music of Western civilization? And, for each of these questions, once more, the "why?" The more extreme the quality of the work, the more difficult the critic's job.

10. The critic, besides all the above functions, is also a kind of performer. A good critic is entertaining, engaging, and encourages his or her audience to read further and deeper in the area of concern.

Most students of music criticism agree that the greatest music critic ever to write in English was George Bernard Shaw. He served as the music critic for The Star from 1888 to 1890 and from 1890 to 1894 for The World. From 1889 to 1890, he wrote under the *nom de plume* of "Corno di Bassetto" ("basset horn"--a somewhat archaic instrument which is rather like a clarinet, but having a lower pitch). His "feuilletons," as he called them, were collected into several volumes.

In his essay "How to Become a Musical Critic" (from How to Become a Musical Critic [by] Bernard Shaw. Dan H. Laurence, ed. New York, Hill and Wang, 1961, pp 2-3, et seq.), Shaw discusses the problem of the professional music critic:

> There are three main qualifications for a musical critic, besides the general qualification of good sense and knowledge of the world. He must have a cultivated taste for music; he must be a skilled writer; and he must be a practiced critic. Any of these three may be found without the others; but the complete combination is indispensable to good work. Take up any of our musical papers--those which are taken in by the organist as The Lancet is taken in by the doctor-- and you will find plenty of articles written by men of unquestionable competence and even eminence as musicians. These gentlemen may write without charm because they have not served their apprenticeship to literature; but they can at all events express themselves at their comparative leisure as well as most journalists do in their feverish haste; and they can depend on the interest which can be commanded by any intelligent man who has ordinary powers of expression, and who is dealing with a subject he understands. Why, then, are they so utterly impossible as musical critics? Because they cannot criticize. They set to work like schoolmasters to prove that this is 'right' and that 'wrong'; they refer disputed points to school authorities who have no more authority in the republic of art than the head master of Eton has in the House of Commons; they jealously defend their pet compositions and composers against rival claims like ladies at a musical at-home; they shew [sic] no sense of the difference between a professor teaching his class to resolve the chord of the dominant seventh and a critic standing in the presence of the whole world and its art, and submitting his analysis of the work of an artist whose authority is at least equal to his own. A man may have counterpoint at his finger ends; but if, being no more than a second-rate music teacher, he petulantly treats composers of European reputation as intrusive and ignorant pretenders who ought to be suppressed--a very different thing from genuine criticism, however unfavorable, of their works--he obviously puts himself

out of the question as a member of the staff of any general newspaper or magazine. . . . A man cannot become an expert in criticism without practicing on art of some kind; and if that art is not music, then he naturally confines himself to the art he is accustomed to handle, writing about it if he has the requisite literary faculty, and if not, teaching it. . . . I need hardly say that it is about as feasible to obtain the services of a fully-qualified musical critic . . . as it would be to obtain a pound of fresh strawberries every day from January to December for five shillings a week. Consequently, to all the qualifications I have already suggested, I must insist on this further one--an independent income, and sufficient belief in the value of musical criticism to sustain you in doing it for its own sake whilst its pecuniary profits are enjoyed by others.

Obviously, the rewards of a "fully-qualified" music critic have increased somewhat since Shaw's writing, otherwise the New York Times and the Los Angeles Times, among other publications, would not have the full time critics of the prominence and stature which they do.

That most music critics, even fine ones (Shaw for example), can err (and err on several occasions) is not disputed. In 1893, Shaw wrote: "Brahms is just like Tennyson, an extraordinary musician, with the brains of a third-rate village policeman." He later publicly repented and recanted. In 1911, he wrote: "I consider that the history of original music, broken off by the death of Purcell, begins again with Sir Edward Elgar." Although he was writing of the "history of original music" in England, the flat out statement does belie a typically narrow view of the world which can still be found among many Britons. Still, his estimates of his contemporaries, as tested by the passage of time, were unusually accurate.

What pains the music critics who follow Shaw, however, is not how often he was accurate--that kind of acumen is not rare. What does gall the critic who has read Shaw on music is how much he could teach and entertain. To have that talent plus the one for drama, and to have lived as long and as well, is almost enough to have made an ordinary music critic behave as badly towards Shaw as Salieri ostensibly did towards Mozart in that wretched "vehicle," Amadeus.

What follows is an enumeration of those biases regarding performance and performers which I bring to this work. There is no defense for some of these biases any more than there is a defense for a taste for pickled herring, *id est quod id est*.

Rather than "biases" here, perhaps "informed opinions" would better express my meaning. I do not expect you to accept every one of these biases; I have too much respect for you to expect that. After all, you had the good sense to consult this book--in itself an indication of taste and informed opinion. In this matter of personal opinion, or biases, I defer to Mr. Shaw's view on the matter:

> People have pointed out evidences of personal feeling in my notices as if they were accusing me of a misdemeanor, not knowing that a criticism written without personal feeling is not worth reading . . . . The artist who accounts for my disparagement by alleging personal animosity on my part is quite right: when people do less than their best, and do that less at once badly and self-complacently, I hate them, loathe them, detest them, long to tear them limb from limb and strew them in gobbets about the stage or platform . . . In the same way, really fine artists inspire me with the warmest personal regard, which I gratify in writing my notices without the smallest reference to such monstrous conceits as justice, impartiality, and the rest of the ideals. When my critical mood is at its height, personal feeling is not the word: it is passion: the passion for artistic perfection--for the noblest beauty of sound, sight, and action--that rages in me. (Shaw on Music: A Selection on the Music Criticism of Bernard Shaw. Eric Bentley, ed. Garden City, NY, Doubleday Anchor Books, 1955, pp 34-35.)

7

Despite Shaw's being renowned as one of the earliest and most famous personages to espouse vegetarianism, one cannot but be struck by the bloodthirstiness of his choice of expression: gobbets, indeed. Enough of justification; on with the codification of informed opinions.

1.   There has never been, and never will be, a performing artist who is equally adept in all the literature appropriate to that type of artist. For example, as wonderfully well as Bruno Walter could conduct Brahms or Beethoven or Mozart, he was never really at home in the Italian or French literature for the orchestra: German music was his metier, and he wisely did not venture far or often from that metier. Another example: Jan DeGaetani is one of the best interpreters of modern vocal music to be found anywhere. But it is unimaginable that, extraordinary mezzo-soprano that she is, she would essay something like the lead in <u>Carmen</u>. Ergo, Walter and DeGaetani are two performers who, being aware of where their talents lie, eschewed areas unsuited to those talents.

On the other hand, unfortunately, not all performers are as wise. Pierre Boulez is quite comfortable conducting his own works and, say, those of Stravinsky. I don't know where to lay the blame, but for some reason CBS Records issued a performance of Boulez (with the New York Philharmonic) of the Beethoven Symphony No.5. The performance is beyond not making sense of the music--it is a prime example of how not to conduct this work: something for which teachers of musical interpretation or conducting ought to consider it. Similarly, Toscanini had a wonderful sense of how to direct Italian opera (particularly the works of Verdi and Puccini). But having read too many of his laudatory press releases and the reviews of sycophantic critics, both of which often described him as the greatest conductor in the world--ever: a conductor who could do no musical wrong, Toscanini began to believe them. As evidence of critical and conductorial error, RCA Victor, many years ago, issued a recording of Toscanini's (with the NBC Symphony) of the Sibelius Symphony No.2. It was just as bad as Boulez' Beethoven 5th, but received relatively good notices.

I could go on and on with this, but the point is: don't purchase a performance of a specific work by a favorite performer on the basis of that performer's efforts in dissimilar works. It is best to listen to it first or, failing that opportunity, rely on the judgment of someone whom you trust.

2.   There is a musical genre commonly known as "Nationalistic" (I find the term abhorrent in that it conjures, for me, images of jingoistic xenophobes. I prefer, and will use instead, the term "Ethnic"). Composers like Smetana, Dvořák, Liszt, Grieg, Sir Hubert Parry, Falla, Bartók, and Ives all fit into the commonly accepted definition of the Ethnic school. Under that definition, an Ethnic composer is one who tends to employ his or her native folk melodies and rhythms; and allusions to, or quotations from, well known musical works of his or her country. Ethnic composers also, supposedly, frequently attempt to emulate musically their native speech patterns. Sibelius and Janáček are two such who attempted this latter effect rather often, and ostensibly did it effectively.

Ethnic compositions are very tricky in performance. Such works require an intimacy with the native culture that most foreigners seldom acquire. That it can be acquired is evidenced in the performances of Central European composers (most notably Enesco and Janáček) by the American born (of Australian parentage) conductor, Sir Charles Mackerras. Mackerras is even capable of obtaining musically informed performances of Janáček's operas, with non-Czech performers--so fine is his grasp of the Central European musical milieu. This apparent anomaly is resolved when one is aware that Mackerras studied conducting with Václav Talich--the preeminent Czech conductor of the first half of this century (also among his students was Karel Ančerl). Mackerras remains, nonetheless, an anomalism (there is more than one).

For an obvious example of how difficult it is to become sufficiently imbued with a foreign culture to be able to interpret its music properly, Gershwin serves our purposes. Gershwin used many jazz elements in everything he wrote, including the concert pieces <u>Rhapsody in Blue</u> and <u>An American in Paris</u>. Most American

9

listeners take this for granted, only unconsciously realizing that Gershwin is among the most "representative" of American composers because of these jazz elements.

American orchestras and instrumentalists have little trouble interpreting Gershwin (and many even overcome the formidable technical difficulties in his piano works)--they "understand" his idiom because it is part of their cultural heritage. Most Americans assume, because of their own familiarity with Gershwin's music, that musicians unfamiliar with American music, Europeans say, ought to be able to play Gershwin as readily, and with the same understanding they bring to the music of Beethoven, or Grieg, or Sir Edward Elgar.

That this is not true goes without saying. Just compare the recording of Gershwin's Second Rhapsody by pianist Teodor Moussov (with the TVR Symphony) with that of almost any American pianist and orchestra. Where has the very essence of Gershwin gone? But then, the inverse is also true. Karel Ančerl's version (with the Czech Philharmonic) of Janáček's Sinfonietta is quite a different work from the performance by Simon Rattle (with the Philharmonia Orchestra). The quality of the performers is not in question. The Philharmonia Orchestra is safely in the first class of the world's orchestras, the Czech Philharmonic is either at the nether end of that rank, or the front rank of the next. It is a matter of, as one of my learned musical friends likes to say, "having the music in your blood and heart, not just in your head."

What this leads to is Rosenberg's Axiom Number 9: "Regarding specific Ethnic music, the best performances will tend to come from members of that Ethnic group." As noted previously, every axiom will have its exceptions or anomalies but, by and large, this one holds.

3.   Rosenberg's Axioms Numbers 1 through 8 do not pertain to music, so here is Number 10: "A composer is not always the best interpreter of his or her own music." Number 11 is the inverse of Number 10 or, rephrased, "A composer is sometimes the best interpreter of his or her own music."

Examples abound for both of these axioms. Ravel could not play his own compositions as well as other pianists or conductors. Although Stravinsky's recorded performances reveal much about Stravinsky as a conductor (and are important historical documents), his work is often better served by conductors like Monteux, or Ansermet, or Boulez, or Bernstein, or Haitink.

Yet Copland does extremely well by his own works, just as (expectedly) Bernstein interprets Bernstein incomparably (and his Copland is outstanding, too). Paganini supposedly was just about the only violinist of his own time who was even willing to play his own excruciatingly difficult violin works. Wagner may well have been the best conductor of Wagnerian operas ever; the same with Mahler and his own works.

The lesson to be learned here is very simple: one should be aware of the composer's limitations as a performing artist and never assume that the composer is the last word on interpreting his or her own compositions.

4.   Every critic has favorite performers, and also a list of performers he or she considers less than tolerable. A good critic can (and, at the drop of a baton, will) tell you why. Not only will a good critic tell you why, but will tell you why honestly and with cogent reasons. If these reasons are less than compelling or convincing to you, at least the ultimate difference between you and that good critic should devolve to a *je ne sais quoi*.

No one should be summarily shot or dismissed on matters of taste. The good critic understands that in matters of art, there is a domain which will always be beyond reason and logic--and that domain is just as valid as reason and logic. The good critic will always hope, however, that his or her powers of persuasion will ultimately prevail; of such things are sporting events and parimutuel betting made. *Basta!*

5.   Since nothing in our human experience is perfect, there is no such thing as a perfect performance. It follows then, that there is no such thing as a perfect recorded performance. Every honest performer knows this and will be glad to tell you, immediately after a performance, just how he or she failed this time. With good

11

performers the failures vary from performance to performance: this is an indication of having learned from previous failures. Bad performers, no matter how honest, just keep making the same mistakes, and their accounts of these failures are performances of a different sort.

There are performances that so closely approximate one's ideal that, for all purposes, they are perfect. When a critic has encountered such a one, he or she still has the obligation to try to imagine how the performance might have been improved. Without this attempt, both critics and performers will ultimately accept the routine as excellent.

This is why so many performers record the same works over and over. Each performance is one from which those performers have learned something, and they do not want to leave a legacy that does not include what was learned. It is a noble effort (in my altruism, I must leave all question of royalties to those who would sully art with such thoughts).

I only wish that those performers who could never properly perform a work to begin with would leave it alone, rather than picking at it as if, miraculously by repetition, tedium, or agony, their efforts will somehow become transmuted into insight or joy. So seldom does it happen that the effort is not worth anyone's time.

6.   Very infrequently a miracle does occur. A performer who is by most lights not considered great, will reach down into himself or herself and come up with a performance ranking with the very best. It does happen, but consider such an accomplishment as rare as turning ordinary American drinking water into something truly potable.

7.   The child prodigy and the overnight success are to be looked upon as creatures who must prove their worth over many successful years of performance, that is, to be eyed initially with suspicion. Eighty percent are accidents. Fifteen percent of the "overnight successes" have been striving at their art for years and were given a large audience by chance. They haven't been hiding--their luck was. Four percent are mistakes of judgment (or the result of very good marketing and promotion). To this rule there are virtually no exceptions (to prevent letters citing this or that *Wunderkind* or

recently discovered "genius," remember, I said "*virtually*" no exceptions). Happily, most of the accidents and mistakes usually disappear as quickly as they arrived, thus giving credibility to Andy Warhol's statement about everyone achieving fame for fifteen minutes. Be of good cheer, however: there still remains that one percent.

      8.   This last item is not so much a bias but a brief discussion on the differences between art and artifice, and emotion and passion.

      Art is a subject which finds its way into everyday parlance so often that most of us tend to assume we know precisely what is meant by it. In the realm of aesthetics there are as many definitions given to the term "art" as there are aestheticians. Philosophically, most of these definitions have kernels of truth in them. As I do not intend this to be a philosophical treatise on aesthetics, let's assume that we understand art to consist of the perceptions of an individual which combine such factors as uniqueness, skill or craft, beauty, etc., and which provide others with an insight into verities or aspects of life which they themselves could not create on such a level. There is, then, in art, something of universality, besides those other factors I mentioned before.

      Artifice, obviously, is not art. Artifice is usually the creation of either an excellent craftsman, sans the inspiration of the artist; or artifice is the work of a trickster who may or may not be a good craftsman. There are many composers and performers who are artificers but not artists. The real genius of the work of artists is as inexplicable as the "explanation" given for the compositions of Mozart created before he was fifteen: it was said, simply, that he had been "kissed by God." Before such genius, this "explanation" will suffice. Artifice, though, is all around us and much of it is kitsch. It can be found in the "music" which is piped into elevators, in the "art" of magazine advertisements, in the way we greet or farewell one another, and on and on.

One can find a great deal of artifice posing as art in music. The majority of the "compositions" of John Cage (and others who practice "aleatory" music--if such an oxymoron can exist) is artifice and audiences are gulled by it. So are such works as the "found" pieces of Fritz Kreisler: works he claimed to have discovered and were ostensibly written by composers of the 18th century, but which were his own, and which lacked the genius of the composers to which they were attributed. So is much of the music written by competent Soviet composers: music skillfully written to satisfy the formulaic requirements of the Soviet state (and some of this artifice, unfortunately, written by men of real talent).

If we can find artifice in the composition of music, we can also find it in the performance of music. Howard Mitchell, the onetime music director of the National Symphony Orchestra (Washington, D.C.), was an artificer. He looked dashing in his tails (and he certainly pleased the eye), could read music, and "led" the National through works of which he seemed to have only the slightest understanding. Currently, in this country, we have placed several such figures on podia before orchestras and assumed them to be men of talent or genius because they "looked right" in these positions. Haven't we done the same with some men elected to the Presidency?

Not only do we have artificers as conductors, we have them as soloists. Van Cliburn is one example, Itzhak Perlman (to some extent) is another. For Van Cliburn there is an excuse: little talent; but for Perlman to waste a real talent because he is loath to practice enough is inexcusable. At least Perlman is capable of turning in a superb performance occasionally, but his work is often that of an artificer because he apparently works just hard enough to get by as a fine, instead of a great, violinist.

Perhaps I'm wrong about Perlman, perhaps the technical facility is there but not the intellect. In contrast, Pinchas Zukerman appears to have not only the technique and intellect, but also the discipline and energy required to be a great musician.

14

I began this section writing not only about art and artifice, but also of passion and emotion. In these two latter there also often appears to be some confusion.

Emotion (when defined as "feeling") is a fine thing and is, to a degree, the commerce of art. I know of no work of art worthy of the name which is without emotion. If a supposed work of art does not inspire emotion it is only a dead and useless exercise. It is the artist's job so to construct his or her work as to evince emotion in his or her audience. Naturally, the truly great artists also imbued their works with intellectual content. As Moby Dick is a tale which is filled with emotion, so is it filled, too, with intellectual perceptions about man and nature and destiny, and how all these are intertwined. Equally emotionally and intellectually laden are the late quartets of Beethoven, or Mozart's opera Don Giovanni, or Rembrandt's The Night Watch, or Goethe's Faust.

It is assumed that the reader is fully cognizant of the differences between true emotion (and its little brother: sentiment) and sentimentality. I offer two musical examples to distinguish between these: the last movement of Tchaikovsky's Sixth Symphony "Pathétique" and MacDowell's "To a Wild Rose" from his Woodland Sketches. The former is, as some are wont to say, "jam packed" with emotion--that is, real feeling (although it can, in incompetent performing hands, seem to wallow in self-pity). The MacDowell work, though, is pure sentimentality, replete with all the symptoms of that malaise: superficiality, a trite "prettiness," and a commonness which is essentially vulgar. Admittedly, the "Wild Rose" may be a bit beguiling when performed with reticence, but such is true of virtually all music which offers no more than sentimentality. Besides, no music ever really suffers from some reticence in performance--that is what provides some of the "aesthetic distance" which is related to the "objective correlative" of the old New Critics (and even Kant).

15

Passion in art, however, is a somewhat different thing from emotion. Passion often transcends what we term emotion. It is unfortunate that we often use passion to mean so transcendent an emotion that it is without intelligence, or imagination, or intellect: such a construction is an error. Passion, at least in art, is the supreme combination of emotion and intellect and imagination. It is the coming together of the best of affective and cognitive creation. We are most used to finding artistic passion in but a few works (Bach's <u>St.</u> <u>Matthew</u> Passion serves as one glorious artistic example, a few of Mozart's and Beethoven's symphonies also so serve). More often we encounter passion in performance, and that but very rarely.

What is interesting about passion in performance is that it is often mistaken for "distance" (in the sense of aloofness) or "coldness" because of its virtual perfection. A high level of cognitive skill coupled with profound affect (no and *pace*, I did not misspell "effect") do not alone combine to form passion: that is where the error lies.

There is another necessary ingredient: an almost unbelievable technical facility. So great must this technical facility be that it calls no attention to itself. Great performing artists put aside (in the sense of not thinking about) technique--they do not have to think about it because it has become a second nature to them. They ultimately think about it probably as often as we think about the physical technicalities involved in walking, or picking up a cup of tea. It is a facility so well learned and practiced that it no longer requires conscious effort (how long it may have taken to develop and maintain such a skill, however, is another matter). Lastly, the performer should simply be the "device" by which all three of these factors are presented to the audience.

Such performers as those of which I am writing are so rare that they are almost non-existent. Technical facility without being coupled to intelligence and imagination, one should remember, is similar to some great Nimrod who cannot distinguish between a properly hunted beast and a human being--our Nimrod may kill either, but the rewards or penalties, depending on the target, are quite different (assuming there is an audience or posse which can offer rewards or impose penalties: in art, this is an epitome of the role of the critic).

Much as I usually dislike his interpretations, many of Toscanini's symphonic performances conveyed something of passion, although very often there was more of zeal than passion. There is true passion, though, in the surpassing fine 1951 Bayreuth performance of the Beethoven Symphony No.9, conducted by Wilhelm Furtwängler. In the Furtwängler recording, the passion is most obvious in the last movement, but it is there throughout the first three movements, too. An oddity in the last movement of this performance is that the passion is so intense, and the orchestra so hard pressed, that some lapses occur; but these are almost endearing because they indicate the intensity of the emotion of the moment. Contrast this recording with that of Toscanini and the NBC Symphony and the absence of true passion in Toscanini's version becomes apparent. Toscanini's reading is excited and even a bit febrile, but it is not passionate, it is too slick and superficial.

The recorded performance of the Beethoven Violin Concerto by Heifetz (with Toscanini)--a live performance of a radio broadcast-- has real passion; here the interplay of conductor and soloist possesses such tautness, intensity, and perfection, that other performances of the work become but mere shadows of the music. So does Fischer-Dieskau's recorded performance (with Furtwängler) of Mahler's Lieder eines fahrenden Gesellen.

Where passionate performances do exist, they are frequently, as I wrote earlier, misconstrued by their audiences. For example, it was often claimed that Heifetz was a "frigid" performer because his playing was so "perfect." Pity for those who could not understand that what Heifetz was bringing to his performances was a combination of technical skill and intellectual and emotional involvement so great and deep that mere posturing or idiosyncrasies would have been obscene and profane. Heifetz was not the only such performer, but he

17

serves well because there were so many who maligned him for what were his attributes, and missed the whole point of what really constitutes the passionate in performance. They fail to understand that mannerisms and affectations are only distractions practiced by the artificer, not the artist.

I have not dwelled on the need for integrity in the performer (i.e., to play the piece as closely as possible to what the composer wrote in the score [and, insofar as possible to ascertain what the composer's wishes were when the latter could not be recorded in the score]) because that should be self-evident. Similarly, the great performers exhibit not only imagination but also, for want of a better word, "taste." This I would define as knowing how much of one's own artistic self to inject into the music and when to stop. It is something which a performer like Jean-Pierre Rampal has but James Galway does not. Taste could also be defined as intelligent restraint, or the kind of modesty which leaves the audience wishing for more (of whatever "it" is, knowing the performer can provide more of "it," but also knowing that getting more would be a surfeit). In the performing arts other than music, there is no better example of intelligent artistic restraint than the late Laurence Olivier.

I have mentioned musical intelligence several times in the foregoing. To recognize it presupposes, if not an intimacy with the score, at least a real familiarity with the music which can come only from hearing it often, and in a variety of performances. What it consists of or how it is evidenced is not easy to describe. A few examples of how it may be found will perhaps provide an idea of what I mean. Take Chopin's Andante Spianato and Grande Polonaise, Op.22 in the version for solo piano--one of his greatest works. Almost any pianist with a recording contract can play all the notes which Chopin put into this piece. This alone, obviously, does not a performance make.

In most of Chopin's music generally, and in the Op.22 specifically, the slow portions can be rendered meaningless or boring by just playing the notes as written. To infuse the music with the emotional content and poetic form of expression which were "built into" the work by the composer requires the kind of intelligence which understands that the relationships of adjacent notes will vary by how much or little silence is allowed between them.

This understanding doesn't come solely by studying the score. It also comes from listening to the performances of others, from trial and error at the instrument, and from sensitivity to nuance. This "spacing" of the notes is somewhat allied to the tempo at which it is taken--and one needs to distinguish between tempo and rhythm (the former is more or less a prerogative of the performer, the latter is a designation most often given by the composer). An aspect of tempo common in Chopin is the use of *rubato*. The application of rubato should be essentially insensible to the listener (unless that listener is a very acute one). If rubato is obvious it is not rubato but an exaggeration which may become either affectation or sentimentality or both. Artur Rubinstein's recording of the Op.22 is a good example of how properly to use rubato.

Another indication of intelligence is the performer's ability to find the "arch" of a melodic line and convey it without distorting those portions of the work which support the arch. That is to say, to present a melody coherently without distracting the listener from the totality of the piece. This ability can be heard in the performances of the Brahms symphonies by Bruno Walter.

A great work of art owns a specific kind of reality which makes sense when it is properly realized. The realities of a Mozart opera and a Bach organ work are very different, but no less real or great for that. The principal duty of a performing artist is to present that specific reality to the audience and, by doing justice to the work, to provide it a "rightness" that is so convincing that the perceptive listener will say to him or her self: "Yes! That is the way it ought to be." A truly great work will allow for an infinity of diversity in performance, but only if those performances bring that reality and rightness with them.

I have discussed numerous aspects of criticism and performance in the foregoing pages, but I have not dealt directly with what is, in the case of this work, the primary topic of that criticism: music.

There are hundreds, if not thousands, of definitions of music and most are, unfortunately, either noninformative or confusing. Most of us know what music is, so I will not add to that profusion of definitional frenzy. Rather, I would ask the reader to keep a few points about music in mind.

Music, in performance, is ephemeral. Unlike a work of literary or graphic art, the details of performed music cannot be lingered over at one's own leisure. Even performed dramatic works, because they are comprised of comprehensible words, can be mulled over as the drama proceeds--not so with music. Like a portion of thread pulled from a large skein, performed music disappears before our ears (a mixed metaphor, but better than none) as the next portion comes forward. In that sense, music in performance is the most demanding of our attention of all the performing arts, with the possible exception of dance (and I'm not too sure about dance, since it is both visual and aural--the involvement of two senses seems to leave less to attention or imagination than that of one).

There are three basic components of music (if one leaves out harmony--something fairly often done nowadays): form, rhythm, and melody. Without all these components being present, one has only the semblance of music ("noise" to purists). The quality of music as an art does not "improve" or "progress" over time or through history. There is movement backward and forward, for example, away from polyphony and, years or centuries later, back to polyphony, etc.

20

Music may evolve and, by accretion, gain additional insights or "rules," but the quality is not disturbed. There are basically but two kinds of music: good and bad. The ultimate determinant of which is which is what is called, in the cliché, "the test of time." As with many clichés, there is sufficient truth in this one for it not to be dismissed offhandedly.

Albeit, as there are good and bad musics, there are good and bad listeners. To be a good listener means to pay attention, to allow the music to stand on its own, and to be open to what is new. Good listeners are also demanding listeners. At one time it was the custom to be sufficiently outraged at a bad performance to boo and hiss the performers. It is too bad that this civilizing custom has given way to obedience to the nonsensical "manners" which dictate that because you spent good money to hear a performance you must politely bear with incompetence. On this point, as on many others, Shaw was right in thinking most audiences to be made up of sheep. The tolerance of mediocrity has spread throughout our entire social structure and is a greater contagion than one might initially think. That it has extended to what most people will accept in music should not be surprising.

There is no injunction prohibiting every person from being his or her own critic. If any such learning is of worth or pleasure, then perhaps the following work (on the next page) by an unknown but contemporary Rumanian poet (translated by this writer) may provide a small indication of the labor required by both the artist and those who would be their own critics:

21

ARS POETICA ET CRITICA

The easiest thing is to quote one's self
        repeatedly
And try to make triumphs of the past.
What a bore. That's the whore's
Way of inspiring passion: do only what worked before.
But newness, the fearful essay into what at
First is fog, and if it maps, explore
The limits until the light fades
And forces the pen to newer plains and caves.
Then, to select those few whose impalpable universality
(And yet which are sufficiently esoteric that
The heart is never accurately guessed)
Gives the critics pause, the poet rest
To work the next.
Still, newness is all but not everything;
There must be recognition's ring
Or else the work is of itself and lost between
Blankets of blindness and weights of narcissistic yeas.
The whites and grays and blacks are only shades
        of shades.
Heat comes after. Heat and fashion.
If not of ardor and of its time, the verse
Means only rime: the poetry dead on the tongue.
And in the end, the cleavage must be such
That thought and art (wrung from what alone the heart knows)
Then combine to leave no seam:
At once real, at once dream.

PERFORMERS: THE GOOD, THE BAD AND THE BORING

This section is an exegesis on several of those performers most often encountered in recorded performances. Many of these are relatively brief but, I hope, incisive. Please remember that the following descriptions are the opinions of the author (and being a reasonable person, he thinks, are open to change or disputation, as necessary). For greater detail on the professional and personal lives of individual musicians, I recommend the latest edition of Baker's Biographical Dictionary of Musicians (Schirmer Books, a Division of Macmillan Publishing Co.) as probably the most authoritative, up-to-date, carefully prepared, and most easily found single reference work of its type.

Symphony Orchestras

Academy of St. Martin-in-the-Fields--organized (in 1959 by Sir Neville Marriner) as a rather large chamber orchestra, it has grown to a virtually full-sized symphony orchestra, but only occasionally essays the orchestral repertoire of the late Romantics, which calls for a larger ensemble (e.g., Brahms or Mahler). It specializes in the literature of the Baroque and Classical periods, and throws in a little early, light Beethoven. It can also be heard in some of the works for smaller groups by those such as Ravel, Debussy, Grieg, etc. It appears to be the most recorded orchestra of its size represented in current catalogs. Its sound is bright and airy and the ensemble tends to eschew period instruments in its performances. For what it does, it does very well, but it is neither equal to any of the world's outstanding full-sized orchestras, nor to some of the very best true chamber orchestras. Many of its recorded performances tend to be on the dull side.

Amsterdam Concertgebouw Orchestra--one of the world's greatest orchestras. It has had a long and distinguished history (its last three conductors were Willem Mengelberg, Eduard van Beinum and Bernard Haitink; its newly appointed music director is Riccardo

23

Chailly) and is renowned for its dark, warm sound. Despite this abundance of warmth, the texture of the orchestra is exceptionally transparent--particularly with extremely good conductors before it. The Concertgebouw is at its ease playing anything in the orchestral repertoire, from Beethoven to Stravinsky and back to Handel. The Concertgebouw is capable of an incredible dynamic range and, despite its overall darkish sound, a great variety of color. It is the only orchestra whose performances I refuse to miss, so long as it is playing within a fifty mile radius of my home. The only caution I would offer concerning Concertgebouw recordings is that, when an Englishman is on the podium, although the orchestra still sounds terrific, it may lack the impetus provided by Continental conductors.

Bavarian Radio Symphony Orchestra--a much recorded and often overrated orchestra. In its palmiest days, under Eugen Jochum, it could attain great heights, but it seldom achieves them anymore. It probably falls in the middle of the second rank of world class orchestras. It has never been less than competent, and the sound it produces is nothing more nor less than that of a typical German orchestra: darker than its American counterparts. Under some conductors (currently and specifically, Sir Colin Davis and Rafael Kubelik), the Bavarian can play over its head, and deliver great performances--but don't count on this happening often. Its new music director is Sir Neville Marriner.

Berlin Philharmonic Orchestra--one of the world's oldest and best. Known for its superb strings, its overall sound is very mellow and warm, but not quite as much as the Vienna Philharmonic, and certainly a bit brighter than the Amsterdam Concertgebouw. The rest of the Berlin's sections are far better than good. It was, for a long period, the domain of Herbert von Karajan. The Berlin is quite responsive to other conductors, and is able to change its character, to some extent, for them. The Berlin is most at home in performing works preceding the 20th century, in particular the music of those such as Beethoven and Brahms. It works well with similar material, e.g., Mahler, Bruckner, Wagner. Occasionally, it will essay such moderns as Stravinsky, but these efforts usually succeed only when an extraordinary conductor is on the podium. Its new conductor, Claudio Abbado, should enable this venerable ensemble to recapture some of the passion and vigor which was lost under von Karajan.

Berlin Radio Symphony Orchestra--a group that is good primarily for accompanying fine soloists. Although well represented in record catalogs, when the Berlin Radio is on its own, this orchestra (usually conducted by nonentities) tends to deserve little notice.

Boston Symphony Orchestra--among the top five orchestras of the United States. The first recognition of its true greatness came primarily during the years that Serge Koussevitzky was its permanent conductor (1924-1949). The Boston has good strings, and the other sections are at least competent (for a time it had unusually fine brasses and flutes). In the last several years, it has lost (mostly through retirement) some of its eminent first desk personnel. It will try any kind of music, and its efforts are never truly bad. Sometimes, when pushed too hard, the orchestra may have ensemble problems. Its overall sound is somewhat "American" (i.e., brighter and cooler than, say, the Berlin or Vienna Philharmonic Orchestras), but the Boston is seldom hard or cold sounding. The Boston is excellent in its interpretations of French, Russian, and American composers. Ordinarily, it doesn't succeed as well with the Germans.

Budapest Philharmonic Orchestra and **Budapest Symphony Orchestra**--two good orchestras which perform the works of Central Europeans with precision and security. Don't count on them for much more.

Chicago Symphony Orchestra--one of the newer of the five best American orchestras (giving its first performances, as the Chicago Orchestra, in 1891). As one of the five best which this country has to offer, I rank it as *primus inter pares*. It has had a succession of extraordinary music directors: Artur Rodzinski, Rafael Kubelik, Fritz Reiner, Jean Martinon, and Sir Georg Solti. The sound of the orchestra is full and brilliant, clear and clean, and the ensemble is, by and large, exquisite--much of this owing to the influence of both Kubelik and Martinon. Daniel Barenboim has been recently selected to succeed Solti, beginning with the 1991-1992 season. It, like the Amsterdam Concertgebouw, can easily perform anything in the orchestral literature. It can handle, with ease, the difficulties of Mahler or Stravinsky or Saint-Saëns, and provide refreshing performances of Tchaikovsky or Beethoven.

Cincinnati Symphony Orchestra--one of the better American "secondary" orchestras, the Cincinnati was founded in 1894 and among its Music Directors were Leopold Stokowski, Fritz Reiner, Sir Eugene Goossens, Max Rudolf, and Thomas Schippers. The high level of musicianship of both Rudolf and Schippers was maintained by Michael Gielen, and the Cincinnati can be counted on for excellent performances of works of the Romantics and modern composers. The orchestra has not yet reached the level of the St. Louis or Detroit, but there are hopes for this ultimately happening under its new music director, Jesús López-Cobos.

Cleveland Orchestra--among the five best American orchestras, and probably was, for a time, the best example of the "American" orchestral sound: bright, accurate and secure, with a plethora of energy. When Lorin Maazel became music director, the Cleveland attained a warmer, more European, sound; but still has that "direct" and forward sound peculiar to the better American orchestras. The Cleveland has been fortunate in having as its last three conductors George Szell, Lorin Maazel, and Christoph von Dohnányi. Although the strings of the Cleveland are good, its real strength has been in its winds. The Cleveland can handle all the traditional repertoire for orchestra, and is quite good with modern music.

Columbia Symphony Orchestra--an orchestra which has varied greatly in quality since its personnel have also varied greatly. A "pickup" orchestra, the Columbia was at its most distinguished under

Bruno Walter. Because of its variability, its overall quality depends essentially on who wields the baton. Walter, Szell and Copland have made some fine recordings with this "orchestra without a home."

Czech Philharmonic Orchestra--in the very front of the second rank (or rear of the first rank). The Czech is peculiar among major orchestras in that its strings almost invariably play pizzicati with no vibrati (most noticeable in the basses and 'celli). It has a rather delicate sound--not precious nor small, but precise and lovely. It tends to sound warmer than American orchestras, but not as darkly colored or warm as its German or Dutch equivalents. Not surprisingly, the Czech does well by music of Bohemian or Czech composers (it does Dvořák and Smetana quite understandingly and beautifully), but it can also handle Beethoven (not so good with Brahms) and many modern composers.

Detroit Symphony Orchestra--in the forefront of the second rank of American orchestras. The Detroit is an almost world class orchestra, but currently lacks world class direction (Günther Herbig is hardly in the class of previous Detroit music directors like Paul Paray or Antal Doráti). It is a very capable orchestra, typical of the "American" type: paying attention to attacks and releases, good winds and adequate strings, and a less warm sound than the best European orchestras. Now, only when the likes of a Doráti is at the helm (who, until his death, was Conductor Laureate) is the Detroit regularly to be expected to make great music.

Dresden State Orchestra--so similar to the Bavarian Radio Symphony Orchestra that the comments there suffice here, too.

Hungarian State Orchestra--the best of the Hungarian orchestras (that still leaves it somewhere in the second rank). Comments for the Budapest orchestras also pertain to the Hungarian State, but its level of playing is higher that either of those other two.

27

Israel Philharmonic Orchestra--a world class orchestra, probably at the front of the second rank. It has varied in quality under different conductors. Its sound can be muddy because of its rather lush strings, but the overall competence is good. It is big, and a bit overly Romantic in its fulsomeness for my tastes, but it does well under Bernstein and Perlman. Its worst features seem to be most apparent when Mehta takes charge.

Leipzig Gewandhaus Orchestra--once headed by Felix Mendelssohn, this orchestra has fallen into disrepair since those days. Once in the very forefront of all orchestras, it is now at the rear of the second rank. There are some who think this a truly distinguished orchestra, but they are wrong. The Leipzig often has poor ensemble, bad intonation in the winds, and is generally limited insofar as the quality of the conductors who record with it.

Leningrad Philharmonic Orchestra--a much overlooked and underestimated orchestra. It exemplifies the best in the Russian style of orchestral playing: solid strings, excellent winds; and the worst: a tendency towards too much vibrato in the trombones (and sometimes in the horns). The sound can be brilliant (not hard), and resembles some of the better French orchestras. Under Mravinsky or Rozhdestvensky, this orchestra can offer truly fine (occasionally great) performances.

London Philharmonic Orchestra--one of the five orchestras based in London (along with the London Symphony, National Symphony Orchestra of London, the New Philharmonic Orchestra, and Royal Philharmonic Orchestras). The London Philharmonic falls, in quality somewhere in the middle of the batch. As with many major British orchestras, there is great competence here. Some of the distinctiveness of English ensembles derives from more vibrato in the woodwinds than Americans are used to or that Germans or even Russians employ. The London Philharmonic is solidly second rank

28

and will vary greatly with its conductors. Its overall sound is moderately warm, but undistinguished. It is an excellent accompanying ensemble.

London Symphony Orchestra--currently the most recorded orchestra in the world. The London Symphony is the best of the London symphonic groups, and it deserves a place in the front rank of world orchestras. It is capable in any repertoire (although the quality will be determined by who is holding the baton), and is possessed of a good, relatively warm, sound. Still, I sometimes find the overripe sound of its double reeds obtrusive. At the time of this writing, Michael Tilson Thomas is taking over the position of principal conductor of the London Symphony--perhaps, with the appointment of this American, some of the "untoward" British sound of the orchestra may be ameliorated.

Los Angeles Philharmonic Orchestra--had a chance to become a great orchestra when Eduard van Beinum took over, but he died soon after his appointment and was succeeded by Zubin Mehta. Since then, it has been the worst primary orchestra of any major city in the U. S. It had a chance to grow under Carlo Maria Giulini, but he didn't stay long enough. It is too early to tell how far Esa-Pekka Salonen, its new director, can bring this group, since Mehta left it as an almost musical joke.

Louisville Orchestra--a delightful and strange ensemble, its recordings being devoted almost exclusively to new composers. It is a somewhat small orchestra (at times verging on chamber size) and its sound is clean, but dry. Its tradition of championing modern composers is noble and, although not everything it plays is worthy of repetition, its efforts are extremely good. It is not nearly a world class orchestra, but is competent and deals with challenges to which not many other orchestras would care to respond regularly. Since 1985, the Louisville's music director has been Lawrence Leighton Smith.

Luxembourg Radio Orchestra--has recorded much and seems to specialize in French and Russian (including Soviet) composers, but has recorded some music of the Hungarian and German masters, too. The general sound of the Luxembourg tends towards the French in its clean winds, but there is a touch of the German in its good string sections. It's a solid second-rate orchestra with but a few pretensions. Some of its recordings are distinguished, most are run-of-the-mill.

Minnesota Orchestra--better than the Detroit is now, but not on par with the American "big five." Until 1968, it was the Minneapolis Symphony Orchestra. It has retained, from its Doráti days (1949-1960) a clean, open sound, and can come up with gangbuster performances. It has always had remarkably fine winds, and its strings are excellent. After the departure of Skrowaczewski (1960-1979), Sir Neville Marriner's stewardship did little to add to its luster. Under Edo de Waart's direction, the Minnesotans may well force the "big five" to become the "big six."

Montreal Symphony Orchestra--since Charles Dutoit took the helm (in 1977), the Montreal has become a major ensemble on the North American continent. Dutoit has fashioned the Montreal into a very polished and truly French-sounding ensemble. It is certainly the leading Canadian orchestra and is in the running with its equivalents in this country (i.e., the New York, Chicago, etc.). It has the wonderful French precision in the winds and a good, but somewhat thin to my liking, set of strings. It is almost definitive in its performances of some works by Ravel (and his French contemporaries) and the late Russians.

Moscow Radio Symphony Orchestra--excellent in its chosen repertoire: Russian and some Central European music. It is big, warm, a little heavy, but clear (without the kind of transparency American orchestras are able to provide), and has much vitality. The Moscow is still not in quite the same league as the American "big five" or the best on the European continent.

National Philharmonic Orchestra of London--a good ensemble of the second level, sometimes hard to take seriously when it attempts major compositions. The National has a bright sound, more vitality than some of its brother orchestras in London, and provides efficient recordings--but seldom inspired ones.

National Symphony Orchestra (Washington, D.C.)--never a first, or even second rank American orchestra, the National does hold prominence simply by being located in Washington, and by having been given the appellation of "The Nation's Orchestra." Its music director is Mstislav Rostropovich, and the orchestra seems to offer its greatest service by performing on the West Lawn of the Capitol each July 4th. Its winds are tenuous, its strings usually competent, and the overall orchestral sound nothing out of the ordinary, given that its permanent home is the Kennedy Center. Given its home town, perhaps the NSO is what Washington deserves. The Principal Associate Conductor of the National is Rafael Frühbeck de Burgos, and under his baton the orchestra is capable of performing at a level which hints at something like greatness. If only Rostropovich would go back to his 'cello full time.

NBC Symphony Orchestra--begun as a broadcasting and recording orchestra specifically to entice Arturo Toscanini to NBC and New York, it is now defunct. Many of its recordings are still in the current catalogs, almost none of them made under any other conductor than Toscanini (it really was "his" orchestra and reflected precisely what he thought the ideal ensemble should sound like). It was usually badly recorded (in the old and infamous Studio 8H) but had a very bright sound. Its musicians were of the highest caliber, but the NBC reflected only Toscanini's personality--it had little character of its own. It was precise, could play quickly (it had to under Toscanini's baton) and with enthusiasm. There has never been anything quite like it since. Since this author is not a Toscanini buff, and since not much of the NBC has been transferred to CD, only a few of its offerings are represented in these pages.

New Philharmonia Orchestra--see Philharmonia Orchestra

New York Philharmonic--among the oldest orchestras in the world, and certainly the oldest orchestra of size or importance in the United States (founded 1842), it began life as the New York Philharmonic Society. In 1928 it amalgamated with New York Symphony Society to become the New York Philharmonic Symphony Orchestra. That it is among the five best orchestras in the United States is indisputable; where it is among those five is another matter (I would place it about third, after the Chicago and Cleveland, others might say first or fourth, after the first two named and the Boston). Regardless, it is a world class orchestra whose fortunes have waned along with its quality, since the departure of Leonard Bernstein as music director. It is a European-sounding ensemble, darker and more lustrous in tone than the others of the top five. It has been notoriously hard on conductors it has felt to be less than first-rate (but the orchestra's collective judgment is often faulty--it seems to have taken Zubin Mehta to its heart), and feels itself to be the premier orchestra of the world (definitely a mistake). Its repertoire excludes nothing, and of late (under Mehta) includes almost nothing it plays in a distinguished manner. When there is someone other than Mehta on the podium, it can still provide superb performances. It has long been well regarded for its recordings of Beethoven, Brahms, and Mahler, in particular. When Bernstein directs it, the orchestra can give exceptionally fine readings, especially of modern American composers. Now, with Mehta's imminent departure, there is real hope that the New York may return to its prior greatness.

Orchestre National de France--a fairly new orchestra which quickly established itself as being in the second rank. Its strengths are the clarity and brightness for which French orchestras are known, but its ensemble can be a bit untidy. It is heard to best advantage in French and Soviet music.

L'Orchestre de la Suisse Romande--founded in 1918 by its longtime music director, Ernest Ansermet. It is based in Geneva and in its prime it was one of the world's finer orchestras, particularly for the interpretation of French, Spanish, and Russian music. Ansermet had premiered, in Paris, works by Stravinsky, Ravel, and Falla, and he brought this intimate knowledge of their music to the Suisse Romande. For a couple of decades its recordings of the first three Stravinsky ballets were the ones of choice for many critics and collectors (they still hold up remarkably well). The Suisse Romande, despite its occasional intonational and attack problems, was a vibrant and exceptional orchestra. Its tone was bright and light, and it had the graces of the French orchestral style. Since Ansermet's departure, in 1966, it has not done very well, and seems to be in a decline.

Orchestre de Paris--another relatively new orchestra, and one which has recorded a surprising amount since its founding. It is at a slightly higher level than the Orchestre National de France, and has the same basic qualities and weaknesses.

Paris Conservatory Orchestra (L'Orchestre de la Société des Concerts du Conservatoire de Paris)--one of the oldest, and best, of the French ensembles. Although no longer represented by a large number of recordings, it is still an exemplar of the French orchestral style, while remaining firmly in the second level of world class orchestras.

Philadelphia Orchestra--founded in 1900 and in the "big five" of American orchestras. The Philadelphia has a distinguished history, especially when Stokowski brought to it his incredible ear for orchestral sound and balance. Stokowski's directorship, from 1912 to 1936, created an orchestra that was without peer for sheer beauty of orchestral sound in this country. His fussing with seating arrangements, especially his particularity regarding the seating of the string sections, was legendary. Also, he introduced non-synchronized bowing, so that string players not only felt more comfortable with their own, idiomatic bowing, but also were able to provide a continuity of string sound in legato passages not possible with unison bowing. Under the stewardship of Stokowski's successor, Eugene Ormandy, the emphasis of the Philadelphia was still on beautiful orchestral sound. What was lost, though, from Stokowski by Ormandy, was the excitement of the incredible springiness of rhythmic approach, and some of the clarity of sound. Ormandy's recorded performances were very seldom exciting, but they were accomplished. The Philadelphia, since Stokowski, has needed a truly great and vital conductor-- Riccardo Muti may be exciting, but he is not great (and probably will not grow much more than he already has). So, the poor Philadelphia is a wonderful sounding instrument which only rarely achieves real performance heights. Besides its splendid sound, it often displays an almost flawless technique.

Philharmonia Orchestra--based in London and originally created by EMI (the huge electronic and recording conglomerate) for its recording purposes, it now gives "live" concerts around the world. The Philharmonia has been, since its founding shortly after World War II, one of the two or three busiest and best recording orchestras in the world. Having virtually no permanent conductor (Otto Klemperer came close), it quickly became the chameleon of first rank orchestras. With every change of conductors, the Philharmonia subtly changed its sound: for von Karajan and Klemperer, one could easily mistake it for a German orchestra (except for the telltale English double reed sound); for Dervaux it sounded French; and for Sir Eugene Goossens, it sounded typically English. At one time in its history, the Philharmonia boasted the following first desk players: Dennis Brain, horn, Leon Goossens, oboe, and Reginald Kell, clarinet. The other sections were also very well chosen and the entity had a fine ensemble sound: basically warm, Continental, and (in contradistinction to many other English orchestras) a deal of liveliness. It is among the very best recording orchestras in the world. The "New" portion of the orchestra's name was employed beginning in 1964, when the orchestra became a self-governing body, and dropped in 1977, when it resumed its old title of Philharmonia Orchestra.

Pittsburgh Symphony Orchestra--an orchestra just behind the most important five in the United States. It has been one of the most German-sounding of American orchestras: round and warm of tone, fullbodied, and accurate. Until André Previn's brief stay with the Pittsburgh, it had not distinguished itself as an orchestra of great excitement (i.e., under the late William Steinberg). Now it is a fully developed organization which has a good, broad repertoire, and it is fortunate to have obtained Lorin Maazel for its new director.

RCA Symphony Orchestra--an orchestra founded, like the Columbia Symphony, for recording purposes. The comments regarding the quality of the Columbia suffice for the RCA as well.

Royal Philharmonic Orchestra--alphabetically the last of the five major London based orchestras. Founded by Sir Thomas Beecham (in 1946), it is among the most recorded orchestras in the world. In quality, it is probably at the bottom of the London pile. It is typically English in sound, but not known for either great élan or accuracy. It is merely a fine, second-rate ensemble. Its principal strength is in its recordings of British composers. Its current music director is Vladimir Ashkenazy and its principal conductor is André Previn.

St. Louis Symphony Orchestra--like the Minnesota, an orchestra which may soon find itself among the first rank of American orchestras. Under Leonard Slatkin, its music director since 1979, the St. Louis has proven itself a truly fine ensemble. It has excitement, precision, and a repertoire that virtually knows no bounds. Its sound is clear and clean--typically American, with no excesses in any of its sections. If music can be said to be alive in America, it is certainly alive in St. Louis.

San Francisco Symphony Orchestra--has never recovered any of its stature since the departure of Pierre Monteux in 1952. Despite a small revitalization under the directorship of Seiji Ozawa (1970-1976), the orchestra still did not come into its own, even during the tenure (1977-1985) of Edo de Waart. Herbert Blomstedt took over in 1985, and the orchestra now seems to be making positive strides in filling out its repertoire and generally improving the quality of its music making. It may well make its way back to being among the best orchestras in the country.

Utah Symphony Orchestra--in the very forefront, along with the Minneapolis and the St. Louis, of American orchestras of the second rank. Under Maurice Abravanel, who was its music director from 1947 to 1979, it developed into one of the most German-sounding of important American orchestras. With him, the orchestra expanded its repertoire to Mahler, Satie, and Gottschalk--in addition to paying attention to the rest of the orchestral literature. Although not faultless, the Utah has a good, round, relatively warm sound--not as bright say, as the Chicago or Cleveland. It is a fine group which is doing well under its new director (since 1983), Joseph Silverstein.

Vienna Philharmonic Orchestra--among the few very best of all world orchestras. One of the oldest orchestras around, it gave its first performance in 1847 (there are some English, one American [the Handel and Haydn Society chorus and orchestra, of Boston, founded in 1815], and a few Continental orchestras that are older). It is in the same class as the Berlin Philharmonic and Amsterdam Concertgebouw Orchestras. Like the Berlin, the Vienna Philharmonic is at its best in works written essentially before 1900 (exceptions are Mahler, Sibelius, and some others who are of the Late Romantic school). It is among the most beautiful sounding ensembles anywhere (some of its champions say it is *the* most beautiful sounding). It has a warm, round, relatively dark and rich sound, and an exquisite sense of ensemble. It can be extremely exciting and powerful, and I would place it next to the Amsterdam Concertgebouw in my list of favorites. Its chief conductor, since 1971, is Claudio Abbado.

Vienna Symphony Orchestra--a second-rate, typically German or Austrian-sounding ensemble, neither particularly distinguished nor exciting. Even when Horenstein conducted it, although the spirit of the music came to life, its full realization was impeded by intonational flubs and a tonal quality which often sounded cheap. It hasn't changed much in the years since Horenstein recorded with it.

Chamber Orchestras

Academy of Ancient Music--an exceedingly fine group which usually employs period ("authentic") instruments. Under Christopher Hogwood (its founder), the Academy is among the most recorded of those groups which perform essentially Baroque and Classical instrumental works (and a few choral compositions) in the styles contemporary with their composition. With Simon Preston conducting, the Academy essays choral works of composers such as Bach, Handel, Haydn and Vivaldi--again, in the style appropriate to the periods. The sound of the Academy is airy, light, and exceptionally good. It is a very stylish ensemble, and displays intelligence and vitality, but sometimes is a bit arch sounding.

Bournemouth Sinfonietta--a decent orchestra, but without real distinction.

Collegium Aureum--one of the finest, and among the most recorded, chamber orchestras in the world. Like the Academy of Ancient Music, it usually employs instruments appropriate to its chosen repertoire: Baroque, Classical, and a smidgen of Early Romantic. It possesses a transparent and warm, but brilliant, sound.

Cologne Musica Antiqua--a very competent group, but not in the league of the Academy of Ancient Music or the Collegium Aureum.

English **Baroque Soloists**--a chamber orchestra which only uses instruments appropriate to Baroque music. The ensemble is good, not great, and it tends to extend the term "Baroque" to include Mozart (and does particularly well by his piano concerti). The English Baroque Soloists suffer only a bit in comparison with some of their more accomplished counterparts.

English **Chamber** Orchestra--possesses some of the worst sonic qualities (particularly in the double reeds, and sometimes the horns) of British ensembles, yet can rise to real heights in interpretation. It is easily the most recorded chamber orchestra in the world, and undertakes performances of works ranging from Mozart to 20th century composers. Despite its usual use of modern instruments it does quite well in its wide repertoire, depending who is on the podium.

English **Concert**--a truly fine group, usually conducted by the impeccable Trevor Pinnock (its founder [in 1973] and also its harpsichordist). Remarkably, for an English orchestra, there is little to mark the English Concert as being specific to any geographic locale. Its sound is relatively open, devoid of any overuse of vibrato, and the period instruments are well used. It often tends, though, to rather fast (to my mind) tempi.

Franz Liszt Chamber Orchestra--based in Budapest, is one of the best Central European orchestras of its size and repertoire. It has an extensive catalog, with composers ranging from Bach to Molter and Stamitz (with heavy doses of Mozart and Vivaldi). It is a clean sounding group, but has an occasional intonational problem. It evidences a real delight in playing and its exuberance often makes up for its lapses.

Hanover Band--is a new ensemble comprised of 29 players, and usually performs without the benefit of a conductor (the concertmistress acting as director). The Hanover uses period instruments (essentially of the late 18th and early 19th centuries), and is extremely careful in its search for accuracy in such details as dynamics, tempi, etc., but its performances never sound arid, pedagogical, or lifeless. Hearing the Hanover perform the Beethoven symphonic repertoire is extremely revealing and pleasurable.

Leonhardt Consort--named for its founder-conductor, Gustav Leonhardt, it was formed essentially for the recording of all the Bach Cantatas. In that role, it has found a real niche and has performed a very valuable service. It has also recorded several other works of Bach, and many of these are outstanding. The ensemble is of a just size and sound for the Bach repertoire.

London Sinfonietta--a capable chamber orchestra, but not one possessed of sufficient quality to recommend it over several others.

Los Angeles Chamber Orchestra--founded by Sir Neville Marriner in 1968, this is the only Los Angeles orchestra of any size worth listening to. Gerard Schwarz has brought it to its current excellence and the ensemble is the equal of any of its type in the U. S., except for the St. Paul Chamber Orchestra.

Lucerne Festival Strings--has only made a couple of recordings worth bothering about: one conducted by Furtwängler (with Menuhin, in the Brahms Violin Concerto) and the other under von Karajan (with Lipatti, in the Mozart Piano Concerto No.21)--the rest are average performances, and better done elsewhere.

Marlboro Festival Ensemble--not to be confused with the Marlboro Festival Orchestra (which is an older group of less quality-- particularly when Casals directed it), is a fine group which is willing to take on any music, from Bach to Webern. It has the best sonic attributes of American players, and invests its performances with dash and care.

Munich Bach Orchestra--a good, solid ensemble, one which does its namesake proud. In the Bach choral works it has recorded, it usually employs top flight vocalists and produces fine performances (even though they are not always stylistically "correct").

Munich Chamber Orchestra--a decent ensemble, and one which records some really unusual works (e.g., Albrechtsberger's Concerti for Jew's Harp and Leopold Mozart's Sinfonia in D with Bagpipes and Hurdy-Gurdy). Not in the running with its Munich Bach Orchestra cousin, nor with the best of the other chamber orchestras.

I Musici--among the very oldest of recording chamber orchestras (ostensibly it was Toscanini's favorite of its kind), and one of the best. It is virtually without peer in its performances of Vivaldi, and can do justice to Mozart and some modern composers. It tends to employ modern instruments, but uses them wisely and well. Few ensembles of any type can invest a work with as much excitement as can I Musici on its best days.

Orpheus (Chamber Orchestra)--usually known simply as "Orpheus." It is among the finest chamber orchestras in the world, and brings impeccable musicianship, vitality, and musical intelligence to a wide range of musical periods, from Bach to Beethoven and Stravinsky. Orpheus, to my lights, has yet to commit any crimes against music in its recordings.

Jean-François Paillard Chamber Orchestra--one of my own particular favorites, despite its use of modern instruments. The Paillard can hold its own, in musicianship and élan with any chamber orchestra, and often makes warhorses sound like colts. Few are the ensembles which can bring as clean and open a sound to their repertoires, and with as fine and sure an intonation. The Paillard must exemplify what Virgil Thomson seems to have loved most about the best of French orchestral timbres and sophistication.

La Petite Bande--a new chamber orchestra which uses period instruments exclusively. They play impeccably and with enthusiasm. The only fault I can find with La Petite Bande is that it hasn't recorded nearly enough.

Saar Chamber Orchestra--a very competent ensemble and one which uses modern instruments. It is better than many though not as good as the best. Its sound is a bit heavy and thick, given its Baroque and Classical repertoire.

St. Paul Chamber Orchestra--among American chamber orchestras, the best. The St. Paul usually uses modern instruments, despite the period of the composition being performed. It has fine technical proficiency, a nicely balanced sound, and is over time, going to have to be reckoned among the world's finest.

I Solisti Veneti--a most capable orchestra and under Claudio Scimone (founded by him in 1959), one which does fine work. Eschewing period instruments, its sound is somewhat more robust than is often warranted.

I Solisti di Zagreb--another capable ensemble (founded in 1950 by 'cellist Antonio Janigro), occasionally obtaining the services of exceptional soloists (Julius Baker, Hubert Jellinek, Jean-Pierre Rampal, Helmut Wobisch, et al.). It has a darker than usual sound for a chamber orchestra, probably due to its use of modern instruments and European training. The Zagreb almost makes it to the first rank, but not quite because of its occasional lackluster performances.

Stuttgart Chamber Orchestra--a rather overrated group (founded in 1945 by Karl Münchinger) which, more often than not, offers precious and mincing performances. The Stuttgart deserves credit, though, for being one of the first chamber orchestras to make a reputation performing Baroque works when there was almost no

41

audience for such music. Being rather small, it has a fine transparency of sound (which is produced on modern instruments), but frequently doesn't do real justice to the works it undertakes.

Württemberg Chamber Orchestra--although often recorded, the Württemberg is a mediocre ensemble and not worth much attention.

Conductors

Abbado, Claudio--born in Italy in 1933, has distinguished himself as an operatic and symphonic conductor. He has it within himself to become a truly great conductor (he has already provided us with a few great recorded performances). He is now the music director of the Vienna Philharmonic (and the Vienna State Opera) and, quite recently, the Berlin Philharmonic.

Abravanel, Maurice--born in Greece (Salonica) in 1903, was the music director of the Utah Symphony Orchestra from 1947 to 1979. His recordings with the Utah of Mahler's symphonies are among the best. His repertoire was extremely large and all of his performances reveal thoroughgoing musicianship.

Ashkenazy, Vladimir--born in the Soviet Union in 1937, is best known as a pianist of huge talent. He began conducting in the late 1970s and, although his ability in that role has improved steadily, he still does not bring to conducting the same genius that he does to his piano playing because he seems to be searching for obscure meanings in the music (which meanings are not always there). He is best in the works of Tchaikovsky and Sibelius.

Barbirolli, Sir John--born in England in 1899, died in 1970. Was principal conductor of the New York Philharmonic from 1937 to 1943. He is best known for his work as music director of the Hallé Orchestra of Manchester, England. He was exceptionally fine in performances of the works of British composers and of Sibelius.

Barenboim, Daniel--born in Argentina in 1942, he began as a very fine pianist and began conducting in 1962. He has distinguished himself in performances of American, French and Russian composers and in modern works, and will become the music director of the Chicago Symphony in 1991.

Baudo, Serge--born in France in 1927, is a very good interpreter of French composers.

Beecham, Sir Thomas--born in England in 1879, died 1961. An exceptional musician who was, for the most part, a self-taught conductor. As the heir to the Beecham's Pills fortune (Beecham's Pills were, and still are, for all I know, a very popular British laxative and panacea), Beecham was able to found several British orchestras, among which were the New Symphony Orchestra and the Royal Philharmonic Orchestra. He was an early champion of the works of Delius and Sibelius, and gave no little impetus to the career of the odd British composer, Lord Berners. Many of his recorded performances are esteemed as definitive. Among these, certainly, are his readings of Delius' works, the Franck Symphony in d, and a few of Sibelius' symphonic works. Despite the eccentricities of his performances of some of the works of Handel and Bach, they are still treasured as insightful. His sharpness of wit, and lack of generosity to hosts, is evidenced in his departure as conductor of the Seattle Symphony by terming Seattle the "cultural dustbin of the universe."

Bernstein, Leonard--born in the United States in 1918, was the first American born musician to be named permanent conductor of a major American orchestra (New York Philharmonic, from 1958 to 1971). He is a brilliant and erratic conductor who attempts to perform everything in the orchestral repertoire, but not with equal success. While his Mahler is outstanding, his Beethoven and Brahms are less so. He is extremely good with works that have a rhythmic base (e.g., some Tchaikovsky, some Ravel, some Liszt) rather than an intellectual one; therefore, he excels in music for dance or that is balletic.

43

Blomstedt, Herbert--born in Denmark in 1927, is a conductor of excellent abilities who specializes in works of Northern European composers. Mr. Blomstedt now has the task of trying to bring the San Francisco back into the ranks of the better American orchestras.

Böhm, Karl--born in Austria in 1894, died in 1981, one of the last of the outstanding great conductors of the Romantic style, specializing in works by Mozart, Beethoven, Brahms, and in those by several modern composers. He was an eminent conductor of opera, ranging from those of Mozart to Richard Strauss.

Bonynge, Sir Richard--born in Australia in 1930, pianist, vocal coach, and husband of the great soprano Dame Joan Sutherland, Bonynge has made a name for himself as an expert conductor, particularly of ballets and *bel canto* operas, such as those of Bellini and Donizetti.

Boulez, Pierre--born in France in 1925, is well known as both a composer and conductor. He specializes in conducting works of the 20th century (e.g., Stravinsky and Schoenberg), and often brings to them an intelligence and vitality few other conductors can.

Boult, Sir Adrian--born in England in 1889, died in 1983, was one of the finest British conductors of the century. Boult's specialties were works by his compatriots, but he was almost as adept in works by Brahms and Rachmaninoff. His approach was gentle (belied in his version of Holst's The Planets) and reflective--even his readings of Elgar's Pomp and Circumstance Marches were more symphonic than martial.

Britten, Benjamin--born in England in 1913, died in 1976, was better known as a composer than conductor. He was infallible in interpreting his own works, but also did well in directing the works of others, particularly Bach and Mozart. He was also a pianist of considerable talent.

Casals, Pablo--born in Spain in 1879, died in 1973, conducted Bach, Mozart, and some of his own works. He had gained his fame as an outstanding 'cellist and should have left well enough alone--his conducting is far too Romantic for modern ears (as were, for many, his 'cello interpretations of such Baroque masters as Bach), and his orchestras were not always comprised of musicians of the caliber required.

Chailly, Riccardo--born in Italy in 1953, is an excellent and enthusiastic conductor of both orchestral and operatic works. He is intelligent and perceptive, and is developing into one of the finest of the younger conductors now practicing. He was appointed music director of the Amsterdam Concertgebouw Orchestra in 1988.

Corboz, Michel--born in Switzerland in 1935, has specialized in Renaissance music, and exhibits much talent in that field.

Davis, Sir Colin--born in England in 1927, is a well regarded conductor, particularly in the works of Sibelius, some modern composers, and as an accompanying conductor. Many of his purely orchestral readings are rather lifeless and dry.

Deller, Alfred--born in England in 1912, died in 1979, was a countertenor of superb abilities and an excellent conductor of Medieval and Renaissance vocal works.

Dervaux, Pierre--born in France in 1917, is a conductor of competence and polish who is particularly good with works by 19th and 20th century French composers.

De Waart, Edo--see Waart, Edo de

Dohnányi, Christoph von--born in Germany in 1929, is the grandson of composer Ernst von Dohnányi and, since 1984, the music director of the Cleveland Orchestra. He is an exceptional musical talent and, in following the fine directorship given the Cleveland by

45

Lorin Maazel, has provided the Cleveland with a warmer, rounder sound than the orchestra previously had. He is extremely fine in both the orchestral and operatic repertoires, and is often a champion of the works of new composers.

Doráti, Antal--born in Hungary 1906, died in 1988. He achieved the reputation of being one of the very best conductors of second half of this century, and as one of the greatest builders of orchestras of any time. He was been the chief conductor of the Stockholm Philharmonic Orchestra, plus being the music director of the Dallas, Minneapolis, National (Washington, D.C.), and Detroit Symphony Orchestras. He was also the principal conductor of the London Philharmonic Orchestra. His reputation as a conductor brought him almost to the ranks of the very greatest, and he participated in the milestone recordings of the complete symphonies of Haydn (with the Hungarica Philharmonia). He was at his best in works of his countrymen and Russian composers, but was also very fine in virtually anything to which he set his baton. I have to add that I believe his recordings of Bartók's orchestral music to be the among the very best.

Dutoit, Charles--born in Switzerland in 1936, is now the music director of the Montreal Symphony Orchestra, which he has brought to a level of true distinction. He is, among living conductors, almost without peer in his interpretations of French composers (his only real competition coming from Bernard Haitink), and is a premier director of Spanish music.

Fennell, Frederick--born in the United States in 1914, is generally considered the finest wind ensemble conductor in the world. An oddity among practicing musicians, Fennell is also an academician (M. M. from the Eastman School of Music and for many years on the faculty of that institution) who first came to attention conducting the Eastman-Rochester Wind Ensemble in a series of recordings now deemed classics. There is virtually nothing in the literature for band that Fennell cannot conduct superbly.

Ferencsik, János--born in Hungary in 1907, is a specialist in the music of his native country. He is equally adept in Hungarian orchestral and operatic works.

Fistoulari, Anatole--born in Russia in 1907 despite the French-Italian sounding name. He is best known as an operatic conductor of no little distinction.

Frühbeck de Burgos, Rafael--born in Spain in 1933 to Spanish and German parents. He is a consummate conductor of Spanish works and, like Giulini, works that include chorus (in Frühbeck's case in particular, Orff's <u>Carmina Burana</u>). His work is infused with enthusiasm and vitality, and orchestra members seem to dote on him.

Furtwängler, Wilhelm--born in Germany in 1886, died in 1954. He is considered one of the handful of truly great conductors of the 20th century (in the same class as Toscanini and Bruno Walter). Furtwängler was at his best in directing the works of Wagner, Beethoven, and Brahms, but his recordings of Haydn and Mozart reveal his talent for music of the Classical period, as well. He was the music director of the Berlin Philharmonic during World War II, and seems to have arrived at some kind of accommodation with the Nazis to be able to continue his career. In 1949, he was invited to conduct the Chicago Symphony but declined when several demonstrations were held protesting his appearance in this country after his "close affiliations" with the Nazi party. In 1955, Furtwängler was asked to bring the Berlin Philharmonic to the U. S.; however, he died the preceding year and Herbert von Karajan, Furtwängler's successor, made the tour (which was a triumphant one).

Gardiner, John Eliot--born in England in 1941, is a scholar and conductor--primarily of Early Classical music and of some works preceding that period. His work shows him to be rather a purist, but one capable of informing his performances with both scholarship and excitement.

Gibson, Sir Alexander--born in Scotland in 1926, Gibson is a conductor who has specialized in the works of British composers and of Sibelius. In particular, he has recorded several of the lesser known works of the Finnish composer, thus placing Sibelius fans in his debt. His work is craftsman like and well considered.

Giulini, Carlo Maria--born in Italy in 1914, he is among the finest working conductors. Unfortunately, due to illness and other problems, he has not maintained a relationship with an orchestra long enough to have gained an even greater following. He is outstanding in choral works (e.g., the Verdi and Mozart Requiems) and in conducting opera. His work in the symphonic repertoire proves him to be among the very best now wielding a baton.

Haitink, Bernard--born in Holland in 1929, Haitink is, to my mind, the best all around conductor now on the podium, and the most likely to join the ranks of the few "immortals." He "inherited" the Concertgebouw Orchestra from Eduard van Beinum in 1962 (van Beinum having died in 1959--decisions of that magnitude are not made quickly in Holland) and relinquished it in 1988. Haitink is an outstanding interpreter of Mozart, Beethoven, Berlioz, Ravel, Debussy, Mahler, Bruckner, and sundry lesser lights. His orchestra was, if not the best in the world, sufficiently close to have allowed him a full demonstration of his prowess. He is also excellent in the operatic repertoire.

Harnoncourt, Nikolaus--born in Berlin in 1929, is the founder of the Vienna Concentus Musicus--among the best of the chamber orchestras now performing. Harnoncourt is both conductor and musicologist, and is recognized for being among the first modern conductors to revive the practice of giving performances of early music on period instruments. Further, he is well known for his performing editions of several works of Monteverdi operas and Bach choral works.

Horenstein, Jascha--born in Russia in 1898, died in 1973, was an estimable conductor. He was well regarded for his interpretations of Mahler, Tchaikovsky, and Dvořák.

Janigro, Antonio--born in Italy in 1918, is the founder of the chamber group called I Solisti di Zagreb (given an Italian name since Janigro thought it would call more attention to itself than a group made up of Yugoslavians with a Yugoslavian name). He is an accomplished 'cellist and a reasonably good conductor. With I Solisti, he has recorded many of the better known works for chamber orchestra, several of which are better served by other ensembles.

Jochum, Eugen--born in Germany in 1902, died in 1987, one of the finest interpreters of Austrian and German music of the last century. His recordings of Mozart, Beethoven, Brahms, Wagner, Mahler, and Bruckner are among the best. Particularly outstanding are his recordings made with the Amsterdam Concertgebouw Orchestra, of which he was co-principal director for several years. He was also superb as a conductor of German opera (from Mozart to Wagner).

Kamu, Okko--born in Finland in 1946, has become recognized as one of the best interpreters of the works of his compatriots (most notably, Sibelius).

Karajan, Herbert von--born in Austria in 1908 and died in 1989, was one of the most highly visible and recognized conductors of the century. His belief in his musical powers knew no bounds, and there is no music that he refused to conduct: from Bach (heavy handed and without taste) to Beethoven (usually lifeless) to Tchaikovsky (usually lacking any balletic quality) to the moderns (which he often does not seem to have fully understood). I often had the feeling, when listening to performances by von Karajan, that I was not so much hearing music qua music, so much as being provided, as it were, an audible postmortem of what had probably been an interesting living entity. As the ostensible successor of the much esteemed Furtwängler, a good deal was expected from von Karajan. For many of his admirers, von Karajan realized those expectations. He was never truly incompetent, was often excellent, and very occasionally superb (for me, in particular, his recordings of the Mozart the Sinfonia Concertante, K.Anh.104 [320e] and the Beethoven Symphony No.2). Still, without all the hype, von Karajan was no greater a conductor than many other, less ballyhooed musicians. In order to ensure that his career in Germany would flourish during the Second World War, von Karajan joined the Nazi party not once, but twice (perhaps to evidence his political seriousness or, more likely, to bring himself to the attention of those then in power--he was well known as an unabashed and unrelenting opportunist).

Kempe, Rudolf--born in Germany in 1910, died in 1976, was musical director of the Dresden State Opera and, after a time, of the Munich State Opera. He became well known as an opera conductor and worked in most of the important opera houses of the world. He was also a superb interpreter of the waltzes of Johann Strauss, Jr.

Kertész, István--born in Hungary in 1929, died in 1973 (drowned while swimming in the Mediterranean), was chiefly known as an excellent interpreter of the works of Dvořák, and that ilk. He was also a fine conductor of Hungarian operatic works.

Kleiber, Carlos--born in Germany in 1930 (son of the great Austrian conductor, Erich Kleiber). The younger Kleiber has produced some exceptional recordings (notably the Beethoven Fifth and Seventh Symphonies and several operas). He has the potential to become one of the conductorial lights of this half century.

Klemperer, Otto--born in Germany in 1885, died in 1973, one of the giants of conducting during the first three-quarters of this century. He has left an incredible legacy of recordings, including all the Beethoven and Brahms symphonies, many Haydn and Mozart Symphonies, an <u>Ein Deutsches Requiem</u> of Brahms essentially without peer, many operatic recordings (especially of Mozart and Beethoven's <u>Fidelio</u>) and sundry other discs that testify to his greatness of spirit and intellect. One of the notable achievements in his recordings is the separation of the first and second violins in the symphonies of Beethoven, etc., placing them respectively on the left and right of the conductor--making it considerably easier to hear them when they are not playing in unison or parallel.

Kondrashin, Kiril--born in Russia in 1914, Kondrashin is among the finest of the Soviet conductors. He has conducted many of the major orchestras of the world, and is at his best in modern Russian compositions.

Kubelik, Rafael--born in Czechoslovakia in 1914, is probably the best living interpreter of the orchestral works of Dvořák. He is a champion of modern music and is a fine operatic conductor. His father was the eminent Czech violinist, Jan Kubelik.

Leinsdorf, Erich--born in Austria in 1912, Leinsdorf is one of the best of the older group of operatic conductors still practicing (he is also an orchestral conductor of considerable talent). He served his apprenticeship as an assistant to both Toscanini and Bruno Walter and his work is marked by sensitivity and intelligence.

Levine, James--born in the United States in 1943, Levine is generally considered both a pianist and conductor of great skill. He became the music director of the Metropolitan Opera at the age of 36--the youngest in its history. He is known as a fine pianist in chamber works, an excellent conductor of the works of Mahler and Brahms, and one of the most vital operatic conductors wielding a baton.

Maazel, Lorin--born in France in 1930, Maazel made his conductorial debut at the age of nine. He is one of the few "child geniuses" to have survived to adulthood with his sanity and abilities intact. Maazel has been the director of the Cleveland, Vienna

Philharmonic, and most recently, the Pittsburgh Symphony Orchestras. His work is notable for its great technical and emotional control, and by a fine sense of orchestral balance.

Mackerras, Sir Charles--born in the United States in 1925, of Australian parents, he studied with Vaclav Talich and became expert in directing works by Central European composers. His recorded cycle of the operas of Janáček is without peer.

Marriner, Sir Neville--born in England in 1924, Marriner was a conducting assistant to Pierre Monteux and founded, in 1959, the orchestra now known as the Academy of St. Martin-in-the-Fields in London. He began by specializing in early chamber orchestra works and expanded to the full orchestral repertoire. Marriner's work is often marred by a lack of vitality, but he almost always is able to achieve good transparency of sound.

Mehta, Zubin--born in India in 1936, Mehta has depended more on physical charm and an ingratiating personality than on the thorough musicianship that many attribute to him. Most of his performances of great orchestral works are egregious and are often salvaged only by the quality of the orchestras he directs.

Menuhin, Sir Yehudi--born in the United States in 1916, Menuhin has been a British subject for several decades. He was once known as a virtuoso violinist (and sometime viola player of no mean expertise), but his numerous other activities (including teaching, studying various religions, travel, etc.) and conducting have taken their toll on his abilities as a soloist. As a conductor, he is at his best in Baroque music.

Monteux, Pierre--born in France in 1875, died in 1964, Monteux was arguably the best interpreter of French music of the Romantic and Impressionistic schools. He was the conductor of choice of Diaghilev's Ballet Russe to direct the world premieres of Stravinsky's Le Sacre du printemps, Petrouchka, and Le Rossignol, along with Debussy's <u>Jeux</u> and Ravel's <u>Daphnis et Chloé</u>. His recordings of such works as several of Tchaikovsky's symphonies, Rimsky-Korsakov's <u>Scheherazade</u> and Franck's Symphony in d are still to be treasured as being insightful and filled with color.

Mravinsky, Evgeny--born in Russia in 1903, died in 1988, was one of the most prominent Soviet conductors, and from 1938 to his death had been the principal conductor of the Leningrad Philharmonic. His readings of the early Tchaikovsky symphonies, and works of Prokofiev and Shostakovich are in the realm of true greatness.

Muti, Riccardo--born in Italy in 1941, inherited the title of Eugene Ormandy, in 1980, as music director of the Philadelphia Orchestra. He has an ear for color and seems to believe that the harder a piece is driven the greater the performance. I place him only a notch above Zubin Mehta in overall talent.

Ormandy, Eugene--born in Hungary in 1899, died in 1986, Ormandy served for what seems an eternity as music director of the Philadelphia Orchestra (1931-1980) and proved to have a fine ear for orchestral color and balance. His performances, however, seem to suffer from avitaminosis.

Ozawa, Seiji--born in Japan in 1935, Ozawa was a student of von Karajan and assistant to Bernstein. His work as music director of the Boston Symphony Orchestra has largely been undistinguished except for such works as Ives' Symphony No.4 and Ravel's <u>Daphnis et Chloé</u>, among a few others. His interpretations are colorful, but sometimes lack musical intelligence and, often, insight (only seldom does he give real due to such composers as Mahler or Beethoven).

Paillard, Jean-François--born in France in 1928, Paillard is the founder of the Jean-François Paillard Chamber Orchestra. His work is always imbued with an obvious sense of both scholarship and musical intelligence, plus vitality and verve.

Pinnock, Trevor--born in England in 1946, Pinnock began as a harpsichordist. His work as a conductor (often from the harpsichord) has been almost exclusively with the chamber orchestra called the English Concert. His ensemble uses period instruments, and their performances mark their conductor's scholarship and "feel" for early music. In sum, he and his band are among the best of those recording Baroque and Pre-Baroque music.

Previn, André--born in Berlin in 1929, Previn is a complete musician. He is a pianist who purveys fine jazz and serious music, a composer of good film music, and a thorough craftsman as a conductor. Although he seldom provides a "great" performance, his work is admirable and intelligent.

Reiner, Fritz--born in Hungary in 1888, died in 1963, Reiner was a tyrant on the podium and possessed a "vest pocket" beat, that is, his baton hardly moved when he was conducting (he claimed he was trying to avoid bursitis). His interpretations of works by his fellow Hungarians (and neighboring Czechs) are brilliant. His recordings of the works of Johann Strauss, Jr. and the overtures of Rossini are essentially faultless. He was among the finest operatic conductors of his generation, and was more than competent in most of the orchestral repertoire. His years as music director of the Chicago Symphony were among the best that orchestra has known.

Rostropovich, Mstislav--born in Azerbaijan (USSR) in 1927, became a Soviet émigré to the United States in 1974. He is acknowledged as probably the greatest living 'cellist and became music director of the National Symphony Orchestra (Washington, D.C.) about 1979. The world of music was far better off when Rostropovich was occupied as a full time 'cellist, but then, the National Symphony Orchestra has never enjoyed palmy days (it came closest when Doráti was its music director). Rostropovich's conducting consists of coaxing lovely playing from his string sections, leaving the rest of the orchestra to fend for itself, and usually producing a strange kind of incoherence in his performances.

Rozhdestvensky, Gennady--born in the Soviet Union in 1931, is one of the most exciting of the younger Soviet conductors. He is fine in works by Russian and Soviet composers, and is exceptional in relatively modern Central European works. He has directed several of the world's finest orchestras, and almost always to great acclaim.

Sargent, Sir Malcolm--born in England in 1895, died in 1967, he was superb as an interpreter of Gilbert and Sullivan, works by British composers, and (as is not unusual with English conductors) very good in the works of Sibelius.

Sawallisch, Wolfgang--born in Germany in 1923, is best known for his work as a very fine conductor of the operas of Wagner.

Skrowaczewski, Stanislaw--born in Poland in 1923, was music director of the Minnesota Orchestra (previously called the Minneapolis Symphony Orchestra) from 1960 to 1979. He is known for excellence in the traditional repertoire and for championing the works of modern composers.

Slatkin, Leonard--born in the United States in 1944 to a musical family (his father was the violinist and conductor Felix Slatkin and his mother the 'cellist, Eleanor Aller), Slatkin is undoubtedly the most brilliant young American conductor of a major American orchestra (St. Louis Symphony) and will surely have a career befitting his great talents. His repertoire seems to know no limits; he always is able to bring color, clarity, and real excitement to most of his interpretations.

Solti, Sir Georg--born in Hungary in 1912, Solti has been the music director of the Chicago Symphony since 1969. Not everyone agrees that he has done well by the Chicago, but few disagree that he is a powerful and knowledgeable conductor. His best work is in the traditional Romantic repertoire and in opera (in which latter he is both expert and inspired).

Stokowski, Leopold--born in England in 1882, died in 1977, this rather mysterious conductor (he affected an indescribable accent, ostensibly Central European, despite having been born and raised in London). He was trained as an organist, and brought the sensibilities and ear of an organist to his conducting. As an orchestral colorist, he was without peer. Often overlooked was his ability to infuse his efforts with excitingly nuanced rhythms. He was termed a charlatan for his orchestral transcriptions of Bach's organ works, but he succeeded in popularizing those works far beyond the dreams of "mere" organists. Any orchestra with which he worked played "over its head" for Stokowski, yet no one who played under his direction can provide a coherent description of Stokowski's incredible conductorial powers. His recordings, even the very earliest ones, indicate a complete musician whose primary aim (usually realized) was the communication of both sound and music.

Szell, George--born in Hungary in 1897, died in 1970, began his career as a pianist and became a conductor of eminence and distinction. His years as music director of the Cleveland Orchestra (1946 to 1970) brought that ensemble into the realm of the finest in the U. S. He was an aristocrat of the baton, equally at ease with Mozart and Beethoven (not so comfortable with Brahms) and in opera. His rhythms tended towards the faster side and he obviously cared greatly for clarity, particularly among the wind sections.

Tennstedt, Klaus--born in Germany in 1926, Tennstedt can be one of the most electrifying conductors in works of composers such as Mahler. He is a thorough musician (who would do better to avoid some of his "Bernsteinian" podium antics) and one to whom audiences and orchestras alike relate with affection and admiration. He needs a major orchestra of his own to realize his powers most fully.

Toscanini, Arturo--born in Italy in 1867, died in 1957, considered by many as the greatest conductor of the 20th century (and by some, as the greatest conductor of all time). Toscanini certainly was among the greatest conductors of the operas of Verdi and Puccini (he was a friend of both). His work tends to indicate not an intellectual approach to music, but rather an emotional one. He was well known for his temper tantrums and the often overly swift tempi with which he directed many works. Although he is not my idea of a complete conductor (his reputation rests almost solely on his interpretations of works by Romantic composers), he was certainly fascinating. Perhaps the worst I can say of him is that his orchestral interpretations seldom reveal anything new to me.

Waart, Edo de--born in Holland in 1941, he is an extremely fine conductor whose repertoire is almost limitless.

Walter, Bruno--born in Germany (real name: Bruno Walter Schlesinger) in 1876 (twenty one years before the death of Brahms), died in 1962, he was undoubtedly one of the greatest interpreters of Beethoven, Brahms, and Mozart of this century. His approach to most music was intellectual, gentle, and in a Viennese style (rather the opposite of Toscanini's). He was also an exceptional conductor of opera. Walter was a student of Mahler, and his interpretations of that composer generally are considered definitive.

<u>Small Chamber Ensembles</u>

Amadeus Quartet a very fine string quartet that specializes in the works of Mozart, Beethoven, and Schubert. Due to the recent death of one its members, the Amadeus has disbanded. It played with good ensemble, intelligence, and a warm overall tone.

American Brass Quintet--despite the popularity of the Canadian Brass, the American is the best of this type of ensemble. They play with exquisite clarity and musicianship, and tend to be extremely well recorded. Their repertoire encompasses all periods and styles. Unlike the Canadian Brass, which tends to involve itself in popular music and humor, etc., the American is a strictly business, no nonsense group.

57

Annapolis Brass Quintet--is an excellent ensemble, but not on par with the American Brass Quintet. Technically, it is a slight notch above the Canadian Brass.

Bartók Quartet--an excellent string quartet for interpreting the works of its namesake, but not in the same league as either the Talich or Tátrai Quartets in the same music.

Beaux Arts Trio--currently the finest working and recording piano trio in the world. Probably soon to be disbanded because of the impending retirement of the 'cellist, Bernard Greenhouse. The Beaux Arts' repertoire includes primarily music from Mozart forward to the recent moderns. It is at its best in the Classical and Romantic periods, but is wonderful in Impressionistic works, as well.

Bell'Arte Trio--a competent piano trio that does not approach the sophistication or musicianship of the Beaux Arts Trio.

Alban Berg Quartet (of Vienna)--a fine string quartet, but not of the first rank. It specializes in Mozart, Beethoven, and Schubert (what string quartet doesn't?), but is outclassed by several others.

Budapest Quartet--once considered the ranking string quartet in the world. Although the Budapest was disbanded several years ago, many of its recordings are still available, both in stereo (not with all the members of the original ensemble) and monophonic. The Budapest was the principal example of the lush and exciting Romantic style of string playing and often eschewed the "proper" stylistic approach to early Romantic music (e.g., Beethoven). The Budapest invested its performances with a bit too much *schmaltz* for my tastes.

Canadian Brass--among the most popular chamber ensembles anywhere. The Canadians are much recorded and will attempt any kind of music. Their performances are more valuable as entertainment farragoes than as good music making.

Cleveland Symphonic Winds--is a large wind ensemble drawn from the members of the Cleveland Orchestra. Its recordings are all conducted by Frederick Fennell, and are without equal.

Concord Quartet--is an excellent ensemble that is outstanding in the modern literature for string quartet.

Fitzwilliam Quartet--a good English string quartet that is at its best in the works of Shostakovich.

Guarneri Quartet--among the world's finest string quartets, the Guarneri is always excellent and sometimes really outstanding. It is a reliable and intelligent ensemble, best in the Classical and Early Romantic literature. I admit to the Guarneri's quality, but their performances often leave me feeling a bit chilly.

Istomin, Stern, Rose Trio--was the best piano trio since the Heifetz, Feuermann, Rubinstein Trio. Disbanded in 1984 on the death of 'cellist Leonard Rose, the Istomin, Stern, Rose Trio was at its best in the Beethoven trios.

Juilliard Quartet--among the finest string quartets, the Juilliard has changed personnel a few times but maintains a high level of performance. Although it has recorded works from almost all periods, it is at its zenith in the works of modern composers.

Kocian Quartet--a very good, relatively new, string quartet that has produced several fine recordings of works by Mozart.

Kohon Quartet--although much recorded, the Kohon is, at best, a solid second class ensemble.

Kronos Quartet--a fine string quartet that performs little known modern works.

LaSalle Quartet--among the best string quartets that specialize in 20th century music.

Lenox Quartet--a solid but second class string quartet, at its best in modern works.

Melos Quartet (of Stuttgart)--a world class string quartet. I find its performances of Mozart most appealing.

Nash Ensemble--is a chamber group of varying size and instrumentation. It is extremely fine, particularly capable in more recent music.

Oistrakh, Knushevitsky, Oborin Trio--a superb piano trio that the Soviets recorded so badly that it is virtually unlistenable. Yet its performances are so good that the poor engineering is enough to make one weep.

Orlando Quartet--a frequently overlooked string quartet of real quality. Its recent recordings deserve more attention and appreciation.

Perlman, Harrell, Ashkenazy Trio--a virtuoso piano trio that has not recorded much. In particular, the musicianship of Lynn Harrell (the 'cellist) and Vladimir Ashkenazy (the pianist) are stellar, and they pull violinist Itzhak Perlman up to their level of performance.

Portland String Quartet--a very good ensemble, the Portland plays with accuracy and musicianship. I would only quibble with the Portland's occasionally hard driving tempi.

Pro Arte Quartet--a really fine string quartet that often verges on being world class.

Quartetto Italiano--during its prime (1960s-1970s), among the reigning string quartets in the world. It was most famous for its Beethoven performances.

Sequoia String Quartet--one of the better of the younger such ensembles, it plays with vigor and a high level of musicianship, but lacks sophistication (which will probably be acquired relatively soon).

Soni Ventorum Wind Quintet--among the best of such ensembles now working. Its range encompasses works from Mozart through some very recent music.

Suk Trio--among the best of the first-rate piano trios. Suk and his colleagues (pianist Jan Panenka and 'cellist Josef Chuchro) play with nice warmth and style, and are the closest rivals to the Beaux Arts Trio.

Talich Quartet--one of the half dozen best string quartets now performing.

Tátrai Quartet--in those works that it has recorded, the Tátrai is my very favorite string quartet. They are absolutely peerless in Bartók and Haydn.

Tokyo String Quartet--a very well regarded ensemble that I have always found to be disappointing because of what seems to me to be a lack of involvement in the music they perform. Still, generally considered among the best.

Westwood Wind Quintet--with the Soni Ventorum Wind Quintet, the Westwood is among the best of this type of chamber ensemble. It tends to favor more recent music, in which it excels.

61

Instrumentalists: A. 'Cellists

Casals, Pablo--born in Spain in 1876, died in 1973. Although Casals' career actually is reckoned from his debut in 1899, performing the Lalo 'Cello Concerto, he is usually considered a soloist who specialized in the works of Bach. He was also a member of the highly acclaimed ensemble called the Cortot-Thibaud-Casals Piano Trio. In his younger days, Casals was acclaimed as the greatest 'cellist of his time. Later, as a soloist, his overly romanticized interpretations of Bach fell out of favor, particularly as his technique waned. I prefer the Bach interpretations of other 'cellists (e.g., Starker, Ma, Harrell) to those of Casals--these others care more for the nuances of the Baroque style.

DuPré, Jacqueline--born in England in 1945, died 1987. She was a performer of immense talent and even greater promise. Her interpretations of almost the entire 'cello repertoire were technically and musically informed. Unfortunately, her concert career was brought to an early end due to multiple sclerosis.

Feuermann, Emanuel--born in Austria in 1902, died in 1942. During his brief career Feuermann established himself as one of the best 'cellists of his time. His was an extraordinary technique coupled to a great musical intelligence. Feuermann was equally adept in the solo and chamber repertoire for his instrument.

Fournier, Pierre--born in France in 1906. Fournier is among the giants of 'cello performance during this century. He is as adept in the French and Rumanian music for his instrument as he is in the works of Bach and Brahms. Although his technique was never in the same realm of that of Feuermann's or Rostropovich's or Starker's, Fournier has made up for that by force of intellect and intensity.

Harrell, Lynn--born in the United States in 1944. After studying with Piatigorsky and Casals, he began his career with a Carnegie Hall debut in 1963. Between 1965-1971, Harrell was the principal 'cellist of the Cleveland Orchestra. He has matured into one of the finest 'cellists of the latter half of the 20th century; he has a formidable technique that is abetted by a sincere musical sensitivity. Harrell can always be depended on for performances that are of the highest caliber.

Ma, Yo-Yo--born in Paris in 1955. Ma is a 'cellist whose career has been one of relatively quiet growth. He has a technique that is imposing and a prepossessing musical intelligence; he does very well with Bach and Beethoven. Ma's talents should grow sufficiently to put him in the forefront of world class 'cellists.

Piatigorsky, Gregor--born in Russia in 1903 and died in 1976. Although regarded as one of the world's greatest 'cellists of his time, his virtuosity did not approach that of Feuermann's nor did his musicianship. He was at his best in music of the late 19th and early 20th centuries. He made several trio (and other chamber ensemble) recordings with Heifetz and Rubinstein. Some of these recordings are among the best of their kind.

Rose, Leonard--born in the United States in 1918 and died in 1984. Rose was a much loved teacher and a greatly admired virtuoso. His tone was relatively robust, his technique excellent, and his musicianship unquestioned. He is best known as a member of the Istomin-Stern-Rose Trio (which was impeccable), but he was also a soloist of great skill. He seemed most at ease in works of the Romantic period.

Rostropovich, Mstislav--born in the Soviet Union in 1927. Rostropovich is (arguably) the greatest living 'cellist. But he has essentially exchanged his career as an extraordinary instrumentalist for that of a mediocre conductor.

Starker, János--born in Hungary in 1924. He is both an outstanding 'cellist and pedagogue. Although his sound is relatively small, his technique is prodigious and his interpretations often faultless, especially in works by his countrymen and those of Bach.

Tortelier, Paul--born in France in 1914. He is recognized as an important and intellectual interpreter of works for his instrument. Artur Rubinstein considered him a "prince of 'cellists."

Instrumentalists: B. Flutists

Preston, Stephen--born in England in 1945. He is an excellent flutist for works of Bach and his predecessors and contemporaries.

Rampal, Jean-Pierre--born in France in 1922. Rampal is probably the best "complete" flutist now practicing. He is at ease in flute music of any period or country, and seems to have recorded all of it. Rampal is stylish, without being showy, and intelligent, not "bright." Unlike Galway, Rampal neither plays down to his audience nor tries to amuse it with ostensible drollery.

Robison, Paula--born in the United States in 1941. Robison is a fine exponent of contemporary music for her instrument.

Sollberger, Harvey--born in the United States in 1938. Sollberger is both a composer and instrumentalist. He excels at interpreting music of the 20th century.

Wilson, Ransom--born in the United States in 1951. He is a solid musician who can play virtually any of the repertoire for the flute.

Zukerman, Eugenia--born in the United States in 1944. This Zukerman (she was once married to violinist Pinchas Zukerman) is a careful and intelligent flutist who seems at her best in Baroque and Classical music.

Instrumentalists: C. Guitarists

Bream, Julian--born in England in 1933. Bream is an accomplished guitarist with a creditable technique and formidable intelligence. He has commissioned several pieces (some of which are gems) and plays Bach and modern works equally well, but I feel his heart is more in tune with the music of this century.

Parkening, Christopher--born in the United States in 1947. Just as some other guitarists are most comfortable in the concerted repertoire, Parkening seems most at ease in miniatures. His technique is probably the best around, and the smaller pieces he does play are exquisitely performed.

Segovia, Andrés--born in Spain in 1893, died in 1987. There is little to be said of Segovia that hasn't already been said: he was the guitarist of guitarists and brought the instrument to serious music when everyone else scoffed. There have been a plethora of pieces written for him, and there was no serious music he could not, or would not, essay, if he thought it befitted his instrument. He is probably best known for his performances of Bach and Spanish composers.

Williams, John--born in England in 1941. Williams is now, with Yepes, among the finest guitarists performing. He has technique aplenty, a beautiful and sonorous tone, and wit.

Yepes, Narciso--born in Spain in 1927. With the death of Segovia, Yepes has the field of Spanish guitar music pretty much to himself. Although I haven't heard him do much Bach (or other Baroque composers), I would be surprised if he does not exhibit the same felicity there that he does in music by his countrymen.

Instrumentalists: D. Harpsichordists

Hogwood, Christopher--born in England in 1941. Hogwood often performs with the Academy of Ancient Music as both instrumentalist and director. His playing is tasteful, not overly embellished, and he ranks with the five or six best harpsichord executants.

Kipnis, Igor--born in Germany in 1930. Kipnis may well be the best harpsichordist now before the public. He is exceptionally intelligent (both as musician and as musicologist), possesses remarkable technical skills, and can display a nice sense of humor when the music warrants. His performances are always lively and informed by a good deal of preparation.

Kirkpatrick, Ralph--born in the United States in 1911. Kirkpatrick is equally well known as both a musicologist and a performer. His index to the works of Domenico Scarlatti (plus Kirkpatrick's analysis of that composer's music) is considered to be a most important effort. Kirkpatrick's interpretations often are a bit stuffy (i.e., pedagogical) for my tastes, but they certainly indicate an active mind and facile technique.

Landowska, Wanda--born in Poland in 1877, died in 1959. What Segovia did for the guitar, Landowska did for the harpsichord: she brought it to the attention of the public and popularized it as the appropriate instrument for those works of Bach that had long been played on the piano. Her performances of Bach tend to be somewhat in the Romantic style (she once countered that charge by saying something to the effect that any man who was the father of 20 children must have been rather romantic), which is pretty much eschewed now. Still, she played Bach and Mozart with panache, and her recordings are true artifacts.

Leonhardt, Gustav--born in Holland in 1928. Leonhardt has recorded most of the Bach works for harpsichord, and conducts a chamber orchestra named for himself (Leonhardt Consort). I find most of his performances stiff and dry, and prefer those of several other instrumentalists to his (he is almost the antithesis of Landowska's style).

Pinnock, Trevor--born in England in 1946. Pinnock is well represented on recordings, mostly with his own ensemble, the English Concert. His skills are akin to those of Christopher Hogwood, and the English Concert is about on par with the Academy of Ancient Music. Pinnock occasionally tends towards rather quick tempi (which keeps the music moving).

Instrumentalists: E. Hornists

Baumann, Hermann--born in Germany in 1934. Herr Baumann is technically the best horn player now practicing. If you don't believe it, listen to his recording of all four of Mozart's Horn Concerti, which Baumann plays on a natural (i.e., valveless) horn. His interpretations are exquisite and, for me, no other horn player comes close.

Brain, Dennis--born in England in 1921, died (in an automobile crash) in 1957. Brain was the son of the fine hornist, Aubrey Brain (first desk horn in the Royal Philharmonic Orchestra), who was his first teacher. The younger Brain became principal hornist of the Philharmonia Orchestra, and had a distinguished, although short, career as a soloist. Brain was considered the finest horn player in the world, and, besides a legacy of exquisite recordings, he left a tradition of wonderful British horn playing, exemplified by such musicians as Alan Civil (who studied formally with Aubrey Brain) and Barry Tuckwell (who learned a good deal from Dennis Brain).

Civil, Alan--born in England in 1929, died in 1989. Civil was an accomplished, no nonsense performer who turned in honest readings of the works he played.

Tuckwell, Barry--born in Australia in 1931. Tuckwell is very similar to Civil in ability, but a tad more "unbuttoned" and relaxed. Both are noted for their performances of "newer" music.

<u>Instrumentalists</u>: F. Oboists

Holliger, Heinz--born in Switzerland in 1939. As a technician, Holliger has no equals. Unfortunately, despite his extremely informed performances, his tone is often unpleasant. Were this otherwise, he would be the oboist of choice every time.

Still, Ray--born in the United States in 1920. Still is the principal oboist of the Chicago Symphony Orchestra and is one of the finest of the "American" style oboists--a quick vibrato and a lovely tone, coupled with excellent musicianship.

<u>Instrumentalists</u>: G. Organists

Alain, Marie-Claire--born in France in 1926. With the death of E. Power Biggs, Alain is now esteemed as one of the, if not the, best organists in the world. Her technique, choices of registrations, musicianship, and nuance are all beyond reproach. Most other organists are given to idiosyncrasies--not Alain. From Bach to the most recent composers for the organ, Alain's performances pleasure the ear and the mind.

Chorzempa, Daniel--born in the United States in 1948. Chorzempa is a quite good organist, one who fits into the place just after Alain.

Preston, Simon--born in England in 1938. A most competent organist and conductor (particularly of choral works) who evidences scholarship and vitality in his playing.

Rogg, Lionel--born in Switzerland in 1936. Rogg is a much recorded organist who, although not an exciting performer, is competent and honest.

Walcha, Helmut--born in Germany in 1907. Walcha is one of the preeminent organists or our time, particularly in his playing of the works of Bach. Wonderful to tell, Walcha is blind, but his handicap seems to be no impediment to performing. His interpretations are imbued with thoughtfulness, study, and an old-worldliness that manifest themselves in the way he takes time to examine works carefully. Although his work is not as exciting say, as Biggs or Alain, Walcha's performances are exceptional.

Instrumentalists: H. Pianists

Argerich, Martha--born in Argentina in 1941. Argerich is a remarkable pianist with technical skill to spare and an almost infallible musical intelligence when it comes to specific composers (e.g., Ravel, Tchaikovsky, and Prokofiev).

Arrau, Claudio--born in Chile in 1903. A great pianist who used to "freeze up" in the recording studio, Arrau's recorded performances have become warmer and more accessible during the last decade or so. His is an aristocratic style, but not without a flair for the Romantic. Despite just acclaim for his Liszt interpretations, his recent recordings of the Beethoven Concerti are lustrous.

Ax, Emanuel--born in the Poland in 1949. Ax is very capable both as a soloist and as a member of a chamber ensemble. He is particularly good in the Romantic repertoire.

Backhaus, Wilhelm--born in Germany in 1884, died in 1969. Despite not being well represented in the catalog of CDs (one hopes more of his recordings will soon be reissued), Backhaus is my own

69

favorite Beethoven interpreter. His technique was legendary, his warmth of feeling exceptional, and his understanding of the "inner" Beethoven extraordinary.

Barenboim, Daniel--born in Argentina in 1942. He is an exceptional soloist and accompanist. Barenboim is very fine in Mozart and Schumann.

Berman, Lazar--born in the Soviet Union in 1930. Berman is a pianist of immense power (both physically and technically) who performs in the "Grand Romantic" manner. His playing can be idiosyncratic, but is certainly musical. Berman's specialties are Liszt and his compatriots.

Bilson, Malcolm--born in the United States in 1935. Bilson is a very fine Mozart pianist who often now records that composer appropriately on the fortepiano, rather than its modern counterpart.

Bolet, Jorge--born in Cuba in 1914. A large bear of a man, Bolet is one of the best interpreters of Liszt and Rachmaninoff currently recording. He is more than proficient technically, and he is very thoughtful about his interpretations.

Brendel, Alfred--born in Moravia in 1931. Brendel is the "utility" (as the term is used in baseball, for example: a "utility infielder") pianist of this age. He is idiosyncratic about his person (e.g., his physiognomy often appears startled by the world at large; before he performs, he puts Band-Aids on his fingertips) but there are no eccentricities in his playing. He is a first-rate technician, and an intellectual musician. If he is not always exciting, his performances are alive and intelligent. At his best, he is among the world's premier pianists.

Browning, John--born in the United States in 1933. Among the finest American-born pianists, Browning's technical skill never gets in the way of his often profound performances. He is superb when he performs the works of modern composers like Ravel, Prokofiev, and Barber; and his Chopin is definitely worth hearing.

Casadesus, Robert--born in France in 1899, died in 1970. Coming from an eminent French musical family, Casadesus was an exceptional interpreter of the music of his countrymen and of Mozart.

Ciccolini, Aldo--born in Italy in 1925. Although he specialized in performances of the piano works of Satie, Ciccolini is also an unqualifiedly fine performer of the music of Debussy and Saint-Saëns.

Cliburn, Van (real name: Harvey LaVan Cliburn, Jr.)--born in the United States in 1934. Despite the big splash Cliburn made by winning the prestigious Tchaikovsky Prize in 1958, and his then remarkable recording of the Tchaikovsky Piano Concerto No.1 (the "popular" one), his career has practically fizzled. He has become a mannered and rather incompetent pianist--one who deserves little attention now.

Curzon, Sir Clifford--born in England in 1907, died in 1982. Curzon was a little known pianist in the United States, but his recordings of the Brahms Piano Concerto No.1, the Beethoven Concerto No.5 ("Emperor"), and the Grieg Piano Concerto indicate a pianist of rare musicianship, intelligence, and technique.

Davis, Ivan--born in the United States in 1932. Like Browning, Davis is a pianist who is underappreciated in his own country. Davis is a technician *sans peur et sans reproche*, and a true musician. His recordings of Liszt and Gottschalk are proof of the treasure that Davis is.

De Larrocha, Alicia--see Larrocha, Alicia De

Dichter, Misha--born in Shanghai in 1945. Although born in China, Dichter is of Russian parentage. He is an accomplished pianist, but not a terribly distinguished one.

Entremont, Philippe--born in France in 1934. Often recorded, Entremont is fully at his ease performing the music of his fellow Frenchmen. His performances are scrupulously honest and technically proficient. He is seldom inspiring, but always correct.

Eschenbach, Christoph--born in Breslau (when it was part of Germany) in 1940. Eschenbach is an exquisite accompanist and occasionally an inspired soloist.

Firkušný, Rudolf--born in Czechoslovakia in 1912. Firkušný is among the preeminent interpreters of Dvořák's piano music. He is equally excellent in works by Janáček. He has a complete grasp of the Czech idiom and the technique to create ingratiating performances.

Fleisher, Leon--born in the United States in 1928. Fleisher was a truly great pianist whose right hand became useless for playing the piano due to a neurological disease. His recordings of the Brahms and Beethoven piano concerti are among the best renditions available. Through great effort and study, Fleisher has become a left-handed virtuoso and has made a career performing the piano repertoire specific to his abilities. He has also become a conductor of some repute.

Frager, Malcolm--born in the United States in 1935. When Frager plays well, he plays well indeed. His way with Chopin is often outstanding.

Gieseking, Walter--born in France (to German parents) in 1895, died in 1956. Gieseking was the Debussy and Ravel pianist nonpareil. In listening to his recordings of the works of these composers, I often feel that Gieseking certainly played an instrument, but not any kind of piano with which I am familiar. His tone (perforce his specific instrument, his touch) and his reticent use of the *sostenuto* pedal--but his deft use of the *una corda* pedal, created an aural image that does not conjure what one usually thinks of as a "piano sound." Gieseking, in short, was a wonder. Also, his recordings of Mozart are occasionally equalled, but never surpassed.

Gilels, Emil--born in Russia in 1916, died in 1985. Gilels was an outstanding, even great, pianist who left a large recorded legacy. His art was made up both of technique and musicianship, and he never lacked in good taste or lapsed into mannerisms that call attention to the performer rather than the music. His repertoire included virtually all the piano literature from Beethoven onwards.

Gould, Glenn--born in Canada in 1932, died in 1982. Gould was a controversial pianist and a true eccentric. His technical ability was never in dispute, but his idiosyncratic playing of almost everything in the piano repertoire (especially Bach) tended to make some critics cringe and others applaud, sometimes simultaneously. Among the habits critics found annoying were his tendency to hum (off key) while playing, and (in recording) his insistence on using an old (and comfortable) swivel chair that squeaked audibly. His extensive scholarship as a musicologist seemed implausible in a performer (the only other pianist who combines that level of scholarship with an excellent, and also eccentric, performance level, is Charles Rosen), and his sense of humor was dry, but could be vastly entertaining. It is doubtful, his detractors notwithstanding, that anyone ever recorded Bach's harpsichord and clavichord works better on the modern piano. For one, I miss Gould greatly.

Gulda, Friedrich--born in Austria in 1930. Early in his career (when he was about 20), Gulda was hailed as one of the potentially greatest Beethoven interpreters of the century. His technique was formidable, but his musical intellect was incredible. In 1955, Gulda virtually gave up performing "serious" music and became a jazz composer and pianist. He has returned to recording the standard piano repertoire, and his performances do not belie the predictions of his ultimate abilities.

Horowitz, Vladimir--born in Russia in 1904, died in 1989. Horowitz has often been called the greatest pianist, certainly of this century, possibly of any time. He is the last of the great piano virtuosi: his technique is usually perfect, and his musicianship is most often faultless. Some critics have noted what they feel are oddities in his performances (e.g., too much or too little pedal; his dependence on a particular Steinway piano that, supposedly, has the hammer felts hardened to provide a more brilliant tone; and an occasionally excessive use of rubato), but most agree that there will never be his like again. Horowitz is best heard in music by Beethoven, Scriabin, Chopin, Schumann, Mussorgsky, and Rachmaninoff. His Mozart is rather lacking in an understanding of the Classical style.

Kempff, Wilhelm--born in Germany in 1895. Kempff is supposed, by many critics, to be one of the great Beethoven interpreters. I find his technique somewhat sloppy, and his tempi so slow that his recordings serve me as soporifics.

Larrocha, Alicia De--born in Spain in 1923. Larrocha is a much overrated performer of Mozart but, as one would expect, an interpreter of Spanish music *par excellence*.

Levine, James--born in the United States in 1943. Levine could have made a great career for himself as a virtuoso. Instead, he chose conducting, and occasional piano recordings, mostly as an accompanist. In his latter role, he is an ingratiating and excellent performer.

Michelangeli, Arturo Benedetti--born in Italy in 1920. Michelangeli is almost reclusive, but his virtuosity is such that his few recordings are gems. He is notorious for his perfectionism, often travelling with two pianos (should one be out of tune) and canceling performances because neither was tuned to his liking. For all that, he is a great artist.

Moore, Gerald--born in England in 1899, died in 1987. Moore brought the role of piano accompanist to a level never before achieved on a regular basis. His technique, he felt, was not sufficient to have brought him the kind of acclaim he might have sought as a soloist. As an accompanist, particularly to singers, his infallible intelligence and good sense made him an indispensable partner, often even transforming mediocre singing performances into quite acceptable ones.

Perahia, Murray born in the United States in 1947. Perahia has, given his fine technique and good musical training, become one of the best Mozart pianists.

Pollini, Maurizio--born in Italy in 1942. Pollini is among the few really great pianists now plying his art. There is nothing in the piano repertoire beyond his technique or intelligence, but his Chopin is something most special.

Richter, Sviatoslav--born in Russia in 1915. Despite his frequent illnesses, Richter is in the forefront of piano virtuosi. His sense of nuance, his technical skill, and his taste, make him a pianist against which to measure most others. He has recorded much, and few of the recordings are less than superb.

Rosen, Charles--born in the United States in 1927. Rosen is a true oddity--he has a graduate degree in music history and a doctorate in French literature. He is an instrumental stylist (many would say eccentric) who never performs a work like any other pianist. His technique is better than adequate, but his intelligence and erudition are phenomena. His writings on music (to be found in books, journals, and newspapers) are real delights--something he shared with Glenn Gould.

Rubinstein, Artur--born in Poland in 1887, died in 1982. Rubinstein has been called one of the greatest pianists of all time--a true exemplar of the Romantic tradition. I do not relish being called a revisionist, but Rubinstein was somewhat careless in his technique, and understood little of the piano repertoire written before Chopin (yes, he was at one time known for his Mozart playing, but I can't understand why). He tended to use rubato with abandon, even when it wasn't called for, and he often depended on his "pianistic" physical appearance, and ultimately his age, to make up for what was wanting in his performances. He was awfully good at Chopin and Schumann-- let's leave it at that.

Sándor, György--born in Hungary in 1912. Sándor is generally considered the outstanding interpreter of the piano works of Bartók and Kodály. He does not often wander from that literature, and wisely so.

Serkin, Peter--born in the United States in 1947. Serkin is a most talented pianist who often excels in performing modern works. He is also a fine Mozart pianist.

Serkin, Rudolf--born in Czechoslovakia in 1903. This Serkin has often been cited as one of the most insightful of pianists. His technical virtuosity is somewhat overrated, and his insight can often prolong a performance by a vacuous search for meaning (or by self-indulgence). Still, he has a large following and does do some works quite well, but not well enough for my taste.

Watts, André--born in Germany in 1946. Watts is a pianist who has attracted much attention because of his incredible technique, heard to best advantage in works by Liszt. He is less a musician than many critics have thought and is, at his best, very flashy (but musically empty).

Weissenberg, Alexis--born in Bulgaria in 1929. Weissenberg is a thoughtful and technically proficient pianist who overcame the handicap of being a child prodigy. He has developed into an important artist whose interpretations of the Romantic piano literature are quite often brilliant.

Zimerman, Krystian--born in Poland in 1956. Zimerman is now a pianist of real achievement, and could easily become a truly great artist. He has technique to spare and interpretive skills that are rare (rhyme unintentional). His performances of Brahms and Chopin are particularly worth hearing.

Instrumentalists: I. Trumpeters

André, Maurice--born in France in 1933. André is an impeccable trumpeter: his technique and musicianship make him the reigning "Prince of the Trumpet." He has recorded almost every work calling for solo trumpet, and all are served brilliantly.

Marsalis, Wynton--born in the United States in 1962. Marsalis is a performer who is equally adept at classical music and jazz. He is known for a unique attack and formidable technique.

Instrumentalists: J. Violists

Suk, Josef--born in Czechoslovakia in 1929. Better known as a violinist, Suk (the great-grandson of Dvořák) is probably one of the two best virtuosi of the viola.

Zukerman, Pinchas--born in Israel in 1948. Like Suk, Zukerman is most readily recognized as a violinist. He is now the other of the two best viola performers.

Instrumentalists: K. Violinists

Accardo, Salvatore--born in Italy in 1937. Accardo is a violinist whose tone, although not extraordinary, is very pleasant. His technique and musical intelligence are up to the demands of the difficult Paganini works in which he specializes.

Chung, Kyung-Wha--born in Korea in 1948. Chung's tone is adequate, likewise her technique. The real problem with Chung as an artist is her inability to indicate the inner sense of the music she plays. She is adept, but does not invest her playing with nuance nor much grace. She occasionally rushes through pieces, as though speed alone were an indication of virtuosity.

Francescatti, Zino--born in France in 1902. Francescatti's father had been a student of Paganini's and was himself little Zino's teacher. Francescatti's playing possesses warmth, suavity, subtlety, and a masterful technique. He is among the best of the century.

Grumiaux, Arthur--born in Belgium in 1921. Not quite up to Francescatti's abilities, Grumiaux is still an extremely fine violinist who thoroughly understands the music he plays, and invests it with personality, grace and affection.

Heifetz, Jascha--born in Russia in 1901, died 1987. Certainly insofar as technique, Heifetz was probably the greatest violinist of all time. His tone was as beautiful and variable as it needed to be to suit whatever music he was performing. His musical acumen was one of real genius--he never failed to understand completely every aspect of the music: every nuance and every inner meaning. To speak of Heifetz is to speak in superlatives--he was without mannerisms, always allowing the music to speak for itself. And when I say music, I mean anything to which he put his attention: there was no particular repertoire in which he excelled: he played everything superbly. Contrary to what some critics refer to as his aloofness, Heifetz had always been totally involved, both emotionally and intellectually, in the music. That controlled emotion, far from aloofness, gives most of his performances a white-hot incandescence which is dazzling. Of all performing musicians, I consider Heifetz to be the closest to faultless.

Kremer, Gidon--born in the Soviet Union in 1947. Kremer is a very capable violinist who has a pleasing tone, but not always infallible intonation. He is worth listening to, but there are several violinists who outclass him.

Laredo, Jaime--born in Bolivia in 1941. Laredo has a somewhat pinched tone, but is intelligent and very good in chamber ensembles.

Menuhin, Sir Yehudi--born in the United States in 1916. Menuhin could well have been one of the great violinists of the century had he not spread himself rather thinly, conducting, teaching, dabbling in Eastern religions and music, etc. When Menuhin is playing well, he has an extraordinarily beautiful tone. He is musically brilliant, but his other activities have taken their toll on his technique and intonation. Still, he is very often well worth listening to.

Milstein, Nathan--born in Russia in 1904. One of the last of the great violinists of the early part of the century who still actively performs, Milstein resembles Heifetz somewhat in his impeccable execution, brilliance, and exquisite tone. Given his age, that he still performs at all, let alone being worth hearing, is almost a miracle.

Mutter, Anne-Sophie--born in Germany in 1963. Mutter was a protégée of conductor Herbert von Karajan. As a child prodigy, she displayed a surprising understanding of the music she performed. It is a given that her technique and tone were exceptional. She has matured into a very good young violinist and she may well become a true virtuoso.

Mintz, Shlomo--born in the Soviet Union in 1957. Much heralded as the successor to David Oistrakh, Mintz has been something of a disappointment. His technique is no more than adequate, his tone is nothing special, and I don't understand what all the fuss was about.

Oistrakh, David--born in Russia in 1908, died in 1974. Along with Heifetz and Milstein, Oistrakh was one of the greatest fiddlers of the century. Oistrakh had a robust and luscious tone, virtually infallible technique, and a full comprehension of the music. He was particularly fine in the music of Bach, Mozart, Beethoven, and modern Soviet composers.

Perlman, Itzhak--born in Israel in 1945. Perlman is still capable of becoming a truly great musician, if only he applies himself to his instrument more. His musical intelligence has often been questioned by some critics, but giving him the benefit of the doubt, I think his faults are due to "coasting": getting by on his natural talents without any real exertion. His tone is gorgeous, he has, on occasion, evidenced technical prowess, but his overall performance level is very uneven. And yet, some of his recordings, especially in the big, Romantic works, are exceptional. If he'd work a little harder, who knows?

Standage, Simon--born in England in 1941. Standage specializes in the Baroque repertoire, and records almost exclusively with the English Concert. In what he essays, Standage is extremely fine.

Stern, Isaac--born in the Soviet Union in 1920 (but raised, from infancy, in the United States). Stern is often considered among the greatest violinists practicing: he is capable of producing a truly beautiful violin tone and has good native musical intelligence. I find that most critics and reviewers are kinder to him than I believe he deserves since he has allowed what was once a better than good technique to deteriorate, and seems to rely primarily on being a musical "personage" rather than a true craftsman or artist. In this regard he reminds me of Itzhak Perlman, with whom he shares a great friendship and often appears. I think both performers owe it to their admirers, and the public generally, to practice and rehearse with greater avidity.

Suk, Josef--born in Czechoslovakia in 1929. Suk is, to my mind, the best practicing violinist in the world. He is a wonderful soloist in virtually all the violin literature (if he has a weakness, it is a tendency to make Mozart a bit Romantic), and his chamber playing is unequaled. His tone is beautiful, his technique without flaw, and his musicianship unquestioned.

Szeryng, Henryk--born in Poland in 1918, died 1988. Szeryng was of the same caliber as Grumiaux: very polished and sophisticated, with a fine tone and excellent technique. Grumiaux had the edge on polish, but Szeryng could sometimes be more exciting.

Zukerman, Pinchas--born in Israel in 1948. Perlman and Zukerman are both graduates of Juilliard and students of the famous violin pedagogue: Ivan Galamian. Unlike his colleague, Zukerman seems to have worked very hard at his craft. This is most telling in Zukerman's approach to the better known works in the violin literature: Zukerman displays both a better technique and a finer understanding of what he plays. Zukerman has become a great violinist, one of the best violists, and a conductor to be taken seriously. One wonders how long anyone can retain one's sanity or ability, juggling so many careers.

Vocalists

Allen, Thomas--born in Wales in 1944. Baritone. Allen is competent, and usually sings secondary operatic roles.

Alva, Luigi--born in Peru in 1927. Tenor. Was especially good in Rossini opera (though seldom in leading roles).

Ameling, Elly--born in Holland in 1938. Soprano. Although not possessed of a big voice, Ameling brings grace, intelligence, and a lovely tonal quality to her work, whether in lieder, opera, or cantatas, etc.

Angeles, Victoria de Los--born in Spain in 1923. Soprano. Angeles (real name is Victoria Gómez Cima) was among the leading sopranos for several decades, and was particularly fine in such roles as Carmen and Mimi in La Bohème.

Augér, Arleen--born in the United States in 1939. Soprano. Augér came into real prominence only recently, and is now recognized for the fine singer she is. She is excellent in Mozart, Mahler, Bach, and Haydn.

Bacquier, Gabriel--born in France in 1924. Baritone. Although Bacquier has been around the block a few times, he still offers workmanlike performances in lighter operatic vehicles such as those of Offenbach and Massenet.

Baker, Dame Janet--born in England in 1933. Mezzo-soprano. Dame Janet is, despite her age, still considered one of the leading mezzos, now best heard in lieder; but her older Mahler, Handel, and Bach recordings indicate how really good she was.

Battle, Kathleen--born in the United States in 1949. Soprano. Battle is a wonderful Mozart soprano with a light, warm, feminine tone and who uses her voice exceedingly well. Battle is known for husbanding her instrument carefully, and it should see many more years of use.

Berbié, Jane--born in France in 1931. Soprano. Berbié's lovely, light voice is perfect for the French repertoire to which she wisely tends to adhere.

Berganza, Teresa--born in Spain in 1935. Mezzo-soprano. One of the best mezzos of the second half of this century, Berganza is my favorite in all the Spanish vocal repertoire, and has been outstanding in Mozart. Her voice possesses just the right weight and color for the music she elects to sing. She uses that voice so appropriately that, even now, one tends to forget just how long she has been practicing her art.

Bergonzi, Carlo--born in Italy in 1926. Tenor. Bergonzi was often given the lead tenor roles in recordings of Italian opera with Renata Tebaldi. He tended to "over sing" and "under act," but was competent and not unpleasant.

Björling, Jussi--born in Sweden in 1911, died in 1960. Tenor. Björling was among the greatest tenors of the century. In fact, he is ranked ahead of Caruso by many critics. His voice was bright, yet fully rounded (without the Italianate thinness), and powerful without being overpowering. His technique was flawless, as was his musical intelligence. He was at his best in such Italian works as those of Puccini, and in several French roles (e.g., those written by Gounod, etc.).

Blegen, Judith--born in the United States in 1941. Soprano. Blegen's pleasant, light, accurate soprano makes for an appealing sound in the non-bravura opera roles, and in Bach and Handel.

Bruson, Renato--born in France in 1936. Baritone. Bruson is a good, solid baritone, who has taken many of the roles that Bacquier used to sing (mainly villains, etc., in Italian opera).

Bryn-Julson, Phyllis--born in the United States in 1945. Soprano. Bryn-Julson is among the finest interpreters of the really difficult, modern art songs of composers like Rorem and Clayton. In this arena, her only competition comes from Jan DeGaetani.

Bumbry, Grace--born in the United States in 1937. Mezzo-soprano. Although now somewhat past her prime, Bumbry was once a leading Wagnerian singer with a heavy, dark mezzo sound that could be both sexy and ethereal.

Caballé, Montserrat--born in Spain in 1933. Soprano. Despite her great general acclaim, I have not been an admirer of Caballé's because she has been given to faulty intonation and sometimes "chewing on the scenery." She is, however, generally regarded as a great mezzo.

Callas, Maria--born in the United States in 1923, died in 1977. Soprano. Regarded as one of the greatest of all "singing actresses," Callas often produced sounds reminiscent of a troubled boiler. Her intonation was often quite apart from the score, and her tone could frequently be described as ugly. However, she could transmit, vocally, the inner thoughts of those personae in whose roles she performed. My own feeling is that, given her arresting and magnetic physical appearance, and her undeniable understanding of stagecraft, she should have been a non-singing actress--she would have been magnificent in the kinds of roles Judith Anderson undertook.

Carreras, José--born in Spain in 1946. Tenor. Carreras possesses a good, solid voice that he uses brilliantly. His upper range is not quite as ringing as Domingo's (or what Pavarotti's used to be), but he is judicious in its use and seems to be husbanding it. His acting is more than adequate, and he is excellent in the Italian opera repertoire.

Caruso, Enrico--born in Italy in 1873, died in 1921. Caruso is usually regarded as the greatest tenor of this century (and accounted by many as possibly the greatest tenor in Romantic roles of any time). He is best known for his work in Italian operas of the Realistic school. His career was as spectacular as his voice (at the height of his powers, he earned over one hundred thousand dollars in one year--just from his recordings), and the voice was truly rare. He began as a baritone but soon discovered that he possessed a robust and full-bodied tenor wonderfully suited to the florid and difficult *bel canto* roles. Since his death, every budding Italian tenor is hailed as the "new Caruso:" there has yet to be a "new Caruso," since no tenor has yet emerged who has displayed the musicianship and natural talent with which the "original" Caruso had in such abundance.

Cotrubas, Ileana--born in Rumania in 1939. Soprano. Now at the height of her career, Cotrubas is a leading soprano in several recordings of Mozart, which suits the timbre and range of her voice quite well.

Crespin, Régine--born in France in 1927. Soprano. Crespin was at her best in Wagnerian opera, to which she brought a lovely tonal quality, accurate intonation, and a voice of sufficient power. She is now well past her prime.

DeGaetani, Jan--born in the United States in 1933, died in 1989. Mezzo-soprano. DeGaetani is among the most remarkable singers this, or any, country has produced. She has a wonderful vocal tone, but this is not what makes her so extraordinary. She is able to sing microtones accurately; to inflect the words of what she is singing with infallible meaning and understanding; and to range from light, frothy music to the very most serious. She is the female interpreter without peer in the modern art song and her recordings of works by Ives, Stephen Foster, Crumb, and Ravel are essentially unrivaled. Only Bryn-Julson comes even close.

Deller, Alfred--born in England in 1912, died in 1979. Countertenor. Deller was among the first of this century to revive an interest in the music written for countertenor. He was an intelligent, and often inspired, singer who is well represented by his recordings, particularly of music by Purcell.

de Los Angeles, Victoria--see **Angeles, Victoria de Los**

Di Stefano, Giuseppe--born in Italy in 1921. Tenor. Di Stefano, whose career is obviously over, was the tenor of choice as Maria Callas' partner in many of her operatic recordings. His voice had a solidity and ringing quality that served him well when contrasted with Callas.

Domingo, Plácido--born in Spain in 1941. Tenor. Domingo is now the reigning tenor in virtually any operatic medium. His range is easily through a top C, and his tonal quality is gorgeous. He is a consummate musician, and has recently begun to conduct seriously.

Esswood, Paul--born in England in 1942. Countertenor. One of the most recorded countertenors now working, Esswood is superb in Bach cantatas and Handel operas.

Fassbaender, Brigitte--born in Germany in 1939. Mezzo-soprano. Fassbaender is among those mezzos who is comfortable in works by Beethoven, Berlioz, Brahms, and Verdi. She has a very fine tonal quality and excellent intonation.

Ferrier, Kathleen--born in England in 1912, died in 1953. Contralto. Ferrier was among the greatest contraltos of the modern era (i.e., after 1900). She was capable of producing a blooming and wonderful tone, exact intonation, and exercised flawless taste in both her repertoire and execution. She was particularly outstanding in works by Mahler, but was also adept in music of Britten and Gluck.

Fischer-Dieskau, Dietrich--born in Germany in 1925. Baritone. Fischer-Dieskau's baritone is relatively light, but extremely expressive. Although now well beyond his best days, Fischer-Dieskau has made what are considered among the best recordings of lieder ever. His thorough understanding of the lyrics, expressiveness, intelligence, and nuance, have made him the male lieder singer without peer. He has now turned to conducting, and has recorded a few very fine symphonic performances.

Flagstad, Kirsten--born in Norway in 1895, died in 1962. Soprano. Flagstad was the very best Wagnerian soprano of the century. Her voice was strong, full, and she had the stamina to endure a full Wagnerian operatic performance without tiring. Her Isolde and Brünnhilde are the measure of all later sopranos attempting those roles.

Forrester, Maureen--born in Canada in 1930. Contralto. Forrester is an extremely well trained contralto and one whose voice is rich and mellow. She is not often to be found in operas so much as in lieder and symphonic works calling for a contralto (e.g., Mahler symphonies). In her chosen domain, she is among the very best.

Freni, Mirella born in Italy in 1935. Soprano. Freni is essentially a lyric soprano whose voice is still fresh and lovely sounding. She has been outstanding in operatic roles by Puccini, Mozart, and Verdi.

Gedda, Nicolai--born in Sweden in 1925. Tenor. Gedda is quite possibly the most recorded tenor of all time. His round, warm, and full tenor suits him to heroic roles by composers from Mozart to Verdi. He is also often to be found in earlier composers like Gluck. His fame is well deserved--he has not, to my knowledge, given a poor performance.

Haefliger, Ernst--born in Switzerland in 1921. Tenor. Haefliger has specialized in works by Bach, Haydn, and Mozart, and in these he has proven to be dependable. His voice is suited to this repertoire by virtue of its lightness and flexibility.

Hagegard, Hakan--born in Sweden in 1945. Baritone. The American public first became generally aware of Hagegard in Ingmar Bergman's sprightly movie of Mozart's <u>Die Zauberflöte</u>. Hagegard has made his way as a lieder singer of real quality. His voice has a fuller texture than Fischer-Dieskau's, and his enunciation is very good.

He is not quite the perfectionist Fischer-Dieskau was, but then, who is? Hagegard is still very much worth hearing, and he may even improve a bit yet.

Hendricks, Barbara--born in the United States in 1948. Soprano. Hendricks is one fine soprano who, despite her age, seems just coming to the fore. Her vocal texture is well suited to Puccini, but she has made some fine recordings of Mozart and Verdi as well.

Hollweg, Werner--born in Germany in 1936. Tenor. The light-voiced Hollweg is admirably cast in Mozart operas and in works by Handel. His intonation is relatively secure and he projects that light voice well.

Horne, Marilyn--born in the United States in 1934. Mezzo-soprano. Horne is now on the down side of her career, but in her prime she was the *bel canto* mezzo without challenge by anyone. She was a marvelous <u>Carmen</u> and was supreme in Rossini roles. As a counter to Dame Joan Sutherland, she was magnificent--that really was a pair of magicians!

Janowitz, Gundula--born in Germany in 1937. Soprano. Although she has recorded works by Haydn, Janowitz has been at her best in music by Bach, Mozart, and Wagner. She is full-voiced, careful of intonation, reliable, and intelligent.

King, James--born in the United States in 1927. Tenor. King has been an excellent Wagnerian tenor--possessing a large voice and a nice command of German inflection.

Kollo, René--born in Germany in 1937. Tenor. Kollo's voice has been put to good use in the service of Wagnerian opera. His large tenor is sweet and sufficiently strong to make its way through the Wagnerian orchestra.

Lear, Evelyn--born in the United States in 1927. Soprano. Lear has recorded a wide range of music, from Bach to Berg. In all she was able to project a clean, full voice coupled to musical integrity and intelligence.

Lloyd, Robert--born in England in 1940. Bass. Lloyd is in great demand for recordings. There seems to be no limit on the range of music he can accommodate. His voice is, as one would expect, dark and somber.

Ludwig, Christa--born in Germany in 1928. Mezzo-soprano. Ludwig has had a long and illustrious career. She is not a *bel canto* mezzo, but a dramatic one, and in that field she has had little competition. Hers is a full and womanly voice, which she has been able to vary with true skill. She has recorded a wide variety of music, and all with intelligence and outstanding artistry.

Luxon, Benjamin--born in England in 1937. Baritone. Luxon is good in Bach, Handel, and music by British composers. His baritone is relatively light and flexible, and he wisely does not tend to push it.

Mathis, Edith--born in Switzerland in 1938. Soprano. Mathis has a lovely soprano that she uses intelligently and with skill. She can be serious or coquettish with equal enthusiasm, and has been excellent in Bach, Haydn, and Mozart.

Milnes, Sherrill--born in the United States in 1935. Baritone. If Brendel is a utility pianist, Milnes is a utility baritone. Give him the music for a baritone, irrespective of period, and Milnes will provide an informed and well-sung performance. There is no baritone role that Milnes does not grace with his musicianship.

Moll, Kurt--born in Germany in 1938. Bass. Moll is a superb Wagnerian bass who is excellent in recordings of <u>Die Meistersinger</u> and <u>Der fliegende Holländer</u>. Moll can also do comic roles such as Baron Ochs in <u>Der Rosenkavalier</u>.

Nilsson, Birgit--born in Sweden in 1918. Soprano. Obviously beyond her public singing days, Nilsson's CD recordings are numerous and, mostly, show off her incredible trumpeting soprano: a voice clear and secure in intonation, and well used in her acting. She is best known for her work in Wagnerian roles.

Norman, Jessye--born in the United States in 1945. Soprano. Norman's voice is a velvety, dark, and dramatic soprano. There is no limit to the roles or songs she can sing. Once heard, Norman's beautiful soprano is one not easily forgotten.

Pavarotti, Luciano--born in Italy in 1935. Tenor. At one time, Pavarotti was favorably compared to Caruso. Pavarotti has never had the musical intelligence of either Caruso or Domingo, but he possessed a tenor of great beauty and range. Too many high Cs and too many sobs and breaks have hastened the deterioration of his wonderful instrument. Pavarotti now pleases audiences through nostalgia and a great warmth of personality rather than by providing the noble vocal thrills of yesteryear.

Popp, Lucia--born in Czechoslovakia in 1939. Soprano. Popp, in her youth, was not only an excellent soprano, but very attractive physically, too. She is a bit plumper now, but her voice is still good and pleasing, and has a sexy edge to it. Her texture was relatively light and is well matched to music by Mozart.

Prey, Hermann--born in Germany in 1929. Baritone. Prey was Fischer-Dieskau's only real competition as a baritone lieder singer. Prey, though, was also very much at home in operatic roles by Mozart and Rossini because his voice had a somewhat darker tone and heavier texture than Fischer-Dieskau's. Given his age, he still sings quite well.

Price, Leontyne--born in the United States in 1927. Soprano. A great dramatic soprano, Price has continued to perform publicly when she really ought to have retired. She had a unique vocal quality: smooth, creamy, dark, and vibrant. She was the best Verdi soprano of her time, and possibly the century.

Ramey, Samuel--born in the United States in 1942. Bass. Ramey's bass is beautiful: rich, strong, and used with intelligence. He is superb in Rossini.

Ricciarelli, Katia--born in Italy in 1946. Soprano. When Ricciarelli is in good voice and in the proper vehicle, she is wonderful. Her best roles have been in Rossini and Verdi, but she does well in Puccini, also. Her soprano is bright, lively, and quite feminine, without being ear piercing.

Schreier, Peter--born in Germany in 1935. Tenor. Schreier's voice is quite light but expressive, and reminiscent of the great Fritz Wunderlich. He is excellent in Bach and Mozart. In recent years, Schreier has turned to conducting and become quite accomplished in this, too.

Shirley-Quirk, John--born in England in 1931. Baritone. Shirley-Quirk is a specialist in works by British composers but uses his light baritone well in Bach and Handel as well.

Sills, Beverly--born in the United States in 1929. Soprano. Now retired from public singing, Sills was a very fine *bel canto* specialist who was one to be relished in works by Donizetti and Bellini. Her voice was supple, but her intonation was not always quite perfect, but she (and, perforce, her audiences) had so much fun that her lapses were never held against her.

91

Söderström, Elisabeth--born in Sweden in 1927. Soprano. Given her age, Söderström has been recording up a storm in the last few years. She has made some magnificent recordings of operas of Janáček, and these may well be her real testament.

Stade, Frederica Von--born in the United States in 1945. Mezzo-soprano. Stade is currently among the most popular of sopranos. Her voice is warm, full, and rich. She uses it with intelligence and skill. She is very good in art songs, and in Mozartean roles.

Sutherland, Dame Joan--born in Australia in 1926. Soprano. One of the most recorded sopranos of all time, Sutherland has been the best *bel canto* soprano of most of this century. Her roulades, trills, runs, melisma--all have provided audiences with goose bumps for decades. She was often compared (unfavorably, by some critics) to Callas, particularly in the roles in <u>Norma</u> and <u>Lucia di Lammermoor</u>. The differences between the two are rather great. Sutherland could sing on pitch, and with a beautiful sound. It is true that her enunciation was poor (due to jaw and teeth problems), but all else was lovely. Her vocal acting was somewhat wooden, but oh, the voice. Callas had difficulty producing beautiful sounds, but she could act. In my opinion, if opera is to be thought of as a musical art, then Sutherland won the battle of the *bel canto* sopranos handily (or vocally).

Talvela, Martti--born in Finland in 1934, died in 1989. Bass. Talvela was probably the best bass recently singing. His was a powerful, rich, compelling voice that can be heard ravishingly in Wagner and in several recordings of the Beethoven Symphony No.9. If only Talvela had recorded <u>Die Meistersinger</u>--what a Hans Sachs he'd have made.

Tear, **Robert**--born in England in 1939. Tenor. Tear is one of the best "white voiced" tenors now singing. He is superb in works that call for a very light, almost countertenor, voice: music in which the voice has to have a bit more weight than that of a countertenor. Tear is exquisite in works by Britten, Handel, and Tippett.

Te Kanawa, Dame Kiri--born in New Zealand in 1944. Soprano. Te Kanawa has made numerous recordings, and they range from popular songs to Brahms to Mozart. In all, her intelligently used, expressive, rather lyric soprano, is extremely pleasing. She is a solid musician and is among the best sopranos now practicing the art.

Vickers, Jon (full name: Jonathan Stewart Vickers)--born in Canada in 1926. Tenor. Vickers is one of the best *Heldentenors* now plying his art. His voice is robust and abundantly rich. Although now virtually at the end of his career, Vickers' recordings (particularly of Wagner and Verdi) are a fine legacy.

Von Stade, Frederica--see Stade, Frederica von

93

ADAM, ADOLPHE-CHARLES
1803-1856

Ballet

{1}   *B*   Giselle (1841)
Royal Opera House Orchestra, Covent Garden; Sir
Richard Bonynge, conductor; London 417 505-2 (2 discs)
[DDD] (TT = 126.22).

ADDINSELL, RICHARD
1904-1977

Concerted

{2}   *A*   Warsaw Concerto for Piano and Orchestra (1941)
(from the film Suicide Squadron, originally released as
Dangerous Moonlight)
Mischa Dichter, piano; Philharmonia Orchestra; Sir
Neville Marriner, conductor; Philips 411 123-2 [DDD]
(TT = 54.10). Includes Chopin's Grand Fantasy on Polish Airs
for Piano and Orchestra, Op.13; Gershwin's Rhapsody in Blue
for Piano and Orchestra (1924), rated A; the Scherzo from
Litolff's Concerto symphonique No.4, Op.102, rated C and
Liszt's Polonaise brilliante, S.367 (c.1851), arranged for piano
and orchestra from Weber's Polacca brilliante for Piano (also
known as "L'Hilarité"), Op.72.

ALBÉNIZ, ISAAC
1860-1909

Concerted

{3}   *C*   Rapsodia española ("Spanish Rhapsody") for
Piano and Orchestra, Op.70 (Orchestrated by Cristobal
Halffter)

Alicia de Larrocha, piano; London Philharmonic Orchestra; Rafael Frühbeck de Burgos, conductor; London 410 289-2 [DDD] (TT=51.32). Includes Falla's <u>Noches en los jardines de España</u> ("Nights in the Gardens of Spain") (1909-1915), rated B; and Turina's <u>Rapsodia sinfónica</u> ("Symphonic Rhapsody") (1931).

Instrumental

{4}   *B*   Suite <u>Iberia</u> (1905-1908)

Alicia De Larrocha, piano; London 417 887-2 (2 discs) [DDD] (TT=126.29). Includes Albéniz' <u>Navarra</u> (1909) (completed by de Séverac) and Suite <u>España</u>, Op.47.

ALBINONI, TOMASO
1671-1759

Concerted

{5}   *C*   Concerto for Oboe and Strings, Op.9 No.8, in g

Heinz Holliger, oboe; I Musici; Philips 420 189-2 [DDD] (TT=60.23). Includes Cimarosa's Concerto for Oboe and Strings (Arranged from Melodics of Cimarosa by Arthur Benjamin, 1942), rated A; Lotti's Concerto for Oboe, in A; Marcello's Concerto for Oboe and Strings, in d (1716), rated A and Giuseppe Sammartini's Concerto for Oboe and Orchestra, in D.

Orchestral

{6}   *A*   Adagio in g (orchestrated by Giazotto)
a

     Jean-François Paillard Chamber Orchestra; Jean-François Paillard, conductor; Erato ECD-88020 [DDD] (TT=47.45). Includes Bach's Chorales from Cantatas BWV 6, <u>Bleib bei uns</u> ("Remain With Us"); BWV 140, <u>Wachet auf, ruft uns die Stimme</u> ("Sleepers Awake"), rated A; BWV 147, <u>Herz und Mund und Tat und Leben</u> ("Heart and Mouth and Deed and Life"), rated A; BWV 167, <u>Ihr Menschen</u> ("Your People");

Chorale Prelude BWV 721, <u>Erbarm dich mein, o Herre Gott</u> ("Take Pity on Me, O Lord"); Bonporti's Concerto a Quattro, Op.11 No.5; Molter's Concerto for Two Trumpets and Strings, in D and Pachelbel's Kanon ("Canon") in D, rated A.

b   Matitiahu Braun, violin; Philharmonia Virtuosi of New York; Richard Kapp, conductor; CBS MK-34544 [ADD] (TT=40.40). Includes Bach's BWV Anh.183, Minuet in G, from <u>Clavier-Büchlein vor Anna Magdalena Bachin</u> ("Keyboard Notebook of Anna Magdalena Bach") (1722), rated B (the work was attributed to Bach but is actually that of Christian Pezold < 1677-1733 > and, in this recording, arranged for orchestra by Thomas Frost; it is among the most popular works from the <u>Anna Magdalena</u> Notebook), Largo from BWV 1056, Concerto for Harpsichord and Strings, in f (with Judith Norell, harpsichord), rated A, Adagio from BWV 1060, Concerto for Violin, Oboe and Strings, in c (with Oscar Ravina, violin and Ronald Roseman, oboe), rated A, and Air from BWV 1068, Suite No.3, in D, for Orchestra, rated A; Campra's "Triumphal March" from <u>Tancrède</u> (1702); Corelli's Gigue ("Jig") from Trio Sonata Op.5 No.9 (with Oscar Ravina, violin), rated B; Handel's Sarabande from the Suite for Harpsichord No.11, rated C (the Sarabande became popular after its use as a theme in the film, <u>Barry Lyndon</u>); Mouret's Rondeau from Symphonic Suite No.1 (1729), rated A (the Rondeau gets an A rating only because of its infernally immense popularity since its use as the theme music for the PBS series <u>Masterpiece Theater</u>); Pachelbel's Kanon ("Canon") in D, rated A.

ALFVÉN, HUGO
1872-1960

Orchestral

{7}   *B*   Swedish Rhapsody No.1 (<u>Midsommarvarka</u>) ("Midsummer Vigil") (1904)

Stockholm Philharmonia Orchestra; Neeme Järvi, conductor; Bis CD-385 [DDD] (TT = 68.18). Includes Alfvén's Symphony No.2, R.28, in D.

ALKAN, CHARLES-MARIE VALENTIN
1813-1888

Instrumental

{8}   *C*   Allegretto ("Fa") from Trente chants ("Thirty Songs"), Op.38 Book 2

Ronald Smith, piano; Arabesque 7.6523 [DDD] (TT = 58.26). Includes Alkan's Barcarolle from Trente chants ("Thirty Songs"), Op.70, Book 5 No.6; Barcarolle from Trente chants ("Thirty Songs"), Op.65, Book 3 No.6; "Cantique des cantiques" ("Song of Songs") (No.13 of Preludes, Op.31); "Carnaval" from Les Mois ("The Months"), Op.74, Book 1 No.2; From Esquisses ("Sketches"), "Les Cloches" ("The Bells") Book 1 No.4, "Délire" ("Frenzy") Book 5 No.29, "Les Enharmoniques" ("Enharmonics") Book 4 No.41, "Increpatio" ("Chiding") Book 1 No.10, "Morituri te Salutamus ("We Who Are About to Die Salute You"), Book 2 No.21, "Le Premier billet doux" ("The First Love Letter") Book 4 No.20, "En Songe" ("In a Dream") Book 4 No.48, and "Les Soupirs" ("The Sighs") Book 1 No.11; Gigue ("Jig") (from Op.24); "Gros temps" ("Foul Times") from Les Mois ("The Months"), Op.74 Book 4 No.1; "Marche" ("March") from Trois Marches ("Three Marches"), Op.37, No.1; Nocturne, Op.22 No.1; Preludes, Op.31: "Assez Lentement" ("Rather Slowly") No.16, "Dans le Genre gothique" ("In the Gothic Style") No.15, "Petit Rien" ("Little Nothing") No.11, and "Le Temps qui n'est plus" ("The Times Which Are No More") No.12; Petit Conte ("Fairy Tale") (1859); Le Tambour bat aux champs ("The Drum Beats a Salute for the Dead"), Op.63; "Toccatina" ("Little Toccata"), Op.75.

ARNAUD, LEO
1904-

Orchestral
{9}   *B*   Three Fanfares ("Olympic Theme," "La Chasse" <"The Hunt">, and "Olympiad") (c.1959)

Cleveland Symphonic Winds; Frederick Fennell, conductor; Telarc CD-80099 [DDD] (TT=59.12). Includes Barber's Commando March (1943); Fučik's Florentiner, Op.214; Grainger's Lincolnshire Posy (1937), rated C, and Shepherd's Hey (1918), rated C; King's Barnum and Bailey's Favorite; Leemans Belgian Paratroopers; Sousa's The Stars and Stripes Forever (1896), rated A; Vaughan Williams' English Folk Song Suite (1923), rated A, and Sea Songs; Johann Strauss, Sr.'s Radetzky March, Op.228, rated A; and Zimmermann's Anchors Aweigh (1907), rated A. Except for the Arnaud work, the rated items on this disc are some of the best known pieces for band. However, the Arnaud Fanfare "Olympic Theme" is the one which has received an immense amount of "air play"--it is the theme used by ABC as, quite literally, the Olympic theme.

AUBER, DANIEL-FRANÇOIS
1782-1871

Orchestral
{10}   *C*   Overture: Fra Diavolo (1830)

Cincinnati Pops Orchestra; Erich Kunzel, conductor; Telarc CD-80116 [DDD] (TT=61.20). Includes Hérold's Overture: Zampa (1831), rated C; Offenbach's Overture: Orphée aux enfers ("Orpheus in the Underworld") (Written by Carl Binder) (1858), rated C; Reznicek's Overture: Donna Diana (1894), rated B; Rossini's Overture: William Tell (1829), rated A; and von Suppé's Overtures: Leichte Kavallerie ("Light Cavalry") (1886), rated B and Dichter und Bauer ("Poet and

Peasant") (1854), rated A. Two of these works gained popularity because of having been the themes for radio series: Rezniček's <u>Donna Diana</u> for <u>Sergeant Preston of the Yukon</u>, and the <u>William Tell</u>, as most know, for <u>The Lone Ranger</u>. Kunzel and his Pops removes the patina of warhorsedom from all these bouncy pieces, and invests them with *brio* and fresh polish.

BACH, CARL PHILIPP EMANUEL
1714-1788

Concerted

{11}   *B*   Concerto for Harpsichord and Orchestra, in G, Wq 43 No.5

Trevor Pinnock, harpsichord; English Concert; Trevor Pinnock, conductor; CRD 4311 [ADD] (TT=51.49). Includes Vivaldi's Concerto for 'Cello and Strings, RV 424, in b, rated B (with Anthony Pleeth, baroque 'cello); Concerto for Transverse Flute and Strings, RV 429, in d (with Stephen Preston, baroque flute), rated A; Concerti for Violin and String Orchestra, Op.8 ("<u>Il Cimento dell' armonia e dell' invenzione</u>") ("The Contest Between Harmony and Invention"), Op.8 (12) Nos.11-12, in D and C (with Simon Standage, baroque violin), rated B.

Orchestral

{12}   *C*   Symphonies for String Orchestra (6) Wq 182: Nos.1-6: in G, B flat, C, A, b, and E

English Concert; Trevor Pinnock, harpsichord and conductor; Archiv 415 300-2 [DDD] (TT=64.48).

BACH, JOHANN SEBASTIAN
1685-1750

Chamber

{13}   *A*   BWV 1014, Sonata for Violin and Harpsichord, in b

Josef Suk, violin; Zuzana Růžičková, harpsichord; Denon CO-1370-1371 (2 discs) [DDD] (TT=106.09). Includes Bach's BWV 1015-1019, Sonatas for Violin, in A, E, c, f and G, all rated A.

{14}   *A*   BWV 1015, Sonata for Violin and Harpsichord, in A -- see entry No.{13}.

{15}   *A*   BWV 1016, Sonata for Violin and Harpsichord, in E -- see entry No.{13}.

{16}   *A*   BWV 1017, Sonata for Violin and Harpsichord, in c -- see entry No.{13}.

{17}   *A*   BWV 1018, Sonata for Violin and Harpsichord, in f -- see entry No.{13}.

{18}   *A*   BWV 1019, Sonata for Violin and Harpsichord, in G -- see entry No.{13}.

{19}   *B*   BWV 1020, Sonata for Flute and Harpsichord, in g

Jean-Pierre Rampal, flute; Trevor Pinnock, harpsichord; Roland Pidoux, 'cello; CBS M2K-39746 (2 discs) [DDD] (TT=97.36). Includes Bach's BWV 1013, Partita for Solo Flute, in a and BWV 1030-1035, Six Sonatas for Flute and Harpsichord, in b, E flat, A, C, e and E, all rated B.

{20}   *C*   BWV 1021, Sonata for Violin and Continuo, in G

Ingrid Seifert, violin; Charles Medlam, double-bass; John Toll, harpsichord; Angel CDC 49203-2 [DDD] (TT=51.15). Includes Bach's BWV 1022, Sonata for Violin and Harpsichord, in F, rated C; BWV 1023, Sonata for Violin and Continuo, in e, rated C; BWV 1024, Sonata for Violin and Continuo, in c, rated C and BWV 1026, Fugue for Violin and Continuo, in g, rated C.

{21}   C   BWV 1022, Sonata for Violin and Harpsichord, in F -- see entry No.{20}.

{22}   C   BWV 1023, Sonata for Violin and Continuo, in e -- see entry No.{20}.

{23}   C   BWV 1024, Sonata for Violin and Continuo, in c -- see entry No.{20}.

{24}   C   BWV 1026, Fugue for Violin and Continuo, in g -- see entry No.{20}.

{25}   B   BWV 1030, Sonata for Flute and Harpsichord, in b -- see entry No.{19}.

{26}   B   BWV 1031, Sonata for Flute and Harpsichord, in E flat -- see entry No.{19}.

{27}   B   BWV 1032, Sonata for Flute and Harpsichord, in A -- see entry No.{19}.

{28}   B   BWV 1033, Sonata for Flute and Harpsichord, in C -- see entry No.{19}.

{29}   B   BWV 1034, Sonata for Flute and Harpsichord, in e -- see entry No.{19}.

{30}   B   BWV 1035, Sonata for Flute and Harpsichord, in E -- see entry No.{19}.

Choral (A. Cantatas)

{31}   *C*   BWV 4, <u>Christ lag in Todesbanden</u> ("Christ Lay in the Bonds of Death")

Dietrich Fischer-Dieskau, baritone; Munich Bach Choir and Orchestra; Karl Richter, conductor; Archiv 413 646-2 (3 discs) [ADD] (TT = 179.34). Includes Bach's Cantatas BWV 26, <u>Ach wie flüchtig, ach wie nichtig</u> ("Ah, How Fleeting, Ah, How Void"), with soloists Edith Mathis, soprano; Trudeliese Schmidt, contralto; Peter Schreier, tenor and Dietrich Fischer-Dieskau, baritone; BWV 51, <u>Jauchzet Gott in allen Landen</u> ("Praise God in All Lands"), rated B, with Edith Mathis, soprano; BWV 56, <u>Ich will den Kreuzstab gerne tragen</u> ("Gladly Will I Bear the Cross"), rated C, with Dietrich Fischer-Dieskau, baritone; BWV 61, <u>Nun komm' der Heiden Heiland</u> ("Come Now, Saviour of the Gentiles"), with Edith Mathis, soprano; Peter Schreier, tenor and Dietrich Fischer-Dieskau, baritone; BWV 80, <u>Ein feste Burg ist unser Gott</u> ("A Mighty Fortress Is Our God"), rated A, with Edith Mathis, soprano; Trudeliese Schmidt, contralto; Peter Schreier, tenor and Dietrich Fischer-Dieskau, baritone; BWV 106, <u>Gottes Zeit ist die allerbeste Zeit</u> ("God's Time Is the Best Time of All"), rated C, with Hertha Töpper, contralto; Ernst Haefliger, tenor and Theo Adam, bass; BWV 147, <u>Herz und Mund und Tat und Leben</u> ("Heart and Mouth and Deed and Life"), rated A, with Ursula Buckel, soprano; Hertha Töpper, contralto; John van Kesteren, tenor and Keith Engen, bass. It should be noted that several sections of BWV 80 are based on Martin Luther's wonderful hymn (i.e., "A Mighty Fortress. . . ."), and that BWV 147 has the well-known melody "Jesu, Joy of Man's Desiring" as its final chorale.

Also -- see entry No.{94}.

{32}   *B*   BWV 51, <u>Jauchzet Gott in allen Landen</u> ("Praise God in All Lands")

Nancy Argenta, soprano; Patrizia Kwella, soprano; Charles Brett, countertenor; Anthony Rolfe-Johnson, tenor;

David Thomas, bass; English Baroque Soloists; John Eliot
Gardiner, conductor; Philips 411 458-2 [DDD] (TT=41.25).
Includes Bach's Magnificat, BWV 243, in D, rated B.
Also -- see entry No.{31}.

{33}　　　　*C*　BWV 56, Ich will den Kreuzstab gerne tragen
("Gladly Will I Bear the Cross") -- see entry No.{31}.

{34}　　　　*A*　BWV 80, Ein feste Burg ist unser Gott ("A Mighty
Fortress Is Our God")

a　　　　　Gabriele Fontana, soprano; Julia Hamari, contralto;
Gösta Winbergh, tenor; Tom Krause, baritone; Hymnus Boys'
Choir, Stuttgart; Stuttgart Chamber Orchestra; Karl
Münchinger, conductor; London 415 045-2 [DDD]
(TT-57.54). Includes Bach's Cantata BWV 140, Wachet auf,
ruft uns die Stimme ("Sleepers Awake"), rated A, with
instrumental soloists Herwig Zack, violin; Lajos Lencsés, oboe
and Hans-Peter Weber, English horn.

b　　　　　Jane Bryden, soprano; Drew Minter, countertenor;
Jeffrey Thomas, tenor; Jan Opalach, bass; Bach Ensemble;
Joshua Rifkin, conductor; L'Oiseau-Lyre 417 250-2 [DDD]
(TT=53.00). Includes Bach's Cantata BWV 147, Herz und
Mund und Tat und Leben ("Heart and Mouth and Deed and
Life"), rated A. In these recordings, the vocal soloists double
as the chorus, each singing a choral voice. This allows for a
very nice transparency of "choral" sound and is quite clean.
However, I still prefer a true chorus which can summon some
of the grandeur which I believe Bach intended.

{35}　　　　*C*　BWV 106, Gottes Zeit ist die allerbeste Zeit
("God's Time Is the Best Time of All") -- see entry No.{31}.

{36}　　　　*A*　Cantata BWV 140, Wachet auf, ruft uns die
Stimme ("Sleepers Awake") -- see entries Nos.{6}a and {34}a.

{37}   *A*   BWV 147, <u>Herz und Mund und Tat und Leben</u> ("Heart and Mouth and Deed and Life") -- see entries Nos.{6}a, {31}, {34}b and {85}.

{38}   *B*   BWV 211, <u>Schweigt stille, plaudert nicht</u> ("Be Quiet, Don't Chatter") (Known as the "Coffee Cantata")

a   Emma Kirkby, soprano; Rogers Covey-Crump, tenor; David Thomas, bass; Lisa Beznosiuk, flute; Anthony Halstead, natural horn; Catherine Mackintosh, violin; Mark Caudle, 'cello; Barry Guy, chamber bass; Christopher Hogwood, harpsichord; The Academy of Ancient Music; Christopher Hogwood, conductor; L'Oiseau-Lyre 417 621-2 [DDD] (TT=51.54). Includes BWV 212, <u>Mer hahn en neue Oberkeet</u> ("We Have a New Squire") (Known as the "Peasant Cantata"), rated B.

b   Julia Varady, soprano; Aldo Baldin, tenor; Dietrich Fischer-Dieskau, baritone; Susan Milan, flute; Timothy Brown, horn; Ian Watson, harpsichord; Denis Vigay, 'cello; Raymond Koster, double-bass; Academy of St. Martin-in-the-Fields; Sir Neville Marriner, conductor; Philips 412 882-2 [DDD] (TT=57.14). Same coupling as recording immediately above. These are two fine performances, but I lean to the Hogwood version for both the quality of its soprano and the sonorities of its period instruments.

c   Ann Monoyios, soprano; Shirley Love, mezzo-soprano; Stephen Oosting, tenor; John Ostendorf, bass-baritone; Daniel Waitzman, flute; Myron Lutske, 'cello; Edward Brewer, harpsichord; Amor Artis Chorale and Baroque Orchestra; Johannes Somary, conductor; Vox Cum Laude MCD 10046 [DDD] (TT=60.08). Includes Bach's Cantatas BWV 53, <u>Schlage doch, gewünschte Stunde</u> ("Strike Then, Awaited Hour") and BWV 158, <u>Der Friede sei mit mir</u> ("The Peace Remains With Me"); and Bach's Motets BWV 226, <u>Der Geist hilft</u> ("The Spirit Helps"), rated B, and BWV 228, <u>Fürchte dich nicht</u> ("Be Not Afraid"), rated C. Of the various recordings of BWV 211 listed here, my favorite is this one. Ann Monoyios has just the fresh and perky voice the work requires, and John Ostendorf sounds put upon as the father. Unfortunately, in those other works Ostendorf has a bit of a wobbly vibrato which can be a little distracting.

{39}   *B*   BWV 212, <u>Mer hahn en neue Oberkeet</u> ("We Have a New Squire") (Known as the "Peasant Cantata") -- see entries Nos.{38}a-b.

Choral (B. Magnificats)
{40}   *B*   BWV 243, in d -- see entry No.{32}.

{41}   *B*   BWV 243a, in E flat
          Emma Kirkby, soprano; Judith Nelson, soprano; Carolyn Watkinson, contralto; Paul Elliott, tenor; David Thomas, bass; Choir of Christ Church Cathedral, Oxford; Academy of Ancient Music; Simon Preston, conductor; L'Oiseau-Lyre 414 678-2 [ADD] (TT = 64.52). Includes Vivaldi's Gloria, RV 589 in D, rated A.

Choral (C. Masses)
{42}   *A*   BWV 232, in b
a   Julianne Baird, soprano; Judith Nelson, soprano; Jeffrey Dooley, countertenor; Frank Hoffmeister, tenor; Jan Opalach, bass; Bach Ensemble; Joshua Rifkin, conductor; Nonesuch 79036-2 (2 discs) [DDD] (TT = 106.29). This version of BWV 232 is, as in many other choral recordings which Rifkin has undertaken, without chorus: the soloists singing the choral parts. Additionally, Rifkin has drawn upon his considerable scholarship to reconstruct the work to what he considers the original probably was like. I admit to being taken by the performance and preferring it to Gardiner's (listed below).
b   Monteverdi Choir; English Baroque Soloists; John Eliot Gardiner, conductor; Archiv 415 514-2 (2 discs) [DDD] (TT = 105.56).

{43}   *B*   BWV 233, in F
Lina Åkerlund, soprano; Sharon Weller, contralto; Guy de Mey, tenor; Stephen Varcoe, bass; Basler Madrigalisten; Linde Consort; Hans-Martin Linde, conductor; Angel CDCB 49222 (2 discs) [DDD] (TT=111.44). Includes Bach's Masses BWV 234, in A; BWV 235, in g and BWV 236, in G, all rated B.

{44}   *B*   BWV 234, in A -- see entry No.{43}.

{45}   *B*   BWV 235, in g -- see entry No.{43}.

{46}   *B*   BWV 236, in G -- see entry No.{43}.

Choral (D. Motets)
{47}   *B*   BWV 225, <u>Singet dem Herrn ein neues Lied</u> ("Sing a New Song unto the Lord"); BWV 226, <u>Der Geist hilft</u> ("The Spirit Helps"), rated B; BWV 227, <u>Jesu, meine Freude</u> ("Jesu, My Joy"); BWV 228, <u>Fürchte dich nicht</u> ("Be Not Afraid"), rated C; BWV 229, <u>Komm, Jesu, komm</u> ("Come, Jesu, Come") and BWV 230, <u>Lobet den Herrn, alle Heiden</u> ("Praise Ye the Lord, All Ye Gentiles")
a   Knabenchor Hannover; Hilliard Ensemble; London Baroque; Paul Hillier, conductor; Angel CDC 49204-2 [DDD] (TT=68.22).
b   Monteverdi Choir; English Baroque Soloists; John Eliot Gardiner, conductor; Erato ECD-88117 (2 discs) [ADD] (TT=123.54). Includes Bach's Cantatas BWV 50, <u>Nun ist das Hell und die Kraft</u> ("Now Is the Light and the Power") and BWV 118 <u>O Jesu Christ, meins Lebens Licht</u> ("O Jesus Christ, Light of My Life").

{48}   *B*   BWV 226, <u>Der Geist hilft</u> ("The Spirit Helps") -- see entries Nos.{38}c and {47}a-b.

{49}   *C*   BWV 228, <u>Fürchte dich nicht</u> ("Be Not Afraid") --
see entries Nos.{38}c and {47}a-b.

Choral (E. Oratorios)
{50}   *A*   BWV 248, <u>Christmas</u>
Gundula Janowitz, soprano; Christa Ludwig, mezzo-
soprano; Fritz Wunderlich, tenor; Franz Crass, bass; Munich
Bach Choir and Orchestra; Karl Richter, conductor; Archiv
413 625-2 (3 discs) [ADD] (TT = 166.08). Recorded in 1965,
Richter's loving performance has in its favor a group of singers,
each of whom was in his or her prime. Lacking are the period
instruments which adorn some other recorded performances,
but this one is still the most persuasive (it's worth it just for the
work of the late Fritz Wunderlich).

Choral (F. Passions)
{51}   *A*   BWV 244, <u>Saint Matthew</u>
Edith Mathis, soprano; Dame Janet Baker, mezzo-
soprano; Peter Schreier, tenor; Dietrich Fischer-Dieskau,
baritone; Matti Salminen, bass; Regensburg Cathedral Choir;
Munich Bach Choir and Orchestra; Karl Richter, conductor;
Archiv 413 613-2 (3 discs) [ADD] (TT = 197.37).

{52}   *B*   BWV 245, <u>Saint John</u>
a   Evelyn Lear, soprano; Hertha Töpper, mezzo-soprano;
Ernst Haefliger, tenor; Herman Prey, baritone; Keith Engen,
bass; Munich Bach Choir and Orchestra; Karl Richter,
conductor; Archiv 413 622-2 (2 discs) [ADD] (TT = 129.01).
b   Gillian Ross, soprano; Michael Chance, countertenor;
Anthony Rolfe-Johnson, tenor; Cornelius Hauptman, bass;
Stephen Varcoe, bass; Monteverdi Choir; English Baroque
Soloists; John Eliot Gardiner, conductor; Archiv 419 324-2 (2
discs) [DDD] (TT = 106.32). The Gardiner recording is
complemented by an instrumental ensemble performing with
period instruments, and vocal soloists of impeccable
qualifications. The older (1964) Richter recording has

exceptional vocalists and an overall warmer, and more affectionate, attitude toward the music than does the newer (1986) Gardiner set.

Concerted

{53}   *A*   BWV 1041, Concerto for Violin and Orchestra, in
    a

a   Jaap Schröder, violin; Academy of Ancient Music; Christopher Hogwood, conductor; L'Oiseau-Lyre 400 080-2 [DDD] (TT=45.09). Includes Bach's BWV 1042, Concerto for Violin and Orchestra, in E and BWV 1043, Concerto for Two Violins and Orchestra ("Double Concerto"), in d (with Christopher Hirons, violin), both rated A (BWV 1043 is a transcription, made by Bach himself, of BWV 1062, Concerto for Two Harpsichords and Strings, in c).

b   Simon Standage, violin; English Concert; Trevor Pinnock, conductor; 413 634-2 [DDD] (TT=150.38). Includes Bach's BWV 1042, Concerto for Violin and Orchestra, in E and BWV 1043, Concerto for Two Violins and Orchestra ("Double Concerto"), in d (with Elizabeth Wilcock, violin), both rated A (BWV 1043 is a transcription, made by Bach himself, of BWV 1062, Concerto for Two Harpsichords and Strings, in c); BWV 1052, Concerto for Harpsichord and Strings, in d, rated A; BWV 1056, Concerto for Harpsichord and Strings, in f, rated A; BWV 1060, Concerto for Two Harpsichords and Strings, rated A; BWV 1061, Concerto for Two Harpsichords and Strings, in C, rated C; BWV 1063, Concerto for Three Harpsichords and Strings, in d, rated C; BWV 1064, Concerto for Three Harpsichords and Strings, in C and BWV 1065, Concerto for Four Harpsichords and Strings, in a, rated A. In the concerti for solo harpsichord, the soloist is Trevor Pinnock; in those requiring two soloists, Pinnock is coupled with Kenneth Gilbert; for those written for three harpsichords, Lars Ulrik Mortensen is added to Pinnock and Gilbert; and in the BWV 1065, the additional soloist is Nicholas Kraemer.

{54}   *A*   BWV 1042, Concerto for Violin and Orchestra, in
E -- see entries Nos.{53}a-b.

{55}   *A*   BWV 1043, Concerto for Two Violins and
Orchestra ("Double Concerto"), in d
        Erick Friedman, violin; Jascha Heifetz, violin; New
Symphony Orchestra of London; Sir Malcolm Sargent,
conductor; RCA 6778-2-RC [ADD] (TT=70.33). Includes
Brahms' Concerto for Violin and 'Cello ("Double Concerto"),
Op.102, in a (with Gregor Piatigorsky, 'cello, and the RCA
Victor Orchestra conducted by Izler Solomon), rated A and
Mozart's Sinfonia Concertante for Violin, Viola and Orchestra,
K.364, in E flat (with William Primrose, viola, and the RCA
Victor Symphony Orchestra conducted by Alfred Wallenstein),
rated A.
        Also -- see entries Nos.{53}a-b.

{56}   *B*   BWV 1044, Concerto for Flute, Violin,
Harpsichord and Strings ("Triple Concerto"), in a
a   Lisa Beznosiuk, flute; Simon Standage, violin; Trevor
Pinnock, harpsichord; English Concert; Trevor Pinnock,
conductor; Archiv 413 731-2 [DDD] (TT=50.50). Includes
Bach's BWV 1055, Concerto for Oboe d'Amore and Strings, in
A, rated C and BWV 1060, Concerto for Oboe, Violin and
Strings, in c, rated A, with David Reichenberg, oboe and
Simon Standage, violin. BWV 1055 is a reconstruction of
BWV 1055, Concerto for Harpsichord and Strings in A, rated
A, BWV 1060 is a reconstruction of BWV 1060, Concerto for
Two Harpsichords and Strings, in c, rated A.
b   Lisa Beznosiuk, flute; Simon Standage, violin; Trevor
Pinnock, harpsichord; English Concert; Trevor Pinnock,
conductor; Archiv 413 629-2 (4 discs) [DDD] (TT=192.26).
Includes Bach's BWV 1046-1051 ("Brandenburg") Concerti for
Various Instrumental Combinations and Orchestra (6) Nos.1-6:
in F, F, G, G, D and B flat and BWV 1066-1069, Suites for
Orchestra (4) Nos.1-4: in C, b, D and D. Both of the additional

sets of works are rated A. The BWV 1066-1069 recordings are [ADD].

{57}   *A*   BWV 1046-1051 ("Brandenburg") Concerti for Various Instrumental Combinations and Orchestra (6) Nos.1-6: in F, F, G, G, D and B flat

a   Amsterdam Baroque Orchestra; Ton Koopman, conductor; MHS 11089H (2 discs) [DDD] (TT = 100.41).

b   Linde Consort; Hans-Martin Linde; conductor; Angel CDC 47045 and CDC-47046 (2 discs) [DDD] (TT = 96.47).

Of the two sets of Brandenburg Concerti listed here (and the one listed in item No.b), my own favorite is the Pinnock one on Archiv. Koopman (on MHS) is a good clean set of readings, but the tempi are somewhat fast. Linde (on Angel), on the other hand, offers slower and more relaxed performances, but there is a trading of tension for beautiful sounds. Pinnock, however, manages a bright, airy sound combined with taut movement. If only Pinnock could have brought a bit of Linde's laid-back feeling, his readings would have been well-nigh perfect.

Also -- see entry No.{56}b.

{58}   *A*   BWV 1046, "Brandenburg" Concerto No.1, in F -- see entries Nos.{57}a-b.

{59}   *A*   BWV 1047, "Brandenburg" Concerto No.2, in F -- see entries Nos.{57}a-b.

{60}   *A*   BWV 1048, "Brandenburg" Concerto No.3, in G

English Concert; Trevor Pinnock, conductor; Archiv Imago 419 410-2 [DDD] and [ADD] (TT = 71.03). Includes selections from Bach's BWV 1067, Suite for Orchestra, No.2, in b (Bourrées Nos.1-2, Polonaise, Menuet and Badinerie) and the Air from BWV 1068, Suite for Orchestra No.3, in D, both works rated A; Handel's Water Music Suite (1717), rated A and the "The Arrival of the Queen of Sheba" from Solomon

(1749), rated B; Pachelbel's Kanon ("Canon"), rated A and Vivaldi's Concerto for Two Mandolins and Strings, RV 532, in G (with James Tyler and Robin Jeffrey, mandolins), rated B and Concerto for Strings, RV 151, in G ("Alla Rustica"), rated B.

Also -- see entries Nos.{57}a-b.

{61}   *A*   BWV 1049, "Brandenburg" Concerto No.4, in G -- see entries Nos.{57}a-b.

{62}   *A*   BWV 1050, "Brandenburg" Concerto No.5, in D -- see entries Nos.{57}a-b.

{63}   *A*   BWV 1051, "Brandenburg" Concerto No.6, in B flat -- see entries Nos.{57}a-b.

{64}   *A*   BWV 1052, Concerto for Harpsichord and Strings, in d

a   Glenn Gould, piano; Academic Symphony Orchestra of Leningrad; Vladislav Slovak, conductor; CBS M2K-42270 (2 discs) ! [AAD] (TT=143.05). Includes Bach's Concerti for Harpsichord and Strings, BWV 1053, in E, BWV 1054, in A, BWV 1056, in f and BWV 1058, in g (Gould is accompanied in these by the Columbia Symphony Orchestra conducted by Vladimir Golschmann, and these recordings are in stereo), BWV 971, Concerto for Solo Harpsichord ("Italian"), rated A, and excerpts from <u>Die Kunst der Fuge</u> ("The Art of the Fugue") (Contrapunctus 1-9), rated A, which excerpts are performed by Gould on the organ (these are also in stereo). All of these performances are *tours de force* which only could have been managed by Gould. Not everyone agrees with Gould's eccentricities of tempi, embellishment, humming along with his playing (which for many is the greatest distraction), etc., but few think that these are performances other than those of a true genius. By the standards of Bach performance now, the orchestral accompaniment given Gould seems rather

111

overripe and somewhat Romantic, still these are one-of-a-kind piano recordings, and even the old (1957) recording of the BWV 1052 stands up well to today's sonic requirements and the CD technology.

b   Trevor Pinnock, harpsichord; English Concert; Trevor Pinnock, conductor; Archiv   4 1 5   9 9 1 - 2   [D D D] (TT = 42.34).   Includes Bach's BWV 1053, Concerto for Harpsichord and Strings, in E, rated A and BWV 1054, Concerto for Harpsichord and Strings, in A, rated A.   As with almost all of Pinnock's work, these are first rate, modern recordings which take into account current scholarship and appropriate performance style.

Also -- see entry No.{53}b.

{65}   *A*   BWV 1053, Concerto for Harpsichord and Strings, in E -- see entries Nos.{64}a-b.

{66}   *A*   BWV 1054, Concerto for Harpsichord and Strings, in A -- see entries Nos.{64}a-b.

{67}   *A*   BWV 1055, Concerto for Harpsichord and Strings, in A

Trevor Pinnock, harpsichord; English Concert; Trevor Pinnock, conductor; Archiv 415 992-2 [DDD] (TT = 53.14). Includes Bach's BWV 1056, Concerto for Harpsichord and Strings, in f, rated A, BWV 1057, Concerto for Harpsichord, Two Recorders and Strings, in F, rated A and BWV 1058, Concerto for Harpsichord and Strings, in g, rated A.

{68}   *C*   BWV 1055, Concerto for Oboe d'Amore and Strings, in A (this is a reconstruction of the BWV 1055, Concerto for Two Harpsichords and Strings) -- see entry No.{56}a.

{69}   *A*   BWV 1056, Concerto for Harpsichord and Strings, in f - see entries Nos.{6}b, {53}b, {64}a and {67}.

{70}   *A*   BWV 1057, Concerto for Harpsichord, Two Recorders and Strings, in F -- see entry No.{67}.

{71}   *A*   BWV 1058, Concerto for Harpsichord and Strings, in g -- see entries Nos.{64}a and {67}.

{72}   *A*   BWV 1060, Concerto for Oboe, Violin and Strings, in c (this is a reconstruction of BWV 1060, Concerto for Two Harpsichords and Strings) -- see entries Nos.{6}b, {53}b and {56}a.

{73}   *C*   BWV 1061, Concerto for Two Harpsichords and Strings, in C -- see entry No.{53}b.

{74}   *C*   BWV 1063, Concerto for Three Harpsichords and Strings, in d
          Trevor Pinnock, harpsichord; Kenneth Gilbert, harpsichord; Lars Ulrik Mortensen, harpsichord; Nicholas Kraemer, conductor; English Concert; Trevor Pinnock, conductor; Archiv 400 041-2 [DDD] (TT=39.42). Includes Bach's BWV 1064, Concerto for Three Harpsichords and Strings, in C, rated C and BWV 1065, Concerto for Four Harpsichords and Strings, in a, rated A.
          Also -- see entry No.{53}b.

{75}   *C*   BWV 1064, Concerto for Three Harpsichords and Strings, in C -- see entries Nos.{53}b and {74}.

{76}   *A*   BWV 1065, Concerto for Four Harpsichords and Strings, in a -- see entries Nos.{53}b and {74}.

Instrumental (A. Solo 'Cello)
{77}   *B*   BWV 1007-1012, Suites for Unaccompanied 'Cello (6) Nos.1-6: in G, d, C, E flat, c and D
          Lynn Harrell, 'cello; London 414 163-2 (2 discs) [ADD? & DDD] (TT=127.46). These are earnest and well thought-

out performances which would have benefited from a bit of a more "unbuttoned" approach; still, they have better lasting qualities than any of the others I have heard.

Instrumental (B. Solo Harpsichord)

{78}   *B*   BWV 722-801, Two-Part Inventions (15) and Three-Part Inventions ("Symphonies") (15)
Glenn Gould, piano; CBS M2K-42269 (2 discs) [AAD & ADD] (TT=131.18). Includes Bach's BWV 910-916, Toccatas (7) Nos.1-7: in f sharp, c, D, d, e, g and G, rated B.
Huguette Dreyfus, harpsichord; Denon C37-7566 [DDD] (TT=49.49).

{79}   *B*   BWV 806-811, Suites ("English") (6) Nos.1-6: in A, a, g, F, e and d
Glenn Gould, piano; CBS MK-42268 (2 discs) [AAD?] (TT=136.05). Includes Bach's BWV 831, Overture ("In the French Style"). These are vintage Gould recordings which, as yet, have little competition on CDs.

{80}   *C*   BWV 812-817, Suites ("French") (6) Nos.1-6: in d, c, b, E flat, G and E
Glenn Gould, piano; CBS MK-42267 [AAD?] (TT=60.44).

{81}   *A*   BWV 846-893, Das Wohltempierte Klavier ("The Well-Tempered Clavier") (48 Preludes Fugues <one for each Major and minor key>, sometimes called "The Mighty 48;" the work is in Two Books, each of twenty four selections)
Glenn Gould, piano; CBS M3K-42266 (3 discs) [AAD?] (TT=212.10).

{82}   *A*   BWV 903, Chromatic Fantasia and Fugue, in d
Igor Kipnis, harpsichord; Arabesque Z6577 [DDD] (TT=62.59). Includes Bach's BWV 903a, Chromatic Fantasia, in d, BWV 904, Fantasia and Fugue in a, BWV 906, Fantasia

and Fugue in c, rated A, BWV 917, "Fantasie duobus subiectis," in g, BWV 918, "Fantasia über ein Rondo," in c, BWV 919, Fantasia, in c, BWV 922, Fantasia, in a, BWV 944, Fantasia and Fugue in a and BWV 961, Fughetta, in c.

{83}   *A*   BWV 906, Fantasia and Fugue in c -- see entry No.{82}.

{84}   *B*   BWV 910-916, Toccatas (7) Nos.1-7: in f sharp, c, D, d, e, g and G -- see entry No.{78}.

{85}   *A*   BWV 971, Concerto for Solo Harpsichord ("Italian")
        Don Dorsey, electronic synthesizers; Telarc CD-80123 [DDD] (TT=46.47). Includes Bach's Toccata and Fugue, in d, BWV 565, rated A (this may be Bach's most famous and popular work for solo organ, and was used in the Disney movie, Fantasia); excerpts from the Two and Three Part Inventions, for Solo Harpsichord BWV 772, 779, 781, 783, 786, 787, 791, 794 and 801, rated B, the Chorale, "Jesu, Joy of Man's Desiring" from the Cantata, BWV 147, Herz und Mund und Tat und Leben ("Heart and Mouth and Deed and Life"), rated A and BWV 1087, Diverse Kanons (on the first eight notes of the Aria ground from BWV 988, the Goldberg Variations for solo harpsichord -- the BWV 988 is rated A). These performances by Dorsey are inventive, do not take themselves seriously, and indicate how flexible the music of Bach truly is.
        Also -- see entry No.{64}a.

{86}   *A*   BWV 988, Goldberg Variations (Aria with 30 Variations)
        Trevor Pinnock, harpsichord; Archiv 415 130-2 [DDD] (TT=56.50).

{87}   *B*   BWV Anh.183, Minuet in G, from Clavier-Büchlein vor Anna Magdalena Bachin ("Keyboard Notebook of Anna Magdalena Bach") (Attributed to Bach but actually that of Christian Pezold) -- see entries Nos.{6}b and {99}.

Instrumental (C. Solo Organ)

{88}   *B*   BWV 525-530, Trio Sonatas for Solo Organ, in E flat, c, d, e, C and G
Marie-Claire Alain, organ; Erato ECD-88146 [DDD] (TT=67.15).

{89}   *B*   BWV 542, Fantasia and Fugue, in g
Marie-Claire Alain, organ; MHS 11086X [DDD] (TT=49.36). Includes Bach's BWV 565, Toccata and Fugue, in d, rated A, BWV 578, Fugue ("Little Fugue"), in g, rated A, BWV 582, Passacaglia and Fugue, in c, rated A and BWV 593, Concerto in a.

{90}   *A*   BWV 565, Toccata and Fugue, in d
Cincinnati Pops Orchestra; Erich Kunzel, conductor; Telarc CD-80129 [DDD] (TT=57.12). Includes Albeniz' Fête-Dieu à Séville; Bach's BWV 578, Fugue ("Little Fugue"), in g, rated A; Beethoven's Adagio sostenuto, from Sonata for Piano No.14, Op.27 No.2 ("Moonlight") (the Op.27 No.14 rated A); Boccherini's Minuet, from Quintet for Strings, Op.11 No.5, in E, rated B; Debussy's La Cathédrale engloutie ("The Engulfed Cathedral") from Préludes, Book I No.10 (1910) and Clair de lune ("Moonlight"), from Suite bergamasque (1890-1905), the Suite rated A; Mussorgsky's Night on Bald Mountain (1860-1866), rated A and Rachmaninoff's Prelude for Piano, Op.23 No.2, in c sharp, rated A. All of the orchestrations on this disc were by Leopold Stokowski, and Kunzel's readings of them sound very much as if the ghost of Stokowski were on the podium. The Rachmaninoff work is the "famous" (or infamous) Prelude once known as "**THE** Rachmaninoff Piece."
Also -- see entry No.{89}.

{91}   *B*   BWV 572, Fantasia for Organ (Part 2, Transcribed for Wind Band by Richard Franko Goldman and Robert Leist)

Cleveland Symphonic Winds; Frederick Fennell, conductor; Telarc CD-80038 [DDD] (TT=43.48). Includes Handel's <u>Royal Fireworks Music</u> (1749), rated A; and Holst's Two Suites for Military Band (2): Op.28 No.1-2, in E flat and F, both rated B.

{92}   *A*   BWV 578, Fugue ("Little Fugue"), in g -- see entries Nos.{89} and {90}.

{93}   *A*   BWV 582, Passacaglia and Fugue, in c -- see entry No.{89}.

{94}   *A*   BWV 645-650, Chorales ("Schübler") (6) Nos.1-6: <u>Wachet auf, ruft uns die Stimme</u> ("Sleepers Awake"), <u>Wo soll ich fliehen hin</u> ("Whither Shall I Flee"), <u>Wer nur den lieben Gott lässt walten</u> ("He Who Allows Himself to Be Guided by the Lord"), <u>Meine Seele erhebt den Herrn</u> ("My Soul Is Raised Unto the Lord"), <u>Ach bleib' bei uns, Herr Jesu Christ</u> ("Oh, Remain With Us, Lord Jesus Christ") and <u>Kommst du nun, Jesu, vom Himmel herunter</u> ("Come Thee Now Down From the Heavens, Jesus")

Marie-Claire Alain, organ; Erato ECD-88030 [DDD] (TT=43.35). Includes Bach's Chorales, <u>Jesu bleibet meine Freude</u> ("Jesu, Joy of Man's Desiring") from BWV 147, <u>Herz und Mund und Tat und Leben</u> ("Heart and Mouth and Deed and Life"), BWV 622, <u>O Mensch, bewein' dein' Sünde gross</u> ("Oh Man, Deplore Thy Great Sin"), BWV 639, <u>Ich ruf' zu dir, Herr Jesu Christ</u> ("I Call to You, Lord Jesus Christ"), BWV 659, <u>Nun komm' der Heiden Heiland</u> ("Come Now, Saviour of the Gentiles"), BWV 680, <u>Wir glauben all' an einen Gott</u> ("We All Believe in One God"), BWV 721, <u>Erbarm dich mein, o Herre Gott</u> ("Take Pity on Me, O Lord") and BWV 734, <u>Nun</u>

freut euch, lieben Christen g'mein ("Let Us Rejoice in What the Lord Has Done").

Instrumental (D. Solo Violin)

{95}   *A*   BWV 1001-1006, Sonatas and Partitas for Solo Violin (Three Each)

a   Jascha Heifetz, violin; RCA 7708-2-RG (2 discs) ! [ADD] (TT=125.05).

b   Shlomo Mintz, violin; DG 413 810-2 (3 discs) [DDD] (TT=142.30).

Although Mintz does a fine job, the Heifetz performances (dating from 1952) are without peer.

Instrumental (E. Unknown)

{96}   *B*   BWV 1079, Musikalische Opfer ("Musical Offering") (Orchestrated by Sir Neville Marriner)

Iona Brown, violin; Roger Garland, violin; Malcolm Latchem, violin; Stephen Shingles, viola; Denis Vigay, 'cello; William Bennett, flute; Nicholas Kraemer, organ and harpsichord; Academy of St. Martin-in-the-Fields, Sir Neville Marriner, conductor; Philips 412 800-2 [DDD] (TT=48.51). BWV 1079 was probably originally written for violin and flute, but it has been transcribed, orchestrated, and otherwise changed so many times that it appears never to be really known in its original "habitat."

{97}   *A*   BWV 1080, Die Kunst der Fuge ("The Art of the Fugue")

Davitt Moroney, harpsichord; Harmonia Mundi 01169-01170 [DDD] (TT=98.47).

Portland String Quartet; Arabesque Z-6519-2 (2 discs) [DDD] (TT=73.17). BWV 1080 was probably written for keyboard, but of that no one is terribly sure. Therefore, it is performed by various solo and ensemble instruments. Both of the cited recordings are good, my own disposition tending towards Moroney.

Orchestral

{98}   *A*   BWV 1066-1069, Suites for Orchestra (4) Nos.1-4: in C, b, D and D

a   Linde Consort; Hans-Martin Linde, conductor; Angel CDC 49025-2 and 49026-2 (2 discs) [DDD] (TT = 116.03). Includes Handel's Concerto for Two Oboes, Bassoon, Four Horns, Organ and Strings, in F (1746-1748); Concerto a Due Cori, in F (1746-1747) and Royal Fireworks Music (1749), rated A. In the Handel works, Linde conducts the Capella Coloniensis.

b   La Petite Bande; Sigiswald Kuijken, Concertmaster and Director; Angel CDS 7 47819-8 (2 discs) [DDD] (TT = 111.53).

c   Stuttgart Chamber Orchestra; Karl Münchinger, conductor; London 414 505-2 (2 discs) [DDD] (TT = 77.59).

Of all four of these recordings, the Pinnock tends to follow the middle ground most closely. Kuijken and his "Little Band" (modeled after Lully's ensemble, *les petits violons*) are rather "laid-back" and relaxed, while Münchinger is somewhat faster (but offers exceptionally clean ensemble playing) and the Suite No.2 (which is really a flute concerto, of sorts) is performed beautifully, with lovely embellishments added to the solo in the last movement (i.e., Badinerie). Linde's readings are solid, if somewhat pedestrian. If I had to choose but one, I suppose I would get the Pinnock because it is a meritorious performance, and the set offers good value for money.

Also -- see entries Nos.{6}b, {56}b and {60}.

Vocal

{99}   *B*   Clavier-Büchlein vor Anna Magdalena Bachin ("Keyboard Notebook of Anna Magdalena Bach") (1722)

Judith Blegen, soprano; Benjamin Luxon, baritone; Catharina Meints, gamba; Igor Kipnis, harpsichord and clavichord; Nonesuch 79020-2 (2 discs) [DDD] (TT = 108.17).

These discs comprise all of the works found in the notebook of works which Bach had compiled for his second wife, Anna Magdalena. Many of the works are not by Bach, but by various other composers (Hasse, Couperin, Pezold, etc.), yet each was thought, by Bach, to warrant inclusion since each had something to teach. The performances here are indeed lustrous.

BARBER, SAMUEL
1910-1981

Chamber
{100}   C   Summer Music for Wind Quintet, Op.31
Westwood Wind Quintet; Crystal CD-750 [DDD] (TT=61.10). Includes Carlson's Nightwings for Wind Quintet and Tape; Ligeti's Six Bagatelles (Transcribed for Wind Quintet by the Composer in 1953) and Mathias' Quintet, Op.22.

Concerted
{101}   B   Concerto for Violin, Op.14
Elmar Oliveira, violin; St. Louis Symphony Orchestra; Leonard Slatkin, conductor; Angel CDC 47850-2 [DDD] (TT=54.50). Includes Hanson Symphony No.2 ("Romantic"), Op.30, rated B.

Orchestral
{102}   A   Adagio for Strings (Second Movement from String Quartet, Op.11,in b, Orchestrated by the Composer)
a   Los Angeles Philharmonic Orchestra; Leonard Bernstein, conductor; DG 413 324-2 [DDD] (TT=50.17). Includes Bernstein's Overture: Candide (1956), rated B; Copland's Appalachian Spring Suite (1944), rated A and William Schuman's Overture: American Festival (1939).
b   I Musici; Philips 416 356-2 [DDD] (TT=51.42).

120

Includes Elgar's Serenade for Strings, Op.20, in e, rated B; Respighi's <u>Ancient Airs and Dances for the Lute</u> (3 sets) (Set 3: 1932), rated B and Rota's Concerto for Strings (1964-1965).

{103}   *B*   <u>First Essay</u> for Orchestra (1938)
Moscow Philharmonic Orchestra; Dmitri Kitayenko, conductor; Sheffield Lab CD-26 [DDD] (60.06). Includes Piston's Ballet Suite <u>The Incredible Flutist</u> (1938), rated B and Shostakovich's Symphony No.1, Op.10, rated B (the Shostakovich is conducted by Lawrence Leighton Smith).

BARTÓK, BÉLA
1881-1945

Chamber
{104}   *A*   String Quartets (6) Nos.1-6: Sz.40, in a; Sz.67, in a; Sz.85; Sz.91, in C; Sz.102, in B flat and Sz.114, in D
Takács Quartet; Hungaroton HCD 12502-04-2 (3 discs) [DDD] (TT=154.22).

{105}   *B*   Divertimento for String Orchestra, Sz.113
Orpheus Chamber Orchestra; DG 415 668-2 [DDD] (TT=50.00). Includes Bartók's Rumanian Folk Dances, Sz.68, rated C and Janáček's <u>Mládí</u> ("Youth") (1924), rated B.

{106}   *C*   Rumanian Folk Dances, Sz.68 -- see entry No.{105}.

Concerted
{107}   *B*   Concerto for Piano No.3, Sz.119, in E
Vladimir Ashkenazy, piano; London Philharmonic Orchestra; Sir Georg Solti, conductor; London 411 969-2 [AAD] (TT=52.58). Includes Prokofiev's Concerto for Piano No.3, Op.26, in C, rated A (in the Prokofiev work, Ashkenazy

is also the soloist and he is assisted by the London Symphony Orchestra with André Previn conducting).

{108}   C   Concerto for Two Pianos, Percussion and Orchestra, Sz.115
          Katia and Marielle Labèque, pianos; City of Birmingham (England) Symphony Orchestra; Simon Rattle, conductor; Angel CDC 47746 [DDD] (TT = 52.09). Includes Bartók's Sonata for Two Pianos and Percussion, Sz.110 (with percussionists Jean-Pierre Drouet and Sylvio Gualda). The Concerto, Sz.115, was orchestrated by Bartók, using the Sonata, Sz.110, as the basis.

{109}   A   Concerto for Violin No.2, Sz.112

          André Gertler, violin; Czech Philharmonic Orchestra; Karel Ančerl, conductor; Sound CD-3432 [AAD] (TT = 37.54).

Operatic
{110}   B   Bluebeard's Castle, Op.11
          Elena Obraztsova, mezzo-soprano; Yevgeny Nesterenko, bass; Hungarian State Opera Chorus and Orchestra; János Ferencsik, conductor; Hungaroton HCD 12254-2 [DDD] (TT = 57.04).

Orchestral
{111}   A   Concerto for Orchestra, Sz.116
a   Amsterdam Concertgebouw Orchestra; Antal Doráti, conductor; Philips 411 132-2 [DDD] (TT = 54.07). Includes Bartók's Two Pictures, Op.10.
b   Chicago Symphony Orchestra; Fritz Reiner, conductor; RCA 5604-2-RC [ADD] (TT = 65.07). Includes Bartók's Music for Strings, Percussion and Celesta, Sz.106, rated A.

{112}   A   Music for Strings, Percussion and Celesta, Sz.106
-- see entry No.{111}b.

BEETHOVEN, LUDWIG VAN
1770-1827

Chamber

{113}   *B*   Septet for Strings and Winds, Op.20, in E flat
Vienna Octet; London 421 093-2 [ADD] (TT=74.05).
Includes Mendelssohn's Octet for Strings, Op.20, in E flat, rated A.

{114}   *A*   Quintet for Piano, Clarinet, Oboe, Horn and Bassoon, Op.16, in E flat
Radu Lupu, piano; George Pieterson, clarinet; Han de Vries, oboe; Vicente Zarzo, horn and Brian Pollard, bassoon; London 414 291-2 [DDD] (TT=51.57). Includes Mozart's Quintet for Piano, Oboe, Clarinet, Horn and Bassoon, K.452, in E flat, rated A.

{115}   *A*   Sonatas for 'Cello and Piano (5) Nos.1-5: Op.5 Nos.1-2, in F and g; Op.69, in A and Op.102 Nos.1-2, in C and D

a   Mstislav Rostropovich, 'cello; Sviatoslav Richter, piano; Philips 412 256-2 (2 discs) [ADD] (TT=108.38).

b   Yo-Yo Ma, 'cello; Emanuel Ax, piano; CBS MK-37251 (contains Nos.1-2) [DDD] (TT=52.05), CBS MK-39024 (contains Nos.3 and 5) [DDD] (TT=50.20) and CBS MK-42121 (contains No.4) [DDD] (TT=51.51). The third disc in this group includes Beethoven's Seven Variations for 'Cello and Piano on Mozart's "Bei Männern, Welch Liebe Fühlen" ("In Men, Who Know the Feeling of Love") from Die Zauberflöte ("The Magic Flute"), WoO 46; Twelve Variations for 'Cello and Piano on Mozart "Ein Mädchen oder Weibchen" ("A Maiden or a Little Wife") from Die Zauberflöte ("The Magic Flute"), Op.66 and Twelve Variations on "See the Conqu'ring Hero Comes" from Handel's Judas Maccabeus, WoO 45.

{116} *A* Sonatas for Violin and Piano (10) Nos.1-10: Op.12 Nos.1-3, in D, A and E flat; Op.23, in a; Op.24, in F ("Spring"); Op.30 Nos.1-3, in A, c and D; Op.47, in A ("Kreutzer") and Op.96, in G

a   Jascha Heifetz, violin; Emanuel Bay, piano (except in Op.47, where Brooks Smith is the pianist); RCA 7704-7706 (3 discs) ! [ADD] (TT=204.44).

b   David Oistrakh, violin; Lev Oborin, piano; Philips 412 570-2 (4 discs) [ADD] (TT=229.26).

    To have two such sets of these works has to be an embarrassment of riches. Being torn between them, all I can write is, take your pick and you'll not go wrong.

{117} *A* Sonata for Violin and Piano No.5, in F ("Spring") -- see entries Nos.{116}a-b.

{118} *A* Sonata for Violin and Piano No.9, in A ("Kreutzer") -- see entries Nos.{116}a-b.

{119} *B* String Quartets Nos.1-6 ("Early"): Op.18 Nos.1-6, in F, G, D, c, A and B flat

    Talich Quartet; Calliope CAL-9633-9634 (2 discs) [AAD] (TT=72.43).

{120} *A* String Quartet No.7, Op.59 No.1, in F ("First Rasumovsky")

    Talich Quartet; Calliope CAL-9636 [AAD] (TT=71.47). Includes Beethoven's String Quartet No.10, Op.74, in B flat ("Harp"), rated B.

{121} *A* String Quartet No.8, Op.59 No.2, in e ("Second Rasumovsky")

    Talich Quartet; Calliope CAL-9637 [AAD] (TT=72.56). Includes Beethoven's String Quartet No.13, Op.130, in B flat, rated A.

{122}   *A*   String Quartet No.9, Op.59 No.3, in C ("Third Rasumovsky")
Talich Quartet; Calliope CAL-9638 [AAD] (TT=72.11). Includes Beethoven's String Quartet No.14, Op.131, in c sharp, rated A.

{123}   *B*   String Quartet No.10, Op.74, in B flat ("Harp") -- see entry No.{120}.

{124}   *B*   String Quartet No.11, Op.95, in f
Talich Quartet; Calliope CAL-9635 [AAD] (TT=73.20). Includes Beethoven's String Quartet No.12, Op.127, in E flat, rated B and String Quartet Fragment <u>Grosse Fuge</u> ("Great Fugue"), Op.133, in B flat, rated A.

{125}   *B*   String Quartet No.12, Op.127, in E flat -- see entry No.{124}.

{126}   *A*   String Quartet No.13, Op.130, in B flat
Fitzwilliam String Quartet; London 411 943-2 [DDD] (TT=63.47). Includes Beethoven's String Quartet Fragment <u>Grosse Fuge</u> ("Great Fugue"), Op.133, in B flat, rated A.
Also -- see entry No.{121}.

{127}   *A*   String Quartet No.14, Op.131, in c sharp -- see entry No.{122}.

{128}   *A*   String Quartet No.15, Op.132, in a
Talich Quartet; Calliope CAL-9639 [AAD] (TT=68.18). Includes Beethoven's String Quartet No.16, Op.135, in F, rated A.

{129}   *A*   String Quartet No.16, Op.135, in a -- see entry No.{128}.

{130} *A* String Quartet Fragment <u>Grosse Fuge</u> ("Great Fugue"), Op.133, in B flat -- see entries Nos.{124}, {126} and {171}c.

{131} *A* Trio for Piano, Violin and 'Cello, Op.97, in B flat ("Archduke")
Joseph Kalichstein, piano; Jaime Laredo, violin; Sharon Robinson, 'cello; MCA MCAD-25193 [DDD] (TT=61.00). Includes Beethoven's Trio for Piano, Violin and 'Cello, Op.121a, in G (Adagio, 10 Variations on <u>Ich bin der Schneider Kakadu</u> <"I Am the Tailor, Kakadu"> and Rondo, in G), rated A.

{132} *A* Trio for Piano, Violin and 'Cello, Op.121a, in G (Adagio, 10 Variations on <u>Ich bin der Schneider Kakadu</u> <"I Am the Tailor, Kakadu"> and Rondo, in G) -- see entry No.{131}.

Choral

{133} *B* Oratorio: <u>Christ on the Mount of Olives</u>, Op.85
Monica Pick-Hieronimi, soprano; James Anderson, tenor; Victor von Halem, bass; Lyon National Chorus and Orchestra; Serge Baudo, conductor; Harmonia Mundi HCM-90 5181 [DDD] (TT=52.41).

{134} *A* Missa Solemnis, Op.123, in D
a   Sylvia McNair, soprano; Janice Taylor, mezzo-soprano; John Aler, tenor; Tom Krause, baritone; Atlanta Symphony Chorus and Orchestra; Robert Shaw, conductor; Telarc CD-80150 (2 discs) [DDD] (TT=139.19). Includes Mozart's Mass, in c ("Great"), K.427, rated A. In the Mozart, the soloists are Edith Wiens, soprano; Delores Ziegler, mezzo-soprano; John Aler, tenor and William Stone, baritone.
b   Edda Moser, soprano; Hanna Schwarz, contralto; René Kollo, tenor; Kurt Moll, bass; Hilversum Radio Choir;

Amsterdam Concertgebouw Orchestra; Leonard Bernstein, conductor; DG 413 780-2 (2 discs) [ADD] (TT=81.18).

Concerted

{135}   *A*   Concerto for Piano No.1, Op.15, in C
a   Alfred Brendel, piano; Chicago Symphony Orchestra; James Levine, conductor; Philips 412 787-2 [DDD] (TT=67.36). Includes Beethoven's Concerto for Piano No.2, Op.19, in B flat, rated B.
b   Maurizio Pollini, piano; Vienna Philharmonic Orchestra; Eugen Jochum, conductor; DG 410 511-2 [DDD] (TT=37.21). Although this recording offers less music (and value) for the money, the performance is better than that of Brendel's, and recommends itself to those whose libraries can afford both.

{136}   *B*   Concerto for Piano No.2, Op.19, in B flat
        Maurizio Pollini, piano; Vienna Philharmonic Orchestra; Eugen Jochum, conductor; DG 413 445-2 [DDD] (TT=60.58). Includes Beethoven's Piano Concerto No.4, Op.58, in G, rated D (the Concerto No.4 is an [ADD] recording).
        Also -- see entry No.{135}a.

{137}   *A*   Concerto for Piano No.3, Op.37, in c
        Maurizio Pollini, piano; Vienna Philharmonic Orchestra; Eugen Jochum, conductor; DG 413 446-2 [ADD] (TT=42.08). Includes Beethoven's Sonata for Piano No.31, Op.110, in A flat, rated A.

{138}   *A*   Concerto for Piano No.4, Op.58, in G
        Claudio Arrau, piano; Dresden State Orchestra; Sir Colin Davis, conductor; Philips 416 144-2 [DDD] (TT=59.51). Includes Beethoven's Variations on an Original Theme, WoO 80, in c.
        Also -- see entry No.{136}.

127

{139}   *A*   Concerto for Piano No.5 ("Emperor"), Op.73, in E
flat
        Claudio Arrau, piano; Dresden State Orchestra; Sir
Colin Davis, conductor; Philips 416 215-2 [DDD] (TT=40.40).

{140}   *A*   Concerto for Violin, Op.61, in D
a   Zino Francescatti, violin; Columbia Symphony
Orchestra; Bruno Walter, conductor; CBS MK-42018 [AAD?]
(TT=43.22).
b   Jascha Heifetz, violin; Boston Symphony Orchestra;
Charles Munch, conductor; RCA RCD1-5402 [AAD]
(TT=72.20). Includes Brahms' Concerto for Violin, Op.77, in
D, rated A.
c   Itzhak Perlman, violin; Philharmonia Orchestra; Carlo
Maria Giulini, conductor; Angel CDC 47002-2 [ADD?]
(TT=43.55).
d   Henryk Szeryng, violin; Amsterdam Concertgebouw
Orchestra; Bernard Haitink, conductor; Philips 416 418-2
[ADD?] (TT=63.17). Includes Beethoven's Two Romances
for Violin and Orchestra, Op.40, in G and Op.50 in F, both
rated C.
        All four of the above are excellent, but Heifetz's is the
best in both concerti, and RCA offers full measure for the
money.

{141}   *B*   Concerto for Violin, 'Cello and Piano, Op.56, in C
("Triple Concerto")
        Anne-Sophie   Mutter, violin; Yo-Yo Ma, 'cello; Mark
Zeltser, piano; Berlin Philharmonic Orchestra; Herbert von
Karajan, conductor; DG 415 276-2 [ADD] (TT=60.54).
Includes Beethoven's Overtures: Coriolan, Op.62; Egmont,
Op.84 and Fidelio, Op.72b, all rated A.

{142}   *C*   Two Romances for Violin and Orchestra, Op.40,
in G and Op.50, in F -- see entry No.{140}c.

Instrumental

{143}   *A*   Albumblatt ("Für Elise"), Bagatelle, WoO 59, in a
Alfred Brendel, piano; Philips 412 227-2 [DDD]
(TT=49.58). Includes Beethoven's Eroica Variations (Fifteen
Variations and Fugue), Op.35, in E flat, rated B; Six
Bagatelles, Op.126 and Six Ecossaises, WoO 83.

{144}   *B*   Eroica Variations (Fifteen Variations and Fugue),
Op.35, in E flat -- see entry No.{143}.

{145}   *C*   Sonata for Piano No.2, Op.2 No.2, in A
Emil Gilels, piano; DG 415 481-2 [DDD] (TT=58.28).
Includes Beethoven's Sonata for Piano No.4, Op.7, in E flat,
rated C.

{146}   *C*   Sonata for Piano No.4, Op.7, in E flat -- see entry
No.{145}.

{147}   *A*   Sonata for Piano No.8, Op.13, in c ("Pathétique")
Vladimir Horowitz, piano; CBS MK-34509 [ADD?]
(TT=58.13). Includes Beethoven's Sonatas for Piano Nos.14,
Op.27 No.2, in c sharp ("Moonlight") and 23, Op.57, in f
("Appassionata"), both rated A.

{148}   *A*   Sonata for Piano No.14, Op.27 No.2, in c sharp
("Moonlight") -- see entry No.{147}.

{149}   *A*   Sonata for Piano No.21, Op.53, in C ("Waldstein")
Emil Gilels, piano; DG 419 162-2 [ADD] (TT=68.10).
Includes Beethoven's Sonatas for Piano Nos.23, Op.57, in f
("Appassionata") and 26, Op.81a, in E flat ("Les Adieux"), both
rated A.

{150}   *A*   Sonata for Piano No.23, Op.57, in f
("Appassionata") -- see entries Nos.{147} and {149}.

{151}   C   Sonata for Piano No.24, Op.78, in F sharp ("Für Therese")
Alfred Brendel, piano; Philips 412 723-2 [ADD] (TT = 40.05). Includes Beethoven's Sonata for Piano No.29, Op.106, in B flat ("Hammerklavier"), rated A.

{152}   A   Sonata for Piano No.26, Op.81a, in E flat ("Les Adieux") -- see entry No.{149}.

{153}   C   Sonata for Piano No.28, Op.101, in A
Maurizio Pollini, piano; DG 419 199-2 (2 discs) [AAD] (TT = 125.04). Includes Beethoven's Sonatas for Piano Nos.29-32, Op.106, in B flat ("Hammerklavier"); Op.109, in E; Op.110, in A flat and Op.111, in c, all rated A.

{154}   A   Sonata for Piano No.29, Op.106, in B flat ("Hammerklavier") -- see entries Nos.{151} and {153}.

{155}   A   Sonata for Piano No.30, Op.109, in E
Emil Gilels, piano; DG 419 174-2 [DDD] (TT = 43.13). Includes Beethoven's Sonata for Piano No.31, Op.110, in A flat, rated A.
Also -- see entry No.{153}.

{156}   A   Sonata for Piano No.31, Op.110, in A flat -- see entries Nos.{153} and {155}.

{157}   A   Sonata for Piano No.32, Op.111, in c
Friedrich Gulda, piano; Philips 412 114-2 [DDD] (TT = 49.30). Includes Gulda's Wintermeditation.
Also -- see entry No.{153}.

Operatic
{158}   A   Fidelio, Op.72
Hildegard Behrens, soprano; Sona Ghazarian, soprano; Peter Hoffman, tenor; Gwynne Howell, bass-baritone; Theo

Adam, bass; Hans Sotin, bass; Chicago Symphony Chorus and Orchestra; Sir Georg Solti, conductor; London 410 227-2 (2 discs) [DDD] (TT = 119.42).

Orchestral

{159}   C   Overture: <u>Consecration of the House</u>, Op.124
a   Bavarian Radio Symphony Orchestra; Sir Colin Davis, conductor; CBS MK-42103 [DDD] (TT = 63.02). Includes Beethoven's Overtures: <u>Coriolan</u>, Op.62, rated B; <u>Egmont</u>, Op.84, rated A; <u>Fidelio</u>, Op.72b, rated A; <u>Leonore</u> No.1, Op.138, rated A; <u>Leonore</u> No.3, Op.72a, rated A; <u>Prometheus</u>, Op.43, rated B; and <u>Ruins of Athens</u>, Op.113, rated C.
b   Philharmonia Orchestra; Otto Klemperer, conductor; Angel CDC 47190-2 [AAD] (TT = 65.07). Includes Beethoven's Overtures: <u>Coriolan</u>, Op.62, rated B; <u>Fidelio</u>, Op.72b, rated A; <u>Leonore</u> No.1, Op.138, rated A; <u>Leonore</u> No.2, Op.72a, rated A and <u>Leonore</u> No.3, Op.72a, rated A.

{160}   B   Overture: <u>Coriolan</u>, Op.62
         London Philharmonic Orchestra; Klaus Tennstedt, conductor; Angel CDC 47086-2 [DDD] (TT = 43.09). Includes Beethoven's Overtures: <u>Egmont</u>, Op.84, rated A; <u>Fidelio</u>, Op.72b, rated A; <u>Leonore</u> No.3, Op.72a, rated A; and <u>Prometheus</u>, Op.43, rated B.
         Also -- see entries Nos.{141}, {159}a-b and {171}b.

{161}   A   Overture: <u>Egmont</u>, Op.84 -- see entries Nos.{141}, {159}a, {160}, {173}a and {174}c.

{162}   A   Overture: <u>Fidelio</u>, Op.72b -- see entries Nos.{141}, {159}a and {160}

{163}   A   Overture: <u>Leonore</u> No.1, Op.138 -- see entries Nos.{159}a-b.

{164}   *A*   Overture: <u>Leonore</u> No.2, Op.72a -- see entries Nos.{159}b and {174}b.

{165}   *A*   Overture: <u>Leonore</u> No.3, Op.72a -- see entries Nos.{159}a-b and {160}.

{166}   *B*   Overture: <u>Prometheus</u>, Op.43 -- see entries Nos.{159}a, {160}, {173}a and {175}c.

{167}   *C*   Overture: <u>Ruins of Athens</u>, Op.113 -- see entry No.{159}a.

{168}   *B*   <u>Wellington's Victory</u>, Op.91
          Cincinnati Symphony Orchestra; Erich Kunzel, conductor; Telarc CD-80079 [DDD] (TT=35.49). Includes Liszt's <u>Hunnenschlacht</u> ("Battle of the Huns"), Symphonic Poem No.11, S.102 and <u>Ungarischer Sturmmarsch</u> ("Hungarian Assault March"), S.119.

Symphonic

{169}   *A*   Symphony No.1, Op.21, in C
a   Columbia Symphony Orchestra; Bruno Walter, conductor; CBS MK-42009 [AAD?] (TT=59.24). Includes Beethoven's Symphony No.2, Op.36, in D, rated A.
b   Academy of Ancient Music; Christopher Hogwood, conductor; L'Oiseau-Lyre 414 338-2. Includes Beethoven's Symphony No.2, Op.36, in D, rated A.

{170}   *A*   Symphony No.2, Op.36, in D -- see entries Nos.{169}a-b.

{171}   *A*   Symphony No.3 ("Eroica"), Op.55, in E flat
a   Cleveland Orchestra; Christoph von Dohnányi, conductor; Telarc CD-80090 [DDD] (TT=48.32).

b   Columbia Symphony Orchestra; Bruno Walter, conductor; CBS MK-42010 [AAD?] (TT=58.03). Includes Beethoven's Overture: <u>Coriolan</u>, Op.62, rated B.

c   Philharmonia Orchestra; Otto Klemperer, conductor; Angel CDC 47186-2 [AAD] (TT=70.02). Includes Beethoven's String Quartet Fragment <u>Grosse Fuge</u> ("Great Fugue"), Op.133, in B flat (Orchestrated by the composer), rated A.

{172}   *A*   Symphony No.4, Op.60, in B flat
         Columbia Symphony Orchestra; Bruno Walter, conductor; CBS MK-42001 [AAD?] (TT=64.36). Includes Beethoven's Symphony No.5, Op.67, in c, rated A.

{173}   *A*   Symphony No.5, Op.67, in c
a   Amsterdam Concertgebouw Orchestra; George Szell, conductor; Philips 420 771-2 PM [ADD] (TT=74.14). Includes Sibelius' Symphony No.2, Op.43, in D, rated A.
b   Hanover Band; Nimbus NI-5007 [DDD] (TT=48.53). Includes Beethoven's   Overture: <u>Egmont</u>, Op.84, rated A and Overture: <u>Prometheus</u>, Op.43, rated B.
c   Philharmonic Symphony Orchestra of London; Artur Rodzinski, conductor; MCA MCAD-2-9806 (2 discs) [AAD] (TT=131.10). Includes Beethoven's Symphony No.9 ("Choral"), Op.125, in d, rated A, with Elizabeth Söderström, soprano; Regina Resnik, contralto; Jon Vickers, tenor; David Ward, bass; London Bach Choir; London Symphony Orchestra; Pierre Monteux, conductor; MCA MCAD-2-9806 (2 discs) [AAD] (TT=131.10), excerpts from the rehearsal for the Op.125, and a fine rehearsal performance of <u>La Marseillaise</u>, by de Lisle, (in, as Monteux puts it, the "*officiel, not arrangéd, version*").
d   Vienna Philharmonic Orchestra; Carlos Kleiber, conductor; DG 415 861-2 [ADD] (33.10).
         Of the five listed performances of this, the most popular and well-known of Beethoven's symphonies: The Hanover

Band's performance is probably as close in style and sound to performances contemporary to Beethoven as we are likely to hear. Kleiber's recording is a robust Romantic one--replete with all exposition repeats, vitality, and the incomparable lush sound of the Vienna Philharmonic at its best. Walter offers a less hard-driving 5th, one not without power, but more introspective. The Rodzinski performance is superb (despite a barely adequate orchestra), and the Symphony No.9 of Monteux is startling for its clarity and incisiveness (it is also a real bargain, since the 2 discs are sold at the price of one mid-priced CD). The Szell recording is extremely fine, but its true value is in the Sibelius 2nd Symphony, for me the best ever recorded. For those either short either of memory or years, it is the four opening notes of the Fifth Symphony which resounded on radio and in movies throughout World War II as one symbol of an anticipated Allied victory (that four note motif, three short notes and one long one, is also Morse code for the letter "V").

Also -- see entry No.{172}.

{174}   *A*   Symphony No.6 ("Pastoral"), Op.72, in F
a   Cleveland Orchestra; Christoph von Dohnányi, conductor; Telarc CD-80145 [DDD] (TT=56.25).
b   Columbia Symphony Orchestra; Bruno Walter, conductor; CBS MK-42012 [AAD?] (TT=56.15). Includes Beethoven's Overture: Leonore No.2, Op.72a, rated A.
c   Philharmonia Orchestra; Otto Klemperer, conductor; Angel CDC 47188-2 [AAD] (TT=69.16). Includes Beethoven's Overture and Incidental Music to Egmont, Op.84 (with soprano Birgit Nilsson), the Overture is rated A, and Overture: Prometheus, Op.43, rated B.
d   Vienna Philharmonic Orchestra; Wilhelm Furtwängler, conductor; Angel CDC 47121-2 [ADD] (TT=44.48).

The recording by the Cleveland has the advantage of full digital engineering, and is a performance of which von Dohnányi can be proud. It does tend, however, to be, despite

134

its relative slowness, "pushed." The advantage of the Klemperer recording, aside from a fine performance, is the Egmont incidental music which, however beautifully done by Nilsson (then in her prime), is not really required in most libraries. Walter displays his usual warm way with the even numbered symphonies of Beethoven, and offers good value. It is the old (i.e., 1953) recording of Furtwängler's which steals the show--this is a "Pastoral" without peer. Unfortunately, the recording is a monophonic one, but the "cleaning up" of the old disc by EMI was scrupulously done, and the lack of stereo need not be a deterrent to anyone seeking the ultimate performance of Beethoven's sunniest (despite the storm sequence) symphony. An abbreviated version of the Pastoral was used in Disney's film, Fantasia.

{175}   *A*   Symphony No.7, Op.92, in A
a   Columbia Symphony Orchestra; Bruno Walter, conductor; CBS MK-42013 [AAD?] (TT=64.49). Includes Beethoven's Symphony No.8, Op.93, in F, rated A.
b   Vienna Philharmonic Orchestra; Carlos Kleiber, conductor; DG 415 862-2 [ADD] (TT=38.20).

{176}   *A*   Symphony No.8, Op.93, in F
             Cleveland Orchestra; Christoph von Dohnányi, conductor; Telarc CD-80091 [DDD] (TT=52.49). Includes Schubert's Symphony No.8 ("Unfinished"), D.759, in b, rated A. Also -- see entry No.{175}a.

{177}   *A*   Symphony No.9 ("Choral"), Op.125, in d
a   Yvonne Kenny, soprano; Sarah Walker, mezzo-soprano; Patrick Power, tenor; Petteri Salomaa, bass; Schütz Choir of London; London Classical Players; Roger Norrington, conductor; Angel CDC 49221-2 [DDD] (TT=62.25).
b   Aase Nordmo Lövberg, soprano; Christa Ludwig, mezzo-soprano; Waldemar Kmentt, tenor; Hans Hotter, baritone; Philharmonia Chorus and Orchestra; Otto

Classical Music and Opera on CDs

Klemperer, conductor; Angel CDC 47189-2 [AAD] (TT=72.06).

c   Janet Price, soprano; Birgit Finnila, contralto; Horst Laubenthal, tenor; Marius Rintzler, bass; Amsterdam Concertgebouw Chorus and Orchestra; Bernard Haitink, conductor; Philips 410 036-2 [DDD] (TT=69.34).

d   Elisabeth Schwarzkopf, soprano; Elisabeth Höngen, contralto; Hans Hopf, tenor; Otto Edelmann, bass; Bayreuth Festival (1953) Chorus and Orchestra; Wilhelm Furtwängler, conductor; Angel CDC 47081-2 [ADD] (TT=74.43).

e   Carol Vaness, soprano; Janice Taylor, mezzo-soprano; Siegfried Jerusalem, tenor; Robert Lloyd, bass; Cleveland Chorus and Orchestra; Christoph von Dohnányi, conductor; Telarc CD-80120 [DDD] (TT=66.24).

Once again, with a stunning performance, Furtwängler steals the show: his relaxed, yet constantly flowing, tempi are completely arresting, and the finale is as exciting as Beethoven could have wished. Once more, the only drawback is a monophonic recording (and, again, as clear and clean as fine engineering could make it). Klemperer is not as exciting, but offers an inner view of the work which only he would find. The Cleveland's recording is winning one for sheer brilliance of sound, and is also very exciting; but the modern recording walks off with the honors is Haitink's with that superb bunch of Amsterdamers. Norrington's fascinating recording attempts to recreate the tempi indicated by Beethoven's metronome markings. It is a valiant and exciting attempt which, ultimately, fails due to lack of intellectual weight.

Also -- see entry No.{173}b.

Vocal

{178}   *B*   An die ferne Geliebte ("To the Distant Beloved") Song Cycle, Op.98

Dietrich Fischer-Dieskau, baritone; Jörg Demus, piano; DG 415 189-2 [ADD?] (TT=70.54). Includes seven Beethoven lieder: Adelaïde, Op.46; L'Amante impaziente ("The Impatient

Love"), Op.82 Nos.3-4; Es war einmal ein König ("There Once Was a King"), Op.75 No.3; In questa tomba oscura ("In This Dark Tomb"), WoO 133; Maigesang ("Maying Song"), Op.52 No.4 and Zärtliche Liebe ("Gentle Love"), WoO 123; and Brahms' Vier ernste Gesänge ("Four Serious Songs"), Op.121, rated B, and six lieder: Alte Liebe ("Old Love"), Op.72 No.1; Auf dem Kirchhofe ("In the Churchyard"), Op.105 No.4; Feldeinsamkeit ("Lonely Fields"), Op.86 No.2; Nachklang ("Echo"), Op.59 No.4; O wüßt'ich doch den Weg zurück ("O That I Knew the Way Back"), Op.63 No.8 and Verzagen ("Despair"), Op.72 No.4.

BELLINI, VINCENZO
1801-1835

Operatic

{179} *B* Norma (1831)

Maria Callas, soprano; Rina Cavallari, mezzo-soprano; Ebe Stignani, mezzo-soprano; Mario Filippeschi, tenor; Nicola Rossi-Lemeni, bass; Chorus and Orchestra of La Scala, Milan; Tullio Serafin, conductor; Angel CDC 47303 (3 discs) ! [AAD] (TT=160.08).

{180} *C* La Sonnambula ("The Sleepwalking Woman") (1831)

Isobel Buchanan, soprano; Dame Joan Sutherland, soprano; Della Jones, mezzo-soprano; Piero de Palma, tenor; Luciano Pavarotti, tenor; Nicolai Ghiaurov, bass; John Tomlinson, bass; London Opera Chorus; National Philharmonic Orchestra; Sir Richard Bonynge, conductor; London 417 424-2 (2 discs) [DDD] (TT=141.57).

BERG, ALBAN
1885-1935

Chamber

{181} *C* Chamber Concerto for Piano, Violin and Thirteen Winds (1925)

Peter Serkin, piano; Isaac Stern, violin; Members of the London Symphony Orchestra; Claudio Abbado, conductor; CBS MK-42139 [DDD] (TT=62.19). Includes Berg's Concerto for Violin ("To the Memory of an Angel") (1935), rated A (this portion of the disc is [AAD], and features Stern with the New York Philharmonic, conducted by Leonard Bernstein).

Concerted

{182} *A* Concerto for Violin ("To the Memory of an Angel") (1935)

Itzhak Perlman, violin; Boston Symphony Orchestra; Seiji Ozawa, conductor; DG 413 725-2 [ADD] (TT=56.59). Includes Stravinsky's Concerto for Violin, in D (1931), rated B.

Also -- see entry No.{181}.

Operatic

{183} *B* Lulu (1928-1934)

Teresa Stratas, soprano; Yvonne Minton, mezzo-soprano; Hanna Schwarz, contralto; Kenneth Riegel, tenor; Robert Tear, tenor; Franz Mazura, baritone; Gerd Nienstedt, bass; Orchestra of the Paris Opera; Pierre Boulez, conductor; DG 415 489-2 (3 discs) [ADD] (TT=169.18).

Orchestral

{184} *B* Lyric Suite (1926)

Cincinnati Symphony Orchestra; Michael Gielen, conductor; MMG MCD-10024 [DDD] (TT=50.50). Includes Berg's Lulu Suite (1934) (with Kathleen Battle, soprano), rated C.

Vocal

{185} *C* Lulu Suite (1934) -- see entry No.{184}.

BERLIOZ, HECTOR
1803-1869

Choral

{186} *A* Grande Messe des Morts (Requiem Mass), Op.5

a John Aler, tenor; Atlanta Symphony Chorus and Orchestra; Robert Shaw, conductor; Telarc CD-80109-2 (2 discs) [DDD] (TT = 126.00). Includes Boïto's Prologue to Mefistofele ("Mephistopheles") (After Goethe's Faust) (1868-1875), rated C (With John Cheek, bass, The Morehouse-Spelman Chorus and The Young Singers of Callanwolde) and Verdi's Te Deum (No.4 of Pezzi Sacrum <"Sacred Pieces">) (1898).

b Ronald Dowd, tenor; Wandsworth School Boys' Choir; John Alldis Choir; London Symphony Chorus and Orchestra; Sir Colin Davis; Philips 416 283-2 (2 discs) [ADD] (TT = 126.26). Includes Berlioz' Symphonie funèbre et triomphale ("Funereal and Triumphal Symphony"), Op.15.

{187} *B* Te Deum, Op.22

Francisco Aiza, tenor; Martin Haselböck, organ; London Philharmonic Choir Boys' Choir; London Symphony Chorus; Woodburn Singers; Boys' Choirs; European Community Youth Orchestra; Claudio Abbado, conductor; DG 410 696-2 [DDD] (TT = 46.53).

Concerted

{188} *A* Harold in Italy, for Viola and Orchestra, Op.16 (After Byron's Childe Harold)

a Wolfram Christ, viola; Berlin Philharmonic Orchestra; Lorin Maazel, conductor; DG 415 109-2 [DDD] (TT = 51.08). Includes Berlioz' Overture Le Carnaval romain ("The Roman Carnival"), Op.9, rated A.

b Nobuko Imai, viola; London Symphony Orchestra; Sir Colin Davis, conductor; Philips 416 431-2 [ADD] (TT = 69.17). Includes Berlioz' Tristia, Op.18, with the John Alldis Choir,

139

and the Prelude to Act II of <u>Les Troyens</u> ("The Trojans"), (1856-1859) (entire work rated C).

Operatic

{189}   *B*   <u>Roméo et Juliette</u>: Dramatic Symphony, Op.17
a   Regina Resnik, mezzo-soprano; André Turp, tenor; David Ward, bass; London Symphony Chorus and Orchestra; Pierre Monteux, conductor; MCA MCAD2-9805-A/B (2 discs) [ADD?] (TT=118.26). Includes Tchaikovsky's <u>Romeo and Juliet</u> (1870), rated A (performed by the Vienna State Opera Orchestra; Hermann Scherchen, conductor).
b   Florence Quivar, mezzo-soprano; Alberto Cupido, tenor; Tom Krause, bass; The Tudor Singers of Montreal; Montreal Symphony Orchestra; Charles Dutoit, conductor; London 417 302-2 (2 discs) [DDD] (TT=130.41). Includes Berlioz' <u>Symphonie funèbre et triomphale</u>, Op.15, with the Montreal Symphony Chorus and Orchestra.

{190}   *C*   <u>Les Troyens</u> ("The Trojans"), (1856-1859)
⋅Berit Lindholm, soprano; Elizabeth Bainbridge, mezzo-soprano; Josephine Veasey, mezzo-soprano; Ryland Davies, tenor; Ian Partridge, tenor; Jon Vickers, tenor; Peter Glossop, baritone; Raimund Herincx, baritone; Roger Soyer, baritone; Wandsworth School Boys' Choir; London Symphony Chorus and Orchestra; Sir Colin Davis, conductor; Philips 416 432-2 (4 discs) [ADD] (TT=239.56). This set runs four seconds shy of four hours of playing time: almost as long as it took to build the famous horse.
Also -- see entry No.{188}b.

Orchestral

{191}   *A*   Overtures: <u>Béatrice et Bénédict</u> (After Shakespeare) (1862); <u>Le Carnaval romain</u> ("The Roman Carnival"), Op.9, rated A; <u>Le Corsaire</u> ("The Pirate"), Op.21, rated A; <u>King Lear</u> (After Shakespeare), Op.4, rated A and <u>Rob Roy</u> (After Scott) (1832), rated A

Scottish National Orchestra; Sir Alexander Gibson, conductor; Chandos CD-8316 [DDD] (TT=52.35).

{192}   *A*   Overture: <u>Le Carnaval romain</u> ("The Roman Carnival"), Op.9 -- see entries Nos.{188}a and {191}.

{193}   *A*   Overture: <u>Le Corsaire</u> ("The Pirate"), Op.21 -- see entry No.{191}.

{194}   *A*   Overture: <u>King Lear</u> (After Shakespeare), Op.4 -- see entry No.{191}.

{195}   *A*   Overture: <u>Rob Roy</u> (After Scott) (1832) -- see entry No.{191}.

Symphonic

{196}   *A*   <u>Symphonie fantastique</u> ("Fantastic Symphony"), Op.14
a   Berlin Philharmonic Orchestra; Herbert von Karajan, conductor; DG 415 325-2 [ADD] (TT=52.36).
b   Cleveland Orchestra; Lorin Maazel, conductor; CBS MK-35867 [DDD] (TT=49.08).
c   Cleveland Orchestra; Lorin Maazel, conductor; Telarc CDC-80076 [DDD] (TT=48.38).
d   Amsterdam Concertgebouw Orchestra; Sir Colin Davis, conductor; Philips 411 425-2 [ADD] (TT=56.38).

For sheer brilliance of sound, the later Maazel recording (which is marginally faster than the one he did for CBS) is astounding. For stylishness and greater depth, the Berlin is recommended. Any of the listed four, however, is quite a safe purchase.

Vocal

{197}   *C*   <u>Nuits d'été</u> ("Summer Nights"): Song Cycle, Op.7
a   Frederica von Stade, mezzo-soprano; Boston Symphony Orchestra; Seiji Ozawa, conductor; CBS MK-39098 [DDD]

(TT=51.49). Includes Debussy's <u>La Damoiselle élue</u> ("The Blessed Damozel," after D.G. Rosetti): Cantata for Female Voices (1887-1888) (with the Tanglewood Festival Chorus), rated C.

b   Dame Kiri Te Kanawa, soprano; Orchestre de Paris; Daniel Barenboim, conductor; DG 410 966-2 [DDD] (TT=52.13). Includes Berlioz' <u>La Mort de Cléopâtre</u>: <u>Scène lyrique</u> ("The Death of Cleopatra: Lyric Scene"): Cantata (1829) (with Jessye Norman, soprano), rated C.

{198}   C   <u>La Mort de Cléopâtre</u>: <u>Scène lyrique</u> ("The Death of Cleopatra: Lyric Scene"): Cantata (1829) -- see entry No.{197}b.

BERNSTEIN, LEONARD
1918-

Choral
{199}   C   <u>Chichester Psalms</u> for Chorus and Orchestra (1965)

Vienna Boys' Choir; Israel Philharmonic Orchestra; Leonard Bernstein, conductor; DG 415 965-2 [ADD] (TT=60.58). Includes Bernstein's <u>Songfest</u> (1977) (performed with the National Symphony Orchestra <Washington, D.C.>, conducted by the composer).

Orchestral
{200}   B   Overture: <u>Candide</u> (1956)

New York Philharmonic; Leonard Bernstein, conductor; CBS MK-42263 [ADD] (TT=54.43). Includes Bernstein's <u>On the Town</u>: Three Dance Episodes (1944); <u>On the Waterfront</u>: Symphonic Suite (1954) and <u>West Side Story</u>: Three Dance Episodes (1956).

Also -- see entry No.{102}a.

BIZET, GEORGES
1838-1875

Operatic

{201}   *A*   Carmen (Based on a Novella by Prosper Mérimée) (1873-1874)

a   Teresa Berganza, soprano; Ileana Cotrubas, soprano; Yvonne Kenny, soprano; Alicia Nafé, mezzo-soprano; Plácido Domingo, tenor; Sherrill Milnes, baritone; Ambrosian Singers; London Symphony Orchestra; Claudio Abbado, conductor; DG 419 636-2 (3 discs) [ADD] (TT = 156.43).

b   Faith Esham, soprano; Lilian Watson, soprano; Julia Migenes-Johnson, mezzo-soprano; Susan Daniel, mezzo-soprano; Plácido Domingo, tenor; Ruggero Raimondi, bass; French Radio Chorus and Children's Chorus; Orchestre National de France; Lorin Maazel, conductor; MHS 110567 (3 discs) [DDD] (TT = 150.48).

The DG issue of Carmen is the more traditional (and, to me, moving) of the two listed. Migenes-Johnson on MHS, however, is the marginally more sexy "Carmen" and is well remembered (as is the rest of the cast on MHS) for the movie version.

Orchestral

{202}   *A*   L'Arlésienne Suites Nos.1-2 (1872) (Incidental Music for a Play by Alphonse Daudet)

a   Montreal Symphony Orchestra; Charles Dutoit, conductor; London 417 839-2 [DDD] (TT = 73.18). Includes Bizet's Carmen Suites, Nos.1-2 (1873-1874), rated A.

b   Royal Philharmonic Orchestra; Sir Thomas Beecham, conductor; Angel CDC 47460 [ADD] (TT = 65.03). Includes Bizet's Symphony No.1, Op.25, in c, rated A.

Both of the listed L'Arlésiennes are terrific: Beecham's is a classic performance, Dutoit's somewhat more exciting--and both have excellent (and needed) works as couplings.

{203}   *A*   Carmen Suites, Nos.1-2 (1873-1874) -- see entry No.{202}a.

Symphonic
{204}   *A*   Symphony No.1, Op.25, in c -- see entry No.{202}b.

BLOCH, MAX
1880-1959

Concerted
{205}   *B*   Schelomo ("Solomon"): Hebraic Rhapsody for 'Cello and Orchestra (1915)
      Lynn Harrel, 'cello; Amsterdam Concertgebouw Orchestra; Bernard Haitink, conductor; London 414 162-2 [DDD] (TT=50.36). Includes Shostakovich Concerto for 'Cello No.1, Op.107, in E flat, rated B.

BOCCHERINI, LUIGI
1743-1805

Chamber
{206}   *B*   Minuet, from Quintet for Strings, Op.11 No.5, in E -- see entry No.{90}.

Concerted
{207}   *C*   Concerto for 'Cello No.9, in B flat
      Jacqueline du Pré, 'cello; English Chamber Orchestra; Daniel Barenboim, conductor; Angel CDC 47840-2 [ADD] (TT=52.53). Includes Haydn's Concerto for 'Cello, Op.101, in D, rated B.

BOÏTO, ARRIGO
1842-1918

Operatic

{208}   *C*   Mefistofele ("Mephistopheles") (After Goethe's Faust) (1868-1875)

Montserrat Caballé, soprano; Mirella Freni, soprano; Della Jones, mezzo-soprano; Piero de Palma, tenor; Luciano Pavarotti, tenor; Nicolai Ghiaurov, bass; Trinity Boys' Choir; London Opera Chorus; National Philharmonic Orchestra of London; Oliviero de Fabritiis, conductor; London 410 175-2 (3 discs) [DDD] (TT = 146.40).

Also -- see entry No.{186}.

BORODIN, ALEXANDER
1833-1887

Chamber

{209}   *B*   String Quartet No.2, in D (1881-1885)

Talich Quartet; Calliope CAL-9202 [DDD] (TT - 57.14). Includes Tchaikovsky's String Quartet No.1, Op.11, in D, rated B.

Two melodies from the Borodin Second Quartet were used in the musical, Kismet, for the songs titled Baubles, Bangles and Beads and This Is My Beloved. The Tchaikovsky gave us the popular 1930s song, The Isle of May.

Orchestral

{210}   *C*   In the Steppes of Central Asia: Musical Picture (1880)

a   Bavarian Radio Symphony Chorus and Orchestra; Esa-Pekka Salonen, conductor; Philips 412 552-2 [DDD] (TT = 45.34). Includes Balakirev's Islamey: Oriental Fantasy (1869); Borodin's Prince Igor: "Polovtsian Dances" (1890),

145

rated A; Glinka's Overture: <u>Russlan and Ludmilla</u> (1838-1841), rated A and Tchaikovsky's Overture: <u>1812</u>, Op.49, rated A.

b   St. Louis Symphony Orchestra; Leonard Slatkin, conductor; Telarc CD-80072 [DDD] (TT=40.38). Includes Glière's "Russian Sailors' Dance" from <u>The Red Poppy</u> (1927), rated B; Glinka's Overture: <u>Russlan and Ludmilla</u> (1838-1841), rated A; Rimsky-Korsakov's Overture: <u>Russian Easter</u>, Op.36, rated B and Tchaikovsky's <u>Marche slave</u>, Op.31, rated A.

{211}   *A*   <u>Prince Igor</u>: "Polovtsian Dances" (1890)
a   Chicago Symphony Orchestra; Daniel Barenboim, conductor; DG Imago 419 407-2 [ADD] (TT=72.15). Includes Mussorgsky's <u>Night on Bald Mountain</u> (Orchestrated by Rimsky-Korsakov) (1860-1866), rated A; Rimsky-Korsakov's Overture: <u>Russian Easter</u>, Op.36, rated B; Tchaikovsky's Overture: <u>1812</u>, Op.49, rated A and <u>Romeo and Juliet</u> (1870), rated A.

b   L'Orchestre de la Suisse Romande; Ernest Ansermet, conductor; London 414 124-2 [AAD] (TT=57.19). Includes Rimsky-Korsakov's <u>Scheherazade</u>, Op.35, rated A.

One of the Polovtsian Dances was used in the musical, <u>Kismet</u>, as the song titled <u>Stranger in Paradise</u>.

Also -- see entry No.{210}a.

BRAHMS, JOHANNES
1833-1897

Chamber
{212}   *A*   Quartets for Piano and Strings (3) Nos.1-3: Op.25, in g; Op.26, in A and Op.60, in c
Cantilena Piano Quartet; Arabesque Z6553-2 (2 discs) [DDD] (TT=125.09).

{213}   *A*   Quartet for Piano and Strings No.2, Op.26, in A -- see entry No.{212}.

{214}   *A*   Quartet for Piano and Strings No.3, Op.60, in c --
see entry No.{212}.

{215}   *B*   Quintet for Piano and Strings, Op.34, in f
André Previn, piano; Musikverein Quartet; Philips 412
608-2 [DDD] (TT=41.17).

{216}   *B*   Sextet for String Quartet, Viola and 'Cello No.1,
Op.18, in B flat
Kocian Quartet; Milan Škampa, viola; Antonin Kohout,
'cello; Supraphon CO-2141 [DDD] (TT=74.13). Includes
Brahms' Sextet for String Quartet, Viola and 'Cello No.2,
Op.36, in G, rated B.

{217}   *B*   Sextet for String Quartet, Viola and 'Cello No.2,
Op.36, in G -- see entry No.{216}.

{218}   *A*   Sonatas for 'Cello and Piano (2) Nos.1-2: Op.38,
in e and Op.99, in F
a   Yo-Yo Ma, 'cello; Emanuel Ax, piano; RCA RCD1-
7022 [DDD] (TT=56.17).
b   Mstislav Rostropovich, 'cello; Rudolf Serkin, piano; DG
410 510-2 [DDD] (TT=57.18).
Both of these recordings are extremely fine, but the Ma
and Ax disc gets my nod.

{219}   *A*   Sonatas for Violin and Piano (3) Nos.1-3: Op.78,
in G; Op.100, in A and Op.108, in d
a   Itzhak Perlman, violin; Vladimir Ashkenazy, piano;
Angel CDC 47403-2 [DDD] (TT=69.02).
b   Josef Suk, violin; Julius Katchen, piano; London 421
092-2 [ADD] (TT=68.23).
c   Pinchas Zukerman, violin; Daniel Barenboim, piano;
DG 415 989-2 [ADD] (TT=72.11).
Of these excellent recordings, Perlman and Ashkenazy
are a shade warmer in sound, while Zukerman and Barenboim

147

are more introspective (either is a good choice). Still, it is the earliest recording of Suk and Katchen (1968) that is a walkaway set of performances.

{220}   *B*   String Quartet No.1, Op.51 No.1, in c
Gabrielli Quartet; Chandos ABRD-1264 [DDD] (TT=61.21). Includes Brahms String Quartet No.2, Op.51 No.2, in a, rated B.

{221}   *B*   String Quartet No.2, Op.51 No.2, in a -- see entry No.{220}.

{222}   *B*   Trio for Clarinet (or Viola), 'Cello and Piano, Op.114, in a flat
Peter Schmidl, clarinet; Friedrich Dolezal, 'cello; Andras Schiff, piano; London 410 114-2 (must be specially ordered) [DDD] (TT=55.20). Includes Brahms' Trio for Horn, Violin and Piano, Op.40, in E flat, rated A.

{223}   *A*   Trio for Horn, Violin and Piano, Op.40, in E flat
Barry Tuckwell, horn; Itzhak Perlman, violin; Vladimir Ashkenazy, piano; London 414 128-2 [AAD] (54.58). Includes Franck's Sonata for Violin and Piano, in A (1886), rated A.
Also -- see entry No.{222}.

{224}   *A*   Trio for Piano, Violin and 'Cello No.1, Op.8, in B
a   Artur Rubinstein, piano; Henryk Szeryng, violin; Pierre Fournier, 'cello; RCA 6260-3-RC [ADD] (TT=63.11). Includes Brahms' Trio for Piano, Violin and 'Cello No.2, Op.101, in c, rated A.
b   Joseph Kalichstein, piano; Jaime Laredo, violin; Sharon Robinson, 'cello; MMG MCD-10042 [DDD] (TT=54.09). Includes Brahms' Trio for Piano, Violin and 'Cello No.2, Op.101, in c, rated A.

{225}   *A*   Trio for Piano, Violin and 'Cello No.2, Op.101, in
c -- see entries Nos.{224}a-b.

Choral
{226}   *A*   <u>Ein Deutsches Requiem</u> ("A German Requiem"),
Op.45

a   Gundula Janowitz, soprano; Tom Krause, baritone;
Vienna State Opera Concert Chorus; Vienna Philharmonic
Orchestra; Philips 411 436-2 (2 discs) [DDD] (TT=92.50).
Includes Brahms' <u>Schicksalslied</u> ("Song of Destiny"), Op.54,
rated C.

b   Elisabeth Schwarzkopf, soprano; Dietrich Fischer-
Dieskau, baritone; Philharmonia Chorus and Orchestra; Otto
Klemperer, conductor; Angel CDC 47238-2 [ADD]
(TT=69.16).

          Klemperer's recording, from 1962, remains the first
choice, but Haitink's is almost as possessed of *Innigkeit* and
authority. Of course, Haitink does have the <u>Schicksalslied</u> as a
lagniappe, and has an effective acoustic (not to waffle, but the
sound of Klemperer's recording belies its age). Larger
libraries should probably own both (I seldom make such a
recommendation).

{227}   *C*   <u>Schicksalslied</u> ("Song of Destiny"), Op.54   see
entry No.{226}a.

Concerted
{228}   *A*   Concerto for Piano No.1, Op.15, in d
          Vladimir Ashkenazy, piano; Amsterdam
Concertgebouw Orchestra; Bernard Haitink, conductor;
London 410 009-2 [DDD] (TT=48.38).

{229}   *A*   Concerto for Piano No.2, Op.83, in B flat
a   Vladimir Ashkenazy, piano; Amsterdam
Concertgebouw Orchestra; Bernard Haitink, conductor;
London 410 199-2 [DDD] (TT=50.58).

b   Wilhelm Backhaus, piano; Vienna Philharmonic
           Orchestra; Karl Böhm, conductor; London 414 142-2 [ADD]
           (TT=48.01).

{230}   *A* Concerto for Violin, Op.77, in D -- see entry
           No.{140}b.

{231}   *A* Concerto for Violin and 'Cello ("Double
           Concerto"), Op.102, in a
           Zino Francescatti, violin; Pierre Fournier, 'cello;
           Columbia Symphony Orchestra; Bruno Walter, conductor;
           CBS MK-42024 [AAD?] (TT=60.00). Includes Schumann's
           Concerto for Piano, Op.54, in a, rated A.
           Also -- see entry No.{55}.

Instrumental

{232}   *B* Ballades for Piano (4) Op.10 Nos.1-4: in d, D, b
           and Stephen Bishop-Kovacevich, piano; Philips 411 103-2.
           Includes Brahms' Eight Pieces for Piano, Op.76 Nos.1-8: in f
           sharp, b, A flat, B flat, c sharp, A, a and C and Scherzo, Op.4,
           in e flat.

{233}   *B* Fantaisies for Piano (7) Op.116 Nos.1-7: in d, a, g,
           E, e, E and d
           Stephen Bishop-Kovacevich, piano; Philips 411 137-2
           [DDD] (TT=51.19). Includes Brahms' Three Intermezzi for
           Piano, Op.117 Nos.1-3: in E flat, b flat and c sharp and
           Klavierstücke ("Piano Pieces") (4): Op.119 Nos.1-4: in b, e, C
           and E flat.

Orchestral

{234}   *A* Hungarian Dances for Orchestra (21) Nos.1-21
           (1868, 1880)
a   Budapest Festival Orchestra; Iván Fischer, conductor;
           Hungaroton HCD 12571-2 [DDD] (TT=54.55).

b   Leipzig Gewandhaus Orchestra; Kurt Masur,
conductor; Philips 411 426-2 [DDD] (TT=53.02).
c   Vienna Philharmonic Orchestra; Claudio Abbado,
conductor; DG 410 615-2 [DDD] (TT=48.16).
          Of the three sets of dances, Fischer's is odd in that a
"gypsy" set of orchestrations (including solo violin and
cimbalom) is favored instead of the "normal" ones. This
recording, vibrant and warm and exciting as it is, smacks a bit
of Russian tearoom ambience. Abbado offers a poker-faced
set of readings which is nice in its reticence. Masur chooses a
middle path, but lacks the rhythmic bounce which these pieces
cry out for.

{235}   *A*   Overture: <u>Academic Festival</u>, Op.80
a   Columbia Symphony Orchestra; Bruno Walter,
conductor; CBS MK-42021 [AAD?] (TT=51.09). Includes
Brahms' Symphony No.2, Op.73, in D, rated A.
b   Hallé Orchestra; Stanislaw Skrowaczewski, conductor;
MCA MCAD-25188 [DDD] (TT=57.56). Includes Brahms'
Symphony No.2, Op.73, in D, rated A.

{236}   *A*   Overture: <u>Tragic</u>, Op.81
          Columbia Symphony Orchestra; Bruno Walter,
conductor; CBS MK 42023 [AAD?] (TT-55.58). Includes
Brahms' Symphony No.4, Op.98, in e, rated A.

{237}   *B*   Serenade No.1, Op.11, in D
          Berlin Philharmonic Orchestra; Claudio Abbado,
conductor; DG 410 654-2 [DDD] (TT=49.13).

{238}   *A*   Variations on a Theme by Haydn, Op.56a.
          Columbia Symphony Orchestra; Bruno Walter,
conductor; CBS MK-42022 [AAD] (TT=52.01). Includes
Brahms' Symphony No.3, Op.90, in F, rated A.

Symphonic
{239}   *A*   Symphony No.1, Op.68, in c
Columbia Symphony Orchestra; Bruno Walter,
conductor; CBS MK-42020 [AAD?] (TT=44.19).

{240}   *A*   Symphony No.2, Op.73, in D -- see entries
Nos.{235}a-b.

{241}   *A*   Symphony No.3, Op.90, in F -- see entry No.{238}.

{242}   *A*   Symphony No.4, Op.98, in e
Vienna Philharmonic Orchestra; Carlos Kleiber,
conductor; DG 400 037-2 [DDD] (TT=39.20).
Also -- see entry No.{236}.

Vocal
{243}   *C*   Liebeslieder Walzer("Love Songs: Waltzes"),
Op.52 and Neue Liebeslieder Walzer ("New Love Songs:
Waltzes"), Op.65: Waltzes for Vocal Quartet and Piano, Four
Hands
Armen Guzelimian and Raul Herrera, piano; Los
Angeles Vocal Arts Ensemble; Nonesuch 79008-2 [DDD]
(TT=46.15).

{244}   *B*   Rhapsody for Alto, Chorus and Orchestra (After
Goethe), Op.53
Alfreda Hodgson, mezzo-soprano; Bavarian Radio
Chorus and Symphony Orchestra; Bernard Haitink, conductor;
Orfeo C-025821 [DDD] (TT=48.13). Includes Brahms'
Begräbnisgesang ("Burial Song"), Op.13; Gesang der Parzen
("Song of the Fates"), Op.89 and Nänie, Op.82.

{245}   *B*   Vier ernste Gesänge ("Four Serious Songs"),
Op.121 -- see entry No.{178}.

BRITTEN, BENJAMIN
1913-1976

Choral

{246}   *B*   Ceremony of Carols, Op.28

Gregg Smith Singers; Dorothy Shaw Hand Bell Choir; Fort Worth Chamber Ensemble; Texas Boys' Choir; Gregg Bragg, conductor; Vox Prima MWCD 7104 [AAD?] (TT=54.58). Includes Ives' A Christmas Carol and twelve traditional carols.

{247}   *B*   War Requiem, Op.66

Galina Vishnevskaya, soprano; Sir Peter Pears, tenor; Dietrich Fischer-Dieskau, baritone; Bach Choir; Highgate School Choir; Simon Preston, organ; Melos Ensemble; London Symphony Chorus and Orchestra; Benjamin Britten, conductor; London 414 383-2 (2 discs) [AAD] (TT=81.21).

Operatic

{248}   *B*   Peter Grimes (After George Crabbe) (1945)

Iris Kells, soprano; Marion Studholme, soprano; Claire Watson, soprano; Lauris Elms, mezzo-soprano; Jean Watson, contralto; John Lanigan, tenor; Raymond Nilsson, tenor; Sir Peter Pears, tenor; Sir Geraint Evans, baritone; James Pease, bass-baritone; Owen Brannigan, bass; Chorus and Orchestra of the Royal Opera House, Covent Garden; Benjamin Britten, conductor; London (3 discs) [ADD] (TT=141.59).

Orchestral

{249}   *B*   Matinées musicales (After Rossini), Op.24

National Philharmonic Orchestra; Sir Richard Bonynge, conductor; London 410 139-2 [DDD] (TT=64.13). Includes Britten's Soirées musicales (After Rossini), Op.9, rated B and Respighi's La Boutique fantasque ("The Fantastic Toyshop") (After Rossini) (1919), rated A.

{250}   *C*   <u>Simple</u> Symphony for String Orchestra, Op.4
a   London Symphony Orchestra; Benjamin Britten, conductor; London 417 509-2 [ADD] (TT=60.54). Includes Britten's <u>Young Person's Guide to the Orchestra</u>, Op.34 and Variations on a Theme of Frank Bridge for String Orchestra, Op.10, rated C (the Symphony and Variations are performed by the English Chamber Orchestra and Britten also conducts these).
b   Northern Sinfonia; Richard Hickox, conductor; ASV CDDCD-591 [DDD] (TT=50.28). Includes Britten's Prelude and Fugue for 18 Strings, Op.29 and Variations on a Theme of Frank Bridge for String Orchestra, Op.10, rated C.

{251}   *B*   <u>Soirées musicales</u> (After Rossini), Op.9 -- see entry No.{249}.

{252}   *A*   <u>Young Person's Guide to the Orchestra</u>, Op.34 -- see entry No.{250}a.

{253}   *C*   Variations on a Theme of Frank Bridge for String Orchestra, Op.10 -- see entries Nos.{250}a-b.

Vocal

{254}   *C*   <u>Les Illuminations</u> for Solo Voice and Orchestra (After Rimbaud), Op.18
              Sir Peter Pears, tenor; English Chamber Orchestra; Benjamin Britten, conductor; London 417 153-2 [ADD] (TT=72.49). Includes Britten's Nocturne for Tenor, Seven Obligato Instruments and Strings, Op.60 and Serenade for Tenor, Horn and Strings, Op.31, rated B (the accompanying orchestra for these latter is the London Symphony Orchestra, the hornist in the Serenade is Barry Tuckwell).

{255}   *B*   Serenade for Tenor, Horn and Strings, Op.31 -- see entry No.{254}.

BRUCH, MAX
1838-1920

Concerted

{256} B Concerto for Violin No.1, Op.26, in g
a   Jascha Heifetz, violin; New Symphony Orchestra of London; Sir Malcolm Sargent, conductor; RCA 6214-2-RC [ADD] (TT=65.11). Includes Bruch's Scottish Fantasy for Violin and Orchestra, Op.46, rated B and Vieuxtemps' Concerto for Violin No.5, Op.37, in a, rated C.

b   Itzhak Perlman, violin; Amsterdam Concertgebouw Orchestra; Bernard Haitink, conductor; Angel CDC 47074-2 [DDD] (TT=51.48). Includes Mendelssohn's Concerto for Violin, Op.64, in e, rated A.

{257} C Kol Nidrei for 'Cello and Orchestra, Op.47
         Lynn Harrell, 'cello; Philharmonia Orchestra; Vladimir Ashkenazy, conductor; London 410 144-2 [DDD] (TT=52.07). Includes Dvořák's Concerto for 'Cello, Op.104, in b rated A.

{258} B Scottish Fantasy for Violin and Orchestra, Op.46
-- see entry No.{256}a.

BRUCKNER, ANTON
1824-1896

Symphonic

{259} C Symphony No.3, in d (1889)
         Berlin Radio Symphony Orchestra; Riccardo Chailly, conductor; London 417 093-2 [DDD] (TT=56.02).

{260} A Symphony No.4 ("Romantic"), in E flat (1880)
         Columbia Symphony Orchestra; Bruno Walter, conductor; CBS MK-42035 [AAD?] (TT=66.31).

{261}   *B*   Symphony No.6, in A (1881)
Bavarian State Orchestra; Wolfgang Sawallisch, conductor; Orfeo C-024821 [DDD] (TT=55.06).

{262}   *A*   Symphony No.7, in E (1883)
Berlin Philharmonic Orchestra; Herbert von Karajan, conductor; DG 419 195-2 [ADD] (TT=64.17).

{263}   *A*   Symphony No.8, in c (1890)
Vienna Philharmonic Orchestra; Carlo Maria Giulini, conductor; DG 415 124-2 (2 discs) [DDD] (TT=87.20).

{264}   *A*   Symphony No.9, in d (1896)
Amsterdam Concertgebouw Orchestra; Bernard Haitink, conductor; Philips 410 039-2 [DDD] (TT=62.30).

CANTELOUBE, JOSEPH
1879-1957

Vocal
{265}   *C*   <u>Chants d'Auvergne</u> ("Songs of the Auvergne") Complete (Four Sets, Comprising Nos.1-27) (1923-1930)
Frederica von Stade, mezzo-soprano; Royal Philharmonic Orchestra; Antonio de Almeida, conductor; CBS MK-37299 [DDD] (TT=51.12) and CBS MK-37837 [DDD] (TT=60.42). The second disc includes Canteloube's <u>Triptyque</u> ("Triptych") (1914).

CHABRIER, EMMANUEL
1841-1894

Orchestral
{266}   *A*   <u>España</u> Rhapsody (1883)

156

a   Cincinnati Pops Orchestra; Erich Kunzel, conductor;
Vox Cum Laude MCD 10017 [DDD] (TT=46.06). Includes
Gould's American Salute (1944), rated C; Liszt's Hungarian
Rhapsody No.2, in c sharp (1847), rated A; Sibelius' Finlandia,
Op.26, rated A; Johann Strauss, Jr.'s Wiener Blut ("Viennese
Blood") Waltz, Op.354, rated A and Tchaikovsky's Marche
slave, Op.31, rated A.

b   L'Orchestre de la Suisse Romande; Ernest Ansermet,
conductor; London 417 691-2 [AAD] (TT=60.10). Includes
Falla's El Amor brujo ("Love, the Warlock") (1915) (with
mezzo-soprano Marina de Gabarain), rated A; Ravel's Boléro
(1927), rated A and Rapsodie espagnole ("Spanish Rhapsody")
(1907) (6) Nos.1-4: Prélude à la nuit ("Prelude in the Fashion
of the Night"); Malagueña; Habañéra and Féria ("Fiesta"),
rated A.

CHAUSSON, ERNEST
1855-1899

Concerted
{267}   *B*   Poème for Violin and Orchestra, Op.25
          Jascha Heifetz, violin; RCA Victor Symphony
Orchestra; Izler Solomon, conductor; RCA 7709-2-RG [DDD]
(TT=63.50). Includes Lalo's Symphonie espagnole ("Spanish
Symphony"), Op.21, rated B; Saint-Saëns' Havanaise for Violin
and Orchestra, Op.83, rated A and Introduction and Rondo
Capriccioso for Violin and Orchestra, Op.28, rated A, and
Sarasate's Zigeunerweisen ("Gypsy Airs") for Violin and
Orchestra, Op.20, rated B. In all but the Chausson work, the
RCA Victor Symphony Orchestra is conducted by William
Steinberg.
          Once again, Heifetz's recordings make any others of the
same works *hors de combat*.

157

CHERUBINI, LUIGI
1760-1842

Operatic
{268}   B   Méedée ("Medea") (1797)
Sylvia Sass, soprano; Magda Kalmár, soprano; Klára Tákacs, mezzo-soprano; Veriano Luchetti, tenor; Kolos Kováts, bass; Hungarian Radio Chorus; Budapest Symphony Orchestra; Lamberto Gardelli, conductor; Hungaroton HCD-11904-11905 (2 discs) [ADD] (137.39).

CHOPIN, FRÉDÉRIC
1810-1849

Concerted
{269}   A   Concerto for Piano No.1, Op.11, in e
Krystian Zimerman, piano; Los Angeles Philharmonic Orchestra; Carlo Maria Giulini, conductor; DG 415 970-2 [ADD] (TT=71.51). Includes Chopin's Concerto for Piano No.2, Op.21, in f, rated A.

{270}   A   Concerto for Piano No.2, Op.21, in f
Cecile Licad, piano; London Philharmonic Orchestra; André Previn, conductor; CBS MK-39153 [DDD] (TT=55.12). Includes Saint-Saëns's Concerto for Piano No.2, Op.22, in g, rated B.
Also -- see entry No.{269}.

Instrumental
{271}   A   Andante spianato and grande polonaise, Op.22
a   Malcolm Frager, piano; Telarc CD-80040 [DDD] (TT=37.09). Includes Chopin's Contredanse, in G flat (1827?); Mazurkas, Op.6 Nos.1-4, in f sharp, c sharp, E and e flat, rated A; Polonaise ("Heroic"), Op.53, in A flat, rated A;

Tarantelle, Op.43, in A flat and <u>Variations brillantes</u> on a the
Rondo from <u>Ludovic</u> by Halévy, Op.12.

b   Artur Rubinstein, piano; RCA 5617-2-RC [ADD]
(TT=67.17). Includes Chopin's Barcarolle, Op.60, in F sharp,
rated B; Berceuse, Op.57, in D flat, rated C; Bolero, Op.19, in
C; <u>Fantaisie impromptu</u>, Op.66, in c sharp, rated A;
Impromptus (3) Nos.1-3: Op.29, in A flat; Op.36, in F sharp
and Op.51, in G flat, all rated A; <u>Trois nouvelles études</u>
("Three New Studies") (1839): in f, A flat and D flat and
Tarentelle, Op.43, in A flat.

{272}   *A*   Ballades (4) Nos.1-4: Op.23., in g; Op.38, in F;
Op.47, in A flat and Op.52, in f
    Artur Rubinstein, piano; RCA RCD1-7156 [ADD?]
(TT=71.21). Includes Chopin's Scherzi (4) Nos.1-4: Op.20, in
b; Op.31, in b flat; Op.39, in c sharp and Op.43, in E, all rated
B.

{273}   *B*   Barcarolle, Op.60, in F sharp -- see entry
No.{271}b.

{274}   *C*   Berceuse, Op.57, in D flat -- see entry No.{271}b.

{275}   *A*   Études (24), Op 10 Nos 1-12 (No.5 is known as the
"Black Key" Étude, and No.12 as the "Revolutionary" Étude)
and Op.25, Nos.1-12
    Maurizio Pollini, piano; DG 413 794-2 [AAD]
(TT=56.06).

{276}   *A*   Études, Op.10 Nos.3, 5 ("Black Key" Étude) and
12 ("Revolutionary" Étude)
    Vladimir Horowitz, piano; CBS MK-42305 [AAD]
(TT=73.17). Includes Bizet-Horowitz <u>Carmen</u> Variations;
Chopin's Polonaise, Op.53 ("Heroic"), in A flat, rated A;
Debussy's "Serenade for the Doll" from <u>Children's Corner</u>
Suite (1906-1908), rated A and <u>L'Isle joyeuse</u> ("The Happy

Island") (1904), rated A; Mozart's "Rondo alla Turca" from Sonata for Piano, K.331, in A, rated A; Moszkowski's Étude, Op.72 No.11, in A flat; Rachmaninoff's Étude-Tableau, Op.33 No.2, in C, rated C and Prelude, Op.32 No.12, in g sharp, rated B; Scarlatti's Sonatas, L.430, in E and L.483, in A, both rated A; Schubert's Impromptu, Op.90 No.3, in G flat, rated B; Schumann's Toccata, Op.7, in C and "Träumerei" ("Dreams") from Kinderszenen ("Childhood Scenes"), Op.15 and Scriabin's Études, Op.2 No.1, in c sharp and Op.8 No.12, in d sharp.

{277}   *A*   Fantaisie, Op.49, in f
Artur Rubinstein, piano; RCA 5616-2-RC [ADD?] (TT = 60.45). Includes Chopin's Sonatas for Piano, No.2 ("Funeral March"), Op.35, in b flat, rated A and No.3, Op.58, in b, rated B.

{278}   *A*   Fantaisie impromptu, Op.66, in c sharp -- see entry No.{271}b.

{279}   *A*   Impromptus (3) Nos.1-3: Op.29, in A flat; Op.36, in F sharp and Op.51, in G flat -- see entry No.{271}b.

{280}   *A*   Mazurkas: Op.7 No.1, in B flat; Op.30 No.4, in c sharp; Op.33 No.4, in b; Op.63 No.2, in f; Op.68 No.2, in a
Ivan Moravec, piano; Vox Cum Laude MCD 10016 [DDD] (TT=50.30). Includes Chopin's Polonaise, Op.26 No.1, in c sharp, rated A; Polonaise fantaisie, Op.61, in A flat, rated B and Waltzes: Op.34 No.2, in a; Op.64 No.2, in c sharp and Op.Posth., in e, all rated A.
Also -- see entry No.{271}a.

{281}   *B*   Nocturnes (19) Nos.1-19
Artur Rubinstein, piano; RCA 5613-2-RC (2 discs) [ADD] (TT = 107.34).

{282}   *B*   Polonaise fantaisie, Op.61, in A flat -- see entries
Nos.{280} and {283}a-b.

{283}   *A*   Polonaises (6) No.1-6: Op.26 Nos.1-2, in c sharp
and e flat; Op.40 Nos.1 ("Military") and 2, in A and c; Op.44, in
f sharp; Op.53 ("Heroic"), in A flat
a   Artur Rubinstein, piano; RCA 5615-2-RC [ADD]
(TT=59.20). Includes Chopin's Polonaise fantaisie, Op.61, in
A flat, rated B.
b   Maurizio Pollini, piano; DG 413 795-2 DG [DDD]
(TT=61.03). Includes Chopin's Polonaise fantaisie, Op.61, in
A flat, rated B.
               Also -- see entries Nos. {271}a and {276}.

{284}   *A*   Préludes, Op.28 (24) Nos.1-24
               Maurizio Pollini, piano; DG 413 796-2 [ADD]
(TT=36.20).

{285}   *B*   Scherzi (4) Nos.1-4: Op.20, in b; Op.31, in b flat;
Op.39, in c sharp and Op.43, in E -- see entry No.{272}.

{286}   *A*   Sonata for Piano No.2 ("Funeral March"), Op.35,
in b flat
               Maurizio Pollini, piano; DG 415 346-2 [DDD]
(TT=51.53). Includes Chopin's Sonata for Piano No.3, Op.58,
in b, rated B.
               Also -- see entry No.{277}.

{287}   *B*   Sonata for Piano No.3, Op.58, in b -- see entries
Nos.{277} and {286}.

{288}   *A*   Waltzes (14) Nos.1-14
               Artur Rubinstein, piano; RCA RCD1-5492 [ADD?]
(TT=49.53).
               Also -- see entry No.{280}.

CIMAROSA, DOMENICO
1749-1801

Concerted
{289}   *A*   Concerto for Oboe and Strings (Arranged from Melodies of Cimarosa by Arthur Benjamin, 1942) -- see entry No.{5}.

CLARKE, JEREMIAH
1673-1707

Orchestral
{290}   *A*   Trumpet Voluntary (Prince of Denmark's March) (1700)
Richard Giangiulio, trumpet; Paul Reido, organ; ensemble (Bert Truax, trumpet; Thomas Booth, trumpet and Douglas Howard, timpani); Crystal CRD-232 [DDD] (TT = 41.01). Includes Buxtehude's Fanfare and Chorus; Charpentier's Prelude and Te Deum; Handel's "La Rejouissance" from Royal Fireworks Music (1749), rated A; Mendelssohn's "Wedding March" from A Midsummer Night's Dream, Op.21 and Op.61, rated A; Mouret's Symphonic Suite No.1 (1729), rated A; Purcell's Introduction and Trumpet Tune (1698), in D, rated A; John Stanley's Trumpet Voluntary (1752); Truax's Fanfare for Trumpet, Organ and Timpani and Wagner's "Wedding March" from Parsifal (1882), rated A.

COLERIDGE-TAYLOR, SAMUEL
1875-1912

Choral
{291}   *C*   Hiawatha's Wedding Feast: Cantata (1898)
Richard Lewis, tenor; Royal Choral Society; Philharmonia Orchestra; Sir Malcolm Sargent, conductor;

Angel CDM 69689 [ADD] (TT=45.52). Includes Coleridge-Taylor's Petite suite de concert (1910) (here the Philharmonia is conducted by George Weldon).

COPLAND, AARON
1900-

Ballet
{292}   *A*   Appalachian Spring Suite (1944)
a   Atlanta Symphony Orchestra; Louis Lane, conductor; Telarc CD-80078 [DDD] (TT=44.15). Includes Copland's Fanfare for the Common Man (1944), rated B and Four Dance Episodes from Rodeo (1942), rated B.
b   Moscow Philharmonic Orchestra; Dmitri Kitayenko, conductor; Sheffield Lab CD-27 [DDD] (TT=62.47). Includes Gershwin's Lullaby, for String Quartet (1919); Glazunov's Valse de Concert ("Concert Waltz"), Op.47, in D; Griffes' White Peacock for Flute and Orchestra (1919), rated B, Ives' The Unanswered Question (1906) rated B and Shostakovich's Festive Overture, Op.96, rated B. The Glazunov and Shostakovich works are conducted by Lawrence Leighton Smith.
     Also -- see entry No.{102}a.

{293}   *B*   Fanfare for the Common Man (1944)
     Detroit Symphony Orchestra; Antal Doráti, conductor; London 414 273-2 [DDD] (TT=50.56). Includes Copland's Dance Symphony (1925), rated C; Four Dance Episodes from Rodeo (1942), rated B and El salón México (1936), rated B.
     Also -- see entry No.{292}.

{294}   *B*   Four Dance Episodes from Rodeo (1942)
     Detroit Symphony Orchestra; Antal Doráti, conductor; London 414 273-2 [DDD] (TT=50.56). Includes Copland's

163

Dance Symphony (1925), rated C; Fanfare for the Common Man (1944), rated B and El salón México (1936), rated B.
Also -- see entry No.{292}.

Orchestral

{295}   *B*   Fanfare for the Common Man (1944) -- see entries Nos.{292} and {293}.

{296}   *C*   Lincoln Portrait (1942)
Katharine Hepburn, speaker; Cincinnati Pops Orchestra; Erich Kunzel, conductor; Telarc CD-80117 [DDD] (TT=50.07). Includes Copland's Ceremonial Fanfare (1969); John Henry (1952); Jubilee Variations (1986); An Outdoor Overture (1938), rated B; Old American Songs (1954) (with Sherrill Milnes, baritone) and "The Promise of Living" from The Tender Land (1954).

{297}   *B*   An Outdoor Overture (1938) -- see entry No.{296}.

{298}   *B*   El salón México (1936) -- see entry No.{293}.

Symphonic

{299}   *C*   Dance Symphony (1925) -- see entry No.{293}.

CORELLI, ARCANGELO
1653-1713

Chamber

{300}   *B*   Gigue ("Jig") from Trio Sonata Op.5 No.9 -- see entry No.{6}b.

Orchestral

{301}   *A*   Concerto Grosso, Op.6 No.8 ("Christmas")

La Petite Bande; Sigiswald Kuijken, conductor; Angel CDCB-47919 (2 discs) [DDD] (TT=136.17). Includes Corelli's Concerti Grossi, Op.6 Nos.1-7, Nos.9-12.

DEBUSSY, CLAUDE
1862-1918

Ballet

{302}   C   Jeux: Poème dansé ("Games: A Dance Poem") (1912)

a   Amsterdam Concertgebouw Orchestra; Bernard Haitink, conductor; Philips 400 023-2 [AAD] (TT=42.24). Includes Debussy's Nocturnes (1893) (3) Nos.1-3: Nuages ("Clouds"); Fêtes ("Festivals") and Sirènes ("Sirens") (includes the Women's Voices of the Collegium Musicum Amstelodamense), rated B.

b   New Philharmonia Orchestra; Pierre Boulez, conductor; CBS MYK-37261 [AAD?] (TT=50.39). Includes Debussy's Prélude à l'après-midi d'un faune ("Prelude to the Afternoon of a Faun") (1892-1894), rated A and La Mer ("The Sea") (1903-1905), rated A.

Chamber

{303}   B   Danse sacrée et profane ("Sacred and Profane Dances") for Harp and Strings (1904)

a   Ossian Ellis, harp; Academy of St. Martin-in-the-Fields; Sir Neville Marriner, conductor; MHS CD DCA 517 [DDD] (TT=60.11). Includes Fauré's Dolly Suite, Op.56, rated C; Ibert's Divertissement (1930), rated B and Ravel's Le Tombeau de Couperin ("Homage to Couperin") (1914-1917), rated A.

b   Frances Tietov, harp; Saint Louis Symphony Orchestra; Leonard Slatkin, conductor; Telarc CD-80071 [DDD] (TT=45.02). Includes Debussy La Mer ("The Sea") (1903-

1905), rated A and <u>Prélude à l'après-midi d'un faune</u> ("Prelude to the Afternoon of a Faun") (1892-1894), rated A.

{304}   *A*   String Quartet, Op.10, in g
a   Alban Berg Quartet; Angel CDC 47347-2 [DDD] (TT=51.52). Includes Ravel's String Quartet, in F (1903), rated A.
b   Cleveland Quartet; Telarc CD-80111 [DDD] (TT=54.27). Includes Ravel's String Quartet, in F (1903), rated A.
c   Orlando Quartet; Philips 411 050-2 [DDD] (TT=55.56). Includes Ravel's String Quartet, in F (1903), rated A.
d   Quatuor Via Nova; Erato ECD-71572 [AAD] (TT=65.14). Includes Ravel's Introduction and Allegro for Harp, Flute, Clarinet and String Quartet (1906) (with Lily Laskine, harp, Alain Marion, flute and Jacques Lancelot, clarinet), rated A and String Quartet, in F (1903), rated A.
           Of these four fine performances, the Alban Berg is the smoothest in both works, the Cleveland is a bit less unhurried, and the Quatuor Via Nova is the most idiomatic.

{305}   *C*   <u>Petite Piece</u> for Clarinet and Piano (1910)
           Roger Fallows, clarinet; Ian Brown, piano; Chandos CHAN-8385 [AAD] (TT=54.56). Includes Debussy's Première Rapsodie for Clarinet and Piano (1909-1910), rated C; Sonata No.2, for Flute, Viola and Harp (1916), with Richard McNicol, flute, Roger Best, viola and Frances Kelly, harp; Sonata No.1, for 'Cello and Piano, in d (1915), with Stephen Orton, 'cello and Ian Brown, piano, rated B; Sonata No.3, for Violin and Piano, in g (1916-1917), with Hugh Maguire, violin and Ian Brown, piano, rated C and <u>Syrinx</u>, for Solo Flute (1912), with Richard McNicol, flute, rated B.

{306}   *C*   Première Rapsodie for Clarinet and Piano (1909-1910) -- see entry No.{305}.

166

{307}   *B*   Sonata No.1, for 'Cello and Piano, in d (1915) --
see entry No.{305}.

{308}   *C*   Sonata No.3, for Violin and Piano, in g (1916-
1917) -- see entry No.{305}.

Instrumental

{309}   *A*   Beau soir ("Beautiful Evening") (1878?)
(Transcribed from the Debussy song by Heifetz)
     Jascha Heifetz, violin; Brooks Smith, piano; RCA 7707-
2-RG [ADD] (TT=63.36). Includes transcriptions by Heifetz
of Debussy's La Chevelure ("A Woman's Hair") (From
Chansons de Bilitis ("Songs of Bilitis") (After Louÿs) (1897),
rated A; Golliwog's Cakewalk from Children's Corner Suite
(1906-1908), rated A and La Fille aux cheveux de lin ("The
Maid with the Flaxen Hair") from Préludes, Book I No.8
(1910) (Transcribed by Arthur Hartmann), rated A; Fauré's
Sonata for Violin and Piano, Op.13, in A, rated B; Ibert's Le
Petit âne blanc ("The Little White Donkey") (1937)
(Transcribed by Heifetz); Poulenc's Mouvements perpétuels
("Perpetual Movements") (1918) (Transcribed by Heifetz);
Ravel's Valses nobles et sentimentales ("Noble and
Sentimental Waltzes") (1911), Nos.6-7 (Transcribed by
Heifetz), rated A; Saint-Saëns' Sonata No.1 for Violin and
Piano, Op.75, in d, rated A and "The Swan" from Carnival of
the Animals (1886) (Transcribed by Heifetz), rated A.

{310}   *A*   La Cathédrale engloutie ("The Engulfed
Cathedral") from Préludes, Book I No.10 (1910) -- see entries
Nos.{90} and {322}.

{311}   *A*   Children's Corner Suite (1906-1908) (6), Nos.1-6:
Doctor ad Gradus Parnassum; Jimbo's Lullaby; Serenade for
the Doll; Snow Is Dancing; The Little Shepherd and Golliwog's
Cakewalk

a   Arturo Benedetti Michelangeli, piano; DG 415 372-2 [ADD] (TT = 45.06). Includes Debussy's Images (Book I) (1905) (3) Nos.1-3: Reflets dans l'eau ("Reflections on the Water"); Hommage à Rameau ("Homage to Rameau") and Mouvement, rated A and Images (Book II) (1907) (3) Nos.1-3: Cloches à travers les feuilles ("Bells Heard Through the Leaves"); Et la lune descend sur le temple qui fut ("And the Moon Descends to the Temple Which Had Been") and Poisson d'or ("Goldfish"), rated A.

b   Alexis Weissenberg, piano; DG 415 510-2 [DDD] (TT = 58.15). Includes Debussy's Estampes ("Engravings") (1903) (3) Nos.1-3: Pagodes ("Pagodas"); Menuet and Jardins sous la pluie ("Gardens in the Rain"), rated A; Étude No.11 (from Twelve Etudes, Book II) (1915); Prélude No.8 (from Twelve Preludes, Book I) (1910): La Fille aux cheveux de lin ("The Maid with the Flaxen Hair"), the set rated A; L'Isle joyeuse ("The Happy Island") (1904), rated A; La Plus que lente ("The Slower the Better") (1910), rated A and Suite bergamasque (1890-1905) (4) Nos.1-4: Prélude, Menuet, Clair de lune ("Moonlight") and Passepied, rated A.

   Also -- see entry No.{276}.

{312} *A* Clair de lune ("Moonlight"), from Suite bergamasque (1890-1905) -- see entries Nos.{90} and {320}.

{313} *A* Estampes ("Engravings") (1903) (3) Nos.1-3: Pagodes ("Pagodas"); Menuet and Jardins sous la pluie ("Gardens in the Rain") -- see entry No.{311}b.

{314} *A* La Fille aux cheveux de lin ("The Maid with the Flaxen Hair") from Préludes, Book I No.8 (1910) -- see entries Nos.{309} and {311}a-b.

{315} *A* Golliwog's Cakewalk from Children's Corner Suite (1906-1908) -- see entry No.{309}.

{316}   *A*   Images (Book I) (1905) (3) Nos.1-3: Reflets dans
l'eau ("Reflections on the Water"); Hommage à Rameau
("Homage to Rameau") and Mouvement -- see entry
No.{311}a.

{317}   *A*   Images (Book II)   (1907) (3) Nos.1-3: Cloches
à travers les feuilles ("Bells Heard Through the Leaves"); Et la
Lune descend sur le temple qui fut ("And the Moon Descends
to the Temple Which Had Been") and Poisson d'or
("Goldfish") -- see entry No.{311}a.

{318}   *A*   L'Isle joyeuse ("The Happy Island") (1904) -- see
entries Nos.{276} and {311}b.

{319}   *A*   La Plus que lente ("The Slower the Better") (1910)
-- see entry No.{311}b.

{320}   *A*   Suite bergamasque (1890-1905) (4) Nos.1-4:
Prélude, Menuet, Clair de lune ("Moonlight") and Passepied --
see entry No.{311}b.

{321}   *B*   Syrinx, for Solo Flute (1912) -- see entry No.{305}.

{322}   *A*   Twelve Preludes, Book I (1910) Nos.1-12:
Danseuses de Delphes ("Ballerinas of Delphi"); Voiles
("Sails"); Le Vent dans la plaine ("The Wind in the Plain"); Les
Sons et les parfums tournent dans l'air du soir ("The Sounds
and the Perfumes Turn in the Evening Air"); Les Collines
d'Anacapri ("The Hills of Anacapri"); Des pas sur la neige
("From the Tread on the Snow"); Ce qu'a vu le vent d'Ouest
("How Good Is the West Wind!"); La Fille aux cheveux de lin
("The Maid with the Flaxen Hair"); Le Sérénade interrompue
("The Interrupted Serenade"); La Danse de Puck ("Puck's
Dance") and Minstrels.
a   Walter Gieseking, piano; Angel CDH 761 004-2 [ADD]
(TT=69.47). Includes Debussy's Twelve Preludes, Book II

169

(1913) Nos.1-12: <u>Brouillard</u> ("Mists"); <u>Feuilles mortes</u> ("Dead Leaves"); <u>La Puerta del vino</u> ("The Gate of Wine"); <u>Fées sont d'exquises danseuses</u> ("The Fairies are Exquisite Dancers"); <u>Bruyères</u> ("Heather"); <u>Général Lavine--eccentric</u> ("General Lavine: The Eccentric"); <u>La Terrasse des audiences du clair de lune</u> ("The Reception Terrace by Moonlight"); <u>Ondine</u>; <u>Hommage à S. Pickwick, Esq., P.P.M.P.C.</u> ("Homage to S. Pickwick, Esq., P.P.M.P.C."); <u>Canope</u> ("Canopus"); <u>Les Tierces alternées</u> ("Alternating Thirds") and <u>Feux d'artifice</u> ("Fireworks").

b   Arturo Benedetti Michalengeli, piano; DG 413 450-2 [AAD] (TT=42.38).

Although Michalengeli gives a wonderful performance (on a comparatively skimpy disc), Gieseking "owns" this music, and to say he performs it on a "piano" is not to be listening to an instrument that is anything its master wishes it to be (despite the analog transfer to digital not being all that one might desire in the way of sound).

{323}   *A*   Twelve Preludes, Book II (1913) Nos.1-12: <u>Brouillard</u> ("Mists"); <u>Feuilles mortes</u> ("Dead Leaves"); <u>La Puerta del vino</u> ("The Gate of Wine"); <u>Fées sont d'exquises danseuses</u> ("The Fairies are Exquisite Dancers"); <u>Bruyères</u> ("Heather"); <u>Général Lavine--eccentric</u> ("General Lavine: The Eccentric"); <u>La Terrasse des audiences du clair de lune</u> ("The Reception Terrace by Moonlight"); <u>Ondine</u>; <u>Hommage à S. Pickwick, Esq., P.P.M.P.C.</u> ("Homage to S. Pickwick, Esq., P.P.M.P.C."); <u>Canope</u> ("Canopus"); <u>Les Tierces alternées</u> ("Alternating Thirds") and <u>Feux d'artifice</u> ("Fireworks") -- see entry No.{322}a.

Operatic

{324}   *B*   <u>Pelléas et Mélisande</u> (1892-1902)

Christine Barbaux, soprano; Frederica von Stade, soprano; Nadine Denize, mezzo-soprano; José van Dam, baritone; Richard Stilwell, baritone; Ruggero Raimondi, bass;

Pascal Thomas, bass; Chorus of the German Opera, Berlin; Berlin Philharmonic Orchestra; Herbert von Karajan, conductor; Angel CDC 49350-2 (3 discs) [ADD] (TT=162.14).

Orchestral

{325}   *A*   Ibéria ("Spain") from Images pour orchestre (1906-1909)
Amsterdam Concertgebouw Orchestra; Bernard Haitink, conductor; Philips 416 444-2 [ADD] (TT=54.07). Includes Debussy's La Mer ("The Sea") (1903-1905), rated A and Prélude à l'après-midi d'un faune ("Prelude to the Afternoon of a Faun") (1892-1894), rated A.

{326}   *A*   La Mer ("The Sea") (1903-1905) -- see entries Nos.{302}b, {303}b and {325}.

{327}   *B*   Nocturnes (1893) (3) Nos.1-3: Nuages ("Clouds"); Fêtes ("Festivals") and Sirènes ("Sirens")
Boston Symphony Orchestra; Claudio Abbado, conductor; DG 415 370-2 [ADD] (TT=66.48). Includes Ravel's Daphnis et Chloé (1909-1912), rated A and Scriabin's Symphony No.4 ("Poem of Ecstasy"), Op.54, rated A.
Also -- see entry No.{302}a.

{328}   *A*   Prélude à l'après-midi d'un faune ("Prelude to the Afternoon of a Faun") (1892-1894) -- see entries Nos.{302}b, {303}b and {325}.

Vocal

{329}   *A*   Beau soir ("Beautiful Evening") (After Bourget) (1878?)
Sarah Walker, mezzo-soprano; Roger Vignoles, piano; Unicorn CD-9035 [DDD] (TT=59.34). Includes Debussy's Chansons de Bilitis ("Songs of Bilitis") (After Louÿs) (1897) (3) Nos.1-3: La Flûte de Pan ("The Flute of Pan"), La Chevelure ("A Woman's Hair") and Le Tombeau des Naïades ("Homage

to the Naiads"), rated A; Trois chansons de France ("Three Songs of France") (After Charles d'Orléans) (1904) (3) Nos.1-3: Rondel, La Grotte ("The Cave") and Rondel; Les Cloches ("The Bells") (No.2 from Deux Romances, after Bourget) (1891); Fêtes galantes Suite II ("Courtly Festivals") (After Verlaine) (1904) and Mandoline (After Verlaine) (1880-1883); Enesco's Sept chansons de Clément Marot, Op.16 and six songs of Roussel.

Also -- see entry No.{309}.

{330}   A   Chansons de Bilitis ("Songs of Bilitis") (After Louÿs) (1897) (3) Nos.1-3: La Flûte de Pan ("The Flute of Pan"), La Chevelure ("A Woman's Hair") and Le Tombeau des Naïades ("Homage to the Naiads") -- see entry No.{329}.

{331}   A   La Chevelure ("A Woman's Hair") (From Chansons de Bilitis ("Songs of Bilitis") (After Louÿs) (1897) -- see entry No.{309}.

{332}   C   La Damoiselle élue ("The Blessed Damozel," after D.G. Rosetti): Cantata for Female Voices (1887-1888)
Jessye Norman, soprano; José Carreras, tenor; Dietrich Fischer-Dieskau, baritone; Stuttgart Radio Women's Chorus; Stuttgart Symphony Orchestra; Gary Bertini, conductor; Pro Arte CDD-128 [DDD] (TT = 54.15). Includes Debussy's L'Enfant prodigue: Scène lyrique ("The Prodigal Child") Cantata (1884), with Ileana Cotrubas, soprano and Glenda Maurice, mezzo-soprano, rated C.

Also -- see entry No.{197}.

{333}   C   L'Enfant prodigue: Scène lyrique Cantata ("The Prodigal Child") (1884) -- see entry No.{332}.

DELIBES, LÉO
1836-1891

Ballet

{334}   *B*   Coppélia (1876)
National Philharmonic Orchestra, London; Sir Richard Bonynge, conductor; London 414 502-2 (2 discs) [DDD] (TT=92.23).

Operatic

{335}   *C*   Lakmé (1880)
Mady Mesplé, soprano; Danielle Millet, mezzo-soprano; Jean-Christoph Benoît, baritone; Charles Burles, tenor; Roger Soyer, bass; Paris Opéra-Comique Chorus and Orchestra; Alain Lombard, conductor; EMI CDS7 49430-2 (2 discs) (must be specially ordered) [ADD] (TT=149.28).

DELIUS, FREDERICK
1862-1934

Orchestral

{336}   *C*   Brigg Fair: "An English Rhapsody" (1907)
Royal Philharmonic Orchestra; Sir Thomas Beecham, conductor; Angel CDS 47509-8 (2 discs) [ADD] (TT=146.44). Includes Delius' Dance Rhapsody No.2 (1916); Intermezzo from Fennimore and Gerda (1908-1910); Florida Suite (1886), rated C; Irmelin Prelude (1932), rated C; Marche Caprice (1888); On Hearing the First Cuckoo in Spring (1912), rated A; Over the Hills and Far Away (1895), rated B; Sleigh Ride (1888), rated C, A Song Before Sunrise (1918); Songs of Sunset (1906-1907) (with Maureen Forrester, contralto; John Cameron, baritone and the Beecham Choral Society) and Summer Evening (Two Pieces Arranged and Edited by Sir Thomas Beecham, in 1946).

{337}   *C*   Florida Suite (1886) -- see entry No.{336}.

{338}   *C*   Irmelin Prelude (1932) -- see entry No.{336}.

173

{339}   *A*   <u>On Hearing the First Cuckoo in Spring</u> (1912) --
see entry No.{336}.

{340}   *B*   <u>Over the Hills and Far Away</u> (1895) -- see entry
No.{336}.

{341}   *C*   <u>Sleigh Ride</u> (1888) -- see entry No.{336}.

DONIZETTI, GAETANO
1797-1848

Choral

{342}   *C*   Miserere, in d (Psalm 50) (1842?)
Júlia Pászthy, soprano; Zsolt Bende, baritone; Slovak
Philharmonic Chorus and Orchestra; József Maklári,
conductor; Hungaroton HCD 12147-2 [ADD] (TT=55.06).

Operatic

{343}   *B*   <u>L'Elisir d'amore</u> ("The Elixir of Love") (1832)
a   Katia Ricciarelli, soprano; Susanna Rigacci, soprano;
José Carreras, tenor; Leo Nucci, baritone; Domenico
Trimarchi, baritone; Chorus and Orchestra of the Turin RAI;
Philips 412 714-2 (2 discs) [DDD] (TT=126.49).
b   Dame Joan Sutherland, soprano; Maria Casula,
soprano; Luciano Pavarotti, tenor; Dominic Cossa, baritone;
Spiro Malas, bass; Ambrosian Opera Chorus; English
Chamber Orchestra; Sir Richard Bonynge, conductor; London
414 461-2 (2 discs) [ADD] (TT=140.51).

{344}   *A*   <u>Lucia de Lammermoor</u> (1835) (After Sir Walter
Scott)
Dame Joan Sutherland, soprano; Luciano Pavarotti,
tenor; Sherrill Milnes, baritone; Nicolai Ghiaurov, bass;
Covent Garden Opera Chorus and Orchestra; Sir Richard
Bonynge, conductor; London (3 discs) [DDD] (TT=140.45).

DOWLAND, JOHN
1563-1626

Vocal

{345}   *C*   Lachrimae, or Seaven Teares Figured in Seaven Passionate Pavans (1604)

Dowland Consort; Jakob Lindberg, conductor; Bis CD-315 [DDD] (TT=65.36). Includes fourteen additional works by Dowland, most importantly: The King of Denmark's Galliard, rated C and Semper Dowland semper dolens ("Always Dowland, Always Grieving"), rated B.

{346}   *C*   The King of Denmark's Galliard -- see entry No.{345}.

{347}   *B*   Semper Dowland semper dolens ("Always Dowland, Always Grieving") -- see entry No.{345}.

DUKAS, PAUL
1865-1935

Orchestral

{348}   *A*   L'Apprenti sorcier ("The Sorcerer's Apprentice") (1897)

Cincinnati Pops Orchestra; Erich Kunzel, conductor; Telarc CD-80115 [DDD] (TT=57.49). Includes Liszt's Les Préludes, Symphonic Poem No.3 (1848), rated A; Rimsky-Korsakov's Dance of the Tumblers from The Snow Maiden (1882), rated B and Procession of the Nobles from Mlada (1872), rated B and Weinberger's Polka and Fugue from Schwanda the Bagpiper (1927), rated B. The Dukas L'Apprenti will be well remembered as the segment in the Disney film Fantasia as the one which featured Michael Mouse as the hapless apprentice.

DUPARC, HENRI
1848-1933

Vocal

{349}   C   L'Invitation au voyage ("Invitation to the Journey") (1870-1871)

Dame Kiri Te Kanawa, soprano; French National Symphony Orchestra; Sir John Pritchard, conductor; Angel CDC 47111-2 [DDD] (TT=44.59). Includes Duparc's Au pays ou se fait la guerre ("To the Land Where War Is Being Waged") (1867); Chanson triste ("Melancholy Song") (1868); Le Manoir de Rosemonde ("The Domain of Rosemonde") (1870?); Phidylé (1868?), rated B; Testament (1872?) and La Vie antérieure ("The Former Life") (1872?), rated C and Ravel's Shéhérazade (Song Cycle) (1925-1926) (3) Nos.1-3: Asie ("Asia"); La Flûte enchantée ("The Enchanted Flute") and L'Indifférent ("The Indifferent Man"), rated B.

{350}   B   Phidylé (1868?) -- see entry No.{349}.

{351}   C   La Vie antérieure ("The Former Life") (1872?) -- see entry No.{349}.

DURUFLÉ, MAURICE
1902-1986

Choral

{352}   C   Requiem, Op.9

Atlanta Symphony Chorus and Orchestra; Robert Shaw, conductor; Telarc CD-80135 [DDD] (TT=74.26). Includes Fauré's Requiem, Op.48, rated A (the Fauré features soloists Judith Blegen, soprano and James Morris, bass).

DVOŘÁK, ANTONÍN
1841-1904

Chamber

{353}   *B*   Serenade for Strings, Op.22, in E
a   Academy of St. Martin-in-the-Fields; Sir Neville
Marriner, conductor; Philips 400 020-2 [DDD] (TT=50.24).
Includes Dvořák's Serenade for Winds, 'Celli and String
Basses, Op.44, in d, rated B.
b   Orpheus Chamber Orchestra; DG 415 364-2 [DDD]
(TT=54.13). Includes Dvořák's Serenade for Winds, 'Celli and
String Basses, Op.44, in d, rated B.
     Of the two above couplings of the same works, the
Orpheus has more vitality and Marriner's has a bit more
polish.

{354}   *B*   Serenade for Winds, 'Celli and String Basses,
Op.44, in d -- see entries Nos.{353}a-b.

{355}   *B*   String Quartet No.12 ("American"), Op.96, in F
     Talich Quartet; Calliope CAL-9617 [AAD]
(TT=56.55).   Includes Dvořák's String Quartet No.11,
Op.61, in C.

{356}   *B*   Trio for Piano, Violin and 'Cello ("Dumky"),
Op.90, in e
     Suk Trio; Denon C37-7057 [DDD] (TT=37.21).
Includes Suk's <u>Elegie</u> for Piano, Violin and 'Cello, Op.23.

Concerted

{357}   *A*   Concerto for 'Cello, Op.104, in b -- see entry
No.{257}.

{358}   *C*   Concerto for Piano, Op.33, in g
     Sviatoslav Richter, piano; Bavarian State Orchestra,
Munich; Carlos Kleiber, conductor; Angel CDC 47967-2

177

[ADD] (TT = 59.24). Includes Schubert's Fantasia ("Wanderer"), D.760, in C, rated A.

{359}   *A*   Concerto for 'Cello, Op.104, in b -- see entry No.{257}.

{360}   *B*   Concerto for Violin, Op.53, in a
Itzhak Perlman, violin; London Philharmonic Orchestra; Daniel Barenboim, conductor; Angel CDC 47168-2 [ADD] (TT = 42.23). Includes Dvořák's Romance for Violin and Orchestra, Op.11, in f.

Operatic
{361}   *C*   <u>Russalka</u>, Op.114
Gabriela Beňáčková-Čápová, soprano; Věra Soukupová, mezzo-soprano; Wiesław Ochman, tenor; Drahomira Drobková, contralto; Richard Novák, bass; Prague Philharmonic Chorus and Orchestra; Václav Neumann, conductor; Supraphon (3 discs) C37-7201-7203 [DDD] (TT = 157.27).

Orchestral
{362}   *A*   Overture: <u>Carnival</u>, Op.92
a   Chicago Symphony Orchestra; Fritz Reiner, conductor; RCA 5606-2-RC [ADD] (TT = 64.08). Includes Dvořák's Symphony No.9 ("From the New World"), Op.95, in e, rated A; Smetana's Overture: <u>The Bartered Bride</u> (1866), rated B and Weinberger's Polka and Fugue from <u>Schwanda the Bagpiper</u> (1927), rated B.
b   Cleveland Orchestra; George Szell, conductor; CBS MYK-36716 [AAD?] (TT = 51.39). Includes Dvořák's Slavonic Dances: Op.46 Nos.1 and 3, in C and A flat, Op.72 Nos.2 and 7, in e and C; Smetana's <u>Vltava</u> ("Moldau") from <u>Má Vlast</u> ("My Fatherland") (1874-1879), rated A and Three Dances from <u>The Bartered Bride</u> (1866), rated A.

{363}   *B*   Scherzo Capriccioso, Op.66
Cleveland Orchestra; Christoph von Dohnányi,
conductor; London 414 422-2 [DDD] (TT=49.04). Includes
Dvořák's Symphony No.8, Op.88, in G, rated A.

{364}   *B*   Slavonic Dances (16) Nos.1-16: Op.46 Nos.1-8, in
c, e, A flat, F, A, D, c and g; Op.72 Nos.9-16, in B, e, F, D flat,
b flat, B flat, C and A flat
Royal Philharmonic Orchestra; Antal Doráti,
conductor; London (2 discs) [DDD] (TT=90.33). Includes
Dvořák's American Suite, Op.98b.
Also -- see entries Nos.{362}b and {367}.

Symphonic
{365}   *B*   Symphony No.6, Op.60, in D
Scottish National Orchestra; Neeme Järvi, conductor;
Chandos CHAN-8530 [DDD] (TT-55.47). Includes Dvořák's
The Noon Witch--Symphonic Poem, Op.108.

{366}   *B*   Symphony No.7, Op.70, in d
Vienna Philharmonic Orchestra; Lorin Maazel,
conductor; DG 410 997-2 [DDD] (TT-36.48).

{367}   *A*   Symphony No.8, Op.88, in G
Cleveland Orchestra; George Szell, conductor; Angel
CDC 47618-2 [ADD] (TT=48.34). Includes Dvořák's Slavonic
Dances Op.46 No.3 and Op.72 No.2.
Also -- see entry No.{363}.

{368}   *A*   Symphony No.9 ("From the New World"), Op.95,
in e -- see entry No.{362}a.

ELGAR, SIR EDWARD
1857-1934

179

Choral

{369}   C   The Dream of Gerontius, Op.30: Oratorio

Alfreda Hodgson, contralto; Robert Tear, tenor; Benjamin Luxon, baritone; Scottish National Orchestra and Chorus; Sir Alexander Gibson, conductor; CRD 33267 (2 discs) [AAD] (TT=89.26).

Chamber

{370}   B   Elegy for Strings, Op.58; Serenade for String Orchestra, Op.20, in e

a   Allegri Quartet; Sinfonia of London; Sir John Barbirolli, conductor; Angel CDC 47537-2 [ADD] (TT=57.47). Includes Elgar's Introduction and Allegro for String Quartet and String Orchestra, Op.47, rated B; Serenade for String Orchestra, Op.20, in e, rated B and Sospiri for Strings, Harp and Organ, Op.70 (the Elegy and Sospiri are performed by the New Philharmonia Orchestra under Barbirolli) and Vaughan Williams' Fantasia on Greensleeves for String Orchestra, Harp and Two Flutes (1934), rated A and Fantasia on a Theme by Thomas Tallis for String Quartet and Double String Orchestra (1910, 1919), rated C.

b   Orpheus Chamber Orchestra; DG 419 191-2 [DDD] (TT=48.47). Includes Elgar's Introduction and Allegro for String Quartet and String Orchestra, Op.47, rated B and Serenade for String Orchestra, Op.20, in e, rated B and Vaughan Williams' Fantasia on Greensleeves for String Orchestra, Harp and Two Flutes (1934), rated A and Fantasia on a Theme by Thomas Tallis for String Quartet and Double String Orchestra (1910, 1919), rated C.

For the works that are common to both of these recordings, I am hard pressed to choose between the discs: Barbirolli elicits a warm, polished, and very "English" sound; the Orpheus readings are springier, brighter and also very polished. I guess it comes down to, do you feel a need for a recording of the Elgar Sospiri: if not, it's a tossup.

{371}   *B*   Introduction and Allegro for String Quartet and
String Orchestra, Op.47 -- see entries Nos.{370}a-b.

{372}   *B*   Serenade for String Orchestra, Op.20, in e
London Philharmonic Orchestra; Sir Adrian Boult,
conductor; Angel CDC 477204-2 [AAD] (TT=69.08). Includes
Elgar's Chanson de nuit, Op.15 No.1; Chanson de matin, Op.15
No.2 and Symphony No.1, Op.55, in A flat, rated C.
Also -- see entries Nos.{102}b and {370}a-b.

Concerted
{373}   *B*   Concerto for 'Cello, Op.85, in e
Jacqueline Du Pré, 'cello; London Symphony Orchestra;
Sir John Barbirolli, conductor; Angel CDC 47329-2 [AAD]
(TT=54.04). Includes Elgar's Sea Pictures (Song Cycle),
Op.37 (with Dame Janet Baker, mezzo-soprano).

Orchestral
{374}   *A*   Enigma Variations, Op.36
a   Hallé Orchestra; Sir John Barbirolli, conductor; Angel
CDM 69185 (must be specially ordered) [ADD] (TT=64.58).
Includes Elgar's Falstaff: A Symphony Study (1913).
b   London Symphony Orchestra; Sir Adrian Boult,
conductor; Angel CDC 47206 2 [AAD] (TT=55.64). Includes
Elgar's Pomp and Circumstance Marches (5) Nos.1-5: in D,
rated A, a, c, g and C. The Pomp and Circumstance No.1 (in
D) is the most famous of the group, having been used in the
United States as a processional in commencement exercises.
In the United Kingdom, "P&C" No.1 is often sung to the words
(which are considered its title), Land of Hope and Glory.

{375}   *A*   Pomp and Circumstance March No.1, in D -- see
entry No.{374}b.

181

Symphonic

{376}   C   Symphony No.1, Op.55, in A flat -- see entry No.{372}.

{377}   C   Symphony No.2, Op.63, in E flat
Philharmonia Orchestra; Bernard Haitink, conductor; Angel CDC 47299-2 [DDD] (TT=59.02).

ENESCO, GEORGES
1881-1955

Orchestral

{378}   A   Rumanian Rhapsody, Op.11 No.1, in A
Philharmonic Orchestra of Monte Carlo; Lawrence Foster, conductor; Erato ECD-75179 [DDD] (TT=51.40). Includes Enesco's Rumanian Rhapsody, Op.11 No.2, in D, rated C and Rumanian Poem for Chorus and Orchestra, Op.1 (with the Men's Chorus of the Colonne Orchestra and the Vocal Audite Nova of Paris).

{379}   C   Rumanian Rhapsody, Op.11 No.2, in D -- see entry No.{378}.

FALLA, MANUEL DE
1876-1956

Ballet

{380}   A   El Amor brujo ("Love, the Warlock") (1915)
a   Teresa Berganza, mezzo-soprano; L'Orchestre de la Suisse Romande; Ernest Ansermet, conductor; [AAD] (TT=43.51). Includes Falla's Interlude and Dance from La Vida breve ("The Short Life") (1914), rated B.
b   Colette Boky, soprano; Huguette Tourangeau, mezzo-soprano; Montreal Symphony Orchestra; Charles Dutoit,

conductor; London 410 008-2 [DDD] (TT = 61.54). Includes Falla's El Sombrero de tres picos ("The Three-Cornered Hat") (1919), rated B.

c   Florence Quivar, mezzo-soprano; Men of the May Festival Chorus; Cincinnati Symphony Orchestra; Jesús López-Cobos, conductor; Telarc CD-80149 [DDD] (TT = 60.16). Includes Falla's Homenajes (1920-1939) and Interlude and Dance from La Vida breve ("The Short Life") (1914), rated B.

Of the three recordings listed above, I prefer Berganza's effort to any of the other mezzos (and the old Ansermet electricity is even more startling because of London's cleaner, more spacious sonics than the original lp provided). For a purer, more authentic "Spanish" feel, however, López-Cobos' has the edge. All three are fine, and each has the merits of very good couplings.

Also -- see entry No.{266}b.

{381}   *B*   El Sombrero de tres picos ("The Three-Cornered Hat") (1919) -- see entry No.{380}b.

Concerted
{382}   *B*   Noches en los jardines de España ("Nights in the Gardens of Spain") (1909-1915) -- see entry No.{3}.

Orchestral
{383}   *B*   La Vida breve ("The Short Life") (1914) -- see entries Nos.{380}a and {380}c.

FAURÉ, GABRIEL
1845-1924

Chamber
{384}   *B*   Sonata for Violin and Piano, Op.13, in A -- see entry No.{309}.

Choral
{385}   *A*   Requiem, Op.48
Kathleen Battle, soprano; Andreas Schmidt, baritone; Philharmonia Chorus and Orchestra; Carlo Maria Giulini, conductor; DG 419 243-2 [DDD] (TT = 48.46). Includes Ravel's <u>Pavane pour une infante défunte</u> ("Pavane for a Dead Princess") (1899), rated A. The Ravel <u>Pavane</u> became well known, in the 1940s, as a popular song titled, <u>The Lamp Is Low</u>.
Also -- see entry No.{352}.

Orchestral
{386}   *C*   <u>Dolly</u> Suite, Op.56 -- see entry No.{303}.

{387}   *C*   <u>Masques et Bergamasques</u> Suite, Op.112
Academy of St. Martin-in-the-Fields; Sir Neville Marriner, conductor; Argo 410 552-2 [DDD] (TT = 42.16). Includes Fauré's Fantaisie, Op.79; Pavane, Op.50, rated A and <u>Pelléas et Mélisande</u> Suite, Op.80, rated B.

{388}   *A*   Pavane, Op.50 -- see entry No.{387}.

{389}   *B*   <u>Pelléas et Mélisande</u> Suite, Op.80
New York City Ballet Orchestra; Robert Irving, conductor; Nonesuch 79135-2 (2 discs) [DDD] (TT = 121.16). Includes excerpts from Fauré's <u>Shylock</u> Suite, Op.57; Hindemith's <u>Four Temperaments</u> (1940); Stravinsky's <u>Agon</u> (1954-1957) and Tchaikovsky's Serenade for Strings, Op.48, in C, rated A.
Also -- see entry No.{387}.

FRANCK, CÉSAR
1822-1890

Chamber

{390}   *A*   Sonata for Violin and Piano, in A (1886)
Jean-Jacques Kantorow, violin; Jacques Rouvier, piano; Denon C37-7079 [DDD] (TT=43.31). Includes Ravel's Sonata for Violin and Piano (1920-1922), rated C.
Also -- see entry No.{223}.

Choral

{391}   *C*   Les Béatitudes ("The Beatitudes"): Oratorio (1880)
Louise Lebrun, soprano; Jane Berbié, mezzo-soprano; Nathalie Stutzmann, contralto; Peter Jeffes, tenor; David Rendall, tenor; Marcel Vanaud, baritone; François Loup, bass; Daniel Ottevaere, bass; French Radio Chorus; New Philharmonic Orchestra; Armin Jordan, conductor; Erato ECD-88217 (2 discs) [DDD] (TT=120.22).

Concerted

{392}   *A*   Variations symphoniques ("Symphonic Variations") for Piano and Orchestra (1885)
Jean-Philippe Collard, piano; Orchestre National du Capitole de Toulouse; Michel Plasson, conductor; Angel CDC 47547 [DDD] (TT=56.06). Includes Franck's Symphony in d (1886-1888), rated A.

Symphonic

{393}   *A*   Symphony in d (1886-1888)
a   Berlin Philharmonic Orchestra; Carlo Maria Giulini, conductor; DG 419 605-2 [DDD] (TT=54.14). Includes Franck's Psyché: Poème symphonique ("Symphonic Poem").
b   Orchestre National de France; Leonard Bernstein, conductor; DG 400 070-2 [DDD] (TT=51.41). Includes Saint-Saëns's Le Rouet d'Omphale: Poème symphonique ("Omphale's Spinning Wheel: Symphonic Poem"), Op.31, rated B.
Also -- see entry No.{392}.

GERSHWIN, GEORGE
1898-1937

Concerted
{394}   *A*   Rhapsody in Blue for Piano and Orchestra (1924)
George Gershwin, piano (1925 piano roll); Columbia
Jazz Band; Michael Tilson Thomas, conductor; CBS MK-42240
[AAD] (TT=71.30). Includes Gershwin's An American in
Paris (1928), rated A; Broadway Overtures: Funny Face; Girl
Crazy; Let 'em Eat Cake; Of Thee I Sing; Oh, Kay! and Strike
Up the Band.
Also -- see entries Nos.{2} and {395}.

Instrumental
{395}   *C*   Cuban Overture (Arranged for Piano, Four
Hands, by George Gershwin) (1932)
Richard and John Contigulia, piano (four hands); MCA
MCAD-6226; [DDD] (TT=58.54). Includes Gershwin's
Embraceable You (1929); Love Walked In (1936) (John
Contigulia, piano solo); The Man I Love (1924) (Richard
Contigulia, piano solo); Porgy and Bess Fantasy (1951)
(Arranged for Two Pianos by Percy Grainger), rated A and
Rhapsody in Blue (Arranged for Two Pianos by George
Gershwin) (1924), rated A.

{396}   *A*   Porgy and Bess Fantasy (1951) (Arranged for Two
Pianos by Percy Grainger) -- see entry No.{395}.

{397}   *A*   Rhapsody in Blue (Arranged for Two Pianos by
George Gershwin) (1924) -- see entries Nos.{394} and {395}.

Operatic
{398}   *B*   Porgy and Bess (1935)
Leona Mitchell, soprano; Florence Quivar, soprano;
McHenry Boatright, bass-baritone; Willard White, bass;

186

Cleveland Chorus and Orchestra; Lorin Maazel, conductor; London 414 559-2 (3 discs) [ADD] (TT=181.44).
Also -- see entries Nos.{395} and {400}.

Orchestral
{399}   *A*   An American in Paris (1928) -- see entry No.{394}.

{400}   *B*   Porgy and Bess: Symphonic Picture (Arranged by Robert Russell Bennett) (1941-1942)
Detroit Symphony Orchestra; Antal Doráti; conductor; London 410 110-2 [DDD] (TT=59.42). Includes Grofé's Grand Canyon Suite (1931), rated A.
Also -- see entries Nos.{395} and {398}.

GILBERT AND SULLIVAN -- SEE SULLIVAN, SIR ARTHUR

GIORDANO, UMBERTO
1867-1948

Operatic
{401}   *B*   Andrea Chenier (1896)
a   Montserrat Caballé, soprano; Astrid Varnay, soprano; Kathleen Kuhlmann, mezzo-soprano; Christa Ludwig, mezzo-soprano; Luciano Pavarotti, tenor; Leo Nucci, baritone; Welsh National Opera Chorus; National Philharmonic Orchestra, London; Riccardo Chailly, conductor; London 410 117-2 (2 discs) [DDD] (TT=106.39).
b   Renata Scotto, soprano; Plácido Domingo, tenor; Sherrill Milnes, baritone; John Alldis Choir; National Philharmonic Orchestra of London; James Levine, conductor; RCA RCD2-2046 (2 discs) [ADD?] (TT=114.24).

GLAZUNOV, ALEXANDER
1865-1936

Concerted
{402}   *C*   Concerto for Violin, Op.82, in a
Jascha Heifetz, violin; RCA Symphony Orchestra; Walter Hendl, conductor; RCA RCD1-7019 [ADD?] (TT = 68.57). Includes Prokofiev's Concerto for Violin No.2, Op.63, in g, rated B (Heifetz is here accompanied by the Boston Symphony Orchestra under Charles Munch) and Sibelius' Concerto for Violin, Op.47, in d, rated A (the accompaniment here provided by the Chicago Symphony Orchestra, conducted by Walter Hendl).

GLIÈRE, REINHOLD
1875-1956

Orchestral
{403}   *B*   "Russian Sailors' Dance" from The Red Poppy (1927) -- see entry No.{210}b.

GLINKA, MIKHAIL
1804-1857

Orchestral
{404}   *A*   Overture: Russlan and Ludmilla (1838-1841)
Moscow Philharmonic Orchestra; Lawrence Leighton, conductor; Sheffield Lab CD-25 [DDD] (TT = 57.49). Includes Mussorgsky's Khovanshchina: Prelude (1872-1880), rated C and Tchaikovsky's Symphony No.5, Op.64, in e, rated A.
Also -- see entries Nos.{210}a-b.

GLUCK, CHRISTOPH WILLIBALD
1714-1787

Operatic

{405}   *B*   Orfeo ed Euridice (1762)
Marjanne Kweksilber, soprano; Magdalena Falewicz, soprano; René Jacobs, countertenor; Ghent Collegium Vocale; La Petite Bande; Sigiswald Kuijken, conductor; Accent ACC-48223 (2 discs) (must be specially ordered) [DDD] (TT = 105.27).

GOLDMARK, KARL
1830-1915

Concerted

{406}   *B*   Concerto for Violin, Op.28, in a
Itzhak Perlman, violin; Pittsburgh Symphony Orchestra; André Previn, conductor; Angel CDC 47846-2 [ADD] (TT=57.46). Includes Korngold's Concerto for Violin, Op.35, in D, rated B.

GOULD, MORTON
1913-

Orchestral

{407}   *C*   American Salute (1944) -- see entry No.{266}.

GOUNOD, CHARLES
1818-1893

Ballet

{408}   *B*   Ballet Music from Faust (1852-1859)

189

Montreal Symphony Orchestra; Charles Dutoit, conductor; London 411 708-2 [DDD] (TT = 59.04). Includes Offenbach's Gaîté parisienne (Arranged by Manuel Rosenthal) (1938), rated A.

Operatic

{409}   *A*   Faust (1852-1859)
Mirella Freni, soprano; Michèle Command, soprano; Jocelyne Taillon, mezzo-soprano; Plácido Domingo, tenor; Thomas Allen, baritone; Marc Vento, baritone; Nicolai Ghiaurov, bass; Chorus and Orchestra of the National Theater of Opera of Paris; Georges Prêtre, conductor; Angel CDS 47493-8 (3 discs) [ADD] (TT = 189.19).

{410}   *C*   Roméo et Juliette ("Romeo and Juliet") (1864)
Catherine Malfitano, soprano; Ann Murray, soprano; Jocelyne Taillon, mezzo-soprano; Charles Burles, tenor; Alfredo Krauss, tenor; Jean-Marie Frémau, baritone; Kurt Ollmann, baritone; Gino Quilico, baritone; Gabriel Bacquier, bass; José van Dam, bass; Jean-Jacques Douméne, bass; Regional Chorus of the Midi-Pyrénées; Chorus of the Capitole de Toulouse; Orchestre National du Capitole de Toulouse; Michel Plasson, conductor; Angel CDCC 47365 (3 discs) [DDD] (TT = 166.03).

GRAINGER, PERCY
1882-1961

Orchestral

{411}   *C*   Lincolnshire Posy (1937) -- see entry No.{9}.

{412}   *C*   Shepherd's Hey (1918) -- see entry No.{9}.

GRANADOS, ENRIQUE
1867-1916

Instrumental
{413}   *C*   Goyescas (1911)
Alicia de Larrocha, piano; London 411 958-2 [AAD?]
(TT=60.25).

GRIEG, EDVARD
1843-1907

Concerted
{414}   *A*   Concerto for Piano, Op.16, in a
Jorge Bolet, piano; Radio Symphony Orchestra of
Berlin; Riccardo Chailly, conductor; London 417 112-2 [DDD]
(TT=64.45). Includes Schumann's Concerto for Piano, Op.54,
in a, rated A.

Orchestral
{415}   *C*   Holberg Suite, Op.40
Berlin Philharmonic Orchestra; Herbert von Karajan,
conductor; DG 400 034-2 [DDD] (TT=52.02). Includes
Mozart's Serenade (Eine kleine Nachtmusik) ("A Little Night
Music") for Strings, in G, K.525, rated A and Prokofiev's
Symphony No.1 ("Classical"), Op.25, in D, rated A.

{416}   *C*   Lyric Suite, Op.54
Gothenburg Symphony Orchestra; Neeme Järvi,
conductor; DG 419 431-2 [DDD] (TT=68.06). Includes
Grieg's Norwegian Dances, Op.35 Nos.1-4, rated B and
Symphonic Dances, Op.64, rated C.

{417}   *B*   Norwegian Dances, Op.35 Nos.1-4 -- see entry
No.{416}.

191

{418}   *A*   Peer Gynt Incidental Music, Complete, Op.46 and 55
Lucia Popp, soprano; Ambrosian Singers; Academy of St. Martin-in-the-Fields; Sir Neville Marriner, conductor; Angel CDC 47003 (TT=33.44).

{419}   *A*   Peer Gynt Suites Nos.1-2, Op.23
Berlin Philharmonic Orchestra; Herbert von Karajan, conductor; DG 410 026-2 [DDD] (TT=64.33). Includes Sibelius' Pelléas and Mélisande Suite, Op.64, rated C.

{420}   *C*   Symphonic Dances, Op.35 Nos.1-4 -- see entry No.{416}.

GRIFFES, CHARLES TOMLINSON
1884-1920

Orchestral
{421}   *B*   White Peacock for Flute and Orchestra (1919) -- see entry No.{292}b.

GROFÉ, FERDE
1892-1972

Orchestral
{422}   *A*   Grand Canyon Suite (1931)
Royal Philharmonic Orchestra; Enrique Bátiz, conductor; Angel CDC 49056 [DDD] (TT=53.44). Includes Grofé's Mississippi Suite (1932), rated C. The Mississippi Suite contains a melody which was transformed into a popular song in the 1940s, Daybreak.
Also -- see entry No.{400}.

{423}   *C*   Mississippi Suite (1932) -- see entry No.{422}.

HANDEL, GEORGE FRIDERIC
1685-1759

Choral

{424}   B   Alexander's Feast (Ode for St. Cecilia's Day) (1736) (Words by John Dryden)
Donna Brown, soprano; Carolyn Watkinson, contralto; Ashley Stafford, countertenor; Nigel Robertson, tenor; Stephen Varcoe, baritone; Monteverdi Choir; English Baroque Soloists; John Eliot Gardiner, conductor; Philips 422 055-2 (2 discs) [DDD] (TT=98.36). Includes Handel's Concerto Grosso (1736) ("Alexander's Feast"), in C, rated B.

{425}   A   L'Allegro, il penseroso ed il moderato for Chorus and Instrumental Ensemble (1740-1741)
Michael Ginn, boy soprano; Patrizia Kwella, soprano; Marie McLaughlin, soprano; Jennifer Smith, soprano; Maldwyn Davies, tenor; Martyn Hill, tenor; Stephen Varcoe, bass; Monteverdi Choir; English Baroque Soloists, John Eliot Gardiner, conductor; Erato ECD-880752 (2 discs) [ADD] (TT=116.12).

{426}   C   Belshazzar: Oratorio (1745)
Felicity Palmer, soprano; Maureen Lehane, mezzo-soprano; Paul Esswood, countertenor; Robert Tear, tenor; Stockholm Chamber Choir; Concentus Musicus of Vienna; Nikolaus Harnoncourt, conductor; Teldec 835326 ZB (3 discs) [AAD] (TT=172.55).

{427}   C   Jeptha: Oratorio (1752)
Elizabeth Gale, soprano; Glenys Linos, soprano; Gabriele Sima, contralto; Paul Esswood, countertenor; Werner Hollweg, tenor; Thomas Thomaschke, baritone; Arnold Schoenberg Choir; Mozart Sängerknaben; Concentus Musicus of Vienna; Nikolaus Harnoncourt, conductor; Teldec 835499 ZB (3 discs) [ADD] (TT=175.46).

{428}   *A*   Messiah: Oratorio (1742)
           Emma Kirkby, soprano; Judith Nelson, soprano;
Carolyn Watkinson, contralto; Paul Elliott, tenor; David
Thomas, bass; Choir of Christ Church Cathedral, Oxford;
Academy of Ancient Music; Christopher Hogwood, conductor;
L'Oiseau-Lyre 411 858-2 (3 discs) [DDD] (TT = 135.48).
           A word about the above: there are several complete
Messiah recordings available on CD. Hogwood's uses the
"Foundling Hospital" version of 1754, which incorporates the
changes which Handel himself introduced into the score for a
performance under his own supervision. Of more importance
than the musicological aspects of the score Hogwood chose is
the performance he elicits from his musicians. This is a moving
and credible Messiah: one which sounds fresh, inspired and
filled with the energy which one always suspects Handel
invested in this work, but which is so seldom encountered in
the realization.

{429}   *A*   Messiah: Oratorio (1742) (Arranged by Wolfgang
Amadeus Mozart, K.572)
           Felicity Lott, soprano; Felicity Palmer, mezzo-soprano;
Philip Langridge, tenor; Robert Lloyd, bass; Huddersfield
Choral Society; Royal Philharmonic Orchestra; Sir Charles
Mackerras, conductor; ASV RPD001R (2 discs) (must be
specially ordered) [DDD] (TT = 127.38).

{430}   *B*   Ode for St. Cecilia's Day (1739)
           Felicity Lott, soprano; Anthony Rolfe-Johnson, tenor;
English Concert Choir; English Concert; Trevor Pinnock,
conductor; Archiv 419 220-2 [DDD] (TT = 50.36).

Concerted
{431}   *B*   Concerti for Organ, Op.4 Nos.1-6, in g; B flat; g;
F; F and B flat (the last is for Organ and Harp)

Simon Preston, organ; Ursula Holliger, harp; English Concert; Trevor Pinnock, conductor; Archiv 413 465-2 (2 discs) [DDD] (TT=90.03).

{432}   *B*   Concerti for Organ, Op.7, Nos.1-6: in B flat; A, B flat; d; g and B flat
Simon Preston, organ; English Concert; Trevor Pinnock, conductor; Archiv 413 468-2 (2 discs) [DDD] (TT=105.16). Includes Handel's Concerti for Organ, HWV 295 ("The Cuckoo and the Nightingale"), in F, rated A and HWV 304, in d.

{433}   *A*   Concerto for Organ, HWV 295 ("The Cuckoo and the Nightingale"), in F -- see entry No.{432}.

                    Instrumental
{434}   *C*   Lesson for Harpsichord, HWV 434, in B flat
Igor Kipnis, harpsichord; Nonesuch 79037-2 [DDD] (TT=51.31). Includes Handel's Fantasia, HWV 576, in C; Prelude and Allegro, HWV 576, in a; Sonata, HWV 580, in g, rated C; Sonatina, HWV 583, in g; Suite No.5 ("The Harmonious Blacksmith"), HWV 430, in E, rated A; Suite No.8, HWV, in G. It is to be noted that the theme of the "Aria con variazioni" which terminates the Lesson, HWV 434, was used by Brahms as the theme for his Variations and Fugue on a Theme by Handel, Op.24.

{435}   *C*   Sonata for Harpsichord, HWV 580, in g -- see entry No.{434}.

{436}   *C*   Sonatas for Recorder (5) Nos.1-5: HWV 360, in g; HWV 362, in a; HWV 365, in C; HWV 369, in F; HWV 367a, in d and HWV 377, in B flat
L'Ecole d'Orphée; CRD 3412 [ADD] (TT=56.33).

195

{437}   *A*   Suite for Harpsichord No.5 ("The Harmonious Blacksmith"), HWV 430, in E -- see entry No.{434}.

{438}   *C*   Suite No.11 for Harpsichord (Sarabande) -- see entry No.{6}b.

Operatic
{439}   *B*   <u>Alcina</u> (1735)
Arleen Augér, soprano; Eiddwen Harrhy, soprano; Patrizia Kwella, soprano; Della Jones, mezzo-soprano; Kathleen Kuhlmann, mezzo-soprano; Maldwyn Davies, tenor; John Tomlinson, bass; Opera Stage Chorus; City of London Baroque Sinfonia; Richard Hickox, conductor; Angel CDS 49771 (3 discs) [DDD] (TT=217.51).

{440}   *C*   <u>Atalanta</u> (1736)
Eva Bártfai-Barta, soprano; Katalin Farkas, soprano; Eva Lax, contralto; János Bándi, tenor; József Gregor, bass; László Polgár, bass; Savaria Vocal Ensemble; Capella Savaria; Nicholas McGegan, conductor; Hungaroton HCD-12612-12614 (3 discs) [DDD] (TT=140.00).

{441}   *B*   <u>Imeneo</u> (1740)
Julianne Baird, soprano; Beverly Hoch, soprano; D'Anna Fortunato, mezzo-soprano; John Ostendorff, bass-baritone; Jan Opalach, bass; Edward Brewer, harpsichord; Brewer Chamber Chorus and Orchestra; Rudolph Palmer, conductor; Vox Cum Laude MCD 10063 (2 discs) [DDD] (TT=112.47).

Orchestral
{442}   *B*   "The Arrival of the Queen of Sheba" from <u>Solomon</u> (1749) -- see entry No.{60}.

{443}   *B*   Concerto Grosso (1736) ("Alexander's Feast"), in C -- see entry No.{424}.

{444}   *A*   Concerti Grossi, Op.3 Nos.1-6: in B flat; B flat, G; F; d and D
English Concert; Trevor Pinnock, conductor; Archiv 413 727-2 [DDD] (TT=56.32).

{445}   *A*   Concerti Grossi, Op.6 Nos.1-12
English Concert; Trevor Pinnock, conductor; Archiv 413 897-413-899-2 (3 discs) [DDD] (TT=165.01).

{446}   *A*   <u>Royal Fireworks Music</u> (1749)
Jean-François Paillard Chamber Orchestra; Jean-François Paillard, conductor; Erato ECD-55011 [AAD] (TT=71.11). Includes Handel's <u>Water Music</u> (1717), rated A. Also -- see entries Nos.{91}, {98}a and {290}.

{447}   *A*   <u>Water Music</u> (1717) -- see entry No.{446}.

{448}   *A*   <u>Water Music</u> Suite (1717) -- see entry No.{60}.

HANSON, HOWARD
1896-1981

Symphonic
{449}   *B*   Symphony No.2 ("Romantic"), Op.30 -- see entry No.{101}.

HAYDN, FRANZ JOSEPH
1732-1809

Chamber
{450}   *B*   String Quartets, Op.33 (Known variously as "Gli scherzi," "Jung ern," or "Russian" Quartets) (6) Nos.1-6: in b, E flat ("The Joke"), C ("The Bird"), B flat, G ("How Do You Do?") and D

Tátrai Quartet; Hungaroton HCD 11887-11888-2 (2 discs) [ADD] (TT = 106.52).

{451}   *C*   String Quartets, Op.54 (3) Nos.1-3: in G, C and E
Tátrai Quartet; Hungaroton HCD 12506-12507-2 (2 discs) [ADD] (TT = 129.02). Includes Haydn's String Quartets, Op.55 (3) Nos.1-3: in A, f ("The Razor") and B flat, rated C.

{452}   *C*   String Quartets, Op.55 (3) Nos.1-3: in A, f ("The Razor") and B flat -- see entry No.{451}.

{453}   *B*   String Quartets, Op.64 ("Tost") (6) Nos.1-6: in C, b, B flat, G, D ("The Lark" or "The Hornpipe") and E flat
Tátrai Quartet; Hungaroton HCD 11838-11839-2 (2 discs) [ADD] (TT = 116.10).

{454}   *C*   String Quartets, Op.71 ("Apponyi") (3) Nos.1-3: in B flat, D and E flat
Tátrai Quartet; Hungaroton HCD 12246-12247-2 (2 discs) [ADD] (TT = 136.25). Includes Haydn's String Quartets, Op.74 ("Apponyi") (3) Nos.1-3: in C, F and G ("The Rider"), rated B.

{455}   *B*   String Quartets, Op.74 ("Apponyi") (3) Nos.1-3: in C, F and G ("The Rider") -- see entry No.{454}.

{456}   *A*   String Quartets, Op.76 ("Erdödy") (6) Nos.1-6: in G, d ("Quinten," includes the "Hexen-Minuet," "The Bell" and "The Donkey"), C ("Kaiser" <"Emperor">), B flat ("L'Aurore" <"Sunrise">), D and E flat
Tátrai Quartet; Hungaroton HCD 12812-12813-2 (2 discs) [ADD] (TT = 126.35).
Also -- see entry No.{457}.

{457}   *A*   String Quartet, Op.76 No.3 ("Kaiser" <"Emperor">), in C

Amadeus Quartet; DG 410 866-2 [DDD] (TT=49.52). Includes Mozart's String Quartet No.17, K.458 (Jagdquartett) ("The Hunt Quartet"), in B, rated A.

Choral

{458}   *A*   Die Jahreszeiten ("The Seasons") (Oratorio) (1801)

Edith Mathis, soprano; Siegfried Jerusalem, tenor; Dietrich Fischer-Dieskau, baritone; Chorus and Academy of St. Martin-in-the-Fields; Sir Neville Marriner, conductor; Philips 411 428-2 (2 discs) [DDD] (TT=134.05).

{459}   *A*   Mass No.7, H.XXII:7, in C ("Missa in tempore belli" or "Paukenmesse") ("Mass in the Time of War" or "Drum Roll Mass") (1796)

a   Judith Blegen, soprano; Brigitte Fassbaender, contralto; Claes Haakan Ahnsjö, tenor; Hans Sotin, bass; Bavarian Radio Symphony Orchestra and Chorus; Leonard Bernstein, conductor; Philips 412 734-2 [DDD] (TT=45.01).

b   Margaret Marshall, soprano; Carolyn Watkinson, contralto; Keith Lewis, tenor; Robert Holl, bass; Leipzig Radio Choir; Dresden State Orchestra; Sir Neville Marriner, conductor; Angel CDC 47425-2 [DDD] (TT=40.10).

{460}   *A*   Mass No.9, H.XXII:9, in C ("Nelson Mass")

Felicity Lott, soprano; Carolyn Watkinson, contralto; Meredith Davies, tenor; David Wilson-Johnson, baritone; English Concert and Choir; Trevor Pinnock, conductor; DG ARC-423 097-2 [DDD] (TT=51.12). Includes Haydn's Te Deum, H.XXXIII:c2, in C.

{461}   *A*   Mass No.11, H.XXII:11, in d ("Missa in angustiis" <"Mass in Difficult Times"> or "Nelson Mass") (1798)

Barbara Hendricks, soprano; Marjana Lipovšek, contralto; Francisco Araiza, tenor; Peter Meven, bass;

199

Bavarian Radio Symphony Chorus and Orchestra; Sir Colin Davis, conductor; Philips 416 358-2 [DDD] (TT = 40.03).

{462}   *A*   Die Schöpfung ("The Creation") (Oratorio) (1798)
a   Edith Mathis, soprano; Aldo Baldin, tenor; Dietrich Fischer-Dieskau, baritone; Chorus and Academy of St. Martin-in-the-Fields; Sir Neville Marriner, conductor; Philips 416 449-2 (2 discs) [ADD] (TT = 108.34).
b   Edith Mathis, soprano; Francisco Araiza, tenor; José van Dam, bass; Wiener Singverein; Vienna Philharmonic Orchestra; Herbert von Karajan, conductor; DG 410 718-2 (2 discs) [DDD] (TT = 114.28).

Concerted

{463}   *B*   Concerto for 'Cello, Op.101, in D -- see entry No.{205}.

{464}   *A*   Concerto for Trumpet, H.VIIe:1, in E flat
          Wynton Marsalis, trumpet; National Philharmonic Orchestra of London; Raymond Leppard, conductor; CBS MK-37846 [DDD] (TT = 39.53). Includes Hummel's Concerto for Trumpet, in E flat (1803), rated B and Leopold Mozart's Concerto for Trumpet, in D (1762), rated C.

{465}   *A*   Sinfonia Concertante, Op.84, in B flat
          Marieke Blankenstein, violin; William Conway, 'cello; Douglas Boyd, oboe; Matthew Wilkie, bassoon; Chamber Orchestra of Europe; Claudio Abbado, conductor; DG 423 105-2 [DDD] (TT = 42.38). Includes Haydn's Symphony No.96 ("Miracle"), in D (1791), rated A.

Instrumental

{466}   *B*   Sonatas for Keyboard, H.XVI:36, in c sharp, 40, in G, 41, in B, 49, in E flat and 50, in C
          Gilbert Kalish, piano; Nonesuch 79162-2 [AAD] (TT = 69.33).

Symphonic

{467}　　　*C*　Symphony No.6 ("Le Matin") ("The Morning"), in D (1761)

Academy of St. Martin-in-the-Fields; Sir Neville Marriner, conductor; Philips [DDD] (TT = 60.21). Includes Haydn's Symphonies Nos.7 ("Le Midi") ("The Afternoon") (1761), in C, rated C and 8 ("Le Soir") ("The Evening") (1761), in G, rated C.

{468}　　　*C*　Symphony No.7 ("Le Midi") ("The Afternoon"), in C (1761) -- see entry No.{467}.

{469}　　　*C*　Symphony No.8 ("Le Soir") ("The Evening"), in G (1761) -- see entry No.{467}.

{470}　　　*C*　Symphony No.43 ("Mercury"), in E flat (c.1772)

Cantilena; Adrian Shepherd, conductor; Chandos CD-8451 [DDD] (TT = 68.02). Includes Haydn's Symphony No.44 ("Trauer") ("Funeral"), in e (1772), rated B and Symphony No.49 ("La Passione") ("The Passionate"), in f (1768), rated A.

{471}　　　*B*　Symphony No.44 ("Trauer") ("Funeral"), in e (1772)

Orpheus Chamber Orchestra; DG 415 365-2 [DDD] (TT = 43.38). Includes Haydn's Symphony No.77, in B flat (c.1782).
Also -- see entry No.{470}.

{472}　　　*A*　Symphony No.49 ("La Passione") ("The Passionate"), in f (1768) -- see entry No.{470}.

{473}　　　*A*　Symphony No.86, in D (1786)

Academy of St. Martin-in-the-Fields; Sir Neville Marriner, conductor; Philips 412 888-2 [DDD] (TT = 47.42). Includes Haydn's Symphony No.87, in A (1785), rated A.

{474}   *A*   Symphony No.87, in A (1785) -- see entry
No.{473}.

{475}   *A*   Symphony No.88, in G (1787)
          Columbia Symphony Orchestra; Bruno Walter,
conductor; CBS MK-42047 [AAD?] (TT=47.49). Includes
Haydn's Symphony No.100 ("Military"), in G (1793-1794), rated
A.

{476}   *A*   Symphony No.91, in E flat (1788)
          Amsterdam Concertgebouw Orchestra; Sir Colin Davis,
conductor; Philips 410 390-2 [DDD] (TT=53.97). Includes
Haydn's Symphony No.92 ("Oxford"), in G (1789), rated A.

{477}   *A*   Symphony No.92 ("Oxford"), in G (1789) see entry
No.{476}.

{478}   *A*   Symphony No.93, in D (1792)
          Amsterdam Concertgebouw Orchestra; Sir Colin Davis,
conductor; Philips 412 871-2 [DDD] (TT=67.47). Includes
Haydn's Symphonies Nos.94 ("Surprise"), in G (1791), rated A
and 96 ("Miracle"), in D (1791), rated A.

{479}   *A*   Symphony No.94 ("Surprise"), in G (1791)
a   Academy of Ancient Music; Christopher Hogwood,
conductor; L'Oiseau-Lyre 414 330-2 [DDD] (TT=49.22).
Includes Haydn's Symphony No.96 ("Miracle"), in D (1791),
rated A.
b   Philharmonia Hungarica; Antal Doráti, conductor;
London 417 718-2 [ADD] (TT=68.48). Includes Haydn's
Symphonies Nos.96 ("Miracle"), in D (1791), rated A and 100
("Military"), in G (1793-1794), rated A.
c   Vienna Philharmonic Orchestra; Leonard Bernstein,
conductor; DG 419 233-2 [DDD] (TT=46.13). Includes
Haydn's Sinfonia Concertante, in B (1792), with soloists Rainer
Küchl, violin; Franz Bartolomey, 'cello; Walter Lehmayer,

oboe and Michael Werba, bassoon.
Also -- see entry No.{478}.

{480}   *A*   Symphony No.96 ("Miracle"), in D (1791) -- see
entries Nos.{465}, {478} and {479}a-b.

{481}   *A*   Symphony No.100 ("Military"), in G (1793-1794)
         Academy of Ancient Music; Christopher Hogwood,
conductor; L'Oiseau-Lyre 411 833-2. Includes Haydn's
Symphony No.104 ("London"), in D (1795), rated A.
         Also -- see entries Nos.{475} and {479}b.

{482}   *A*   Symphony No.101 ("Clock"), in D (1793-1794)
         Scottish Chamber Orchestra; Raymond Leppard,
conductor; Erato ECD-88079 [DDD] (TT=58.48). Includes
Haydn's Symphony No.104 ("London"), in D (1795), rated A.

{483}   *A*   Symphony No.102, in B flat (1794)
         London Philharmonic Orchestra; Sir Georg Solti,
conductor; London 414 673-2 [DDD] (TT=55.25). Includes
Haydn's Symphony No.103 ("Drum Roll"), in E flat (1795),
rated A.

{484}   *A*   Symphony No.103 ("Drum Roll"), in E flat (1795)
-- see entry No.{483}.

{485}   *A*   Symphony No.104 ("London"), in D (1795) -- see
entries Nos.{481} and {482}.

HENZE, HANS WERNER
1926-

Chamber
{486}   *C*   Sonatina for Solo Trumpet (1976)
         Thomas Stevens, trumpet; Crystal CD-665 [DDD]

(TT=66.29). Includes Antheil's Sonata for Trumpet and Piano (1952) (with Thomas Stevens, trumpet and Zita Carno, piano); Leonard Bernstein's <u>Rondo for Lifey</u> (1949) (with Thomas Stevens, trumpet and Zita Carno, piano); Peter Maxwell Davies' Sonata for Trumpet and Piano (1955) (with Thomas Stevens, trumpet and Zita Carno, piano); Charles Dodge's <u>Extensions</u> for Trumpet and Tape (1973) (with Thomas Stevens, trumpet); Ibert's <u>Impromptu</u> (1951) (with Thomas Stevens, trumpet and Zita Carno, piano); Kupferman's <u>Three Ideas</u> (1967) (with Thomas Stevens, trumpet and Chet Swiatkowski, piano); Thomas Stevens' <u>A New Carnival of Venice</u> (based on Arban) (1985) (with Boyde Hood, trumpet; Donald Green, trumpet; Rob Roy McGregor, trumpet; Thomas Stevens, trumpet and David Wheatley, piano), <u>Triangles</u> (1987) (with Donald Green, trumpet; Rob Roy McGregor, trumpet and Thomas Stevens, trumpet), and <u>Variations on Clifford Intervals</u> (1983) (with Thomas Stevens, trumpet; Charlie Shoemake, vibraphone and Barry Lieberman, contrabass); Tomasi's <u>Triptyque</u> (1957) (with Thomas Stevens, trumpet and Zita Carno, piano).

HÉROLD, LOUIS-JOSEPH FERDINAND
1791-1833

Orchestral

{487}   C   Overture: <u>Zampa</u> (1831) -- see entry No.{10}.

HINDEMITH, PAUL
1895-1963

Chamber

{488}   C   Sonata for Trumpet and Piano (1939)
        Anthony Plog, trumpet; Sharon Davis, piano; Crystal CD-663 [DDD] (TT=60.13). Includes Campo's Two Studies

for Trumpet and Guitar (1985) (with Jack Sanders, guitar); Erickson's <u>Kryl</u>; Petrassi's Fanfare for Three Trumpets (1944) (joining Plog are trumpeters Robert Karon and G. Burnette Dillon); Plog's <u>Animal Dittles</u> (1983); Stevens' Sonata for Trumpet and Piano (1953-1956), rated C and Tull's <u>Profiles</u> for Solo Trumpet.

Concerted
{489}   *B*   <u>Der Schwanendreher</u> ("The Swanherd") Concerto Based on a Folk Theme for Viola and Orchestra (1935)

Daniel Benyamini, viola; Orchestre de Paris; Daniel Barenboim, conductor; DG 423 241-2 [ADD] (TT=70.11). Includes Hindemith's Concert Music for Strings and Woodwinds, Op.50 and <u>Mathis der Maler</u> Symphony ("Mathias <Mathias Grünewald>, the Painter") (1934), rated B.

Symphonic
{490}   *B*   <u>Mathis der Maler</u> Symphony ("Mathias <Mathias Grünewald>, the Painter") (1934) -- see entry No.{489}.

{491}   *A*   Symphonic Metamorphosis on Themes by Weber (1943)

Philadelphia Orchestra; Eugene Ormandy, conductor; Angel CDC 47615 [ADD] (38.12). Includes Hindemith's Concert Music, Op.50.

HOLST, GUSTAV
1874-1934

Orchestral
{492}   *A*   <u>The Planets</u>, Op.32
a   Geoffrey Mitchell Choir; London Philharmonic Orchestra; Sir Adrian Boult, conductor; Angel CDM 69045 [ADD] (TT=48.57).

b   French Radio Chorus Women's Voices; Orchestre
National de France; Lorin Maazel, conductor; CBS MK-37249
[DDD] (TT=49.20).

c   Brighton Festival Chorus' Women's Voices; Royal
Philharmonic Orchestra; André Previn, conductor; Telarc CD-
81033 [DDD] (TT=50.59).
           Of the three <u>Planets</u> above, I lean towards the Boult
recording, despite its age (1979). It is not, however, as
powerful as Previn's. Somehow, Maazel's interpretation is
somewhat less three-dimensional and flat in comparison to
Previn's; this difference becomes most obvious in the "Jupiter"
movement, and most especially in the big hymn tune therein.
Maazel has some fine introspective insights and a care for the
score going for him. Still, all are excellent readings and very
well recorded.

{493}   *B*   Two Suites for Military Band (2): Op.28 No.1-2, in
E flat and F -- see entry No.{91}.

HONNEGER, ARTHUR
1892-1955

Symphonic
{494}   *C*   Symphony No.3 (<u>Liturgique</u>) (1945-1945)
           Berlin Philharmonic Orchestra; Herbert von Karajan,
conductor; DG 423 242-2 [ADD] (TT=59.09). Includes
Honneger's Symphony No.2 for String Orchestra and Trumpet
Obbligato (1942).

HOVHANESS, ALAN
1911-

Symphonic

{495}   *C*   Symphony No.21 (Symphony Etchmiadzin),
Op.234
Royal Philharmonic Orchestra; Alan Hovhaness,
conductor; Crystal CD-804 [DDD] (TT = 63.43). Includes
Hovhaness' Armenian Rhapsody No.3, Op.189, Fra Angelico
Op.220 and Mountains and Rivers Without End (Chamber
Symphony for 10 Players), Op.225.

{496}   *C*   Symphony No.24 (Majun), Op.273
Martyn Hill, tenor; John Wilbraham, trumpet; Sidney
Sax, violin; John Alldis Choir; National Philharmonic
Orchestra of London; Alan Hovhaness, conductor; Crystal CD-
803 [DDD] (TT – 48.00).

HUMMEL, JOHANN NEPOMUK
1778-1837

Concerted

{497}   *B*   Concerto for Trumpet, in E flat (1803) -- see entry
No.{464}.

HUMPERDINCK, ENGELBERT
1854-1921

Operatic

{498}   *B*   Hänsel und Gretel, (1893)
Arleen Augér, soprano; Helen Donath, soprano; Anna
Moffo, soprano; Lucia Popp, soprano; Charlotte Berthold,
mezzo-soprano; Christa Ludwig, mezzo-soprano; Dietrich
Fischer-Dieskau, baritone; Tölzer Knabenchor; Munich Radio
Broadcasting Orchestra; Kurt Eichhorn, conductor; Eurodisc
610 266-232 (2 discs) [DDD] (TT = 102.00).

IBERT, JACQUES
1890-1962

Ballet

{499} *B* Divertissement (1930) -- see entry No.{303}.

IVES, CHARLES
1874-1954

Orchestral

{500} *B* The Unanswered Question (1906)
Chicago Symphony Chorus and Orchestra; Michael Tilson Thomas, conductor; CBS MK 42381 [DDD] (TT=62.58). Includes Ives' Central Park in the Dark (1898-1899) and Symphony: Holidays (1913) (4) Nos.1-4: Decoration Day; Fourth of July; Thanksgiving and Washington's Birthday, rated B.
Also -- see entry No.{292}b.

Symphonic

{501} *B* Symphony: Holidays (1913) (4) Nos.1-4: Decoration Day; Fourth of July; Thanksgiving and Washington's Birthday -- see entry No.{500}.

JANÁČEK, LEOŠ
1854-1928

Chamber

{502} *B* Mládí ("Youth") (1924) -- see entry No.{105}.

{503} *B* String Quartet No.1 ("Kreutzer Sonata") (1923)
Smetana Quartet; Supraphon CO-1130 [DDD] (TT=40.34). Includes Janáček's String Quartet No.2 ("Intimate Pages") (1927-1928), rated A.

{504}   *A*   String Quartet No.2 ("Intimate Pages") (1927-1928) -- see entry No.{503}.

Choral

{505}   *B*   Glagolitic Mass (also known as the Slavonic Mass) (1926)

a   Libuše Domanínská, soprano; Věra Soukupová, mezzo-soprano; Beno Blachut, tenor; Eduard Haken, bass; Czech Singers' Chorus; Czech Philharmonic Orchestra; Karel Ančerl, conductor; Fidelio CD-855 [ADD] (TT=41.02).

b   Elisabeth Söderström, soprano; Drahomira Drobková, contralto; František Livora, tenor; Richard Novák, bass; Czech Philharmonic Chorus and Orchestra; Sir Charles Mackerras, conductor; Supraphon C37-7448 [ADD] (TT=40.19).

Although the Ančerl performance is essentially peerless, the Mackerras is almost as good, and has the benefit of better female singers.

Operatic

{506}   *B*   The Cunning Little Vixen (1921-1923)

Lucia Popp, soprano; Éva Randová, mezzo-soprano; Dalibor Jedlička, bass; Vienna State Opera Chorus; Bratislava Children's Choir; Vienna Philharmonic Orchestra; Sir Charles Mackerras, conductor; London 417 129-2 (2 discs) [DDD] (TT=108.45).

{507}   *A*   Jenůfa (1894-1903)

Lucia Popp, soprano; Elisabeth Söderström, soprano; Peter Dvorský, tenor; Wiesław Ochman, tenor; Dalibor Jedlička, bass; Vienna State Opera Chorus; Vienna Philharmonic Orchestra; Sir Charles Mackerras, conductor; London 414 483-2 (2 discs) [DDD] (TT=130.22).

Orchestral

{508}   *B*   Sinfonietta (1926)

Czech Philharmonic Orchestra; Václav Neumann,

conductor; Supraphon CO-1041 [DDD] (TT=46.01). Includes Janáček's Taras Bulba (Slavonic Rhapsody after Gogol) (1918), rated C.

{509}   C   Taras Bulba (Slavonic Rhapsody after Gogol) (1918) -- see entry No.{508}.

KHACHATURIAN, ARAM
1903-1978

Ballet
{510}   A   Suite -- Khachaturian»Gayne Suite (1942)
Royal Philharmonic Orchestra; Yuri Temirkanov, conductor; Angel CDC 47348-2 [DDD] (TT=51.07). Includes Khachaturian's Spartacus Suite (1953), rated B.
Also -- for Gayne Suite (1942): "Sabre Dance" see entry No.{511}.

{511}   A   Gayne Suite (1942): "Sabre Dance"
Bolshoi Theatre Orchestra; Mark Ermler, conductor; Mobile Fidelity (Melodia) MFCD 2-862 (2 discs) [DDD] (TT=84.16). Includes Glière's "Hymn to the Great City" from The Bronze Horseman Ballet Suite (1948-1949); Karev's Procession from Seven Beauties; Khachaturian's Waltz from the Masquerade Ballet (1941), rated A, and "Adagio of Spartacus and Phrygia" from the Spartacus Ballet (1954, 1968), rated B (the Adagio is an eminently recognizable piece which has been used for a variety of purposes, and was used by more than one competitor for ice skating background music in the 1988 Olympics) and the Dance of the Gaditan Maidens and Spartacus' Victory from the Spartacus Ballet (1954, 1968); Khrennikov's Procession from the Seven Beauties Ballet; Melnikov's Adagio from Suite No.1 ("Legends About Love"); Prokofiev's March from the opera Love for Three Oranges, Op.33, rated A; "Gavotte, Dance of the West Indian Girls,

Montagues and Capulets" from the Romeo and Juliet Ballet, Op.64, rated A and Waltz from the opera War and Peace (1946); Shchedrin's "Dance of Maidens, and Russian Quadrille" from the Humpback Horse Ballet; Shostakovich "Romance" from the film, The Gadfly, Op.97, rated A (the Gadfly "Romance" became very popular after its use as the theme music for the PBS TV series, Reilly, Ace of Spies) and Svirdov's "Old Romance" from the film, Snowstorm and Introduction from the film, Time Forever. The March from the Love for Three Oranges was the theme for the radio program, The FBI in Peace and War.

{512}   *B*   Masquerade Ballet (1941): Waltz -- see entry No.{511}.

{513}   *B*   Spartacus Ballet (1954, 1968): -- see entries Nos.{510} and {511}.

KODÁLY, ZOLTÁN
1882-1967

Chamber
{514}   *C*   String Quartet No.1, Op.2
        Kodály Quartet; Hungaroton HCD 12362-2 [DDD] (TT = 56.05). Includes Kodály's String Quartet No.2, Op.10, rated B.

{515}   *B*   String Quartet No.2, Op.10 -- see entry No.{514}.

Choral
{516}   *B*   Psalmus Hungaricus for Tenor, Chorus and Orchestra, Op.13
        József Simándy, tenor; Budapest Chorus; Hungarian Radio and Television Children's Chorus; Hungarian State Orchestra; Antal Doráti, conductor; Hungaroton HCD 11392-2

211

[ADD] (TT=47.50). Includes Kodály's Variations on an Hungarian Folk Song (Peacock), Op.13, rated C.

Operatic

{517}   C   Háry János, Op.15

Mária Sudlik, soprano; Katalin Mészöly, mezzo-soprano; Klára Takács, soprano; Sándor Palcsó, tenor; Balázs Póka, baritone; Sándor Sólyom-Nagy, baritone; József Gregor, bass; Hungarian Radio and Television Children's Chorus; Hungarian State Opera Chorus and Orchestra; János Ferencsik, conductor; Hungaroton HCD 12387-12388 (2 discs) [ADD] (TT=85.34).

Orchestral

{518}   A   Háry János Suite (1927)

Budapest Philharmonic Orchestra; János Ferencsik, conductor; HCD 12190-2 [ADD] (TT=42.10). Includes Kodály's Concerto for Orchestra (1939) (this latter is performed by Zoltán Döry, violin; Anna Mauthner, viola; Tamás Koó, 'cello; and the Hungarian State Orchestra, again conducted by Ferencsik).

{519}   C   Variations on an Hungarian Folk Song (Peacock), Op.13 -- see entry No.{516}.

KORNGOLD, ERICH WOLFGANG
1897-1957

Concerted

{520}   B   Concerto for Violin, Op.35, in D -- see entry No.{406}.

LALO, ÉDOUARD
1823-1892

Concerted

{521}   *B*   Concerto for 'Cello and Orchestra, in d (1876)
a   Lynn Harrell, 'cello; Berlin Radio Symphony Orchestra;
Riccardo Chailly, conductor; London 414 387-2 [DDD]
(TT=51.45). Includes Fauré's Elegie, Op.24 and Saint-Saëns'
Concerto for 'Cello and Orchestra No.2, Op.119, in d, rated B.
b   Yo-Yo Ma, 'cello; Orchestre National de France; Lorin
Maazel, conductor; CBS MK-35848 [DDD] (TT=46.06).
Includes Saint-Saëns' Concerto for 'Cello and Orchestra No.1,
Op.33, in a, rated B.

{522}   *A*   Symphonie espagnole ("Spanish Symphony") for
Violin and Orchestra, Op.21
            Itzhak Perlman, violin; Orchestre de Paris; Daniel
Barenboim, conductor; DG 400 032-2 [DDD] (TT=40.06).
Includes Berlioz' Reverie et Caprice for Violin and Orchestra,
Op.8.
            Also -- see entry No.{267}.

LEHÁR, FRANZ
1870-1948

Operatic

{523}   *A*   Die lustige Witwe ("The Merry Widow") (1905)
            Elisabeth Schwarzkopf, soprano; Hanny Steffek,
soprano; Kurt Equiluz, tenor; Nicolaï Gedda, tenor; Hans
Strohbauer, tenor; Josef Knapp, baritone; Eberhard Wächter,
baritone; Philharmonia Chorus and Orchestra; Lovro von
Matačič, conductor; Angel CDC 47177 (2 discs) [AAD]
(TT=79.42).

{524}   *C*   Der Zarewitsch ("The Czar's Son") (1927)

            Elfriede Höbarth, soprano; Lucia Popp, soprano;
Hartmut Brosius, tenor; René Kollo, tenor; Ivan Rebroff, bass;

Bavarian Radio Chorus; Munich Radio Orchestra; Heinz Wallberg, conductor; Eurodisc 258-359.

LEONCAVALLO, RUGGERO
1857-1919

Operatic
{525}   *A*   <u>Pagliacci</u> (1892)
Teresa Stratas, soprano; Florindo Andreolli, tenor; Plácido Domingo, tenor; Juan Pons, baritone; Alberto Rinaldi, baritone; Chorus and Orchestra of La Scala, Milan; George Prêtre, conductor; Philips 411 484-2 [DDD] (TT=70.40).

LISZT, FRANZ
1811-1886

Choral
{526}   *B*   <u>Christus</u> (Oratorio) (1855-1859)
Veronika Kincses, soprano; KIára Takács, mezzo-soprano; János B. Nagy, tenor; Sándor Sólyom-Nagy, baritone; László Polgár, bass; Hungarian Radio and Television Chorus; Nyiregyháza Children's Chorus; András Virágh, harmonium; Bertalan Hock, organ; Hungarian State Orchestra; Antal Doráti, conductor; Hungaroton (3 discs) [DDD] (TT=180.28).

{527}   *C*   Mass: <u>Hungarian Coronation</u> (1867)
Veronika Kincses, soprano; Klára Takács, mezzo-soprano; Dénes Gulyás, tenor; László Polgár, bass; Hungarian Radio and Television Chorus; Gábor Lehotka, organ; Budapest Symphony Orchestra; György Lehel, conductor; Hungaroton HCD 12148-2 [ADD] (TT=47.54).

{528}   *C*   Mass: Requiem (1868-1871)
Alfonz Bartha, tenor; Sándor Palcsó, tenor; Zsolt

Bende, baritone; Péter Kovács, bass; Male Chorus of the Hungarian People's Army; Sándor Margittay, organ; János Ferencsik, conductor; Hungaroton HCD 112267-2 [ADD] (TT=50.06).

Concerted

{529}   *A*   Concerto for Piano No.1, in E flat (1830-1850)
Sviatoslav Richter, piano; London Symphony Orchestra; Kiril Kondrashin, conductor; Philips 412 006-2 [ADD] (TT=41.14). Includes Liszt's Concerto for Piano No.2, in A (1830-1856), rated A.

{530}   *A*   Concerto for Piano No.2, in A (1830-1856) -- see entry No.{529}.

{531}   *A*   Fantasia on Hungarian Folk Themes for Piano and Orchestra (1852)
Jorge Bolet, piano; London Symphony Orchestra; Ivan Fischer, conductor; London 414 079-2 [DDD] (TT=46.54). Includes Liszt's Malédiction for Piano and Orchestra (1840) and Totentanz ("Dance of Death") for Piano and Orchestra (Paraphrase on Dies Irae) (1838-1859), rated C.

{532}   *C*   Totentanz ("Dance of Death") for Piano and Orchestra (Paraphrase on Dies Irae) (1838-1859) -- see entry No.{531}.

Instrumental

{533}   *B*   Années de pèlerinage (Première année -- Suisse) ("Years of Pilgrimage") ("First Year -- Switzerland") (1855)
Jorge Bolet, piano; London 410 160-2 [DDD] (TT=50.00).

{534}   *B*   Années de pèlerinage (Deuxième année -- Italie) ("Years of Pilgrimage") ("Second Year -- Italy") (1858)

Jorge Bolet, piano; London 410 161-2 [DDD] (TT=50.49).

{535}   *A*   Études d'exécution transcendante (12) ("Transcendental Etudes") Nos.1-12 (1851)
Claudio Arrau; Philips 416 458-2 [ADD] (TT=66.32).

Orchestral

{536}   *A*   Hungarian Rhapsody No.2, in c sharp (1847) -- see entry No.{266}.

{537}   *A*   Les Préludes, Symphonic Poem No.3 (1848)
a   Hungarian State Orchestra; János Ferencsik, conductor; Hungaroton HCD 12446-2 [DDD] (TT=47.45). Includes Liszt's Orpheus, Symphonic Poem No.4 (1854) and Tasso, Lamento e Trionfo, Symphonic Poem No.2 (1854). Les Préludes became quite well known (albeit subliminally) as some of the most substantial background music used in the radio and television versions of The Lone Ranger series (of yesteryear. . .).
b   Berlin Philharmonic Orchestra; Herbert von Karajan, conductor; DG 413 587-2 [DDD] (TT=63.55). Includes Liszt's Hungarian Rhapsody No.5 ("Héroïde-Élégiaque"), in e (1853), rated B; Rossini's Overture: William Tell (1829), rated A; Smetana's Vltava ("Moldau") from Má Vlast ("My Fatherland") (1874-1879), rated A and Weber's Invitation to the Dance (Orchestrated by Berlioz), Op.65, rated A.

Vocal

{538}   *B*   A Faust Symphony (1854-1857)
John Aller, tenor; Rotterdam Philharmonic Chorus and Orchestra; James Conlon, conductor; Erato ECD-88060 [DDD] (TT=73.40).

216

LITOLFF, HENRY CHARLES
1818-1891

Concerted
{539}   *C*   Concerto symphonique No.4, Op.102 (Scherzo) --
see entry No.{2}.

LUTOSLAWSKI, WITOLD
1913-

Concerted
{540}   *C*   Double Concerto for Oboe, Harp and Chamber
Orchestra (1980)
    Heinz Holliger, oboe; Ursula Holliger, harp; Cincinnati
Symphony Orchestra; Michael Gielen, conductor; Vox Cum
Laude MCD 10006 [DDD?] (TT=43.59). Includes Richard
Strauss' Concerto for Oboe and Small Orchestra, in d (1945,
1948).

Symphonic
{541}   *C*   Symphony No. 3 (1983)
a   Berlin Philharmonic Orchestra; Witold Lutoslawski,
conductor; Philips 416 387-2 [DDD] (TT=44.26). Includes
Lutoslawski's Les espaces du sommeil ("Sleep's Spaces") for
Baritone and Orchestra (1975), rated B (with baritone Dietrich
Fischer-Dieskau).
b   Los Angeles Philharmonic Orchestra; Esa-Pekka
Salonen, conductor; CBS M2K-42271 (2 discs) (TT=124.38).
Includes Lutoslawski's Les espaces du sommeil ("Sleep's
Spaces") for Baritone and Orchestra (1975), rated B (with
baritone John Shirley-Quirk) and Messiaen's Turangalîla-
Symphonie for Piano, Ondes Martenot and Orchestra (1946),
rated B, with Paul Crossley, piano and Tristan Murail, Ondes
Martenot.

Vocal

{542}   *B*   Les espaces du sommeil ("Sleep's Spaces") for
Baritone and Orchestra (1975) -- see entries Nos.{541}a-b.

MAHLER, GUSTAV
1860-1911

Symphonic

{543}   *A*   Symphony No.1 ("Titan"), in d (1888)
London Philharmonic Orchestra: Klaus Tennstedt;
Angel CDC 47884-2 [ADD] (TT=53.59).

{544}   *A*   S y m p h o n y   N o . 2   ("A u f e r s t e h u n g")
("Resurrection"), in c (1894)
a   Kathleen Battle, soprano; Maureen Forrester,
contralto; St. Louis Symphony Chorus and Orchestra; Leonard
Slatkin, conductor; Telarc CD-8 (2 discs) [DDD] (TT=81.24).
b   Emilia Cundari, soprano; Maureen Forrester, contralto;
Westminster College Choir; Columbia Symphony Orchestra;
Bruno Walter, conductor; CBS M2K-42032 (2 discs) [AAD?]
(TT=79.52).

{545}   *B*   Symphony No.3, in d (1895)
a   Marilyn Horne, mezzo-soprano; Women of the Chicago
Symphony Orchestra Chorus; Glen Ellyn Children's Chorus;
Chicago Symphony Orchestra; James Levine, conductor; RCA
RCD2-1757 (2 discs) [DDD] (TT=103.42).
b   Christa Ludwig, mezzo-soprano; Kuhn Children's
Chorus; Prague Philharmonic Chorus; Czech Philharmonic
Orchestra; Václav Neumann, conductor; Supraphon C37-7288-
7299 (2 discs) [DDD] (TT=90.34).

{546}   *A*   Symphony No.4, in G (1900)
a   Roberta Alexander, soprano; Amsterdam
Concertgebouw Orchestra; Bernard Haitink, conductor; Philips

412 119-2 [DDD] (TT=55.33).
b   Lucia Popp, soprano; London Philharmonic Orchestra; Klaus Tennstedt, conductor; Angel CDC 47024-2 [DDD] (TT=54.55).

{547}   *B*   Symphony No.5, in c sharp (1902)
a   Amsterdam Concertgebouw Orchestra; Bernard Haitink, conductor; Philips 416 469-2 [ADD] (TT=60.45).
b   London Philharmonic Orchestra; Klaus Tennstedt, conductor; Angel CDS-47104-2 (2 discs) [ADD] (TT=103.25). Includes Mahler's Symphonic Movement, Adagio and Symphony No.10 ("Unfinished") (Reconstructed by Deryck Cooke), in F, (1910), rated C.

{548}   *C*   Symphony No.6, in a (1904)
            Christa Ludwig, mezzo-soprano; Berlin Philharmonic Orchestra; Herbert von Karajan, conductor; DG 415 099-2 (2 discs) [ADD] (TT=102.04). Includes Mahler's Kindertotenlieder ("Songs on the Deaths of Children") (1902), rated A.

{549}   *B*   Symphony No.7, in e (1905)
a   Amsterdam Concertgebouw Orchestra; Bernard Haitink, conductor; Philips 410 398-2 (2 discs) [DDD] (TT=80.49).
b   Chicago Symphony Orchestra; Sir Georg Solti, conductor; London 414 675-2 (2 discs) [ADD] (TT=93.53). Includes Mahler's Des Knaben Wunderhorn ("The Youth's Magic Horn") (1892-1895), rated B (with vocal soloist Yvonne Minton, mezzo-soprano).

{550}   *B*   Symphony No.8 ("Symphony of a Thousand"), in E flat (1906)
a   Arleen Augér, soprano; Heather Harper, soprano; Lucia Popp, soprano; Yvonne Minton, mezzo-soprano; Helen Watts, contralto; René Kollo, tenor; John Shirley-Quirk,

219

baritone; Martti Talvela, bass; Chorus of the Vienna State Opera; Vienna Singverein, Vienna Boys' Choir; Chicago Symphony Orchestra; Sir Georg Solti, conductor; London 414 493-2 (2 discs) [ADD] (TT=79.36).

b   Elisabeth Connell, soprano; Felicity Lott, soprano; Trudeliese Schmidt, soprano; Edith Wiens, soprano; Nadine Denize, contralto; Richard Versalle, tenor; Jorma Hynninen, baritone; Hans Sotin, bass; Tiffin School Boys' Choir; London Philharmonic Choir and Orchestra; Klaus Tennstedt, conductor; Angel CDS 47625-8 (2 discs) [DDD] (TT=82.09).

If your library requires an absolutely state-of-the-art recording, then the Tennstedt is the one to have; if an amazingly exciting performance (provided with superb engineering) is what you need, the Solti wins, hands down.

{551}   *C*   Symphony No.9, in D (1909)
Columbia Symphony Orchestra; Bruno Walter, conductor; CBS M2K-42033 (2 discs) [AAD?] (TT=78.10).

{552}   *C*   Symphony No.10 ("Unfinished") (Reconstructed by Deryck Cooke), in F, (1910) -- see entry No.{547}b.

Vocal

{553}   *A*   Kindertotenlieder ("Songs on the Deaths of Children") (1902)

a   Dietrich Fischer-Dieskau, baritone; Berlin Philharmonic Orchestra; Rudolf Kempe, conductor; Angel CDC 47657-2 ! [ADD] (TT=62.29). Includes Mahler's Lieder eines fahrenden Gesellen ("Songs of a Wayfaring Youth") (1883), rated B (in this work, Fischer-Dieskau is accompanied by the Philharmonia Orchestra conducted by Wilhelm Furtwängler) and Rückertlieder (Five "Songs on Poems of Rückert") Nos.1-5 (1902), rated B (in these, the only stereo recordings on this disc, Fischer-Dieskau is accompanied by pianist Daniel Barenboim).

b   Dietrich Fischer-Dieskau, baritone; Berlin Philharmonic Orchestra; DG 415 191-2 [ADD] (TT=59.32). This disc has exactly the same program as entry No.{553}a, but is entirely in stereo and employs the orchestral, rather than piano, accompaniment for the Rückertlieder. My own nod goes to entry No.{553}a, despite entry No.{553}b's fresher stereo sound: in any event, both are superb.
Also -- see entry No.{548}.

{554}   C   Das klagende Lied ("The Song of Lament") (1898)
Helena Döse, soprano; Alfreda Hodgson, mezzo-soprano; Robert Tear, tenor; Sean Rae, baritone; City of Birmingham (England) Symphony Chorus and Orchestra; Simon Rattle, conductor; Angel CDC 47089 [DDD] (TT=65.11).

{555}   B   Des Knaben Wunderhorn ("The Youth's Magic Horn") (1892-1895)
a   Lucia Popp, soprano; Bernd Weikl, baritone; London Philharmonic Orchestra; Klaus Tennstedt, conductor; Angel CDC 49045 [DDD] (TT=52.52).
b   Elisabeth Schwarzkopf, soprano; Dietrich Fischer-Dieskau, baritone; London Symphony Orchestra; George Szell, conductor; Angel CDC 47277 [ADD] (TT=50.26).
Also -- see entry No.{549}.

{556}   A   Das Lied von der Erde ("The Song of the Earth") (1908)
a   Kathleen Ferrier, contralto; Julius Patzak, tenor; Vienna Philharmonic Orchestra; Bruno Walter, conductor; London 414 194-2 ! [ADD] (TT=60.19).
b   Brigitte Fassbaender, mezzo-soprano; Francisco Araiza, tenor; Berlin Philharmonic Orchestra; Carlo Maria Giulini, conductor; DG 413 459-2 [DDD] (TT=64.19).

c   Mildred Miller, mezzo-soprano; Ernst Haefliger, tenor; Columbia Symphony Orchestra; Bruno Walter, conductor; [AAD?] (TT=63.15).

Of the three above, No.{556}a is an historical recording of incredible poignancy and artistry. No.{556} is an exceptionally fine stereo version, but the last of the three holds its own very well (Fassbaender is better than Miller but Araiza has been bettered by both Patzak and Haefliger).

{557}   *B*   <u>Lieder eines fahrenden Gesellen</u> ("Songs of a Wayfaring Youth") (1883) -- see entries Nos.{553}a-b.

{558}   *B*   <u>Rückertlieder</u> (Five "Songs on Poems of Rückert") Nos.1-5 (1902) -- see entries Nos.{553}a-b.

MARCELLO, ALESSANDRO
1669-1747

Concerted
{559}   *A*   Concerto for Oboe and Strings, in d (1716) -- see entry No.{5}.

MASCAGNI, PIETRO
1863-1945

Operatic
{560}   *C*   <u>L'Amico Fritz</u> (1891)

Mirella Freni, soprano; Laura Didier Gambardella, mezzo-soprano; Luciano Pavarotti, tenor; Vicenzo Sardinero, baritone; Royal Opera Chorus and Orchestra, Covent Garden; Gianandrea Gavazzeni, conductor; Angel CDCB 47905 (2 discs) [ADD] (TT=92.48).

{561}   *A*   <u>Cavalleria Rusticana</u> (1890)
Renata Scotto, soprano; Plácido Domingo, tenor; Pablo Elvira, baritone; Ambrosian Opera Chorus; National Philharmonic Orchestra of London; James Levine, conductor; RCA RCD2-3091 [ADD] (TT=70.50).

MASSENET, JULES
1842-1912

Operatic
{562}   *B*   <u>Manon</u> (1884)
Ileana Cotrubas, soprano; Ghyslaine Raphael, soprano; Martine Mahé, mezzo soprano; Charles Burles, tenor; Alfredo Kraus, tenor; Gino Quilico, baritone; Jean-Marie Frémaux, baritone; José van Dam, bass-baritone; Toulouse Capitole Chorus and Orchestra; Michel Plasson, conductor; Angel CDS 49610 (3 discs) [DDD] (TT=154.22).

MENDELSSOHN, FELIX
1809-1847

Chamber
{563}   *A*   Octet for Strings (Orchestral Version), Op.20, in E flat
St. Paul Chamber Orchestra; Pinchas Zukerman, conductor; Philips 412 212-2 [DDD] (TT=61.57). Includes Mendelssohn's Concerto for Violin, Op.64, in e, rated A (with Pinchas Zukerman as both soloist and conductor).
Also -- see entry No.{113}.

{564}   *A*   Trios for Piano, Violin and 'Cello (2), Nos.1-2: Op.49, in d and Op.66, in c

Joseph Kalichstein, piano; Jaime Laredo, violin; Sharon Robinson, 'cello; Vox Cum Laude MCD 10023 [DDD] (TT = 57.59).

Choral

{565}   *B*   Oratorio Elijah, Op.70
Elly Ameling, soprano; Anneliese Rothenberger, soprano; Peter Schreier, tenor; Theo Adam, bass; Leipzig Radio Chorus; Leipzig Gewandhaus Orchestra; Wolfgang Sawallisch, conductor; Philips 420 106-2 (2 discs) [AAD] (TT = 130.47).

Concerted

{566}   *A*   Concerto for Violin, Op.64, in e
Jascha Heifetz, violin; Boston Symphony Orchestra; Charles Munch, conductor; RCA 5933-2 RC [ADD] (TT = 64.29). Includes Tchaikovsky's Concerto for Violin, Op.35, in D (performed by Heifetz with the Chicago Symphony Orchestra, Fritz Reiner conducting), rated A, Sérénade mélancolique for Violin and Orchestra, Op.26, rated B and Waltz from Serenade in C, Op.48 (Arranged for Violin and Orchestra) (these last 2 items performed by Heifetz with a "chamber orchestra" and no conductor given), rated A.
Also -- see entries Nos.{256} and {563}.

Orchestral

{567}   *A*   A Midsummer Night's Dream, Op.21 and Op.61
Heather Harper, soprano; Dame Janet Baker, mezzo-soprano; Philharmonia Chorus and Orchestra; Otto Klemperer, conductor; Angel CDC 47230-2 [ADD] (TT = 48.29).

{568}   *A*   Overture: A Midsummer Night's Dream, Op.21
London Symphony Orchestra; Claudio Abbado, conductor; DG 415 973-2 [DDD] (TT = 65.12). Includes

Mendelssohn's Overture: <u>Fair Melusine</u>, Op.32 and Symphony No.3 ("Scottish"), Op.56, in a, rated A.

{569} *A* "Wedding March" from <u>A Midsummer Night's Dream</u>, Op.21 -- see entry No.{290}.

Symphonic
{570} *A* Symphony No.3 ("Scottish"), Op.56, in a -- see entry No.{568}.

{571} *A* Symphony No.4 ("Italian"), Op.90, in Λ

a   London Symphony Orchestra; Claudio Abbado, conductor; DG 415 974-2 [DDD] (TT=58.54). Includes Mendelssohn's Symphony No.5 ("Reformation"), Op.107, in D, rated B.

b   Philharmonia Orchestra; Giuseppe Sinopoli, conductor; DG 410 862-222 [DDD] (TT-61.09). Includes Schubert's Symphony No.8 ("Unfinished"), D.759, in b, rated A.

c   USSR Symphony Orchestra; Yevgeny Svetlanov, conductor; Mobile Fidelity (Melodia) MFCD 863 [DDD] (TT=43.18). Includes Rossini's Overture: <u>William Tell</u> (1829), rated A.

{572} *B* Symphony No.5 ("Reformation" Symphony), Op.107, in D -- see entry No.{571}a.

MENOTTI, GIAN CARLO
1911-

Operatic
{573} *A* <u>Amahl and the Night Visitors</u> (1946)

James Rainbird, treble; Lorna Haywood, soprano; John Dobson, tenor; Donald Maxwell, baritone; Curtis Watson, bass; Chorus and Orchestra of the Royal Opera House, Covent

Garden; David Syrus, conductor; MCA MCAD-6218 [DDD] (TT=49.22).

MESSIAEN, OLIVIER
1908-

Chamber

{574}   *A*   Quatuor pour la fin du temps ("Quartet for the End of Time") for Clarinet, Violin, 'Cello and Piano (1941)
Claude Desurmont, clarinet; Luben Yordanoff, violin; Albert Tétard, 'cello; Daniel Barenboim, piano; DG 423 247-2 [ADD] (TT=49.11).

Symphonic

{575}   *B*   Turangalîla-Symphonie for Piano, Ondes Martenot and Orchestra (1946) -- see entry No.{541}b.

MILHAUD, DARIUS
1892-1974

Ballet

{576}   *B*   Le Boeuf sur le toit ("The Nothing-Doing Bar") (1919)
Orchestra of Radio Luxembourg; Louis de Froment, conductor; Vox Prima MWCD 7152 [ADD?] (TT=50.34). Includes Poulenc's Les Biches ("The Unsullied Wanton Young Ladies") (1923), rated C and Satie's Parade (1917), rated B.

{577}   *B*   La Création du monde ("The Creation of the World") (1923)
Sinfonia da Camera; Ian Hobson, conductor; Arabesque Z6569 [DDD] (TT=46.39). Includes Milhaud's Caramel mou (1920) (with Ian Hobson, piano), Suite for Violin, Clarinet and Piano (1936) (with Catherine Tait, violin;

226

Howard Klug, clarinet and Ian Hobson, piano), <u>Scaramouche</u>, for Two Pianos (1937) (with Claude Hobson, piano and Ian Hobson, piano) and <u>Three Rag Caprices</u> (1922) (with Ian Hobson, piano).

MONTEVERDI, CLAUDIO
1567-1643

Operatic

{578} *B* <u>L'Orfeo</u> ("Orpheus") (1607)
Chiaroscuro (Vocal Ensemble); London Baroque; London Cornett and Sackbut Ensemble; Charles Medlam, conductor; Angel CDCC 47141 (2 discs) [DDD] (TT – 104.13).

{579} *A* "Lamento di Penelope" from <u>Il Ritorno d'Ulisse in Patria</u> ("The Return of Ulysses to His Homeland") (1641) -- see entry No.{580}.

Vocal

{580} *C* <u>O Bone Jesu</u> for 2 Sopranos and Continuo (1622)
Emma Kirkby, soprano; Evelyn Tubb, soprano; Consort of Musicke; Anthony Rooley, conductor; MCA MCAD-25189 [DDD] (TT=68.04). Includes Monteverdi's <u>Cantate Domino</u> for 2 Sopranos and Continuo (1620), <u>Chimoe d'oro</u> for 2 Voices and Continuo (1619), <u>O Come sei gentile</u> for 2 Sopranos and Continuo (1619), <u>Exulta filia Sion</u> for Soprano and Continuo (1622?) (with Emma Kirkby, soprano, as soloist), <u>Io son pure vezzosetta</u> for 2 Sopranos and Continuo (1619), <u>Iste confessor Domini sacratus</u> (Secondo) for 2 Sopranos and Continuo from <u>Selva Morale e Spirituale</u> ("Moral and Spiritual Forest" -- Venetian Vesper Music) (1640), rated C, "Lamento di Penelope" from <u>Il Ritorno d'Ulisse in Patria</u> ("The Return of Ulysses to His Homeland") (1641) (with Evelyn Tubb, soprano, as soloist), rated A, <u>Laudate Dominum</u> for 1 Voice and Continuo (1651) (with Evelyn Tubb, soprano, as soloist), <u>Non é</u>

de gentil core for 2 Sopranos and Continuo (1619), <u>Ohimé, dov'é il mio ben</u> for 2 Sopranos and Continuo (1619), <u>Sancta Maria</u> for 2 Sopranos and Continuo (1627), <u>Se pur destina</u> for 1 Voice and Continuo (1631?) and <u>Venite, venite sitientes ad aquas Domini</u> for 2 Sopranos and Continuo (1624).

{581}   C   Hymnus, Motet and Psalm 109 from <u>Selva Morale e Spirituale</u> ("Moral and Spiritual Forest" -- Venetian Vesper Music) (1640)
        Emma Kirkby, soprano; Rogers Covey-Crump, tenor; Nigel Rogers, tenor; Taverner Choir, Consort and Players; Andrew Parrott, conductor; Angel CDC 47016-2 [DDD] (TT=66.39).
        Also -- see entry No.{580}.

{582}   B   <u>Vespro della Beata Virgine</u> ("Vespers of the Blessed Virgin") (1610)
        Emma Kirkby, soprano; Nigel Rogers, tenor; Taverner Choir, Consort and Players; Andrew Parrott, conductor; Angel CDCB 47077 (2 discs) [DDD] (TT=105.38).

MOURET, JEAN-JOSEPH
1682-1738

Orchestral
{583}   A   Symphonic Suite No.1 (1729) -- see entries Nos.{6}b and {290}.

MOZART, LEOPOLD
1719-1787

Concerted
{584}   C   Concerto for Trumpet, in D (1762) -- see entry No.{464}.

MOZART, WOLFGANG AMADEUS
1756-1791

Chamber

{585}   *C*   Divertimento <u>Ein musikalischer Spass</u> ("A Musical Joke"), K.522

Gerd Seifert, horn; Manfred Klier, horn; Amadeus Quartet; DG 400 065-2 [DDD] (TT=36.42). Includes Mozart's Serenade (<u>Eine kleine Nachtmusik</u>) ("A Little Night Music") for Strings, in G, K.525, rated A, with Rainer Zepperitz, double-bass, Amadeus Quartet.

{586}   *B*   Duo for Violin and Viola, K.424, in B flat

Ani Kavafian, violin; Ida Kavafian, viola; Nonesuch 79117-2 [DDD] (TT=46.19). Includes Moszkowski's Suite for Two Violins and Piano, Op.71, in g and Sarasate's <u>Navarra</u> (Spanish Dance) for Two Violins and Piano, Op.33 (in the Moszkowski and Sarasate works, the Kavafian sisters both play violins, and the pianist is Jonathan Feldman).

{587}   *A*   Quartet for Piano and Strings, K.478, in g

Beaux Arts Trio; Bruno Giuranna, viola; Philips 410 391-2 [DDD] (TT=61.07). Includes Mozart's Quartet for Piano and Strings, K.493, in E flat, rated A.

{588}   *A*   Quartet for Piano and Strings, K.493, in E flat -- see entry No.{587}.

{589}   *A*   Quintet for Clarinet and String Quartet, K.581, in A

Bohuslav Zahradnik, clarinet; Talich Quartet; Calliope CAL 9628 [AAD] (TT=73.11). Includes Mozart's Sonatas for Violin and Piano, K.376, in F and K.481, in E flat, both rated A.

{590}   *A*   Quintet for Piano, Oboe, Clarinet, Horn and Bassoon, K.452, in E flat -- see entry No.{114}.

{591}   *B*   Rondo for Horn and Orchestra, K.371, in E flat
          Elizabeth Halloin, horn; Chicago Chamber Brass; Dallas Wind Symphony; Howard Dunn, conductor; Crystal CD 431 [DDD] (TT=68.32). Includes Artunian's Concerto for Trumpet and Band (1950) (with Paul Johnson, trumpet); Bozza's Rustiques for Trumpet and Band (with William Camp, trumpet); Clarke's The Bride of the Waves, for Tuba and Band (with Richard Frazier, tuba); Jacob's Music for a Festival, for Brass and Band (1951) and Llewellyn's My Regards (with Steven Gamble, trombone).

{592}   *B*   Serenade No.5, K.204, in D
          Collegium Aureum; Fransjosef Maier, conductor; Angel CDC 47823-2 [DDD] (TT=43.43).

{593}   *A*   Serenade ("Serenata notturna") No.6, K.239, in D
          I Musici; Philips 412 120-2 [DDD] (TT=46.14). Includes Mozart's Divertimenti K.136, in D; K.137, in B flat and K.138, in F.

{594}   *B*   Serenade ("Posthorn") No.9, K.320, in D
          Michael Laird, posthorn; Academy of St. Martin-in-the-Fields, Sir Neville Marriner, conductor; Philips 412 752-2 [DDD] (TT=51.46). Includes Mozart's Marches, K.352 Nos.1-2, in D and D.

{595}   *A*   Serenade No.10, K.361, for 13 Wind Instruments, in B flat
          Orpheus Chamber Orchestra; DG 324 061-2 [DDD] (TT=50.43).

{596}   *A*   Serenade (Eine kleine Nachtmusik) ("A Little Night Music") for Strings, in G, K.525

Guarneri Quartet; Julius Levine, double-bass; RCA RCD1-5167 [DDD] (TT=57.23). Includes Schubert's Piano Quintet (<u>Die Forelle</u>) ("Trout"), D.667, in A, rated A. The pianist in the Schubert is Emanuel Ax.
Also -- see entries Nos.{415} and {585}.

{597}   *B*   Sonata for Violin and Piano, K.296, in C
Itzhak Perlman, violin; Daniel Barenboim, piano; DG 415 102-2 [DDD] (TT=54.01). Includes Mozart's Sonatas for Violin and Piano, K.305, in A, rated A and K.306, in D, both rated A.

{598}   *A*   Sonata for Violin and Piano, K.301, in G
Itzhak Perlman, violin; Daniel Barenboim, piano; DG 410 896-2 [DDD] (TT=46.53). Includes Mozart's Sonatas for Violin and Piano, K.302, in E flat; K.303, in C and K.304, in e, all rated A.

{599}   *A*   Sonata for Violin and Piano, K.302, in E flat -- see entry No.{598}.

{600}   *A*   Sonata for Violin and Piano, K.303, in C -- see entry No.{598}.

{601}   *A*   Sonata for Violin and Piano, K.304, in e -- see entry No.{598}.

{602}   *A*   Sonata for Violin and Piano, K.305, in A -- see entry No.{597}.

{603}   *A*   Sonata for Violin and Piano, K.306, in D -- see entry No.{597}.

{604}   *A*   Sonata for Violin and Piano, K.376, in F -- see entry No.{589}.

{605}   *A*   Sonata for Violin and Piano, K.454, in B flat
               Sergiu Luca, violin; Malcolm Bilson, fortepiano;
Nonesuch 79112-2 [DDD] (TT=60.42). Includes Mozart's
Sonatas for Violin and Piano, K.526, in A and K.547, in F, both
rated A.

{606}   *A*   Sonata for Violin and Piano, K.481, in E flat -- see
entry No.{589}.

{607}   *A*   Sonata for Violin and Piano, K.526, in A -- see
entry No.{605}.

{608}   *A*   Sonata for Violin and Piano, K.547, in F -- see
entry No.{605}.

{609}   *C*   String Quartet No.3, K.156, in G
               Sequoia String Quartet; Nonesuch 79026-2 [DDD]
(TT=51.35). Includes Mozart's String Quartets Nos.4, K.157,
in C; 8, K.168, in F and 13, K.173, in d, all rated C.

{610}   *C*   String Quartet No.4, K.157, in C -- see entry
No.{609}.

{611}   *C*   String Quartet No.8, K.168, in F -- see entry
No.{609}.

{612}   *C*   String Quartet No.13, K.173, in d -- see entry
No.{609}.

{613}   *B*   String Quartet No.14, K.387, in G
               Kocian Quartet; Denon C37-7228 [DDD] (TT=60.26).
Includes Mozart's String Quartet No.15, K.421, in d, rated B.

{614}   *B*   String Quartet No.15, K.421, in d -- see entry
No.{613}.

{615}   *A*   String Quartet No.17 (<u>Jagdquartett</u>) ("The Hunt Quartet"), K.458, in B flat
Salomon Quartet; Hyperion A66234 [DDD] (TT=68.08). Includes Mozart's String Quartet No.18, K.464, in A, rated A.
Also -- see entry No.{457}.

{616}   *A*   String Quartet No.18, K.464, in A -- see entry No.{615}.

{617}   *A*   String Quartet No.21, K.575, in D
Orlando Quartet; Philips 412 121-2 [DDD] (TT=49.51). Includes Mozart's String Quartet No.22, K.589, in B flat, rated A.

{618}   *A*   String Quartet No.22, K.589, in B flat -- see entry No.{617}.

{619}   *A*   String Quintets (6) Nos.1-6: K.174, in B flat; K.515, in C; K.516, in g; K.406, in c; K.593, in D and K.614, in E flat
Grumiaux Trio; Arpad Géreca, violin; Max Lesueur, viola; Eva Czako, 'cello; Philips 416 486-2 (3 discs) [ADD] (TT=170.03).

Choral

{620}   *B*   <u>Ave, verum corpus</u> ("Hail, True Flesh"), K.618
Dame Kiri Te Kanawa, soprano; Elizabeth Bainbridge, mezzo-soprano; Ryland Davies, tenor; Gwenny Howell, bass; London Symphony Chorus and Orchestra; Sir Colin Davis, conductor; Philips 412 873-2 [ADD] (TT=56.10). Includes Mozart's <u>Exsultate, jubilate</u> ("Rejoice, Be Jubilant!") (Motet for Soprano and Orchestra), K.165, rated A, <u>Kyrie</u>, in d, K.341, rated C and <u>Vesperae solennes de confessore</u> ("Solemn Vespers of the Confessor"), K.339, rated A.

{621}   *C*   K̲y̲r̲i̲e̲, in d, K.341 -- see entry No.{620}.

{622}   *B*   Mass ("Coronation"), K.317
          Margaret Marshall, soprano; Ann Murray, mezzo-
soprano; Rogers Covey-Crump, tenor; David Wilson-Johnson,
bass; King's College Choir, Cambridge (England); English
Chamber Orchestra; Stephen Cleobury, conductor; Argo 411
904-2 [DDD] (TT=49.27). Includes Mozart's Missa Solemnis,
K.337, rated B.

{623}   *A*   Mass, in c ("Great"), K.427
          Barbara Hendricks, soprano; Janet Perry, soprano;
Peter Schreier, tenor; Benjamin Luxon, baritone; Vienna
Singverein der Gesellschaft der Musikfreunde; Berlin
Philharmonic Orchestra; Herbert von Karajan, conductor; DG
400 067-2 [DDD] (TT=58.23).
          Also -- see entry No.{134}a.

{624}   *B*   Missa Solemnis, K.337 -- see entry No.{622}.

{625}   *A*   Requiem, K.626 (Completed by Süssmayr)
a   Arleen Augér, soprano; Delores Ziegler, mezzo-
soprano; Jerry Hadley, tenor; Tom Krause, bass; Atlanta
Symphony Chorus and Orchestra; Robert Shaw, conductor;
Telarc CD-80128 [DDD] (TT=51.46).
b   Edith Mathis, soprano; Julia Hamari, contralto;
Wiesław Ochman, tenor; Karl Ridderbusch, bass; Vienna State
Opera Chorus; Vienna Philharmonic Orchestra; Karl Böhm,
conductor; DG 413 553-2 [ADD] (TT=64.26).

{626}   *A*   V̲e̲s̲p̲e̲r̲a̲e̲ ̲s̲o̲l̲e̲n̲n̲e̲s̲ ̲d̲e̲ ̲c̲o̲n̲f̲e̲s̲s̲o̲r̲e̲ ("Solemn
Vespers of the Confessor"), K.339 -- see entry No.{620}.

                    Concerted
{627}   *A*   Concerto for Clarinet, K.622, in A

                        234

Charles Neidich, basset horn; Orpheus Chamber Orchestra; DG 423 377-2 [DDD] (TT = 48.15). Includes Mozart's Concerti for Horn, Nos.1 and 4, K.412, in D, rated A and K.495, in E flat, rated A (the horn soloist is David Jolley).

{628}   *A*   Concerto for Flute, Harp and Orchestra, K.299, in C

Jean-Pierre Rampal, flute; Lily Laskine, harp; Jean-François Paillard Chamber Orchestra; Jean-François Paillard, conductor; Erato ECD-88069 [AAD] (TT = 66.29). Includes Boieldieu's Concerto for Harp, (c.1799), in C and Pierné's Konzertstück for Harp and Orchestra, Op.39, in G sharp.

{629}   *A*   Concerti for Horn and Orchestra (4) Nos.1-4: K 412, in D; K.417, in E flat; K.417, in E flat and K.495, in E flat

Herrmann Baumann, horn; St. Paul Chamber Orchestra; Pinchas Zukerman, conductor; Philips 412 7337-2 [DDD] (TT = 55.57).
Also -- see entry No.{627}.

{630}   *A*   Concerto for Oboe and Orchestra, K.314, in C
Heinz Holliger, oboe; Academy of St. Martin-in-the-Fields, Sir Neville Marriner, conductor; Philips 411 132-2 [DDD] (TT = 48.06). Includes Mozart's Sinfonia Concertante for Flute, Oboe, Horn, Bassoon and Orchestra, K.297b, in E flat, rated A (with Aurèle Nicolet, flute; Heinz Holliger, oboe; Hermann Baumann, horn and Klaus Thuneman, bassoon).

{631}   *B*   Concerto for Piano and Orchestra No.9 ("Jeunehomme"), K.271, in E flat
Malcolm Bilson, fortepiano; English Baroque Soloists, John Eliot Gardiner, conductor; Archiv 410 905-2 [DDD] (TT = 52.53). Includes Mozart's Concerto for Piano and Orchestra No.11, K.413, in F, rated B.

{632}   *B*   Concerto for Piano and Orchestra No.11, K.413, in F -- see entry No.{631}.

{633}   *A*   Concerto for Piano and Orchestra No.12, K.414, in A
a   Vladimir Ashkenazy, piano; Philharmonia Orchestra; Vladimir Ashkenazy, conductor; London 410 214-2 [DDD] (TT = 55.04). Includes Mozart's Concerto for Piano and Orchestra No.13, K.415, in C, rated B.
b   Malcolm Bilson, fortepiano; English Baroque Soloists; John Eliot Gardiner, conductor; Archiv 413 463-2 [DDD] (TT = 45.26). Includes Mozart's Concerto for Piano and Orchestra No.14, K.449, in E flat, rated B.

{634}   *B*   Concerto for Piano and Orchestra No.13, K.415, in C -- see entry No.{633}a.

{635}   *B*   Concerto for Piano and Orchestra No.14, K.449, in E flat -- see entry No.{633}b.

{636}   *B*   Concerto for Piano and Orchestra No.15, K.450, in B flat
           Alfred Brendel, piano; Academy of St. Martin-in-the-Fields, Sir Neville Marriner, conductor; Philips 400 018-2 [DDD] (TT = 51.56). Includes Mozart's Concerto for Piano and Orchestra No.21 ("Elvira Madigan"), K.467, in C, rated A.

{637}   *A*   Concerto for Piano and Orchestra No.17, K.453, in G
           Murray Perahia, piano; English Chamber Orchestra; Murray Perahia, conductor; CBS MK-36686 [DDD] (TT = 59.00). Includes Mozart's Concerto for Piano and Orchestra No.18, K.456, in B flat, rated B.

{638}   *B*   Concerto for Piano and Orchestra No.18, K.456, in B flat -- see entry No.{637}.

{639}   *A*   Concerto for Piano and Orchestra No.19, K.459, in F

a   Murray Perahia, piano; English Chamber Orchestra; Murray Perahia, conductor; CBS MK-39064 [DDD] (TT=56.00). Includes Mozart's Concerto for Piano and Orchestra No.23, K.488, in A, rated A.

b   Vladimir Ashkenazy, piano; Philharmonia Orchestra; Vladimir Ashkenazy, conductor; London 414 433-2 [ADD] (TT=61.23). Includes Mozart's Concerto for Piano and Orchestra No.24, K.491, in c, rated A.

{640}   *A*   Concerto for Piano and Orchestra No.20, K.466, in d

a   Sir Clifford Curzon, piano; English Chamber Orchestra; Benjamin Britten, conductor; London 417 288-2 [ADD] (TT=65.03). Includes Mozart's Concerto for Piano and Orchestra No.27, K.595, in B flat, rated A.

b   Steven Lubin, fortepiano; Mozartean Players; Arabesque Z6530 [DDD?] (TT=55.13). Includes Mozart's Concerto for Piano and Orchestra No.23, K.488, in A, rated A.

{641}   *A*   Concerto for Piano and Orchestra No.21 ("Elvira Madigan"), K.467, in C -- see entry No.{636}.

{642}   *A*   Concerto for Piano and Orchestra No.23, K.488, in A -- see entries Nos.{639}a and {640}b.

{643}   *A*   Concerto for Piano and Orchestra No.24, K.491, in c -- see entry No.{639}b.

{644}   *A*   Concerto for Piano and Orchestra No.25, K.503, in C

a   Malcolm Bilson, fortepiano; English Baroque Soloists; John Eliot Gardiner, conductor; DG 423 119-2 [DDD] (TT=61.21). Includes Mozart's Concerto for Piano and Orchestra No.26 ("Coronation"), K.537, in D, rated A.

237

b   Murray Perahia, piano; English Chamber Orchestra; Murray Perahia, conductor; CBS MK-37267 [DDD] (TT=53.29). Includes Mozart's Concerto for Piano and Orchestra No.5, K.175, in D.

{645}   *A*   Concerto for Piano and Orchestra No.26 ("Coronation"), K.537, in D
           Murray Perahia, piano; English Chamber Orchestra; Murray Perahia, conductor; CBS MK-39224 [DDD] (TT=51.33). Includes Mozart's Rondos for Piano and Orchestra, K.382, in D and K.386, in A, the latter rated C.
           Also -- see entry No.{644}a.

{646}   *A*   Concerto for Piano and Orchestra No.27, K.595, in B flat -- see entry No.{640}a.

{647}   *B*   Concerto for Violin and Orchestra No.1, K.207, in B flat
           Gidon Kremer, violin; Vienna Philharmonic Orchestra; Nikolaus Harnoncourt, conductor; DG 413 461-2 [DDD] (TT=55.09). Includes Mozart's Sinfonia Concertante for Violin, Viola and Orchestra, K.364, in E flat, rated A, with Gidon Kremer, violin and Kim Kashkashian, viola.

{648}   *B*   Concerto for Violin and Orchestra No.2, K.211, in D
a   Iona Brown, violin; Academy of St. Martin-in-the-Fields; Iona Brown, conductor; MHS 11143A [DDD] TT=49.44). Includes Mozart's Sinfonia Concertante for Violin, Viola and Orchestra, K.364, in E flat, rated A.
b   Itzhak Perlman, violin; Vienna Philharmonic Orchestra; James Levine, conductor; DG 415 975-2 [DDD] (TT=42.17). Includes Mozart's Concerto for Violin and Orchestra No.4, K.218, in D, rated A.

Both of these performances are extremely fine. What can break the tie is which coupling is more important for your library.

{649}   *B*   Concerto for Violin and Orchestra No.3, K.216, in G

a   Zino Francescatti, violin; Columbia Symphony Orchestra; Bruno Walter, conductor; CBS MK 42030 [AAD?] (TT=52.27). Includes Mozart's Concerto for Violin and Orchestra No.4, K.218, in D, rated A.

b   Arthur Grumiaux, violin; London Symphony Orchestra; Sir Colin Davis, conductor; Philips 412 250-2 [ADD] (TT=49.00). Includes Mozart's Concerto for Violin and Orchestra No.5 ("Turkish"), K.219, in G, rated A.

{650}   *A*   Concerto for Violin and Orchestra No.4, K.218, in D -- see entries Nos.{648}b and {649}a.

{651}   *A*   Concerto for Violin and Orchestra No.5 ("Turkish"), K.219, in G -- see entry No.{649}b.

{652}   *C*   Rondo for Piano and Orchestra, K.386, in A -- see entry No.{645}.

{653}   *A*   Sinfonia Concertante for Flute, Oboe, Horn, Bassoon and Orchestra, K.297b, in E flat -- see entry No.{630}.

{654}   *A*   Sinfonia Concertante for Violin, Viola and Orchestra, K.364, in E flat -- see entries Nos.{55}, {647} and {648}a.

Instrumental

{655}   *B*   Adagio for Piano, K.540, in b
Claudio Arrau, piano; Philips 411 136-2 [DDD] (TT=40.06). Includes Mozart's Sonatas for Piano Nos.16, K.570, in B flat and 17, K.576, in D, both rated A.

{656}   *A*   Fantasia, K.475, in c
Andras Schiff, piano; London 417 149-2 [ADD]
(TT = 63.10). Includes Mozart's Sonatas for Piano Nos.13,
K.333 in B flat; 14, K.457, in c and 15, K.545, in C, all rated A.

{657}   *A*   Sonata for Piano No.8, K.310, in a
Claudio Arrau, piano; Philips 416 648-2 [DDD]
(TT = 48.14). Includes Mozart's Sonata for Piano No.10, K.330,
in C, rated A.

{658}   *A*   Sonata for Piano No.10, K.330, in C -- see entry
No.{657}.

{659}   *A*   Sonata for Piano No.11, K.331, in A
Mitsuko Uchida, piano; Philips 412 123-2 [DDD]
(TT = 49.48). Includes Mozart's Sonata for Piano No.12, K.332,
in F, rated A. The K.331 has, for its last movement, the
popular rondo: Alla Turca.
Also -- see entry No.{276}.

{660}   *A*   Sonata for Piano No.12, K.332, in F -- see entry
No.{659}.

{661}   *A*   Sonata for Piano No.13, K.333, in B flat -- see
entry No.{656}.

{662}   *A*   Sonata for Piano No.14, K.457, in c -- see entry
No.{656}.

{663}   *A*   Sonata for Piano No.15, K.545, in C -- see entry
No.{656}.

{664}   *A*   Sonata for Piano No.16, K.570, in B flat -- see
entry No.{655}.

{665}   *A*   Sonata for Piano No.17, K.576, in D -- see entry No.{655}.

Operatic

{666}   *A*   Così fan tutte ("Thus Are All Women"), K.588
a   Montserrat Caballé, soprano; Ileana Cotrubas, soprano; Dame Janet Baker, mezzo-soprano; Nicolaï Gedda, tenor; Wladimiro Ganzarolli, baritone; Richard Van Allan, bass; Chorus and Orchestra of the Royal Opera House, Covent Garden (London); Sir Colin Davis, conductor; Philips 416 633-2 (3 discs) [DDD] (182.40).

b   Elisabeth Schwarzkopf, soprano; Hanny Steffek, soprano; Christa Ludwig, mezzo-soprano; Alfredo Kraus, tenor; Giuseppe Taddei, baritone; Walter Berry, bass; Philharmonia Chorus and Orchestra; Karl Böhm, conductor; Angel CMS 69330 (3 discs) [ADD] (TT = 165.23).

c   Carol Vaness, soprano; Lillian Watson, soprano; Delores Ziegler, soprano; John Aler, tenor; Dale Duesing, baritone; Claudio Desderi, bass; Glyndebourne Chorus; London Philharmonic Orchestra; Bernard Haitink, conductor; Angel CDCC 47727 (3 discs) [DDD] (TT = 186.07).
          Of the above 3 Cosìs: Davis' is safe, Böhm's is great, and Haitink's is superb (it has the edge on sound, too).

{667}   *A*   Don Giovanni, K.527
a   Elisabeth Schwarzkopf, soprano; Graziella Sciutti, soprano; Dame Joan Sutherland, soprano; Luigi Alva, tenor; Piero Cappuccilli, baritone; Giuseppe Taddei, baritone; Eberhard Wächter, baritone; Gottlob Frick, bass; Philharmonia Chorus and Orchestra; Carlo Maria Giulini, conductor; Angel CDCC 47260 (3 discs) [ADD] (TT = 162.10).

b   Kathleen Battle, soprano; Anna Tomowa-Sintow, soprano; Agnes Baltsa, mezzo-soprano; Gösta Winbergh, tenor; Paata Burchuladze, bass; Ferruccio Furlanetto, bass; Alexander Malta, bass; Samuel Ramey, bass; Chorus of the German Opera, Berlin; Berlin Philharmonic Orchestra;

Herbert von Karajan, conductor; DG 419 179-2 (3 discs) [DDD] (TT=178.50).

c   Edda Moser, soprano; Dame Kiri Te Kanawa, soprano; Teresa Berganza, mezzo-soprano; Kenneth Riegel, tenor; Malcolm King, bass; John Macurdy, bass; Ruggero Raimondi, bass; José Van Dam, bass; Chorus and Orchestra of the Théâtre de l'Opera, Paris; Lorin Maazel, conductor; CBS M3K 35192 (3 discs) [AAD?] (TT=168.02).

Of the 3 above listed "**Giovannis**," the Giulini has the best Don (Wächter--who brings just the right touch of febrile masculinity); the Maazel version has excellent singers in the female leads; and von Karajan tends to overload his fine cast with tempi which are a shade slow. My own favorite is the Giulini, but then, it's not "state-of-the-art" digital (but its sound does not belie its age).

{668}   *A*   Die Entführung aus dem Serail ("The Abduction from the Seraglio"), K.384

Yvonne Kenny, soprano; Lillian Watson, soprano; Wilfried Gamlich, tenor; Peter Schreier, tenor; Matti Salminen, bass; Wolfgang Reichmann, speaker; Zurich Opera House Chorus; Zurich Mozart Orchestra; Nikolaus Harnoncourt, conductor; Teldec 835673 ZB (3 discs) [DDD] (TT=135.22).

{669}   *B*   Idomeneo, ré di Creta ("Idomeneo, King of Crete"), K.366

Felicity Palmer, soprano; Trudeliese Schmidt, soprano; Rachel Yakar, soprano; Kurt Equiluz, tenor; Werner Hollweg, tenor; Robert Tear, tenor; Simon Estes, bass; Zurich Opera House Chorus; Zurich Mozart Orchestra; Nikolaus Harnoncourt, conductor; Teldec CDT 35547 (3 discs) [DDD] (TT=194.27).

{670}   *A*   Le Nozze di Figaro ("The Marriage of Figaro"), K.492

Gundula Janowitz, soprano; Edith Mathis, soprano; Tatiana Troyanos, mezzo-soprano; Dietrich Fischer-Dieskau, baritone; Hermann Prey, baritone; Chorus and Orchestra of the German Opera, Berlin; Karl Böhm, conductor; DG 415 520-2 (3 discs) [ADD] (TT=173.08).

{671}   *A*   Die Zauberflöte ("The Magic Flute"), K.620
a   Edita Gruberova, soprano; Brigitte Lindner, soprano; Lucia Popp, soprano; Marilyn Richardson, soprano; Ortrun Wenkel, mezzo-soprano; Doris Soffel, contralto; Siegfried Jerusalem, tenor; Waldemar Kmentt, tenor; Heinz Zednik, tenor; Wolfgang Brendel, baritone; Norman Bailey, bass; Roland Bracht, bass; Aage Haugland, bass; Erich Kunz, bass; André von Mattoni, speaker; Tölzer Knabenchor; Bavarian Radio Chorus and Symphony Orchestra; Bernard Haitink, conductor; Angel CDCC 47951 (3 discs) [DDD] (TT=158.25).
b   Hanneke van Bork, soprano; Christina Deutekom, soprano; Renate Holm, soprano; Pilar Lorengar, soprano; Yvonne Minton, mezzo-soprano; Hetty Plümacher, contralto; Stuart Burrows, tenor; Kurt Equiluz, tenor; René Kollo, tenor; Gerhard Stolze, tenor; Hermann Prey, baritone; Herbert Lackner, bass; Hans Sotin, bass; Martti Talvela, bass; Dietrich Fischer-Dieskau, speaker; Wolfgang Zimmer, speaker; Vienna Boys' Choir; Vienna State Opera Chorus; Vienna Philharmonic Orchestra; Sir Georg Solti, conductor; London 414 568-2 (3 discs) [ADD] (TT=156.06).

The Solti "Flute" has a good deal of "presence" (actually, a bit much for my liking) and Deutekom has more vibrato than is necessary. Still, there are many who seem to dote on that recording. Haitink's version has everything I want in this work: good singers, excellent direction, and a feeling of ensemble.

Orchestral
{672}   *A*   Overture: Così fan tutte ("Thus Are All Women"), K.588

Academy of St. Martin-in-the-Fields; Sir Neville Marriner, conductor; Angel CDC 47014 [DDD] (TT=49.46). Includes Mozart's Overtures: <u>Clemenza di Tito</u> ("Clemency of Titus"), K.621, rated B; <u>Don Giovanni</u>, K.527, rated A; <u>Die Entführung aus dem Serail</u> ("The Abduction from the Seraglio"), K.384, rated A; <u>Idomeneo, ré di Creta</u> ("Idomeneo, King of Crete"), K.366, rated B; <u>Lucio Silla</u>, K.135, rated C; <u>Le Nozze di Figaro</u> ("The Marriage of Figaro"), K.492, rated A; <u>Der Schauspieldirektor</u> ("The Impresario"), K.486, rated A and <u>Die Zauberflöte</u> ("The Magic Flute"), K.620, rated A.

{673}   B   Overture: <u>Clemenza di Tito</u> ("Clemency of Titus"), K.621 -- see entry No.{672}.

{674}   A   Overture: <u>Don Giovanni</u>, K.527 -- see entry No.{672}.

{675}   A   Overture: <u>Die Entführung aus dem Serail</u> ("The Abduction from the Seraglio"), K.384 -- see entry No.{672}.

{676}   B   Overture: <u>Idomeneo, ré di Creta</u> ("Idomeneo, King of Crete"), K.366 -- see entry No.{672}.

{677}   C   Overture: <u>Lucio Silla</u>, K.135 -- see entry No.{672}.

{678}   A   Overture: <u>Le Nozze di Figaro</u> ("The Marriage of Figaro"), K.492 -- see entry No.{672}.

{679}   A   Overture: <u>Der Schauspieldirektor</u> ("The Impresario"), K.486 -- see entry No.{672}.

{680}   A   Overture: <u>Die Zauberflöte</u> ("The Magic Flute"), K.620 -- see entry No.{672}.

Symphonic
{681}   A   Symphony No.25, K.183, in g

Academy of Ancient Music; Christopher Hogwood, conductor; L'Oiseau-Lyre 414 631-2 [ADD] (TT=58.40). Includes Mozart's Symphony No.29, K.201, in A, rated A.

{682}   *A*   Symphony No.29, K.201, in A, rated A -- see entry No.{681}.

{683}   *A*   Symphony No.31 ("Paris"), K.297, in D
Orchestra of the Eighteenth Symphony; Frans Brüggen, conductor; Philips 416 490-2 [DDD] (TT=40.03). Includes Mozart's Symphony No.35 ("Haffner"), K.385, in D, rated A.

{684}   *A*   Symphony No.35 ("Haffner"), K.385, in D
Columbia Symphony Orchestra; Bruno Walter, conductor; CBS MK 42026 [AAD?] (TT=46.10). Includes Mozart's Symphony No.39, K.453, in B flat, rated A.
Also -- see entry No.{683}.

{685}   *A*   Symphony No.36 ("Linz"), K.425, in C
a   Columbia Symphony Orchestra; Bruno Walter, conductor; CBS MK 42027 [AAD?] (TT=51.25). Includes Mozart's Symphony No.38 ("Prague"), K.504, rated A.
b   Prague   Chamber Orchestra; Sir Charles Mackerras, conductor; Telarc CD-80148 [DDD] (TT=66.14). Includes Mozart's Symphony No.38 ("Prague"), K.504, rated A.
I find it hard to choose between these two recordings: Walter's is old-fashioned and Romantic and warm, Mackerras' provides numerous repeats and moves at a proper pace. I guess, if I want to hear a glowing Mozart it's Walter, if I want to hear more closely what Mozart intended (i.e., the *da capi*), it's Mackerras.

{686}   *A*   Symphony No.38 ("Prague"), K.504, in D
Academy of Ancient Music; Christopher Hogwood, conductor; L'Oiseau-Lyre 410 233-2 [DDD] (TT=62.01).

245

Includes Mozart's Symphony No.39, K.453, in B flat, rated A. Also -- see entries Nos.{685}a-b.

{687}   *A*   Symphony No.39, K.453, in B flat -- see entries Nos.{684} and {686}.

{688}   *A*   Symphony No.40, K.550, in g
a   Columbia Symphony Orchestra; Bruno Walter, conductor; CBS MK 42028 [AAD?] (TT=56.11). Includes Mozart's Symphony No.41 ("Jupiter"), K.551, in G, rated A.
b   Philharmonia Orchestra; Otto Klemperer, conductor; Angel CDC 47852-2 [ADD] (TT=55.24). Includes Mozart's Symphony No.41 ("Jupiter"), K.551, in G, rated A.
c   Prague Chamber Orchestra; Sir Charles Mackerras, conductor; Telarc CD-80139 [DDD] (TT=71.10). Includes Mozart's Symphony No.41 ("Jupiter"), K.551, in G, rated A.
              The first two listed of the three couplings of the "last" two Mozart symphonies (actually, there are more, but not available to us) are superb. I find it difficult to choose between them. Klemperer has better recorded sound and a better orchestra. Walter has a bit more warmth (of the Viennese type). Mackerras, however has the advantages of being newly recorded digitally and including the repeats. My heart goes to Klemperer, but Mackerras is my preference for a modern recording.

{689}   *A*   Symphony No.41 ("Jupiter"), K.551, in G -- see entries No.{688}a-c.

Vocal
{690}   *A*   Exsultate, jubilate ("Rejoice, Be Jubilant!") (Motet for Soprano and Orchestra), K.165 -- see entry No.{620}.

MUSSORGSKY, MODEST
1839-1881

Instrumental

{691}   *A*   Pictures at an Exhibition (Piano Version) (1874)
Vladimir Ashkenazy, piano; London 414 386-2 [DDD]
(TT = 66.39). Includes Mussorgsky's Pictures at an Exhibition
(Orchestrated by Ravel) (1874), rated A.
Also -- see entry No.{695}.

Operatic

{692}   *A*   Boris Godounov (1874)
a   Elena Shkolnikova, soprano; Irina Arkhipova, mezzo-
soprano; Glafira Koroleva, mezzo-soprano; Nina Grigorieva,
mezzo-soprano; Anatoli Mishutin, tenor; Vladislav Piavko,
tenor; Andrei Sokolov, tenor; Alexander Voroshilo, baritone;
Artur Eisen, bass; Vladimir Matorin, bass; Alexander
Vernikov, bass; "Spring" Studio Children's Chorus; U.S.S.R.
TV and Radio Large Chorus and Symphony Orchestra;
Vladimir Fedoseyev, conductor; Philips 412 281-2 9 (3 discs)
[ADD] (TT = 198.07).
b   Ekaterina Geuorguieva, soprano; Evelyn Lear, soprano;
Méla Bougarinovitch, mezzo-soprano; Mira Kalin, mezzo-
soprano; John Lanigan, tenor; Dimitr Ouzounov, tenor; Milem
Pauutnov, tenor; Boris Christoff, bass; Jacques Mars, bass;
Kostadine Schekerlisky, bass; Chorus of the National Opera of
Sofia; Orchestre de la Société des Concerts du Conservatoire;
André Cluytens, conductor; Angel CDCC 47993 (3 discs)
[ADD] (TT = 202.57).
          The Boris on the Philips label pretty much adheres to
the revised version made by Mussorgsky himself. The Angel
recording employs the Rimsky-Korsakov reworking.
Fedoseyev's performance has a more "old Russian" feel, but
Cluytens has a better cast.

Orchestral

{693}   *C*   Khovanshchina: Prelude (1872-1880)
L'Orchestre de la Suisse Romande; Ernest Ansermet,
conductor; London 414 139-2 [AAD] (TT = 47.40). Includes

247

Mussorgsky's <u>Night on Bald Mountain</u> (Orchestrated by Rimsky-Korsakov) (1860-1866), rated A and <u>Pictures at an Exhibition</u> (Orchestrated by Ravel) (1874), rated A.
Also -- see entry No.{404}.

{694}   *A*   <u>Night on Bald Mountain</u> (Orchestrated by Rimsky-Korsakov) (1860-1866)

a   Cleveland Orchestra; Lorin Maazel, conductor; Telarc CD-80042 [DDD] (TT=40.52). Includes Mussorgsky's <u>Pictures at an Exhibition</u> (Orchestrated by Ravel) (1874), rated A.

b   St. Louis Symphony Orchestra; Leonard Slatkin, conductor; Vox Cum Laude MCD 10014 [ADD?] (TT=42.52). Includes Mussorgsky's <u>Pictures at an Exhibition</u> (Orchestrated by Ravel) (1874), rated A.

Of all the <u>Night</u> and <u>Pictures</u> couplings, I prefer the Ansermet performances; for a more recent (and truly digital) version, Maazel takes the honors. <u>Night on Bald Mountain</u> was used in the classic Disney film, <u>Fantasia</u>.
Also -- see entries Nos.{90}, {211}a and {693}.

{695}   *A*   <u>Pictures at an Exhibition</u> (Orchestrated by Ravel) (1874) -- see entries Nos.{691}, {693} and {694}a-b.

NIELSEN, CARL
1865-1931

Orchestral
{696}   *C*   <u>Helios</u> Overture, Op.17
New Stockholm Chamber Orchestra; Esa-Pekka Salonen, conductor; CBS MK42093 [DDD] (TT=46.16). Includes Nielsen's Symphony No.4 ("The Inextinguishable"), Op.29, rated B (the Symphony no.4 is performed by the Swedish Radio Symphony Orchestra).

{697}   *B*   <u>Little</u> Suite, Op.1, in a
Swedish Radio Symphony Orchestra; Esa-Pekka Salonen, conductor; CBS MK 42321 [DDD] (TT=48.14). Includes Nielsen's Symphony No.1, Op.1, in g, rated C.

Symphonic

{698}   *C*   Symphony No.1, Op.1, in g -- see entry No.{697}.

{699}   *B*   Symphony No.4 ("The Inextinguishable"), Op.29
Berlin Philharmonic Orchestra; Herbert von Karajan; DG 413 313-2 [DDD] (TT=38.26).
Also -- see entry No.{696}.

OFFENBACH, JACQUES
1819-1880

Ballet

{700}   *A*   <u>Gaîté parisienne</u> (Arranged by Manuel Rosenthal) (1938)
Boston Pops Orchestra; Arthur Fiedler, conductor; RCA RCD1-5478 [ADD?] (TT=69.42). Includes Offenbach's Overture: <u>La Belle Hélène</u> ("The Fair Helen") (1864), rated B; Galop from <u>Geneviève de Brabant</u> (1875); Overture: <u>La Grande-Duchesse de Gérolstein</u> (1867), rated C; Overture: <u>Orphée aux enfers</u> ("Orpheus in the Underworld") (Written by Carl Binder) (1858), rated C and Intermezzo (including Introduction, Minuet and Barcarolle) to <u>Les Contes d'Hoffmann</u> ("Tales of Hoffmann") (1881), rated A.
Also -- see entry No.{408}.

Operatic

{701}   *B*   <u>Les Contes d'Hoffmann</u> ("Tales of Hoffmann") (1881)
Dame Joan Sutherland, soprano; Huguette Tourangeau, mezzo-soprano; Hugues Cuénod, tenor; Plácido Domingo,

tenor; Gabriel Bacquier, baritone; Paul Plishka, bass; Radio Suisse Romande Chorus; Pro Arte of Lausanne Chorus; Du Brassus Chorus; L'Orchestre de la Suisse Romande; Sir Richard Bonynge, conductor; London 417 363-2 (2 discs) [ADD?] (TT = 142.29).

Orchestral

{702}   *B*   Overture: La Belle Hélène ("The Fair Helen") (1864) -- see entry No.{700}.

{703}   *A*   Intermezzo (including Introduction, Minuet and Barcarolle) to Les Contes d'Hoffmann ("Tales of Hoffmann") (1881) -- see entry No.{700}.

{704}   *B*   Overture: La Grande-Duchesse de Gérolstein (1867), C -- see entry No.{700}.

{705}   *C*   Overture: Orphée aux enfers ("Orpheus in the Underworld") (Written by Carl Binder) (1858) -- see entries Nos.{10} and {700}.

ORFF, CARL
1895-1982

Choral

{706}   *A*   Carmina Burana (Scenic Cantata) (1935-1936)
a   June Anderson, soprano; Philip Creech, tenor; Bernd Weikl, baritone; Chicago Symphony Chorus and Orchestra; James Levine, conductor; DG 415 136-2 [DDD] (TT = 62.00).
b   Judith Blegen, soprano; William Brown, tenor; Hakan Hagegard, baritone; Atlanta Boy Choir; Atlanta Symphony Chorus and Orchestra; Robert Shaw, conductor; Telarc CD-80056 [DDD] (TT = 60.36).
c   Lucia Popp, soprano; Gerhard Unger, tenor; John Noble, baritone; Raymond Wolansky, baritone; Wandsworth

School Boys' Choir; New Philharmonia Chorus and Orchestra; Rafael Frühbeck de Burgos, conductor; Angel CDM 69060 [ADD] (TT = 61.44).

Many may find it hard to choose between these two recordings of Orff's best known work--my choice is for the Chicagoans on DG for a fully digital recording (but the Shaw gives Levine a run for his money), but Frühbeck de Burgos' is still the best performance.

PACHELBEL, JOHANN
1653-1706

Orchestral

{707} *A* Kanon ("Canon") in D -- see entries Nos.{6}a-b and {60}.

PAGANINI, NICCOLÒ
1782-1840

Concerted

{708} *A* Concerto for Violin No.1, Op.6, in D

a Salvatore Accardo, violin; London Philharmonic Orchestra; Charles Dutoit, conductor; DG 415 378-2 [ADD] (TT = 68.42). Includes Paganini's Concerto for Violin No.2 ("La Campanella") ("The Small Bell"), Op.7, in b, rated B.

b Sir Yehudi Menuhin, violin; Royal Philharmonic Orchestra; Alberto Erede, conductor; Angel CDC 47088-2 [ADD] (TT = 61.02). Includes Paganini's Concerto for Violin No.2 ("La Campanella") ("The Small Bell"), Op.7, in b, rated B.

c Itzhak Perlman, violin; Royal Philharmonic Orchestra; Lawrence Foster, conductor; Angel CDC 47101-2 [ADD] (TT = 45.51). Includes Sarasate's <u>Carmen Fantasy</u> for Violin and Orchestra, Op.25, rated B.

I think the oldest of the Paganini concerti recordings is the best: those of Menuhin. The Accardo is there if you need something more recently recording, and the Perlman because of his lovely performance of the Paganini and the Sarasate. The Paganini 2nd Concerto, by the way, is called the "Little Bell" because the score calls for the use of one.

{709}   *B*   Concerto for Violin No.2 ("La Campanella") ("The Small Bell"), Op.7, in b -- see entries Nos.{708}a-b.

Instrumental
{710}   *A*   Caprices for Solo Violin (24), Op.1 Nos.1-24
        Itzhak Perlman, violin; Angel CDC 47171-2 [ADD] (TT=72.28).

PALESTRINA, GIOVANNI
c.1525-1594

Choral
{711}   *A*   Missa <u>Papae Marcelli</u> ("Pope Marcellus' Mass") (1567)
a   Regensburger Domspatzen; Georg Ratzinger, conductor; Angel CDC 47528-2 [DDD] (TT=59.59). Includes Palestrina's Motets: <u>Ascendit Deus; Hodie Christus natus est; Dum complerentur; Dum ergo essent; Ego sum panis vivus; Laudate Dominum; Pueri Hebraeorum; Rorate coeli; Terra tremuit; Tu est Petrus</u> (1572), rated A.
b   Westminster Abbey Choir; Simon Preston, conductor; Archiv 415 517-2 [DDD] (TT=59.08). Includes Palestrina's Motet: <u>Tu est Petrus</u> (1572), rated A; Allegri's <u>Miserere</u>; Anerio's <u>Venite ad me omnes</u>; Giovannelli's <u>Jubilate Deo</u> and Nanino's <u>Haec dies</u>.

{712}   *A*   Motet: <u>Tu est Petrus</u> (1572) -- see entries Nos.{711}a-b.

252

PERGOLESI, GIOVANNI BATTISTA
1710-1736

Choral
{713}　　　C　Stabat Mater (1736)
Margaret Marshall, soprano; Lucia Valentini-Terrani, mezzo-soprano; London Symphony Orchestra; Claudio Abbado, conductor; DG 415 103-2 [DDD] (TT=42.44).

PISTON, WALTER
1894-1976

Ballet
{714}　　　B　The Incredible Flutist (1938) -- see entry No.{103}.

PONCHIELLI, AMILCARE
1834-1886

Operatic
{715}　　　B　La Gioconda (1876)
a　　　　　Montserrat Caballé, soprano; Agnes Baltsa, mezzo-soprano; Alfreda Hodgson, mezzo-soprano; Luciano Pavarotti, tenor; Sherrill Milnes, baritone; Nicolai Ghiaurov, bass; London Opera Chorus; National Philharmonic Orchestra of London; Bruno Bartoletti, conductor; London 414 349-2 (3 discs) [DDD] (TT=170.34).
b　　　　　Maria Callas, soprano; Fiorenza Cossotto, mezzo-soprano; Pier Miranda Ferraro, tenor; Piero Cappuccilli, baritone; Chorus and Orchestra of La Scala, Milan; Antonino Votto, conductor; Fonit-Cetra CDC-9 (3 discs) [AAD] (TT=167.23).

Gioconda is well known both in and of itself as an opera, and as the source of the often performed ballet

253

sequence called "Dance of the Hours" which was featured as a segment in the Disney film, Fantasia (remember the ballet sequence with a hippopotamus being courted by an alligator?).

POULENC, FRANCIS
1899-1963

Ballet
{716}   *C*   Les Biches ("The Unsullied Wanton Young Ladies") (1923) -- see entry No.{576}.

Choral
{717}   *B*   Gloria, in G (1961)
Sylvia McNair, soprano; Atlanta Symphony Chorus and Orchestra; Robert Shaw, conductor; Telarc CD-80105 [DDD] (TT=45.25). Includes Stravinsky's Symphony of Psalms (1930), rated A.

{718}   *C*   Stabat Mater (1950)
Michele Lagrange, soprano; Lyons National Choir and Orchestra; Serge Baudo, conductor; Harmonia Mundi 905149 [ADD] (TT=42.25). Includes Poulenc's Litanies à la Vierge Noire de Rocamadour (1936) and Salve Regina (1941).

Concerted
{719}   *B*   Aubade for Piano and 18 Instruments (1929)
François-René Duchable, piano; Rotterdam Philharmonic Orchestra; James Conlon, conductor; Erato ECD-88140 [DDD] (TT=60.23). Includes Poulenc's Concerto for Piano and Orchestra, in c sharp (1949) and Concerto for Two Pianos and Orchestra, in d (1932), rated B (the second pianist is Jean-Philippe Collard).

{720}   *B*   Concerto for Two Pianos and Orchestra, in d (1932) -- see entry No.{719}.

Operatic

{721}   *B*   <u>Dialogues des Carmelites</u> (1953-1956)
Régine Crespin, soprano; Denise Duval, soprano; Denise Scharley, mezzo-soprano; Paul Finel, tenor; Xavier Desprez, bass; Paris Opéra Chorus and Orchestra; Pierre Dervaux, conductor; Angel CDC 49332 (2 discs) ! [ADD] (TT = 143.57).

PROKOFIEV, SERGEI
1819-1953

Ballet

{722}   *B*   <u>Cinderella</u>, Op.87
Cleveland Orchestra; Vladimir Ashkenazy, conductor; London 410 162-2 (2 discs) [DDD] (TT = 107.36).

{723}   *B*   <u>Cinderella</u> Suite, Op.87
London Symphony Orchestra; André Previn, conductor; Angel CDC 47969-2 [DDD] (TT = 71.01).

{724}   *A*   <u>Romeo and Juliet</u>, Op.64
a   Cleveland Orchestra; Lorin Maazel, conductor; London 417 510-2 (2 discs) [ADD?] (TT = 140.41).
b   London Symphony Orchestra; André Previn, conductor; Angel CD3 49012-8 (2 discs) [ADD] (TT = 148.42).

{725}   *A*   <u>Romeo and Juliet</u> Suites, Op.64
Cleveland Orchestra; Yoel Levi, conductor; Telarc CD-80089 [DDD] (TT = 50.05).
Also -- for "Gavotte, Dance of the West Indian Girls, Montagues and Capulets" -- see entry No.{511}.

{726}   *B*   <u>Scythian</u> Suite, Op.20
Scottish National Orchestra; Neeme Järvi, conductor; Chandos ABRD 1275 [DDD] (TT = 60.24). Includes

Prokofiev's Symphony No.5, Op.100, in B flat Cantata: Alexander Nevsky (From the Film of the Same Name), Op.78 (with Linda Finnie, soprano, and the Scottish National Chorus), rated A.

{727} *A* Waltz Suite, Op.110
     Scottish National Orchestra; Neeme Järvi, conductor; Chandos CD-8576 [DDD] (TT=43.58). Includes Prokofiev's Symphony No.5, rated A; Opera War and Peace, Op.91 and Lermontov (Music for the Film), 1941.

Chamber
{728} *C* String Quartet No.1, Op.50, in b
     Sequoia String Quartet; Nonesuch 79048 [DDD] (TT=46.21). Includes Prokofiev's String Quartet No.2, Op.92, in F, rated B.

{729} *B* String Quartet No.2, Op.92, in F -- see entry No.{728}.

Choral
{730} *A* Cantata: Alexander Nevsky (From the Film of the Same Name), Op.78
     Elena Obraztsova, mezzo-soprano; London Symphony Chorus and Orchestra; Claudio Abbado, conductor; DG 419 603-2 [ADD] (TT=58.14). Includes Prokofiev's Lieutenant Kijé Suite (from the Film of the Same Name), Op.60, rated A. In addition to its original film use, the Kijé Suite was used as the score for the Sir Alec Guinness film, The Horse's Mouth. Also -- see entry No.{726}.

Concerted
{731} *A* Concerto for Piano No.3, Op.26, in C
     Martha Argerich, piano; Berlin Philharmonic Orchestra; Claudio Abbado, conductor; MHS 11201F [ADD] (TT=62.31). Includes Tchaikovsky's Concerto for Piano No.1,

Op.23, in b flat (wherein Argerich is accompanied by the Royal Philharmonic Orchestra, conducted by Charles Dutoit), rated A.
Also -- see entry No.{107}.

{732}   *B*   Concerto for Violin No.1, Op.19, in D
Itzhak Perlman, violin; BBC Symphony Orchestra; Gennady Rozhdestvensky, conductor; Angel CDC 47025-2 [DDD] (TT=48.39).

{733}   *B*   Concerto for Violin No.2, Op.63, in g -- see entries Nos.{402} and {732}.

Orchestral

{734}   *A*   Lieutenant Kijé Suite (from the Film of the Same Name), Op.60 -- see entry No.{730}.

{735}   *A*   Love for Three Oranges, Op.33: March -- see entry No.{511}.

{736}   *A*   Peter and the Wolf, Op.67
Hermione Gingold, narrator; Vienna Philharmonic Orchestra; Karl Böhm, conductor; DG 415 351-2 [ADD] (TT-54.05). Includes Saint-Saëns' Carnival of the Animals (Grand Zoological Fantasy) for Two Pianos and Orchestra (1886) (With Verses by Ogden Nash), rated A. In the Saint-Saëns, the two pianists are Alfons Kontarsky and Aloys Kontarsky. No.13 of the Carnival of the Animals is "The Swan" (sometimes called "The Dying Swan") and the solo 'cellist is Wolfgang Herzer.

Symphonic

{737}   *A*   Symphony No.1 ("Classical"), Op.25, in D -- see entry No.{415}.

257

{738}   *B*   Symphony No.4, Op.47, in C
Scottish National Orchestra; Neeme Järvi, conductor;
Chandos CD-8401 [DDD] (TT=59.08). Includes Prokofiev's
Symphony No.3, Op.44, in c.

{739}   *A*   Symphony No.5, Op.100, in B flat
Concertgebouw Orchestra; Vladimir Ashkenazy,
conductor; London 417 314-2 [DDD] (TT=51.26). Includes
Prokofiev's Rêves; Symphonic Tableau ("Dreams"), Op.6.
Also -- see entry No.{727}.

PUCCINI, GIACOMO
1858-1924

Choral
{740}   *C*   Messa di gloria (1880)
José Carreras, tenor; Hermann Prey, baritone;
Ambrosian Singers; Philharmonia Orchestra; Claudio
Scimone, conductor; Erato ECD-88022 [DDD] (TT=47.50).

Operatic
{741}   *A*   La Bohème (1896)
a   Lucine Amara, soprano; Victoria de Los Angeles,
soprano; Jussi Björling, tenor; Robert Merrill, baritone; John
Reardon, baritone; Fernando Corena, bass; Giorgio Tozzi,
bass; Columbus Boychoir; RCA Victor Chorus and Orchestra;
Sir Thomas Beecham, conductor; Angel CDCB 47235 (2 discs)
! [ADD] (TT=108.04).
b   Gianna D'Angelo, soprano; Renata Tebaldi, soprano;
Carlo Bergonzi, tenor; Ettore Bastianini, baritone; Cesare
Siepi, bass-baritone; Fernando Corena, bass; Chorus and
Orchestra of the Accademia di Santa Cecilia, Rome; Tullio
Serafin, conductor; London 411 868-2 (2 discs) [AAD]
(TT=111.31).

c   Mirella Freni, soprano; Elizabeth Harwood, soprano;
Luciano Pavarotti, tenor; Nicolai Ghiaurov, bass;
Schöneberger Boys' Choir; Berlin Opera Chorus; Berlin
Philharmonic Orchestra; Herbert von Karajan, conductor;
London 421 049-2 (2 discs) [ADD] (TT = 110.05).
The Beecham set on Angel is a grand and classic
recording, while the Serafin is a gorgeously sung and acted
performance with better sound. Von Karajan has Freni and
Pavarotti at the top of their careers and his is a slightly
eccentric performance--but a very moving one.

{742}   *A*   Madama Butterfly (1904)
Renata Scotto, soprano; Gillian Knight, mezzo-soprano;
Plácido Domingo, tenor; Ingvar Wixell, baritone; Ambrosian
Opera Chorus; Philharmonia Orchestra; Lorin Maazel,
conductor; CBS M2K 35181 (2 discs) (TT = 139.22).

{743}   *B*   Manon Lescaut (1893)
a   Montserrat Caballé, soprano; Plácido Domingo, tenor;
Vicente Sardinero, bass; Ambrosian Opera Chorus; New
Philharmonia Orchestra; Bruno Bartoletti, conductor; Angel
CDCB 47736 (2 discs) [ADD] (TT = 116.08).
b   Mirella Freni, soprano; Plácido Domingo, tenor;
Renato Bruson, baritone; Chorus of the Royal Opera House,
Covent Garden; Philharmonia Orchestra; Giuseppe Sinopoli,
conductor; DG 413 893-2 (2 discs) [DDD] (TT = 123.26).

{744}   *B*   La Rondine ("The Swallow") (1917)
Dame Kiri Te Kanawa, soprano; Mariana Nicolescu,
soprano; Lillian Watson, soprano; Gillian Knight, mezzo-
soprano; Plácido Domingo, tenor; David Rendall, tenor; Leo
Nucci, baritone; Ambrosian Opera Chorus; London Symphony
Orchestra; Lorin Maazel, conductor; CBS M2K 37852 (2 discs)
[DDD] (TT = 103.00).

{745}   *A*   Tosca (1900)
a   Montserrat Caballé, soprano; José Carreras, tenor;
Ingvar Wixell, baritone; Samuel Ramey, bass; Chorus and
Orchestra of the Royal Opera House, Covent Garden; Sir
Colin Davis, conductor; Philips 412 885-2 (2 discs) [ADD]
(TT = 118.24).
b   Dame Kiri Te Kanawa, soprano; Giacomo Aragall,
tenor; Leo Nucci, baritone; Malcolm King, bass; Welsh
National Opera Chorus; Children of the Royal Opera, Covent
Garden; National Philharmonic Orchestra of London; Sir
Georg Solti, conductor; London 414 597-2 (2 discs) [DDD]
(TT = 114.10).

{746}   *A*   Turandot (1926)
a   Eva Marton, soprano; Katia Ricciarelli, soprano; José
Carreras, tenor; Waldemar Kmentt, tenor; John- Paul Bogart,
bass; Wiener Sängerknaben; Chorus and Orchestra of the
Vienna State Opera; Lorin Maazel, conductor; CBS M2K
39160 (2 discs) [DDD] (TT = 122.43).
b   Montserrat Caballé, soprano; Dame Joan Sutherland,
soprano; Luciano Pavarotti, tenor; Sir Peter Pears, tenor;
Nicolai Ghiaurov, bass; John Alldis Choir; Wandsworth School
Boys' Choir; London Philharmonic Orchestra; Zubin Mehta,
conductor; London 414 274-2 (2 discs) [ADD] (TT = 117.37).

PURCELL, HENRY
1659-1695

Choral
{747}   *A*   Music for the Funeral of Queen Mary (1694)
          Felicity Lott, soprano; Charles Brett, countertenor;
John Williams, countertenor; Thomas Allen, baritone;
Monteverdi Choir; Equale Brass Ensemble; Monteverdi
Orchestra; John Eliot Gardiner, conductor; Erato ECD-88071

[DDD] (TT=44.06). Includes Purcell's <u>Music for Queen Mary</u> ("Come, Ye Sons of Art") (1695), rated A.

{748}   *A*   <u>Music for Queen Mary</u> ("Come, Ye Sons of Art") (1695) -- see entry No.{747}.

{749}   *A*   <u>Ode on St. Cecilia's Day</u> ("Hail! Bright Cecilia") (1692)
Taverner Choir; Taverner Consort; Taverner Players; Andrew Parrott, conductor; Angel CDC 47490-2 [DDD] (TT=56.43).

Operatic
{750}   *A*   <u>Dido and Aeneas</u> (1689)
a   Emma Kirkby, soprano; Judith Nelson, soprano; Davit Thomas, bass; Taverner Choir; Taverner Players; Andrew Parrott, conductor; Chandos CD-8306 [DDD] (TT=53.53).
b   Marie McLaughlin, soprano; Jessye Norman, soprano; Thomas Allen, baritone; Anonymous Chorus; English Chamber Orchestra; Raymond Leppard, conductor; Philips 416 299-2 [DDD] (TT=58.18).

{751}   *B*   <u>King Arthur</u> (1691)
Jennifer Smith, soprano; Gillian Fisher, soprano; Ashley Stafford, contralto; Paul Elliott, tenor; Stephen Varcoe, baritone; Monteverdi Choir; English Baroque Soloists; John Eliot Gardiner, conductor; Erato ECD-88056 (2 discs) [DDD] (TT=91.44).

RACHMANINOFF, SERGEI
1873-1943

Chamber
{752}   *A*   Sonata for 'Cello and Piano, Op.19, in g

Lynn Harrell, 'cello; Vladimir Ashkenazy, piano; London 414 340-2 [DDD] (TT=56.19). Includes Altschuler's Melodie on a Theme by Rachmaninoff; Rachmaninoff's Two Pieces for 'Cello and Piano, Op.2 Nos.1-2 ("Prelude" and "Oriental Dance"); Romance (1890), in f and Vocalise, Op.34 No.14, rated A.

{753}   *A*   Vocalise, Op.34 No.14 -- see entry No.{752}.

Choral
{754}   *B*   The Bells (After Poe), Op.35
Natalia Troitskaya, soprano; Ryszard Karczykowski, tenor; Tom Krause, baritone; Chorus of the Amsterdam Concertgebouw Orchestra; Amsterdam Concertgebouw Orchestra; Vladimir Ashkenazy, conductor; London 414 455-2 [DDD] (TT=49.52). Includes Rachmaninoff's Three Russian Songs, Op.41.

Concerted
{755}   *B*   Concerto for Piano No.1, Op.1, in f sharp
Sergei Rachmaninoff, piano; Philadelphia Orchestra; Eugene Ormandy, conductor; RCA 6659-2-RC ! [ADD] (TT=71.56). Includes Rachmaninoff's Concerto for Piano No.4, Op.40, in g, rated B and Rhapsody on a Theme of Paganini, Op.43 (here Rachmaninoff is accompanied by the Philadelphia Orchestra with Leopold Stokowski conducting), rated A. It is the 18th variation in the Rhapsody which usually catches audiences unaware--knowing the melody (which is the inversion of the Paganini theme), but knowing not its origin. This recording is quite an historical document, despite the occasional ticks, pops and hissiness.

{756}   *A*   Concerto for Piano No.2, Op.18, in c
a   Vladimir Ashkenazy, piano; Amsterdam Concertgebouw Orchestra; Bernard Haitink, conductor;

London 414 475-2 [DDD] (TT = 62.07). Includes
Rachmaninoff's Concerto for Piano No.4, Op.40, in g, rated B.

b   Gary Graffman, piano; New York Philharmonic;
Leonard Bernstein, conductor; CBS MYK 36722 [AAD?]
(TT = 56.57). Includes Rachmaninoff's Rhapsody on a Theme
of Paganini, Op.43, rated A.

c   Cecile Licad, piano; Chicago Symphony Orchestra;
Claudio Abbado, conductor; CBS MK 38672 [DDD?]
(TT = 57.19). Includes Rachmaninoff's Rhapsody on a Theme
of Paganini, Op.43, rated A.

d   Sergei Rachmaninoff, piano; Philadelphia Orchestra;
Leopold Stokowski, conductor; RCA 5997-2-RC ! [ADD]
(TT = 66.08). Includes Rachmaninoff's Concerto for Piano
No.3, Op.30, in d, rated A (in the Third Concerto, the
conductor is Eugene Ormandy).

This is Rachmaninoff's most popular concerto (made
even more so by Freddy Martin's pop band arrangement of the
big theme in the last movement, called Full Moon and Empty
Arms). Licad does wonderful readings of both works on her
recording--not too much schmaltz, but still enough warmth and
longing. The Rachmaninoff disc, again, is a historical
document filled with fire and phenomenal technical displays.
Graffman's offers fine, journeyman level jobs and Ashkenazy
provides a bit more poetry than Graffman, but seems lacking in
ardor.

{757}   *A*   Concerto for Piano No.3, Op.30, in d
Vladimir Ashkenazy, piano; Amsterdam
Concertgebouw Orchestra; Bernard Haitink, conductor;
London 417 239-2 [DDD] (TT = 43.28).
Also -- see entry No.{756}d.

{758}   *B*   Concerto for Piano No.4, Op.40, in g -- see entries
Nos.{755} and {756}a.

{759}   *A*   Rhapsody on a Theme of Paganini, Op.43
Bella Davidovich, piano; Amsterdam Concertgebouw Orchestra; Neeme Järvi, conductor; 410 052-2 [DDD] (TT=46.13). Includes Saint-Saëns' Concerto for Piano No.2, Op.22, in g, rated B.
Also -- see entries Nos.{755} and {756}b-c.
This is usually considered Rachmaninoff's finest work for piano and orchestra. Of the various listed performances, my own favorites are those which have either Licad or Rachmaninoff as the pianist. Graffman, Ashkenazy and Davidovich offer very good readings, and one's choice should be determined by which additional works one needs for one's library--all are substantial.

Instrumental
{760}   *C*   Étude-Tableau, Op.33 No.2, in C -- see entry No.{276}.

{761}   *A*   Prelude for Piano, Op.23 No.2, in c sharp (Orchestral version) -- see entry No.{90}.

{762}   *B*   Prelude, Op.32 No.12, in g sharp -- see entry No.{276}.

{763}   *A*   Preludes, Op.23 and Op.32 (23): Nos.1-23
Vladimir Ashkenazy, piano; London 414 417-2 (2 discs) [ADD] (TT=106.14). Includes Rachmaninoff's Sonata for Piano No.2, Op.36, in b flat, rated B.

{764}   *B*   Sonata for Piano No.2, Op.36, in b flat -- see entry No.{763}.

Orchestral
{765}   *C*   <u>Isle of the Dead</u> (Symphonic Poem), Op.29

Amsterdam Concertgebouw Orchestra; Vladimir
Ashkenazy, conductor; London 410 124-2 [DDD] (TT=54.16).
Includes Rachmaninoff's <u>Symphonic Dances</u>, Op.45, rated B.

{766}   *B*   <u>Symphonic Dances</u>, Op.45
USSR TV and Radio Large Symphony Orchestra;
Vladimir Fedoseyev, conductor; Mobile Fidelity (Melodia)
MFCD 858 [DDD] (TT=38.27). Includes the Intermezzo from
<u>Aleko</u> (1893).
Also -- see entry No.{765}.

Symphonic
{767}   *C*   Symphony No.1, Op.13, in d
Amsterdam Concertgebouw Orchestra; Vladimir
Ashkenazy, conductor; London 411 657-2 [DDD] (TT=42.19).

{768}   *A*   Symphony No.2, Op.27, in e
a   Amsterdam Concertgebouw Orchestra; Vladimir
Ashkenazy, conductor; London 400 081-2 [DDD] (TT=55.04).
b   London Symphony Orchestra; André Previn, conductor;
Angel CDC 47159-2 [ADD?] (TT=58.52).
c   Royal Philharmonic Orchestra; André Previn,
conductor; Telarc CD-80113 [DDD] (62.47).
It is odd that Previn's Angel recording is described as
"complete version" on the cover, while his performance on
Telarc is almost 4 minutes longer. Actually, the Telarc reading
is slower and more lush in both sound and performance.
Ashkenazy's is somewhat more "Slavic" and less romantic.

{769}   *B*   Symphony No.3, Op.44, in a
Amsterdam Concertgebouw Orchestra; Vladimir
Ashkenazy, conductor; London 410 231-2 [DDD] (TT=52.23).
Includes the fragment (one movement only) Symphony
("Youth") (1891), in d.

RAVEL, MAURICE
1875-1937

Ballet

{770}   *A*   Daphnis et Chloé (1909-1912)
Montreal Symphony Chorus and Orchestra; Charles
Dutoit, conductor; London 400 055-2 [DDD] (TT=56.02).

{771}   *A*   Daphnis et Chloé Suite No.2 (1909-1912)
Amsterdam Concertgebouw Orchestra; Bernard
Haitink, conductor; Philips 416 495-2 [ADD] (TT=53.40).
Includes Ravel's Boléro (1927), rated A; Pavane pour une
infante défunte ("Pavane for a Dead Princess") (1899), rated A
and Rapsodie espagnole ("Spanish Rhapsody") (1907) (4)
Nos.1-4: Prélude à la nuit ("Prelude in the Fashion of the
Night"); Malagueña; Habanera and Feria ("Fiesta"), rated A.
Also -- see entry No.{327}.

{772}   *A*   Ma Mère l'Oye ("Mother Goose") (1908-1911): (6)
Nos.1-6: Prélude; Danse du Rouet et Scène ("Danse of the
Spinning Wheel"); Pavane de la Belle au bois dormant
("Pavane of Sleeping Beauty"); Les entretiens de la Belle et de
la Bête ("The Conversations of Beauty and the Beast"); Petit
Poucet ("Tom Thumb"); Laideronette, Impératrice des
Pagodes ("Little Ugly One, Empress of the Pagodas") and Le
Jardin féerique ("The Enchanted Garden")
Montreal Symphony Orchestra; Charles Dutoit,
conductor; London 410 254-2 [DDD] (TT=66.53). Includes
Ravel's Pavane pour une infante défunte ("Pavane for a Dead
Princess") (1899), rated A; Le Tombeau de Couperin
("Homage to Couperin") Orchestral Suite (1914-1917), rated A
and Valses nobles et sentimentales ("Noble and Sentimental
Waltzes") (1911), rated A.

Chamber

{773}   *A*   Introduction and Allegro for Harp, Flute, Clarinet and String Quartet (1906) -- see entry No.{304}d.

{774}   *C*   Sonata for Violin and Piano (1920-1922) -- see entry No.{390}.

{775}   *A*   String Quartet, in F (1903) -- see entries Nos.{304}a-d.

{776}   *A*   Trio for Violin, 'Cello and Piano (1914)
      Beaux Arts Trio; Philips 411 141-2 [DDD] (TT=60.21). Includes Chausson's Trio for Violin, 'Cello and Piano, Op.33.

Concerted

{777}   *A*   Concerto for Piano (1930-1931), in G
a   Jean-Philippe Collard, piano; Orchestre National de France; Lorin Maazel, conductor; Angel CDC 47386-2 [ADD] (TT=64.26). Includes Concerto for Piano, for the Left Hand (1930-1931), in D, rated A; Jeux d'eau ("Games of the Water") (1901), rated B; Pavane pour une infante défunte ("Pavane for a Dead Princess") (1899) (Piano Version), rated A and La Valse ("The Waltz") (1921) (Two Piano Version) (with Michel Béroff, piano), rated A.

b   Pascal Rogé, piano; Montreal Symphony Orchestra; Charles Dutoit, conductor; London 410 230-2 [DDD] (TT=56.52). Includes Ravel's Concerto for Piano, for the Left Hand (1930-1931), in D, rated A; Une Barque sur l'océan from Miroirs ("A Boat on the Ocean" from "Mirrors") (1905), rated A; Menuet antique ("Antique Minuet") (1895), rated B and Fanfare from L'Éventail de Jeanne (1927).

      Both of these are excellent recordings, I tend to favor the Rogé in the Concerti, but Collard is not far behind (particularly for the superb performance of the two piano version of La Valse).

{778}   *A*   Concerto for Piano, for the Left Hand (1930-1931) -- see entries Nos.{777}a-b.

{779}   *A*   <u>Tzigane</u> ("Gypsies") for Violin and Orchestra (1924)
Kyung-Wha Chung, violin; Royal Philharmonic Orchestra; Charles Dutoit, conductor; London 417 118-2 [ADD] (TT=45.29). Includes <u>Havanaise</u> for Violin and Orchestra, Op.83, rated A.

Instrumental
{780}   *A*   <u>Gaspard de la nuit</u> ("Gaspard of the Night" -- after Bertrand) (1908) (3) Nos.1-3: <u>Ondine</u>; <u>Le Gibet</u> ("The Gibbet") and <u>Scarbo</u>
Vladimir Ashkenazy, piano; London 410 255-2 [DDD] (TT=41.48). Includes Ravel's <u>Pavane pour une infante défunte</u> ("Pavane for a Dead Princess") (1899) (Piano Version), rated A and <u>Valses nobles et sentimentales</u> ("Noble and Sentimental Waltzes") (1911) (Piano Version), rated A.

{781}   *B*   <u>Jeux d'eau</u> ("Games of the Water") (1901) -- see entries Nos.{777}a and {780}.

{782}   *A*   <u>Pavane pour une infante défunte</u> ("Pavane for a Dead Princess") (1899) (Piano Version) -- see entry No.{777}a.

{783}   *A*   <u>La Valse</u> ("The Waltz") (1921) (Two Piano Version) -- see entry No.{777}a.

{784}   *A*   <u>Valses nobles et sentimentales</u> ("Noble and Sentimental Waltzes") (1911) (Piano Version) -- see entry No.{780}.

{785}   *A*   <u>Valses nobles et sentimentales</u> ("Noble and Sentimental Waltzes") (1911), Nos.6-7 (Transcribed by Heifetz) -- see entry No.{309}.

Operatic

{786}   *B*   L'Enfant et les sortilèges ("The Child and the Sorceries") (1920-1925)

Colette Alliot-Lucaz, soprano; Audrey Michael, soprano; Elisabeth Vidal, soprano; Arlette Chedel, mezzo-soprano; Isabel Garcisanz, mezzo-soprano; Michel Sénéchal, tenor; Philippe Huttenlocher, baritone; Michel Brodard, bass; La Manécanterie Conservatoire Populaire de Musique, Geneva; Suisse Romande Radio Chorus; L'Orchestre de la Suisse Romande; Armin Jordan, conductor; Erato ECD-75312 [DDD] (TT=44.05).

Orchestral

{787}   *A*   Alborada del gracioso ("Morning Song of the Jester") (1905)

a   Montreal Symphony Orchestra; Charles Dutoit, conductor; London 410 010-2 [DDD] (TT=50.36). Includes Ravel's Boléro (1927), rated A; Rapsodie espagnole ("Spanish Rhapsody") (1907) (4) Nos.1-4: Prélude à la nuit ("Prelude in the Fashion of the Night"); Malagueña; Habanera and Feria ("Fiesta"), rated A and La Valse ("The Waltz") (1921), rated A.

b   L'Orchestre de la Suisse Romande; Ernest Ansermet, conductor; London 414 046-2 [AAD] (TT=64.24). Includes Ravel's Boléro (1927), rated A; Rapsodie espagnole ("Spanish Rhapsody") (1907) (4) Nos.1-4: Prélude à la nuit ("Prelude in the Fashion of the Night"); Malagueña; Habanera and Feria ("Fiesta"), rated A; La Valse ("The Waltz") (1921), rated A and Valses nobles et sentimentales ("Noble and Sentimental Waltzes") (1911), rated A.

{788}   *A*   Une Barque sur l'océan from Miroirs ("A Boat on the Ocean" from "Mirrors") (1905) -- see entry No.{777}b.

{789}   *A*   Boléro (1927) -- see entries Nos.{266}b, {771} and {787}a-b.

{790}   *B*   Menuet antique ("Antique Minuet") (1895) -- see entry No.{777}b.

{791}   *A*   Pavane pour une infante défunte ("Pavane for a Dead Princess") (1899) -- see entries Nos.{385}, {771} and {772}.

{792}   *A*   Pavane pour une infante défunte ("Pavane for a Dead Princess") (1899) (Piano Version) -- see entry No.{777}a.

{793}   *A*   Rapsodie espagnole ("Spanish Rhapsody") (1907) (4) Nos.1-4: Prélude à la nuit ("Prelude in the Fashion of the Night"); Malagueña; Habanera and Feria ("Fiesta") -- see entries Nos.{266}b, {771} and {787}a-b.

{794}   *A*   Le Tombeau de Couperin ("Homage to Couperin") (1914-1917) -- see entries Nos.{303} and {772}.

{795}   *A*   La Valse ("The Waltz") (1921) -- see entries Nos.{787}a-b.

{796}   *A*   La Valse ("The Waltz") (1921) (Two Piano Version) -- see entry No.{777}a.

{797}   *A*   Valses nobles et sentimentales ("Noble and Sentimental Waltzes") (1911) -- see entries Nos.{772} and {787}b.

Vocal

{798}   *B*   Shéhérazade (Song Cycle) (1925-1926) (3) Nos.1-3: Asie ("Asia"); La Flûte enchantée ("The Enchanted Flute") and L'Indifférent ("The Indifferent Man") -- see entry No.{349}.

RESPIGHI, OTTORINO
1879-1936

Ballet
{799}   *B*   Ancient Airs and Dances for the Lute (3 sets) (Sets 1-3) (1917-1932)
Los Angeles Chamber Orchestra; Sir Neville Marriner, conductor; Angel CDC 47116-2 [ADD] (TT=47.25).

{800}   *B*   Ancient Airs and Dances for the Lute (3 sets) (Set 2: 1923) -- see entry No.{799}.

{801}   *B*   Ancient Airs and Dances for the Lute (3 sets) (Set 3: 1932)   see entries Nos.{102}b and {799}.

Orchestral
{802}   *B*   Feste Romane ("Roman Festivals") (1929)
Montreal Symphony Orchestra; Charles Dutoit, conductor; London 410 145-2 [DDD] (TT=61.36). Includes Respighi's Fontane de Roma ("Fountains of Rome") (1917), rated A and I Pini di Roma ("The Pines of Rome") (1924), rated A.

{803}   *A*   Fontane de Roma ("Fountains of Rome") (1917) -- see entry No.{802}.

{804}   *A*   I Pini di Roma ("The Pines of Rome") (1924) -- see entry No.{802}.

REZNIČEK, EMIL NIKOLAUS VON
1860-1945

Orchestral
{805}   *B*   Overture: Donna Diana (1894) -- see entry No.{10}.

RIMSKY-KORSAKOV, NIKOLAI
1844-1908

Orchestral

{806}   *A*   Capriccio espagnol ("Spanish Caprice"), Op.34
Montreal Symphony Orchestra; Charles Dutoit, conductor; London 410 253-2 [DDD] (TT=61.11). Includes Rimsky-Korsakov's Scheherazade, Op.35, rated A.

{807}   *B*   Le Coq d'or ("The Golden Cockerel") Suite (1906-1907)
Rotterdam Philharmonic Orchestra; David Zinman, conductor; Philips 411 435-2 [DDD] (TT=46.05). Includes Rimsky-Korsakov's Tsar Sultan Suite, Op.57, rated B. The Tsar Sultan contains the "Flight of the Bumblebee."

{808}   *B*   Dance of the Tumblers from The Snow Maiden (1882) -- see entry No.{348}.

{809}   *B*   Procession of the Nobles from Mlada (1872) -- see entry No.{348}.

{810}   *B*   March from the Tsar Sultan Suite, Op.57
Royal Philharmonic Orchestra; André Previn, conductor; Telarc CD-80107 [DDD] (TT=50.59). Includes Tchaikovsky's Symphony No.5, Op.64, in e, rated A.

{811}   *B*   Overture: Russian Easter, Op.36 -- see entries Nos.{210}b and {211}a.

{812}   *A*   Scheherazade, Op.35
London Symphony Orchestra; John Mauceri, conductor; MCA MCAD-25187 [DDD] (TT=47.13).
Also -- see entries Nos.{211}b and {806}.

{813}   *B*   Tsar Sultan Suite, Op.57 -- see entry No.{807}.

Symphonic
{814}   *B*   Symphony No.2 ("Antar"), Op.9, in f sharp
Pittsburgh Symphony Orchestral, André Previn, conductor; Telarc CD-80131 [DDD] (TT=67.32). Includes Tchaikovsky's Symphony No.2 ("Little Russian"), Op.17, in c, rated A.

RODRIGO, JOAQUÍN

Concerted
{815}   *A*   Concierto de Aranjuez for Guitar and Orchestra (1939)

a   John Williams, guitar; Philadelphia Orchestra; Eugene Ormandy, conductor; CBS MYK 36717 [AAD?] (TT=42.46). Includes Rodrigo's Fantasía para un gentilhombre ("Fantasy for a Gentleman") for Guitar and Orchestra (1954), rated B.

b   John Williams, guitar; Philharmonia Orchestra; Louis Frémaux, conductor; CBS MK 37848 [DDD] (TT=43.05). Includes Rodrigo's Fantasía para un gentilhombre ("Fantasy for a Gentleman") for Guitar and Orchestra (1954), rated B.

Despite Williams being the soloist in both recordings, there are differences: the Ormandy has greater sensitivity, the Frémaux, being more recent, possesses better sound.

{816}   *B*   Fantasía para un gentilhombre ("Fantasy for a Gentleman") for Guitar and Orchestra (1954) -- see entries Nos.{815}a-b.

ROSSINI, GIOACCHINO
1792-1868

Choral
{817}   *B*   Stabat Mater (1832)

a   Katia Ricciarelli, soprano; Lucia Valentini-Terrani, mezzo-soprano; Dalmacio Gonzalez, tenor; Ruggero Raimondi, bass; Philharmonia Chorus and Orchestra; Carlo Maria Giulini, conductor; DG 410 034-2 [DDD] (TT-65.21).

b   Sung-Sook Lee, soprano; Florence Quivar, mezzo-soprano; Kenneth Riegel, tenor; Paul Plishka, bass; Cincinatti May Festival Chorus; Cincinatti Symphony Orchestra; Thomas Schippers, conductor; Vox Cum Laude MCD-10060 [AAD] (TT=57.04).

{818}   *B*   Petite messe solenelle (1863)

Kari Lövass, soprano; Brigitte Fassbaender, mezzo-soprano; Peter Schreier, tenor; Dietrich Fischer-Dieskau, baritone; Munich Volksolisten; Reinhard Raffalt, harmonium; Hans Ludwig Hirsch, piano; Wolfgang Sawallisch, piano; Wolfgang Sawallisch, conductor; Eurodisc 610 263 (2 discs) [AAD] (TT=54.57).

Operatic

{819}   *A*   Il Barbiere di Siviglia ("The Barber of Seville") (1816)

a   Agnes Baltsa, mezzo-soprano; Sally Burgess, mezzo-soprano; Francisco Araiza, tenor; Thomas Allen, baritone; Domenico Trimarchi, baritone; Robert Lloyd, bass; Ambrosian Opera Chorus; Academy of St. Martin-in-the-Fields; Sir Neville Marriner, conductor; Philips 411 058-2 (3 discs) [DDD] (TT=146.51).

b   Teresa Berganza, mezzo-soprano; Stefania Malagu, mezzo-soprano; Luigi Alva, tenor; Hermann Prey, baritone; Enzo Dara, bass; Ambrosian Opera Chorus; London Symphony Orchestra; Claudio Abbado, conductor; DG 415 695-2 (2 discs) [ADD] (TT=138.43).

The older Abbado recording has a first rate class (the Marriner performance is also classy, but not quite on par) and has the advantage of being on fewer discs. Marriner is fully digital and a little more relaxed, but I'll keep Prey's inimitable Figaro.

{820}   *B*   La Cenerentola ("Cinderella") (1817)
Teresa Berganza, mezzo soprano; Luigi Alva, tenor; Renato Capecchi, baritone; Paolo Montarsolo, baritone; Ugo Trama, bass; Scottish Opera Chorus; London Symphony Orchestra; Claudio Abbado, conductor; DG 415 698-2 (3 discs) [ADD] (TT = 144.20).

{821}   *B*   L'Italiana in Algeri ("The Italian Woman in Algiers") (1816)
Kathleen Battle, soprano; Marilyn Horne, mezzo-soprano; Ernesto Palacio, tenor; Domenico Trimarchi, baritone; Nicola Zaccaria, bass; Prague Philharmonic Chorus; I Solisti Veneti; Claudio Scimone, conductor; ECD 88200 (2 discs) [AAD] (TT = 141.21).

{822}   *C*   Il Turco in Italia ("The Turk in Italy") (1814)
Maria Callas, soprano; Jolanda Gardino, mezzo-soprano; Nicolaï Gedda, tenor; Piero de Palma, tenor; Franco Calabrese, bass; Nicola Rossi-Lemeni, bass; Mariano Stabile, bass; Chorus and Orchestra of La Scala, Milan; Gianadrea Gavazzeni, conductor; Angel CDC 49344 ! (2 discs) [ADD] (TT = 112.39).

{823}   *A*   William Tell (1829)
Mirella Freni, soprano; Elizabeth Connell, mezzo-soprano;Della Jones, mezzo-soprano; Luciano Pavarotti, tenor; Sherrill Milnes, baritone; Nicolai Ghiaurov, bass; Franco Mazzoli, bass; Ambrosian Opera Chorus; National Philharmonic Orchestra of London; Riccardo Chailly, conductor; London 417 154-2 (4 discs) [ADD] (TT = 232.22).

Orchestral

{824}   *A*   Overture: Il Barbiere di Siviglia ("The Barber of Seville") (1816)

National Philharmonic Orchestra of London; Riccardo Chailly, conductor; London 414 407-2 [DDD] (TT = 56.16). Includes Rossini's Overtures: La Cambiale di matrimonio ("The Marriage Contract") (1810), rated B; Otello ("Othello") (1816), rated B; Semiramide (1823), rated A; Le Siège de Corinthe ("The Siege of Corinth") (1826), rated B; Tancredi (1813), rated B and Torvaldo e Dorliska (1815), rated C.

{825}   *A*   La Boutique fantasque ("The Fantastic Toyshop") (Arranged by Respighi) (1919) -- see entry No.{249}.

{826}   *B*   Overture: La Cambiale di matrimonio ("The Marriage Contract") (1810) -- see entry No.{824}.

{827}   *A*   Overture: La Gazza ladra ("The Thieving Magpie") (1817)

National Philharmonic Orchestra of London; Riccardo Chailly, conductor; London 400 049-2 [DDD] (TT = 56.05). Includes Rossini's Overtures: L'Italiana in Algeri ("The Italian Woman in Algiers") (1816), rated A; La Scala di seta ("The Silken Ladder") (1812), rated A; Il Signor Bruschino (1813), rated B; Il Turco in Italia ("The Turk in Italy") (1814), rated B; Il Viaggio a Reims ("The Journey to Reims") (1825), rated B and William Tell (1829), rated A.

{828}   *A*   Overture: L'Italiana in Algeri ("The Italian Woman in Algiers") (1816) -- see entry No.{827}.

{829}   *B*   Overture: Otello ("Othello") (1816) -- see entry No.{824}.

{830}   *A*   Overture: La Scala di seta ("The Silken Ladder") (1812) -- see entry No.{827}.

{831}   *A*   Overture: <u>Semiramide</u> (1823) -- see entry No.{824}.

{832}   *B*   Overture: <u>Le Siège de Corinthe</u> ("The Siege of Corinth") (1826) -- see entry No.{824}.

{833}   *B*   Overture: <u>Il Signor Bruschino</u> (1813) -- see entry No.{827}.

{834}   *B*   Overture: <u>Tancredi</u> (1813) -- see entry No.{824}.

{835}   *C*   Overture: <u>Torvaldo e Dorliska</u> (1815) -- See entry No.{824}.

{836}   *B*   Overture: <u>Il Turco in Italia</u> ("The Turk in Italy") (1814) -- see entry No.{827}.

{837}   *B*   Overture: <u>Il Viaggio a Reims</u> ("The Journey to Reims") (1825) -- see entry No.{827}.

{838}   *A*   Overture: <u>William Tell</u> (1829) -- see entries Nos.{10}, {537}b, {571}c and {827}.

SAINT-SAËNS, CAMILLE
1835-1921

Chamber
{839}   *A*   Sonata No.1 for Violin and Piano, Op.75, in d -- see entry No.{309}.

Concerted
{840}   *A*   <u>Carnival of the Animals</u> (Grand Zoological Fantasy) for Two Pianos and Orchestra (1886)
    Christina Ortiz, piano; Pascal Rogé, piano; London Sinfonietta; Charles Dutoit, conductor; London 414 460-2

[ADD] (TT=46.53). Includes Saint-Saëns' <u>Danse macabre</u> ("Macabre Dance"), Symphonic Poem After Henri Cazalis, Op.40, rated A; <u>Phaéton</u>, Op.39 and <u>Le Rouet d'Omphale:</u> <u>Poème symphonique</u> ("Omphale's Spinning Wheel: Symphonic Poem"), Op.31, rated B. No.13 of the <u>Carnival of the Animals</u> is "The Swan" (sometimes called "The Dying Swan").

Also -- see entry No.{736}.

For "The Swan" from <u>Carnival of the Animals</u> (1886) (Transcribed by Heifetz) -- see entry No.{309}.

{841}   *B*   Concerto for 'Cello and Orchestra No.1, Op.33, in a

Lynn Harrell, 'cello; Cleveland Orchestra; Sir Neville Marriner, conductor; London 410 019-2 [DDD] (TT=44.26). Includes Schumann's Concerto for 'Cello, Op.129, in a, rated A.

Also -- see entry No.{521}b.

{842}   *B*   Concerto for 'Cello and Orchestra No.2, Op.119, in d -- see entry No.{521}a.

{843}   *C*   Concerto for Piano No.1, Op.17, in D

Pascal Rogé, piano; Philharmonia Orchestra; Charles Dutoit, conductor; London 417 351-2 (2 discs) [ADD] (TT=138.44). Includes Saint-Saëns' Concerto for Piano No.2, Op.22, in g, rated B; Concerto for Piano No.3, Op.29, in E flat (the ensemble here is the London Philharmonic Orchestra), rated B; Concerto for Piano No.4, Op.44, in c, rated A and Concerto for Piano No.5 ("Egyptian"), Op.103, in F, rated B (here Dutoit conducts the Royal Philharmonic Orchestra), rated B.

{844}   *B*   Concerto for Piano No.2, Op.22, in g

Jean-Philippe Collard, piano; Royal Philharmonic Orchestra; André Previn, conductor; Angel CDC 49051-2

[DDD] (TT=60.06). Includes Saint-Saëns' Concerto for Piano No.5 ("Egyptian"), rated B.
Also -- see entries Nos.{270}, {759} and {843}.

{845}   *B*   Concerto for Piano No.3, Op.29, in E flat -- see entry No.{843}.

{846}   *A*   Concerto for Piano No.4, Op.44, in c -- see entry No.{843}.

{847}   *B*   Concerto for Piano No.5 ("Egyptian"), Op.103, in F -- see entries Nos.{843} and {844}.

{848}   *A*   Havanaise for Violin and Orchestra, Op.83 -- see entries Nos.{267} and {779}.

{849}   *A*   Introduction and Rondo Capriccioso for Violin and Orchestra, Op.28 -- see entry No.{267}.

Instrumental
{850}   *A*   "The Swan" from Carnival of the Animals (1886) (Transcribed by Heifetz) -- see entry No.{309}.

Operatic
{851}   *B*   Samson et Dalila ("Samson and Delilah"), Op.47
Rita Gorr, mezzo-soprano; Jon Vickers, tenor; Ernest Blanc, baritone; Anton Diakov, bass; René Duclos Chorus; Orchestra of the National Opera Theater of Paris; Georges Prêtre, conductor; Angel CDCB 47895 (2 discs) [AAD] (TT=120.14).

Orchestral
{852}   *A*   Bacchanale from Samson et Dalila, Op.47
Orchestre de Paris; Daniel Barenboim, conductor; DG 415 847-2 [ADD] (TT=56.30). Includes Saint-Saëns' Danse macabre ("Macabre Dance"), Symphonic Poem After Henri

Cazalis, Op.40, rated A; Le Déluge: Biblical Poem, Op.45; and Symphony No.3 ("Organ"), Op.78, in c, rated A. In the Symphony, Barenboim conducts the Chicago Symphony Orchestra, and the organist is Gaston Litaize.

{853}   *A*   Danse macabre ("Macabre Dance"), Symphonic Poem After Henri Cazalis, Op.40 -- see entries Nos.{840} and {852}.

{854}   *B*   Le Rouet d'Omphale: Poème symphonique ("Omphale's Spinning Wheel: Symphonic Poem"), Op.31 -- see entries Nos.{393}b and {840}. Le Rouet was used for the theme music for the old radio program, "The Shadow."

Symphonic
{855}   *A*   Symphony No.3 ("Organ"), Op.78, in c
Michael Murray, organ; Philadelphia Orchestra; Eugene Ormandy, conductor; Telarc CD-80051 [DDD] (TT=34.59).
Also -- see entry No.{852}.

SARASATE, PABLO DE
1844-1908

Concerted
{856}   *B*   Carmen Fantasy for Violin and Orchestra, Op.25 -- see entry No.{708}c.

{857}   *B*   Zigeunerweisen ("Gypsy Airs") for Violin and Orchestra, Op.20 -- see entry No.{267}.

SATIE, ERIK
1866-1925

Ballet
{858}   *B*   Parade (1917) -- see entry No.{576}.

Instrumental
{859}   *C*   Avant-dernières pensées ("Penultimate
Thoughts") (3) Nos.1-3 (1915)

a   Laurence Allix, piano; Ensayo 3402 [DDD]
(TT=61.50). Includes Satie's La Diva de l'Empire ("The
Leading Female Singer of 'The Empire'") (c.1904); Sports et
divertissements ("Sports and Entertainments") (1914); Trois
Gnossiennes ("Three Little Gnostics") (3) Nos.1-3 (1888), rated
B; Trois Gymnopédies ("Three 'Barefooted' Dances") (3)
Nos.1-3 (1888), rated A; Trois Morceaux en forme de poire
("Three Pieces in the Shape of a Pear") (3) Nos.1-3 (1903),
rated B; Trois Sarabandes ("Three Sarabands") (3) Nos.1-3,
(1887) and Les Trois Valses distinguées du précieux dégoûté
("The Three Waltzes of an Affected, Disgusted Man") (3)
Nos.1-3 (1914), rated C.

b   Aldo Ciccolini, piano; Angel CDC 47474-2 [DDD]
(TT=71.04). Includes Satie's La Belle excentrique ("The
Eccentric Beautiful Lady") for Two Pianos (1920) (with Aldo
Ciccolini and Gabriel Tacchino, pianos), rated B; Cinq
Nocturnes ("Five Nocturnes") (5) Nos.1-5 (1919); Croquis et
agaceries d'un gros bonhomme en bois ("Sketches and
Exasperations of a Big Wooden Blockhead") (1913), rated C;
Embryons desséchés ("Dessicated Embryos") (1913), rated C;
Six Gnossiennes ("Six Little Gnostics") (6) Nos.1-6 (1888-1893),
rated D; Sonatine bureaucratique ("Bureaucratic Sonatina")
(1917); Trois Gymnopédies ("Three 'Barefooted' Dances") (3)
Nos.1-3 (1888), rated A; Trois Morceaux en forme de poire
("Three Pieces in the Shape of a Pear") (For Piano, Four
Hands) (with Aldo Ciccolini and Gabriel Tacchino, piano) (3)
Nos.1-3 (1903), rated B and Véritables préludes flasques (pour
un chien) ("Truly Flabby Preludes <For a Dog>") (3) Nos.1-3
(1912), rated C.

{860}   *B*   <u>La Belle excentrique</u> (("The Eccentric Beautiful Lady") for Two Pianos (1920) -- see entry No.{859}b.

{861}   *C*   <u>Croquis et agaceries d'un gros bonhomme en bois</u> ("Sketches and Exasperations of a Big Wooden Blockhead") (1913) -- see entry No.{859}b.

{862}   *C*   <u>Embryons desséchés</u> ("Dessicated Embryos") (1913)

Pascal Rogé, piano; London 410 220-2 [DDD] (TT = 60.46). Includes Satie's <u>Je te veux</u> ("I Want You") (1900); <u>Le Picadilly</u> (1904); <u>Prélude en tapisserie</u> ("Prelude in Tapestry") (1906), rated C; <u>Quatre Préludes flasques</u> ("Four Flabby Preludes") (1893); <u>Quatrième Prélude</u> ("Fourth Prelude") (1919); <u>Six Gnossiennes</u> ("Six Little Gnostics") (6) Nos.1-6 (1890-1893), rated B; <u>Sonatine bureaucratique</u> ("Bureaucratic Sonatina") (1917); <u>Trois Gnossiennes</u> ("Three Little Gnostics") (1888), rated B; <u>Trois Gymnopédies</u> ("Three 'Barefooted' Dances") (1888), rated A and <u>Vieux sequins et vielles cuirasses</u> ("Old Sequins and Breast-Plates") (1913).
Also -- see entry No.{859}b.

{863}   *C*   <u>Prélude en tapisserie</u> ("Prelude in Tapestry") (1906) -- see entry No.{862}.

{864}   *B*   <u>Six Gnossiennes</u> ("Six Little Gnostics") (6) Nos.1-6 (1888-1893) -- see entries Nos.{859}b and {862}.

{865}   *B*   <u>Trois Gnossiennes</u> ("Three Little Gnostics") (1888) -- see entry No.{859}a.

{866}   *A*   <u>Trois Gymnopédies</u> ("Three 'Barefooted' Dances") (1888) -- see entries Nos.{859}a and {862}.

{867}   *B*   Trois Morceaux en forme de poire ("Three Pieces in the Shape of a Pear") (3) Nos.1-3 (1903) -- see entries Nos.{859}a-b.

{868}   *C*   Les Trois Valses distinguées du précieux dégoûté ("The Three Waltzes of an Affected, Disgusted Man") (1914) -- see entry No.{859}a.

{869}   *C*   Véritables préludes flasques (pour un chien) ("Truly Flabby Preludes <For a Dog>") (3) Nos.1-3 (1893) -- see entry No.{859}b.

SCARLATTI, DOMENICO
1685-1757

Instrumental
{870}   *A*   Sonata, L.430, in E -- see entry No.{276}.

{871}   *A*   Sonata, L.483, in A -- see entry No.{276}.

SCHOENBERG, ARNOLD
1874-1951

Chamber
{872}   *A*   Verklärte Nacht ("Transfigured Night"), Op.4
Schoenberg Ensemble; Philips 416 306-2 [DDD] (TT=51.22). Includes Schoenberg's Trio for Strings, Op.45. Also -- for Orchestral Version see entry No.{875}.

Choral
{873}   *B*   Gurrelieder ("Gurre Songs") (1900-1901)
Jessye Norman, soprano; Tatiana Troyanos, mezzo-soprano; James McCracken, tenor; David Arnold, baritone; Werner Klemperer, speaker; Tanglewood Festival Chorus;

Boston Symphony Orchestra; Seiji Ozawa, conductor; Philips 212 511-2 (2 discs) [ADD] (TT = 102.43).

Operatic

{874}   *B*   Moses und Aron ("Moses and Aaron") (1954)
Barbara Bonney, soprano; Mira Zakai, contralto; Daniel Harper, tenor; Philip Langridge, tenor; Franz Mazura, baritone; Aage Haugland, bass; Chicago Symphony Chorus and Orchestra; Sir Georg Solti, conductor; London 414 264-2 (2 discs) [DDD] (TT = 96.24).

Orchestral

{875}   *C*   Variations for Orchestra, Op.31
Berlin Philharmonic Orchestra; Herbert von Karajan, conductor; DG 415 326-2 [ADD] (TT = 52.04). Includes Schoenberg's Verklärte Nacht ("Transfigured Night") (Orchestral Version), Op.4, rated A.

{876}   *A*   Verklärte Nacht ("Transfigured Night") (Orchestral Version), Op.4 -- see entry No.{875}.

SCHUBERT, FRANZ
1797-1828

Chamber

{877}   *A*   Adagio for Piano, Violin and 'Cello ("Notturno") ("Nocturne"), D.897, in E flat
Beaux Arts Trio; Philips 412 620-2 (2 discs) [DDD] (TT = 98.49). Includes Schubert's Trio for Piano, Violin and 'Cello No.1, D.898, in B flat, rated A; Trio for Piano, Violin and 'Cello in One Movement ("Sonata"), D.28, in B flat, rated C and Trio for Piano, Violin and 'Cello No.2, D.100, in E flat, rated A.

{878}   *A*   Octet for Strings and Winds, D.803
          Boston Symphony Chamber Players; Nonesuch 79046-2
          [DDD] (TT=59.08).

{879}   *A*   Piano Quintet (Die Forelle) ("Trout"), D.667, in A
a   Borodin Quartet; Sviatoslav Richter, piano; Georg
          Hörtnagel, double-bass; Angel CDC 47009-2 [DDD]
          (TT=44.08).
b   Cleveland Quartet; Alfred Brendel, piano; James van
          Demark, double-bass; Philips 400 078-2 [ADD?] (TT=38.16).
          Also -- see entry No.{596}.

{880}   *C*   String Quartet No.9, D.173, in g
          Tokyo String Quartet; RCA 7750-2-RC [DDD]
          (TT=55.21). Includes Schubert's String Quartet No.13
          ("Rosamunde"), D.804, in a, rated A.

{881}   *A*   String Quartet No.12 ("Quartettsatz"), D.703, in c
a   Amadeus Quartet; DG 410 024-2 [DDD] (TT=47.18).
          Includes Schubert's String Quartet No.14 (Der Tod und das
          Mädchen) ("Death and the Maiden"), D.804, in d, rated A.
b   Portland String Quartet; Arabesque Z6536 [DDD]
          (TT=49.17). Includes Schubert's String Quartet No.14 (Der
          Tod und das Mädchen) ("Death and the Maiden"), D.804, in d,
          rated A.
c   Tokyo String Quartet; Vox Cum Laude MCD-10004
          [DDD] (TT=44.58). Includes Schubert's String Quartet No.14
          (Der Tod und das Mädchen) ("Death and the Maiden"), D.804,
          in d, rated A.

{882}   *A*   String Quartet No.13 ("Rosamunde"), D.804, in a
          Alban Berg Quartet; Angel CDC 47333-2 [DDD]
          (TT=72.28). Includes Schubert's String Quartet No.14 (Der
          Tod und das Mädchen) ("Death and the Maiden"), D.804, in d,
          rated A.
          Also -- see entry No.{880}.

{883}   *A*   String Quartet No.14 (Der Tod und das Mädchen) ("Death and the Maiden"), D.804, in d -- see entries Nos.{881}a-c and {882}.

{884}   *A*   String Quartet No.15, D.887, in G
          Alban Berg Quartet; Angel CDC 49082-2 [DDD] (TT=45.53).

{885}   *B*   String Quintet, D.956, in C
          Amadeus Quartet; Robert Cohen, 'cello; DG 419 611-2 [DDD] (TT=59.46).

{886}   *A*   Trio for Piano, Violin and 'Cello No.1, D.898, in B flat -- see entry No.{877}.

{887}   *C*   Trio for Piano, Violin and 'Cello in One Movement ("Sonata"), D.28, in B flat -- see entry No.{877}.

{888}   *A*   Trio for Piano, Violin and 'Cello No.2, D.100, in E flat -- see entry No.{877}.

Choral
{889}   *B*   Mass No.6, D.950, in E flat
          Helen Donath, soprano; Brigitte Fassbaender, mezzo-soprano; Francisco Araizo, tenor; Dietrich Fischer-Dieskau, baritone; Bavarian Radio Chorus and Orchestra; Wolfgang Sawallisch, conductor; Angel CDM 69223 [ADD] (TT=55.36).

Instrumental
{890}   *A*   Fantasia ("Wanderer"), D.760, in C -- see entry No.{358}.

{891}   *B*   Impromptu, Op.90 No.3, in G flat -- see entry No.{276}.

{892}   *C*   Sonata for Piano, D.537, in a
         Alfred Brendel, piano; Philips 410 605-2 [DDD]
         (TT=47.49). Includes Schubert's Sonata for Piano, D.664, in
         A, rated B.

{893}   *B*   Sonata for Piano, D.664, in A -- see entry
         No.{892}.

{894}   *B*   Sonata for Piano, D.784, in a
a   Alfred Brendel, piano; Philips 422 063-2 [DDD]
         (TT=63.42). Includes Schubert's Sonata for Piano, D.850, in
         D, rated A.
b   Howard Shelley, piano; MHS 1108H [DDD]
         (TT=53.36). Includes Schubert's Sonata for Piano, D.894, in
         G, rated A.

{895}   *A*   Sonata for Piano, D.850, in D -- see entry
         No.{894}a.

{896}   *B*   Sonata for Piano, D.894, in G -- see entry
         No.{894}b.

{897}   *A*   Sonata for Piano, D.959, in A
         Alfred Brendel, piano; Philips 411 777-2 [ADD]
         (TT=49.29). Includes Schubert's Ländler (12) Nos.1-12,
         D.790.

Orchestral
{898}   *A*   Rosamunde (Incidental Music for the Play by
         Helmina von Chézy), D.797
         Elly Ameling, soprano; Leipzig Radio Chorus; Leipzig
         Gewandhaus Orchestra; Kurt Masur, conductor; Philips 412
         432-2 [DDD] (TT=60.44).

Symphonic
{899}   *A*   Symphony No.4 ("Tragic"), D.417, in c

287

Academy of St. Martin-in-the-Fields; Sir Neville Marriner, conductor; Philips 410 045-2 [DDD] (TT=59.25). Includes Schubert's Symphony No.5, D.485, in B flat, rated A.

{900}   *A*   Symphony No.5, D.485, in B flat
Columbia Symphony Orchestra; Bruno Walter, conductor; CBS MK 42048 [AAD?] (TT=53.13). Includes Schubert's Symphony No.8 ("Unfinished"), D.759, in b, rated A. Also -- see entry No.{899}.

{901}   *A*   Symphony No.8 ("Unfinished"), D.759, in b -- see entries Nos.{176}, {571}b and {900}.

{902}   *A*   Symphony No.9 ("Great"), D.944, in C
a   Cleveland Orchestra; Christoph von Dohnányi, conductor; Telarc CD-80110 [DDD] (TT=49.43).
b   Columbia Symphony Orchestra; Bruno Walter, conductor; CBS MK 42049 [AAD?] (TT=52.26).
c   Vienna Philharmonic Orchestra; Sir Georg Solti, conductor; London 400 082-2 [DDD] (TT=55.24).
Dohnányi's performance is taut and well recorded, but lacks a bit of the "Viennese" feel of Schubert. Walter's orchestra is a little less than great (while Solti's is, of course, wonderful), and the recording displays some of its age--I'd rather keep all three for different reasons. If I must choose one, then it's Solti because of its sumptuous sound and fine performance.

Vocal

{903}   *B*   Im Abendrot ("At Dusk"), D.799
a   Dietrich Fischer-Dieskau, baritone; Alfred Brendel, piano; Philips 411 421-2 [DDD] (TT=53.15). Includes Schubert's songs: Auflösung ("Redemption"), D.807, rated C; Der Einsame ("The Solitary Man"), D.800, rated A; Gesänge des Harfners ("The Harper's Songs") (3) Nos.1-3, D.478, rated B; Gruppe aus dem Tartarus ("Group in Tartarus"), D.583,

rated C; <u>Herbst</u> ("Autumn"), D.945, rated A; <u>Hippolitis Lied</u> ("Hippolytus' Song"), D.890, rated B; <u>Nachtstücke</u> ("Nocturne"), D.672, rated B; <u>Nacht und Träume</u> ("Night and Dreams"), D.827, rated B; <u>Über Wildemann</u> ("Over Wildemann"), D.884, rated A and <u>Der Wanderer an dem Mond</u> ("The Wanderer Addresses the Moon"), D.870, rated A.

b   Dietrich Fischer-Dieskau, baritone; Gerald Moore, piano; DG 415 188-2 [ADD] (TT=68.37). Includes Schubert's songs: <u>Die Forelle</u> ("The Trout"), D.550, rated A; <u>Heidenröslein</u> ("Little Heath-Rose"), D.257, rated A; <u>An die Musik</u> ("To Music"), D.547, rated A; <u>An Silvia</u> ("To Sylvia"), D.891, rated A; <u>Schwanengesang</u> ("Swan Song") (Song Cycle after Ludwig Rellstab), D.957, rated A and <u>Der Tod und das Mädchen</u> ("Death and the Maiden"), D.531, rated A.

{904}   C   <u>Auflösung</u> ("Redemption"), D.807 -- see entry No.{903}a.

{905}   A   {903}<u>Der Einsame</u> ("The Solitary Man"), D.800 -- see entry No.{903}a.

{906}   A   <u>Die Forelle</u> ("The Trout"), D.550 -- see entry No.{903}b.

{907}   B   <u>Gesänge des Harfners</u> ("The Harper's Songs") (3) Nos.1-3, D.478 -- see entry No.{903}a.

{908}   C   <u>Gruppe aus dem Tartarus</u> ("Group in Tartarus"), D.583 -- see entry No.{903}a.

{909}   A   <u>Heidenröslein</u> ("Little Heath-Rose"), D.257 -- see entry No.{903}b.

{910}   A   <u>Herbst</u> ("Autumn"), D.945 -- see entry No.{903}a.

289

{911}   *B*   Hippolitis Lied ("Hippolytus' Song"), D.890 -- see entry No.{903}a.

{912}   *A*   An die Musik ("To Music"), D.547 -- see entry No.{903}b.

{913}   *B*   Nachtstücke ("Nocturne"), D.672 -- see entry No.{903}a.

{914}   *B*   Nacht und Träume ("Night and Dreams"), D.827 -- see entry No.{903}a.

{915}   *A*   Die schöne Müllerin ("The Miller's Beautiful Daughter") (Song Cycle After Wilhelm Müller), D.795
          Dietrich Fischer-Dieskau, baritone; Gerald Moore, piano; DG 415 186-2 [DDD] (TT=62.09).

{916}   *A*   Schwanengesang ("Swan Song") (Song Cycle after Ludwig Rellstab), D.957
          Ernst Haefliger, tenor; Jörg Ewald Dähler, fortepiano; Claves CD-8506 [DDD] (TT=50.40). Schwanengesang contains a few of Schubert's most justly popular songs, including: Ständchen ("Serenade"), Abschied ("Farewell") and Doppelgänger ("The Double").
          Also -- see entry No.{903}b.

{917}   *A*   An Silvia ("To Sylvia"), D.891 -- see entry No.{903}b.

{918}   *A*   Der Tod und das Mädchen ("Death and the Maiden"), D.531 -- see entry No.{903}b.

{919}   *A*   Über Wildemann ("Over Wildemann"), D.884 -- see entry No.{903}a.

{920}   *A*   Der Wanderer an dem Mond ("The Wanderer Addresses the Moon"), D.870 -- see entry No.{903}a.

{921}   *A*   Winterreise ("Winter Journey") (Song Cycle After Wilhelm Müller), D.911

a   Dietrich Fischer-Dieskau, baritone; Gerald Moore, piano; DG 415 187-2 [ADD] (TT = 71.41).

b   Ernst Haefliger, tenor; Jörg Ewald Dähler, fortepiano; Claves CD-8008/9 [DDD] (TT = 68.52).

c   Martti Talvela, bass; Ralf Gothóni, piano; Bis CD-253/4 [DDD] (TT = 71.21).

SCHUMANN, ROBERT
1810-1856

Chamber

{922}   *B*   Quartet for Piano and Strings, Op.47, in E flat
Emanuel Ax, piano; Members of the Cleveland Quartet; RCA 6498-2 [DDD] (TT = 56.43). Includes Schumann's Quintet for Piano and Strings, Op.44, in E flat, rated A (here the entire Cleveland Quartet are used, along with Ax).

{923}   *A*   Quintet for Piano and Strings, Op.44, in E flat -- see entry No.{922}.

Concerted

{924}   *A*   Concerto for 'Cello, Op.129, in a -- see entry No.{841}.

{925}   *A*   Concerto for Piano, Op.54, in a -- see entries Nos.{231} and {414}.

Instrumental

{926}   *A*   Arabeske, Op.18, in C

Maurizio Pollini, piano; DG 410 916-2 [DDD] (TT=38.36). Includes Schumann's Symphonic Études in the Form of Variations, Op.13, rated A.

{927}   *A*   Bunte Blätter ("Variegated" or "Multicolored Leaves"), Op.99 (14) Nos.1-2 and 4
Maria João Pires, piano; Erato ECD-88092 [DDD] (TT=51.46). Includes Schumann's Kinderszenen ("Childhood Scenes"), Op.15, rated A and Waldszenen ("Forest Scenes"), Op.28, rated B.

{928}   *A*   Fantasia for Piano, Op.17, in C
Alfred Brendel, piano; Philips 411 049-2 [DDD] (TT=58.00). Includes Schumann's Fantasiestücke, Op.12, rated B.

{929}   *B*   Fantasiestücke ("Fantasy Pieces"), Op.12 -- see entries Nos.{927} and {928}.

{930}   *A*   Kinderszenen ("Childhood Scenes"), Op.15
Martha Argerich, piano; DG 410 653-2 [DDD] (TT=52.25). Includes Schumann's Kreisleriana, Op.16, rated A.

{931}   *A*   Kreisleriana, Op.16 -- see entry No.{930}.

{932}   *A*   Symphonic Études in the Form of Variations, Op.13 -- see entry No.{926}.

{933}   *A*   "Träumerei" ("Dreams") from Kinderszenen ("Childhood Scenes"), Op.15 -- see entry No.{276}.

{934}   *B*   Waldszenen ("Forest Scenes"), Op.28 -- see entry No.{927}.

Symphonic

{935}   *A*   Symphony No.1 ("Spring"), Op.38, in B flat
Amsterdam Concertgebouw Orchestra; Bernard Haitink, conductor; Philips 416 126-2 (2 discs) [DDD] (TT=121.53). Includes Schumann's Symphony No.2, Op.61, in C, rated C; Symphony No.3 ("Rhenish"), Op.97, in E flat, rated B and Symphony No.4, Op.120, in d, rated A.

{936}   *C*   Symphony No.2, Op.61, in C -- see entry No.{935}.

{937}   *B*   Symphony No.3 ("Rhenish"), Op.97, in E flat -- see entry No.{935}.

{938}   *A*   Symphony No.4, Op.120, in d -- see entry No.{935}.

Vocal

{939}   *A*   Dichterliebe ("Loves of a Poet") (Song Cycle After Heinrich Heine), Op.48
Dietrich Fischer-Dieskau; Christoph Eschenbach, piano; DG 415 190-2 [ADD] (TT=67.10). Includes Schumann's Liederkreis ("Song Cycle" After Joseph von Eichendorff), Op.39, rated A and Myrten ("The Myrtles") (Song Cycle), Op.25 (26) Nos.1-3, 7-8, 13 and 24, rated C.

{940}   *A*   Frauenliebe und -leben ("Woman's Love and Life") (Song Cycle After Adelbert von Chamisso), Op.42

a   Brigitte Fassbaender, mezzo-soprano; Irwin Gage, piano; DG 415 519-2 [DDD] (TT=56.50). Includes Schumann's Liederkreis ("Song Cycle" After Joseph von Eichendorff), Op.39, rated A; Tragödie ("Tragedy") (Song Cycle After Heinrich Heine), Op.64 No.3 (3) and Three Lieder, Op.45, No.3; Op.142 No.1 and Op.142 No.4.

b   Jessye Norman, soprano; Irwin Gage, piano; Philips 420 784-2 [ADD] (TT=53.58). Includes Schumann's Liederkreis ("Song Cycle" After Joseph von Eichendorff), Op.39, rated A.

293

{941}   *A*   Liederkreis ("Song Cycle" After Joseph von Eichendorff), Op.39 -- see entries Nos.{939} and {940}a-b.

{942}   *C*   Myrten ("The Myrtles") (Song Cycle), Op.25 -- see entry No.{939}.

{943}   *C*   Tragödie ("Tragedy") (Song Cycle After Heinrich Heine), Op.64 No.3 (3) Nos.1-3 -- see entry No.{940}b.

SCRIABIN, ALEXANDER
1872-1915

Symphonic
{944}   *B*   Symphony No.3 ("The Divine Poem"), Op.43
Amsterdam Concertgebouw Orchestra; Kiril Kondrashin, conductor; Etcetera KTC 1027 [ADD?] (TT=45.59).

{945}   *A*   Symphony No.4 ("Poem of Ecstasy"), Op.54 -- see entry No.{327}.

SHOSTAKOVICH, DMITRI
1906-1975

Chamber
{946}   *A*   Quintet for Piano and Strings, Op.57, in g
Vladimir Ashkenazy, piano; Fitzwilliam String Quartet; London 411 940-2 [DDD] (TT=63.53). Includes Shostakovich's Seven Romances on Poems of Alexander Blok (with Elisabeth Söderström, soprano), Op.127 and Two Pieces for String Quartet (1931).

Concerted
{947}   *B*   Concerto for 'Cello No.1, Op.107, in E flat

Yo-Yo Ma, 'cello; Philadelphia Orchestra; Eugene Ormandy, conductor; CBS MK 37840 [DDD] (TT=45.58). Includes Kabalevsky's Concerto for 'Cello No.1, Op.49, in g. Also -- see entry No.{205}.

Orchestral

{948}   *B*   Festive Overture, Op.96 -- see entry No.{292}b.

{949}   *A*   The Gadfly (Film), Op.97: "Romance" -- see entry No.{511}.

{950}   *C*   Overture on Hebrew Folk Themes, Op.115
Amsterdam Concertgebouw Orchestra; Bernard Haitink, conductor; London 411 939 2 (2 discs) [DDD] (TT=102.42). Includes Shostakovich's Symphony No.6, Op.54, in b, rated B and Symphony No.11 ("In the Year 1905"), Op.103, in g, rated B.

Symphonic

{951}   *B*   Symphony No.1, Op.13, in f
London Philharmonic Orchestra; Bernard Haitink, conductor; London 414 677-2 [DDD] (TT=57.23). Includes Shostakovich's Symphony No.9, Op.70, in E flat, rated B. Also -- see entry No.{103}.

{952}   *A*   Symphony No.5, Op.47, in D
a   Amsterdam Concertgebouw Orchestra; Bernard Haitink, conductor; London 410 017-2 [DDD] (TT=49.34).
b   Berlin Philharmonic Orchestra; Semyon Bychkov, conductor; Philips 420 069-2 [DDD] (TT=48.22).
c   Cleveland Orchestra; Lorin Maazel, conductor; Telarc CD-80067 [DDD] (TT=47.09).
           Although the other two recordings are excellent (Bychkov for his *echt* Slavic "feel" and Maazel for the tension and fine sound), Haitink's wins by a neck.

{953}   *B*   Symphony No.6, Op.54, in b -- see entry No.{950}.

{954}   *C*   Symphony No.8, Op.65, in c
Amsterdam Concertgebouw Orchestra; Bernard
Haitink, conductor; London 411 616-2 [DDD] (TT=61.40).

{955}   *B*   Symphony No.9, Op.70, in E flat -- see entry
No.{951}.

{956}   *C*   Symphony No.10, Op.93, in e
Berlin Philharmonic Orchestra; Herbert von Karajan,
conductor; DG 513 361-2 [DDD] (TT=51.22).

{957}   *B*   Symphony No.11 ("In the Year 1905"), Op.103, in
g -- see entry No.{950}.

{958}   *C*   Symphony No.15, Op.141, in A
USSR State Symphony Orchestra; Gennady
Rozhdestvensky, conductor; JVC/Melodia VDC-528 [DDD]
(TT=43.01).

SIBELIUS, JEAN
1865-1957

Chamber
{959}   *C*   Romance for String Orchestra, Op.42, in C
Gothenburg Symphony Orchestra; Neeme Järvi,
conductor; Bis CD-252 [DDD] (TT=47.21). Includes
Sibelius's Symphony No.2, Op.43, in D, rated A.

{960}   *C*   String Quartet (1894), in a
Sibelius Academy Quartet; Finlandia FACD-345
[DDD] (TT=59.40). Includes Sibelius' String Quartet, Op.4, in
B flat, rated C.

{961}   *C*   String Quartet, Op.4, in B flat -- see entry No.{960}.

Concerted

{962}   *A*   Concerto for Violin, Op.47, in d

Itzhak Perlman, violin; Pittsburgh Symphony Orchestra; André Previn, conductor; Angel CDC 47167 [ADD] (TT = 44.58). Includes Sinding's Suite for Violin and Orchestra, Op.10, in a, rated B.

Also -- see entry No.{402}.

Operatic

{963}   *C*   The Maiden in the Tower: Opera in One Act (1896)

Mari-Ann Häggander, soprano; Tone Kruse, contralto; Erland Hagegård, tenor; Jorma Hynninen, baritone; Gothenburg Concert Hall Choir; Gothenburg Symphony Orchestra; Neeme Järvi, conductor; Bis CD-250 [DDD] (TT = 52.24). Includes Sibelius' Karelia Suite, Op.11, rated A.

Orchestral

{964}   *A*   Finlandia, Op.26

a   Gothenburg Symphony Orchestra; Neeme Järvi, conductor; Bis CD-2221 [DDD] (TT = 47.23). Includes Sibelius' Symphony No.1, Op.39, in e, rated A.

b   Hallé Orchestra; Sir John Barbirolli, conductor; Angel CDM 69205 [ADD] (TT = 50.23). Includes Sibelius' Karelia Suite, Op.11, rated A; Leminkäinen's Return from Four Legends from The Kalevala, Op.22, rated A; Pohjola's Daughter, Op.49, rated B and Valse triste from Kuolema, Op.44, rated A.

Also -- see entry No.{266}.

{965}   *A*   Four Legends from The Kalevala, Op.22

Gothenburg Symphony Orchestra; Neeme Järvi, conductor; Bis CD-294 [DDD] (TT = 48.52). Opus 22 is

297

comprised of four parts: <u>Lemminkäinen and the Maidens of the Island</u>; <u>Lemminkäinen in Tuonela</u>; <u>Lemminkäinen's Return</u> and <u>The Swan of Tuonela</u>.

{966}   *B*   Overture: <u>Karelia</u>, Op.10
Gothenburg Symphony Orchestra; Neeme Järvi, conductor; Bis CD-222 [DDD] (TT=46.57). Includes Sibelius' <u>Andante Festivo</u> (1922) and Symphony No.5, Op.82, in E flat, rated A.

{967}   *A*   <u>Karelia</u> Suite, Op.11 -- see entries Nos.{963} and {964}b.

{968}   *B*   <u>King Kristian II</u> Suite (After Adolf Paul), Op.27
Gothenburg Symphony Orchestra; Neeme Järvi, conductor; Bis CD-228 [DDD] (TT=54.48). Includes Sibelius' Symphony No.3, Op.52, in C, rated A.

{969}   *C*   <u>Kullervo</u>, Op.7
Karita Mattila, soprano; Jorma Hynninen, baritone; Laulun Ystävät Male Choir; Gothenburg Symphony Orchestra; Neeme Järvi, conductor; Bis CD-313 [DDD] (TT=67.48).

{970}   *B*   <u>Kuolema</u> ("Death") Incidental Music, Op.44 and Op.62
Gothenburg Symphony Orchestra; Neeme Järvi, conductor; Bis CD-311 [DDD] (TT=56.53). Includes Sibelius' <u>Night-ride and Sunrise</u>, Op.55, rated C and Symphony No.7, Op.105, in C, rated A. The famous <u>Valse triste</u> comes from the <u>Kuolema</u>, Op.44.

{971}   *A*   <u>Lemminkäinen and the Maidens of the Island</u> -- see entry No.{965}.

{972}   *A*   <u>Lemminkäinen in Tuonela</u> -- see entry No.{965}.

{973}   *A*   Lemminkäinen's Return -- see entries Nos.{964}b and {965}.

{974}   *C*   Night-ride and Sunrise, Op.55 -- see entry No.{970}.

{975}   *B*   The Oceanides, Op.73
Gothenburg Symphony Orchestra; Neeme Järvi, conductor; Bis CD-263 [DDD] (TT=51.51). Includes Sibelius' Canzonetta, Op.62 No.1 and Symphony No.4, Op.63, in a, rated A.

{976}   *C*   Pelléas and Mélisande Suite, Op.46
Gothenburg Symphony Orchestra; Neeme Järvi, conductor; Bis CD-237 [DDD] (TT=56.09). Includes Sibelius' Symphony No.6, Op.104, in d, rated B.
Also -- see entry No.{419}.

{977}   *B*   Pohjola's Daughter, Op.49
Gothenburg Symphony Orchestra; Neeme Järvi, conductor; Bis CD-312 [DDD] (TT=54.14). Includes Impromptu for String Orchestra ("Andante lirico"), Op.5 No.25-6; Rakastava, Op.14, rated C and Tapiola, Op.112. rated A.
Also -- see entry No.{964}b.

{978}   *C*   Rakastava, Op.14 -- see entry No.{977}.

{979}   *B*   En Saga ("A Saga"), Op.9
Gothenburg Symphony Orchestra; Neeme Järvi, conductor; Bis CD-295 [DDD] (TT=54.35). Includes Sibelius' Scènes historiques, Op.25 and Op.66, rated C.

{980}   *C*   Scènes historiques, Op.25 and Op.66 -- see entry No.{979}.

{981}   *A*   <u>The Swan of Tuonela</u> -- see entry No.{965}.

{982}   *A*   <u>Tapiola</u>, Op.112 -- see entry No.{977}.

{983}   *A*   <u>Valse triste</u> from <u>Kuolema</u>, Op.44 -- see entries Nos.{964}b and {970}.

Symphonic

{984}   *A*   Symphony No.1, Op.39, in e -- see entry No.{964}a.

{985}   *A*   Symphony No.2, Op.43, in D -- see entries Nos.{173} and {959}.

{986}   *A*   Symphony No.3, Op.52, in C -- see entry No.{968}.

{987}   *A*   Symphony No.4, Op.63, in a -- see entry No.{975}.

{988}   *A*   Symphony No.5, Op.82, in E flat -- see entry No.{966}.

{989}   *B*   Symphony No.6, Op.104, in d -- see entry No.{976}.

{990}   *A*   Symphony No.7, Op.105, in C -- see entry No.{970}.

SINDING, CHRISTIAN
1856-1941

Concerted

{991}   *B*   Suite for Violin and Orchestra, Op.10, in a -- see entry No.{962}.

Instrumental

{992}   *A*   Rustles of Spring, Op.23 No.3
Jerome Lowenthal, piano; Arabesque Z6578 [DDD]
(TT = 47.51).   Includes Sinding's Alla marcia; Capriccio;
Caprice; Con fuoco; Irrlicht; Marche grotesque; Melodie;
Pomposo; Serenade and Sonata for Piano, Op.91, in b, rated B.

{993}   *B*   Sonata for Piano, Op.91, in b -- see entry
No.{992}.

SMETANA, BEDŘICH
1824-1884

Operatic

{994}   *B*   The Bartered Bride (1886)
Gabriela Beňáčková-Čápová, soprano; Peter Dvorský,
tenor; Richard Novák, tenor; Czech Philharmonic Chorus and
Orchestra; Zdeněk Košler, conductor; Supraphon C37-7309-11
(3 discs) [DDD] (TT = 136.53).

Orchestral

{995}   *B*   Overture: The Bartered Bride (1866) -- see entry
No.{362}a.

{996}   *A*   Three Dances from The Bartered Bride (1866) --
see entry No.{362}b.

{997}   *A*   Vltava ("Moldau") from Má Vlast ("My
Fatherland") (1874-1879) -- see entries Nos.{362}b and
{537}b.

SOUSA, JOHN PHILIP
1854-1932

Orchestral

{998}   *A*   <u>El Capitán</u> (1896)

Eastman Wind Ensemble; Frederick Fennell, conductor; Mercury 416 147-2 [ADD] (TT = 63.46). Includes Sousa's <u>Bullets and Bayonets</u> (1918); <u>The Glory of the Yankee Navy</u> (1909); <u>The Gridiron Club</u> (1926); <u>Hands Across the Sea</u> (1899), rated B; <u>The High School Cadets</u> (1890), rated A; <u>The Invincible Eagle</u> (1901); <u>The Kansas Wildcats</u> (1931); <u>King Cotton</u> (1895), rated B; <u>The Liberty Bell</u> (1893); <u>The National Game</u> (1925); <u>Manhattan Beach</u> (1893), rated A; <u>The Picadore</u> (1889); <u>The Pride of the Wolverines</u> (1926); <u>The Rifle Regiment</u> (1886); <u>Riders for the Flag</u> (1927); <u>Sabre and Spurs</u> (1918); <u>Sound Off</u> (1885), rated C; <u>The Stars and Stripes Forever</u> (1897), rated A; <u>The Thunderer</u> (1889), rated A; <u>U.S. Field Artillery</u> (1917), rated A and <u>The Washington Post</u> (1889), rated A.

{999}   *B*   <u>Hands Across the Sea</u> (1899) -- see entry No.{998}.

{1000}   *A*   <u>The High School Cadets</u> (1890) -- see entry No.{998}.

{1001}   *B*   <u>King Cotton</u> (1895) -- see entry No.{998}.

{1002}   *A*   <u>Manhattan Beach</u> (1893) -- see entry No.{998}.

{1003}   *A*   <u>The Stars and Stripes Forever</u> (1897) -- see entries Nos.{9} and {998}.

{1004}   *A*   <u>The Thunderer</u> (1889) -- see entry No.{998}.

{1005}   *A*   <u>U.S. Field Artillery</u> (1917) -- see entry No.{998}.

{1006}   *A*   <u>The Washington Post</u> (1889) -- see entry No.{998}.

STEVENS, HALSEY
1908-

Chamber
{1007}   *C*   Sonata for Trumpet and Piano (1953-1956) -- see entry No.{488}.

STRAUSS, JOHANN, JR.
1825-1899

Operatic
{1008}   *A*   Die Fledermaus ("The Bat") (1874)
Eva Lind, soprano; Lucia Popp, soprano; Agnes Baltsa, mezzo-soprano; Plácido Domingo, tenor; Peter Seiffert, tenor; Wolfgang Brendel, baritone; Kurt Rydl, bass; Bavarian Radio Chorus; Munich Radio Orchestra; Plácido Domingo, conductor; Angel CDCB 47480 (2 discs) [DDD] (TT = 136.12).

{1009}   *C*   Der Zigeunerbaron ("The Gypsy Baron") (1885)
Julia Varady, soprano; Hanna Schwarz, mezzo-soprano; Josef Protschka, tenor; Dietrich Fischer-Dieskau, baritone; Walter Berry, bass; Bavarian Radio Chorus; Munich Radio Orchestra; Willi Boskovsky, conductor; Angel CDCB 49231 (2 discs) [DDD] (TT = 115.15).

Orchestral
{1010}   *B*   Annen ("Anna's") Polka, Op.117
Hungarian State Orchestra; János Ferencsik, conductor; Hungaroton HCD-12600 [DDD] (TT = 58.55). Includes Strauss' Frühlingsstimmen ("Voices of Spring") Waltz, Op.410, rated A; Kunstlerleben ("Artist's Life") Waltz, Op.316, rated A; Morgenblätter ("Morning Papers") Waltz, Op.279, rated A; Rosen aus dem Süden ("Roses from the South") Waltz, Op.388, rated A; An der schönen blauen Donau ("On the Beautiful Blue Danube") Waltz, Op.314, rated A; Tik-Tak ("Tick-Tock")

Polka, Op.365, rated C and Johann Strauss, Sr.'s <u>Radetzky</u> March, Op.228, rated A.

{1011}   *B*   <u>Auf der Jagd</u> Polka ("At the Hunt"), Op.373
Cincinnati Pops Orchestra; Erich Kunzel, conductor; Telarc CD-80098 [DDD] (TT=48.08). Includes Strauss' <u>Banditen</u> ("Bandits") Galop, Op.378; <u>Champagne</u> Polka, Op.43, rated B; <u>Explosions</u> Polka, Op.43, rated B; <u>Geschichten aus dem Wienerwald</u> ("Tales from the Vienna Woods") Waltz, Op.325, rated A; <u>Im Krapfenwald</u> ("In the Little Jelly Doughnut Woods") Polka, Op.336, rated B; <u>An der schönen blauen Donau</u> ("On the Beautiful Blue Danube") Waltz, Op.314, rated A; <u>Unter Donner und Blitz</u> ("Under Thunder and Lightning") Polka, Op.324, rated B; Eduard Strauss' <u>Bahn frei</u> ("Clear Track") Polka, Op.45; Johann Strauss, Sr.'s <u>Radetzky</u> March, Op.228, rated A; Josef Strauss' <u>Feuerfest</u> ("Fire Festival") Polka, Op.269 and Johann and Josef Strauss' <u>Pizzicato</u> Polka (1870), rated A.

{1012}   *B*   <u>Champagne</u> Polka, Op.43 -- see entry No.{1011}.

{1013}   *B*   <u>Explosions</u> Polka, Op.43 -- see entry No.{1011}.

{1014}   *A*   Overture: <u>Die Fledermaus</u> ("The Bat") (1874)
Budapest Philharmonic Orchestra; János Ferencsik, conductor; Hungaroton HCD-12353 [ADD] (TT=54.56). Includes Strauss' <u>Geschichten aus dem Wienerwald</u> ("Tales from the Vienna Woods") Waltz, Op.325, rated A; <u>Kaiser</u> ("Emperor's") Waltz, Op.437, rated A; <u>Pizzicato</u> Polka (1870), rated A; <u>Tritsch-Tratsch</u> Polka, Op.214, rated A; <u>Wiener Blut</u> ("Viennese Blood") Waltz, Op.354, rated A and Overture: <u>Der Zigeunerbaron</u> ("Gypsy Baron") (1885), rated B.

{1015}   *A*   <u>Frühlingsstimmen</u> ("Voices of Spring") Waltz, Op.410 -- see entry No.{1010}.

{1016}   *A*   Geschichten aus dem Wienerwald ("Tales from the Vienna Woods") Waltz, Op.325 -- see entries Nos.{1011} and {1014}.

{1017}   *A*   Kaiser ("Emperor's") Waltz, Op.437 -- see entry No.{1014}.

{1018}   *B*   Im Krapfenwald ("In the Little Jelly Doughnut Woods") Polka, Op.336 -- see entry No.{1011}.

{1019}   *A*   Kunstlerleben ("Artist's Life") Waltz, Op.316 -- see entry No.{1010}.

{1020}   *A*   Morgenblätter ("Morning Papers") Waltz, Op.279 -- see entry No.{1010}.

{1021}   *A*   Pizzicato Polka (1870) -- see entries Nos.{1011} and {1014}.

{1022}   *A*   Rosen aus dem Süden ("Roses from the South") Waltz, Op.388 -- see entry No.{1010}.

{1023}   *A*   An der schönen blauen Donau ("On the Beautiful Blue Danube") Waltz, Op.314 -- see entries Nos.{1010} and {1011}.

{1024}   *C*   Tik-Tak ("Tick-Tock") Polka, Op.365 -- see entry No.{1010}.

{1025}   *A*   Tritsch-Tratsch Polka, Op.214 -- see entry No.{1014}.

{1026}   *B*   Unter Donner und Blitz ("Under Thunder and Lightning") Polka, Op.324 -- see entry No.{1011}.

{1027}   *A*   <u>Wiener Blut</u> ("Viennese Blood") Waltz, Op.354 -- see entries Nos.{266} and {1014}.

{1028}   *B*   Overture: <u>Der Zigeunerbaron</u> ("Gypsy Baron") (1885) -- see entry No.{1014}.

STRAUSS, JOHANN, SR.
1804-1849

Orchestral
{1029}   *A*   <u>Radetzky</u> March, Op.228 -- see entries Nos.{9}, {1010} and {1011}.

STRAUSS, RICHARD
1864-1949

Concerted
{1030}   *B*   Concerto for Horn No.1, Op.11, in E flat
a   Hermann Baumann, horn; Leipzig Gewandhaus Orchestra; Kurt Masur, conductor; Philips 412 237-2 [DDD] (TT=49.15). Includes Strauss' Concerto for Horn No.2 (1942), in E flat, rated B and Weber's Concertino for Horn and Orchestra, Op.45, in e.
b   Dennis Brain, horn; Philharmonia Orchestra; Wolfgang Sawallisch, conductor; Angel CDC 47834 ! [ADD] (TT=53.17). Includes Hindemith's Concerto for Horn (1950) and Strauss' Concerto for Horn No.2 (1942), in E flat, rated B.

{1031}   *B*   Concerto for Horn No.2 (1942), in E flat -- see entries Nos.{1030}a-b.

Operatic
{1032}   *B*   <u>Ariadne auf Naxos</u> ("Ariadne at Naxos"), Op.60

Edith Gruberová, soprano; Julie Kaufmann, soprano; Eva Lind, soprano; Jessye Norman, soprano; Julia Varady, soprano; Marianne Rerholm, mezzo-soprano; Martin Finke, tenor; Paul Frey, tenor; Olaf Bär, baritone; Dietrich Fischer-Dieskau, baritone; Gerd Wolf, bass; Rudolf Asmus, speaker; Leipzig Gewandhaus Orchestra; Kurt Masur, conductor; Philips 422 084-2 (2 discs) [DDD] (TT = 118.31).

{1033}   *B*   Elektra, Op.58
Birgit Nilsson, soprano; Regina Resnik, mezzo-soprano; Gerhard Stolze, tenor; Tom Krause, baritone; Vienna Philharmonic Orchestra; Sir Georg Solti, conductor; London 417 345-2 (2 discs) [ADD] (TT = 107.50).

{1034}   *C*   Die Frau ohne Schatten ("The Woman Without a Shadow"), Op.65
Birgit Nilsson, soprano; Leonie Rysanek, soprano; Ruth Hesse, mezzo-soprano; James King, tenor; Walter Berry, baritone; Chorus and Orchestra of the Vienna State Opera; Karl Böhm, conductor; DG 415 472-2 (3 discs) [ADD] (TT = 175.06).

{1035}   *A*   Der Rosenkavalier ("The Cavalier of the Rose"), Op. 59
a   Régine Crespin, soprano; Helen Donath, soprano; Emmy Loose, soprano; Anne Howells, mezzo-soprano; Yvonne Minton, mezzo-soprano; Anton Dermota, tenor; Murray Dickie, tenor; Kurt Equiluz, tenor; Luciano Pavarotti, tenor; Otto Wiener, baritone; Manfred Jungwirth, bass; Vienna State Opera Chorus; Vienna Philharmonic Orchestra; Sir Georg Solti, conductor; London 417 493-2 (3 discs) [ADD] (TT = 199.48).
b   Elisabeth Schwarzkopf, soprano; Teresa Stich-Randall, soprano; Ljuba Welitsch, soprano; Christa Ludwig, mezzo-soprano; Nicolaï Gedda, tenor; Eberhard Wächter, baritone; Otto Edelmann, bass; Loughton High School for Girls' Choir;

Bancroft School's Choir; Philharmonia Chorus and Orchestra; Herbert von Karajan, conductor; Angel CDCC 49354 (3 discs) [ADD] (TT=191.23).

Both Rosenkavaliers are exceptional in the quality of the casts and the conductorial attention to detail. Given their ages, both sound wonderful. Schwarzkopf and Ludwig sound as though their parts were written for them, but Solti's orchestra is superb (and Crespin and Minton bring much to their roles). If pressed, I go with Karajan's because I know it better and even love its few flaws.

{1036}   *B*   Salome, Op.54
Birgit Nilsson, soprano; Josephine Veasey, mezzo-soprano; Grace Hoffman, contralto; Waldemar Kmentt, tenor; Gerhard Stolze, tenor; Eberhard Wächter, baritone; Vienna Philharmonic Orchestra; Sir Georg Solti, conductor; London 414 414-2 (2 discs) [AAD] (TT=99.26).

Orchestral

{1037}   *A*   Also sprach Zarathustra ("Thus Spake Zarathustra"), Op.30

a   Berlin Philharmonic Orchestra; Herbert von Karajan, conductor; DG 410 959-2 [DDD] (TT=53.45). Includes Strauss' Don Juan, Op.20, rated A.

b   Chicago Symphony Orchestra; Fritz Reiner, conductor; RCA 5721-2 [ADD?] (TT=71.03). Includes Strauss' Le Bourgeois gentilhomme ("The Would-Be Gentleman") Suite (After Molière), Op.60, rated C.

c   New York Philharmonic Orchestra; Giuseppe Sinopoli, conductor; DG 423 576-2 [DDD] (TT=66.09). Includes Strauss' Tod und Verklärung ("Death and Transfiguration"), Op.24, rated B.

The opening of "Also sprach" became well known through its use in the film 2001.

{1038}   *C*   Le Bourgeois gentilhomme Suite, Op.60 -- see entry No.{1037}b.

{1039}   *A*   Dance of the Seven Veils from Salome, Op.54
           Cleveland Orchestra; Vladimir Ashkenazy, conductor; London 417 184-2 [DDD] (TT=50.32). Includes Strauss' Don Quixote, Op.35, rated B (with Lynn Harrell, 'cello and Robert Vernon, viola).

{1040}   *A*   Don Juan, Op.20
a   Amsterdam Concertgebouw Orchestra; Bernard Haitink, conductor; Philips 411 442-2 [DDD] (TT=59.19). Includes Strauss' Til Eulenspiegel's lustige Streiche ("Til Eulenspiegel's Merry Pranks"), Op.28, rated A and Tod und Verklärung ("Death and Transfiguration"), Op.24, rated B.
b   Cleveland Orchestra; Lorin Maazel, conductor; CBS MK 35826 [DDD] (TT=54.45). Includes Strauss' Til Eulenspiegel's lustige Streiche ("Til Eulenspiegel's Merry Pranks"), Op.28, rated A and Tod und Verklärung ("Death and Transfiguration"), Op.24, rated B.
c   Cleveland Orchestra; George Szell, conductor; CBS MYK 36721 [AAD?] (TT=54.21). Includes Strauss' Til Eulenspiegel's lustige Streiche ("Til Eulenspiegel's Merry Pranks"), Op.28, rated A and Tod und Verklärung ("Death and Transfiguration"), Op.24, rated B.
           Also -- see entry No.{1037}a.

{1041}   *B*   Don Quixote, Op.35 -- see entry No.{1039}.

{1042}   *B*   Ein Heldenleben ("A Hero's Life"), Op.40
a   Cleveland Orchestra; Vladimir Ashkenazy, conductor; London 414 292-2 [DDD] (TT=43.35).
b   Dresden State Orchestra; Rudolf Kempe, conductor; Angel CDM 69171 [ADD] (TT=64.22). Includes Strauss' Macbeth, Op.23.

{1043}   C   Symphonia domestica ("Domestic Symphony"),
Op.53
        Scottish National Orchestra; Neeme Järvi, conductor;
Chandos ABRD-1267 [DDD] (TT=65.13). Includes Strauss'
Til Eulenspiegel's lustige Streiche ("Til Eulenspiegel's Merry
Pranks"), Op.28, rated A and two songs: Zueignung
("Dedication"), Op.10 No.1 and Die heiligen drei Könige aus
Morgenland ("The Three Holy Kings from the Orient"), Op.56
No.6, rated C (sung by Felicity Lott, soprano).

{1044}   A   Til Eulenspiegel's lustige Streiche ("Til
Eulenspiegel's Merry Pranks"), Op.28 -- see entries
Nos.{1040}a-c and {1043}.

{1045}   B   Tod und Verklärung ("Death and
Transfiguration"), Op.24 -- see entries Nos.{1037}c and
{1040}a-c.

Vocal

{1046}   C   Freundliche Vision ("Friendly Vision"), Op.48
No.1
        Elisabeth Schwarzkopf, soprano; Berlin Radio
Symphony Orchestra; George Szell, conductor; Angel CDC
47276 [AAD] (TT=63.43). Includes Strauss' songs: Das
Bachlein ("The Little Brook"), Op.88 No.1; Die heiligen drei
Könige ("The Three Holy Kings"), Op.56 No.6, rated C;
Meinem Kinde ("My Child"), Op.37 No.3, rated B; Morgen
("Tomorrow"), Op.27 No.1, rated A; Muttertändelei ("A
Mother's Dallying"), Op.43 No.2, rated A; Das Rosenband
("The Rose Chain"), Op.36 No.1, rated C; Vier letzte Lieder
("Four Last Songs") (Im Abendrot <"At Dusk">; Beim
Schlafengehen <"At Bedtime">; Frühling <"Spring"> and
September), Op. Posth., rated A; Waldseligkeit ("Woodland
Bliss"), Op.49 No.1; Wiegenlied ("Cradle Song" or "Lullaby"),
Op.41 No.1, rated A; Winterwehe ("Winter Dedication"),

Op.48 No.4 and Zueignung ("Dedication"), Op.10 No.1, rated A.

{1047}   C   Die heiligen drei Könige ("The Three Holy Kings"), Op.56 No.6 -- see entry No.{1046}.

{1048}   B   Meinem Kinde ("My Child"), Op.37 No.3 -- see entry No.{1046}.

{1049}   A   Morgen ("Tomorrow"), Op.27 No.1
Dame Kiri Te Kanawa, soprano; London Symphony Orchestra; Andrew Davis, conductor; CBS MK 35140 [DDD] (TT=41.51). Includes Strauss' songs: Befreit ("Released"), Op.39 No.4; Morgen ("Tomorrow"), Op.27 No.1, rated A; Muttertändelei ("A Mother's Dallying"), Op.43 No.2, rated A; Ruhe, meine Seele ("Rest, My Soul"), Op.27 No.1, rated A; Vier letzte Lieder ("Four Last Songs") (Im Abendrot <"At Dusk">; Beim Schlafengehen <"At Bedtime">; Frühling <"Spring"> and September), Op. Posth., rated A; Wiegenlied ("Cradle Song" or "Lullaby"), Op.41 No.1, rated A and Zueignung ("Dedication"), Op.10 No.1, rated A.
Also -- see entry No.{1046}.

{1050}   A   Muttertändelei ("A Mother's Dallying"), Op.43 No.2 -- see entries Nos.{1046} and {1049}.

{1051}   C   Das Rosenband ("The Rose Chain"), Op.36 No.1 -- see entry No.{1046}.

{1052}   A   Ruhe, meine Seele ("Rest, My Soul"), Op.27 No.1 -- see entry No.{1049}.

{1053}   A   Vier letzte Lieder ("Four Last Songs") (Im Abendrot <"At Dusk">; Beim Schlafengehen <"At Bedtime">; Frühling <"Spring"> and September), Op. Posth. -- see entries Nos.{1046} and {1049}.

311

{1054}   *A*   Wiegenlied ("Cradle Song" or "Lullaby"), Op.41
No.1 -- see entries Nos.{1046} and {1049}.

{1055}   *A*   Zueignung ("Dedication"), Op.10 No.1 -- see
entries Nos.{1046} and {1049}.

STRAVINSKY, IGOR
1882-1971

Ballet
{1056}   *A*   L'Oiseau de feu ("The Firebird") (1910)
New Philharmonia Orchestra; Ernest Ansermet,
conductor; London 414 141-2 [AAD] (TT=47.38).

{1057}   *A*   Pétrouchka (1911)
a   London Philharmonic Orchestra; Bernard Haitink,
conductor; Philips 420 491-2 [ADD] (TT=68.46). Includes
Stravinsky's Le Sacre du printemps ("The Rite of Spring")
(1913), rated A.
b   London Symphony Orchestra; Claudio Abbado,
conductor; DG 400 042-2 [DDD] (TT=34.22).
The reason the DG version is listed is to show how
niggardly a recording company can be in how they may or may
not fill a disc: slightly more than half a hour on a medium
which can provide upwards of 75 minutes is hardly an example
of largess. Besides, the Haitink performance (in addition to
giving value for money) is a more incisive one, and beautifully
recorded.

{1058}   *A*   Le Sacre du printemps ("The Rite of Spring")
(1913)
a   Cleveland Orchestra; Riccardo Chailly, conductor;
London 417 325-2 [DDD] (TT=41.19). Includes Stravinsky's
Four Norwegian Moods (1942).

b   Cleveland Orchestra; Lorin Maazel, conductor; Telarc CD-80054 [DDD] (TT=33.45).

c   Montreal Symphony Orchestra; Charles Dutoit, conductor; London 414 202-2 [DDD] (TT=40.03). Includes Stravinsky's Symphony for Winds (1920), rated B.

Once again, because the Stravinsky ballets are highly desirable as spectacular orchestral works to display the wonders of the compact disc, many recording companies have tended not to provide a full measure (insofar as time) of music on a disc. All of the above listed recordings are excellent, but for true monetary worth and recorded sound and performance, once again the Haitink version (entry No.{1057}a) wins.

Also -- see entry No.{1057}a.

Concerted

{1059}   *B*   Concerto for Violin, in D (1931) -- see entry No.{182}.

{1060}   *A*   <u>Symphony of Psalms</u> (1930) -- see entry No.{717}.

Choral

{1061}   *A*   Symphony of Psalms (1930)

Berlin Radio Symphony Chorus and Orchestra; Riccardo Chailly, conductor; London 414 078-2 [DDD] (TT=50.37). Includes Stravinsky's <u>Feux d'artifice</u> ("Fireworks"), Op.4, rated B; <u>King of the Stars</u> (1911-1912) and <u>Le Chant du rossignol</u> ("The Song of the Nightingale") (1914), rated B.

Operatic

{1062}   *C*   <u>Oedipus Rex</u> ("Oedipus the King") (1927)

Jessye Norman, soprano; Thomas Moser, tenor; Alexandru Ionita, tenor; Roland Bracht, bass; Siegmund Nimsgern, bass; Michel Piccoli, narrator; Bavarian Radio Male Chorus; Bavarian Radio Symphony Orchestra; Sir Colin Davis, conductor; Orfeo C-071831 [DDD] (TT=49.24).

{1063}   C   The Rake's Progress (1951)
Cathryn Pope, soprano; Astrid Varney, soprano; Sarah Walker, mezzo-soprano; John Dobson, tenor; Philip Langridge, tenor; Stafford Dean, bass; Samuel Ramey, bass; London Sinfonietta Chorus; London Sinfonietta; Riccardo Chailly, conductor; London 411 644-2 (2 discs) [DDD] (TT = 135.18).

Orchestral
{1064}   B   Feux d'artifice ("Fireworks"), Op.4 -- see entry No.{1061}.

{1065}   B   Le Chant du rossignol ("The Song of the Nightingale") (1914) -- see entry No.{1061}.

Symphonic
{1066}   A   Symphony (1940), in C
L'Orchestre de la Suisse Romande; Charles Dutoit, conductor; London 414 272-2 [DDD] (TT = 49.03). Includes Stravinsky's Symphony in Three Movements (1945), rated A.

{1067}   B   Symphony for Winds (1920) -- see entry No.{1058}.

{1068}   A   Symphony in Three Movements (1945) -- see entry No.{1066}.

Vocal
{1069}   C   L'Histoire du soldat ("The Soldier's Tale") (1918)
Jean Cocteau, speaker; Jean-Marie Fertey, speaker; Peter Ustinov, speaker; Instrumental Ensemble; Igor Markevitch, conductor; Philips 420 773-2 PM [ADD] (TT = 54.23).

SULLIVAN, SIR ARTHUR
1842-1900

Operatic

{1070}   *B*   The Gondoliers (1889)
Dawn Bradshaw, soprano; Mary Sansom, soprano; Jennifer Toye, soprano; Ceinwen Jones, mezzo-soprano; Gillian Knight, mezzo-soprano; Joyce Wright, mezzo-soprano; Dorothy Gill, contralto; Jeanette Roach, contralto; Joseph Riordan, tenor; Thomas Round, tenor; John Reed, baritone; Jeffrey Skitch, baritone; Kenneth Sandford, baritone; Alan Styler, baritone; Michael Wakeham, baritone; George Cook, bass; D'Oyly Carte Opera Chorus; New Symphony Orchestra of London; Isidore Godfrey, conductor; London 417 254-2 (2 discs) [ADD] (TT = 128.53).

{1071}   *A*   H.M.S. Pinafore (1878)
a   Nellie Briercliffe, soprano; Elsie Griffin, soprano; Bertha Lewis, contralto; Charles Goulding, tenor; George Baker, baritone; Sydney Granville, baritone; Stuart Robertson, baritone; Henry Lytton, bass-baritone; D'Oyly Carte Opera Chorus and Orchestra; Sir Malcolm Sargent, conductor; Arabesque Z8052-2 (2 discs) ! [ADD] (TT=51.42). Includes Sullivan's Trial by Jury (1866) (with soloists Winifred Lawson, soprano; Derek Oldham, tenor; Arthur Hosking, baritone; Leo Sheffield, baritone and George Baker, baritone and the D'Oyly Carte Opera Chorus and Orchestra conducted by Harry Norris), rated B.
b   Elsie Morison, soprano; Monica Sinclair, contralto; Marjorie Thomas, contralto; Richard Lewis, tenor; George Baker, baritone; John Cameron, baritone; John Milligan, bass-baritone; Owen Brannigan, bass; Glyndebourne Festival Chorus; Pro Arte Orchestra; Sir Malcolm Sargent, conductor; Angel CDS 47779 (2 discs) [ADD] (TT = 111.03). Includes Sullivan's Trial by Jury (1866) (with soloists Elsie Morison, soprano; Richard Lewis, tenor; George Baker, baritone; John Cameron, baritone; Bernard Turageon, baritone and Owen Brannigan, bass), rated B.

315

Classical Music and Opera on CDs

c   Elizabeth Ritchie, soprano; Linda Ormiston, mezzo-soprano; Janine Roebuck, mezzo-soprano; Christopher Gillett, tenor; Nicholas Grace, baritone; Paul Parfitt, baritone; Gordon Sandison, baritone; Thomas Lawlor, bass; New Sadler's Wells Opera Chorus and Orchestra; Simon Phipps, conductor; MCA MCAD2-11012 (2 discs) [DDD] (TT=81.14).

In those instances where three versions of a G&S opera are listed, the Arabesque label issue is monophonic and of historic interest, the Angel recording is by Malcolm Sargent and usually has better ensembles than the London discs, which latter are the "officially sanctioned" D'Oyly Carte Company performances. I prefer the Sargent performances for their exceedingly fine casts and solid orchestra, but the other two have the merits described.

{1072}   *A*   Iolanthe (1882)

Elsie Morison, soprano; Monica Sinclair, contralto; Marjorie Thomas, contralto; Alexander Young, tenor; George Baker, baritone; John Cameron, baritone; Ian Wallace, bass; Glyndebourne Festival Chorus; Pro Arte Orchestra; Sir Malcolm Sargent, conductor; Angel CDCB 47831 (2 discs) [ADD] (TT=93.22).

{1073}   *A*   The Mikado (1885)

a   Brenda Bennett, soprano; Josephine Curtis, mezzo-soprano; Marjorie Eyre, mezzo-soprano; Elizabeth Nickell-Lean, contralto; Derek Oldham, tenor; Sydney Granville, baritone; Martyn Green, baritone; Leslie Rands, baritone; Darrell Fancourt, bass; D'Oyly Carte Opera Chorus and Orchestra; Isidore Godfrey, conductor; Arabesque Z8051-2 ! [ADD] (TT=82.10).

b   Valerie Masterson, soprano; Peggy Ann Jones, mezzo-soprano; Pauline Wales, mezzo-soprano; Lyndsie Holland, contralto; Colin Wright, tenor; Michael Rayner, baritone; John Reed, baritone; Kenneth Sandford, baritone; John Ayldon, bass; John Broad, bass; D'Oyly Carte Opera Chorus; Royal

Philharmonic Orchestra; Royston Nash, conductor; London 417 296-2 (2 discs) [AAD] (TT=89.36).

c   Elsie Morison, soprano; Jeannette Sinclair, soprano; Monica Sinclair, contralto; Marjorie Thomas, contralto; Richard Lewis, tenor; John Cameron, baritone; Sir Geraint Evans, baritone; Ian Wallace, baritone; Owen Brannigan, bass; Glyndebourne Festival Chorus; Pro Arte Orchestra; Sir Malcolm Sargent, conductor; Angel CDS 47773 (2 discs) [AAD] (TT=90.52).

{1074}   *B*   Patience (1881)

Heather Harper, soprano; Elsie Morrison, soprano; Elizabeth Harwood, soprano; Monica Sinclair, contralto; Marjorie Thomas, contralto; Alexander Young, tenor; George Baker, baritone; John Cameron, baritone; John Shaw, baritone; Trevor Anthony, bass; Glyndebourne Festival Chorus; Pro Arte Orchestra; Sir Malcolm Sargent, conductor; Angel CDS 47783 (2 discs) [ADD] (TT=113.04). Includes Sullivan's Symphony ("Irish") (1866), in E (performed by the Royal Philharmonic Orchestra conducted by Sir Charles Grove).

{1075}   The Pirates of Penzance (1879)

a   Nellie Briercliffe, soprano; Elsie Griffin, soprano; Dorothy Gill, contralto; Nellie Walker, contralto; Derek Oldham, tenor; George Baker, baritone; Stuart Robertson, baritone; Leo Sheffield, baritone; Peter Dawson, bass-baritone; D'Oyly Carte Opera Chorus and Orchestra; Isidore Godfrey, conductor; Arabesque Z8068-2 (2 discs) ! [ADD] (TT=118.14). Includes an abridged version of Sullivan's The Sorcerer (1877) (with soloists Muriel Dickson, soprano; Alice Moxon, soprano; Anna Bethell, mezzo-soprano; Dorothy Gill, contralto; Derek Oldham, tenor; George Baker, baritone; Stuart Robertson, baritone and Darrell Fancourt, bass. The ensemble is conducted by Isidore Godfrey), rated C.

b   Heather Harper, soprano; Elsie Morison, soprano; Monica Sinclair, contralto; Marjorie Thomas, contralto; Richard Lewis, tenor; George Baker, baritone; John Cameron, baritone; James Milligan, bass-baritone; Owen Brannigan, bass; Glyndebourne Festival Chorus; Pro Arte Orchestra; Sir Malcolm Sargent, conductor; Angel CD 47785 (2 discs) [ADD] (TT=112.34). Includes Sullivan's Overtures: Cox and Box (1875); The Sorcerer (1877) and Princess Ida (1884) and the Concert Overture ("In Memoriam") (1866), this last performed by the City of Birmingham (England) Symphony Orchestra conducted by Sir Vivian Dunn.

c   Valerie Masterson, soprano; Christene Palmer, soprano; Pauline Wales, mezzo-soprano; Philip Potter, tenor; John Reed, baritone; Donald Adams, bass; Owen Brannigan, bass; George Cook, bass; D'Oyly Carte Opera Chorus; Royal Philharmonic Orchestra; Isidore Godfrey, conductor; London 414 286-2 (2 discs) [AAD] (TT=93.55).

{1076}   *B*   Ruddigore (1887)

Elizabeth Harwood, soprano; Elsie Morison, soprano; Pamela Bowden, contralto; Monica Sinclair, contralto; Richard Lewis, tenor; George Baker, baritone; Harold Blackburn, bass; Owen Brannigan, bass; Joseph Rouleau, bass; Glyndebourne Festival Chorus; Pro Arte Orchestra; Sir Malcolm Sargent, conductor; Angel CDS 47787 (2 discs) [ADD] (TT=123.33). Includes Sullivan's The Merchant of Venice (Suite) (1871) and The Tempest (Incidental Music), Op.1, both performed by the City Of Birmingham (England) Symphony Orchestra conducted by Sir Vivian Dunn.

{1077}   *C*   The Sorcerer (1877) (Abridged Version) -- see entry No.{1075}a.

{1078}   *B*   Trial by Jury (1866) -- see entries Nos.{1071}a and {1071}c.

{1079}   *B*   The Yeomen of the Guard (1888)
Doreen Hume, soprano; Elsie Morison, soprano; Monica Sinclair, contralto; Marjorie Thomas, contralto; Richard Lewis, tenor; Alexander Young, tenor; John Cameron, baritone; John Carol Case, baritone; Denis Dowling, baritone; Sir Geraint Evans, baritone; Owen Brannigan, bass; Glyndebourne Festival Chorus; Pro Arte Orchestra; Sir Malcolm Sargent, conductor; Angel CDS 47781 (2 discs) [ADD] (TT=93.32).

SUPPÉ, FRANZ VON
1819-1895

Orchestral

{1080}   *C*   Overture: Banditenstreiche ("Jolly Robbers") (1887)
Montreal Symphony Orchestra; Charles Dutoit, conductor; London 414 408-2 [DDD] (TT=56.23). Includes von Suppé's Overtures: Dichter und Bauer ("Poet and Peasant") (1854), rated A; Fatinitza (1876); Ein Morgen, ein Mittag und ein Abend in Wien ("A Morning, Noon and Night in Vienna") (1844), rated A; Pique Dame ("The Queen of Spades") (1862), rated C and Die schöne Galathée ("The Beautiful Galatea") (1865), rated A.

{1081}   *A*   Overture: Dichter und Bauer ("Poet and Peasant") (1854) -- see entries Nos.{10} and {1080}.

{1082}   *B*   Overture: Leichte Kavallerie ("Light Cavalry") (1886) -- see entries Nos.{10} and {1080}.

{1083}   *A*   Overture: Ein Morgen, ein Mittag und ein Abend in Wien ("A Morning, Noon and Night in Vienna") (1844) -- see entry No.{1080}.

{1084}   *C*   Overture: <u>Pique Dame</u> ("The Queen of Spades") (1862) -- see entry No.{1080}.

{1085}   *A*   Overture: <u>Die schöne Galathée</u> ("The Beautiful Galatea") (1865) -- see entry No.{1080}.

TCHAIKOVSKY, PIOTR ILYICH
1840-1893

Ballet
{1086}   *A*   <u>The Nutcracker</u>, Op.71
a   Ambrosian Choir; Philharmonia Orchestra; Christopher Plummer, reader; Michael Tilson Thomas, conductor; Caedmon Z128-2 (2 discs) [DDD] (TT=144.17).
b   Ambrosian Singers; Royal Philharmonic Orchestra; André Previn, conductor; Angel CDS 472678 (2 discs) [DDD] (TT=87.54).
c   London Symphony Orchestra; Sir Charles Mackerras, conductor; Telarc CD-80137 (2 discs) [DDD] (TT=87.34).

Depending on what one wishes, these are performances of one of Tchaikovsky's finest ballets of which the performers can be proud. Tilson Thomas has Christopher Plummer reading an English translation of E.T.A. Hoffmann's story (on which the ballet is based) and a fine performance by the choir and orchestra. Previn's is a full-bodied and well-paced reading which includes the choir and orchestra. Mackerras' recording gives us the orchestral only version, which is the preference of many who find the choir intrusive.

{1087}   *A*   <u>The Nutcracker</u> Suite, Op.71a
a   Academy of St. Martin-in-the-Fields; Sir Neville Marriner, conductor; Philips 411 471-2 [DDD] (TT=51.40). Includes Tchaikovsky's Serenade for Strings, Op.48, in C, rated A.

b   Cleveland Orchestra; Lorin Maazel, conductor; Telarc
         CD-80068 [DDD] (TT=40.11). Includes Tchaikovsky's <u>Romeo
         and Juliet</u> (1870), rated A.
c   Israel Philharmonic Orchestra; Zubin Mehta,
         conductor; London 410 551-2 [DDD] (TT=47.25). Includes
         Tchaikovsky's <u>Swan Lake</u> Suite, Op.20, rated A.

{1088}   *A*   <u>Sleeping Beauty</u>, Op.66
         Amsterdam Concertgebouw Orchestra; Antal Doráti,
         conductor; Philips 420 792-2 (3 discs) [ADD] (TT=161.22).

{1089}   *A*   <u>Swan Lake</u> Suite, Op.20 -- see entry No.{1087}c.

Chamber
{1090}   *B*   String Quartet No.1, Op.11, in D -- see entry
         No.{209}.

{1091}   *B*   Trio for Piano, Violin and 'Cello, Op.50, in a
         Vladimir Ashkenazy, piano; Itzhak Perlman, violin;
         Lynn Harrell, 'cello; Angel 47988 [ADD] (TT=48.59).

Concerted
{1092}   *A*   Concerto for Piano No.1, Op.23, in b flat -- see
         entry No.{731}.

{1093}   *B*   Concerto for Piano No.2, Op.44, in G
         Jerome Lowenthal, piano; London Symphony
         Orchestra; Sergiu Comissiona, conductor; Arabesque Z6583
         [DDD] (TT=58.42). Includes Tchaikovsky's Concerto for
         Piano No.3, Op.75, in E flat, rated C.

{1094}   *C*   Concerto for Piano No.3, Op.75, in E flat -- see
         entry No.{1093}.

{1095}   *A*   Concerto for Violin, Op.35, in D -- see entry
         No.{566}.

{1096}   *B*   Sérénade mélancolique for Violin and Orchestra, Op.26 -- see entry No.{566}.

{1097}   *A*   Waltz from Serenade in C, Op.48 (Arranged for Violin and Orchestra) -- see entry No.{566}.

Operatic
{1098}   *A*   Eugen Onegin, Op.24
Teresa Kubiak, soprano; Julia Hamari, contralto; Stuart Burrows, tenor; Michel Sénéchal, tenor; Bernd Weikl, baritone; Nicolai Ghiaurov, bass; John Alldis Choir; Royal Opera House Chorus and Orchestra; Sir Georg Solti, conductor; London 417 423-2 (2 discs) [ADD] (TT=144.11).

{1099}   *B*   La Pique Dame ("The Queen of Spades"), Op.78
Tamara Milashkina, soprano; Galina Borisova, mezzo-soprano; Valentina Levko, mezzo-soprano; Vladimir Atlantov, tenor; André Fedoiseyev, baritone; Valery Yarosalvtsev, bass; Chorus and Orchestra of the Bolshoi Theatre, Moscow; Mark Ermler, conductor; Philips 420 375-2 (3 discs) [ADD] (TT=159.35).

Orchestral
{1100}   *A*   Capriccio italien ("Italian Caprice"), Op.45
Detroit Symphony Orchestra; Antal Doráti, conductor; London 414 494-2 [ADD] (TT=41.53). Includes Tchaikovsky's Overture: 1812, Op.49, rated A and Marche slave, Op.31, rated A.

{1101}   *A*   Overture: 1812, Op.49 -- see entries Nos.{210}a, {211}a and {1100}.

{1102}   *A*   Polonaise from Eugen Onegin, Op.24
Cleveland Orchestra; Christoph von Dohnányi, conductor; Telarc CD-80130 [DDD] (TT=49.25). Includes

Tchaikovsky's Symphony No.6 ("Pathétique"), Op.74, in b, rated A.

{1103}   *B*   Francesca da Rimini, Op.32
a   Cleveland Orchestra; Riccardo Chailly, conductor; London 414 159-2 [DDD] (TT=42.30). Includes Tchaikovsky's Romeo and Juliet (1870), rated A.
b   USSR TV Radio Large Symphony Orchestra; Vyacheslav Ovchinnikov, conductor; Mobile Fidelity (Melodia) MFCD 864 [DDD] (TT=42.58). Includes Tchaikovsky's Romeo and Juliet (1870), rated A.

{1104}   *B*   Manfred Symphony, Op.58
Amsterdam Concertgebouw Orchestra; Riccardo Chailly, conductor; London 421 441-2 [DDD] (TT=56.12).

{1105}   *A*   Marche slave, Op.31 -- see entries Nos.{210}b, {266} and {1100}.

{1106}   *A*   Romeo and Juliet (1870)
Philharmonia Orchestra; Riccardo Muti, conductor; Angel 47867 [ADD] (TT=51.53). Includes Tchaikovsky's Symphony No.2 ("Little Russian"), Op.17, in c, rated A.
Also -- see entries Nos.{189}a, {211}a-b, {1103}a-b and {1087}b.

{1107}   *B*   Sérénade mélancolique for Violin and Orchestra, Op.26 -- see entry No.{566}.

{1108}   *A*   Serenade for Strings, Op.48, in C -- see entries Nos.{1087} and {389}.

{1109}   *C*   Voyevode ("The Voyevoda"), Op.78
Chicago Symphony Orchestra; Claudio Abbado, conductor; CBS MK 42094 [DDD] (TT=57.19). Includes Tchaikovsky's Symphony No.5, Op.64, in e, rated A.

Symphonic

{1110}   *B*   Symphony No.1 ("Winter Daydreams"), Op.1, in g
            Olso Philharmonic Orchestra; Mariss Jansons,
            conductor; Chandos CD-6139 [DDD] (TT=43.57).

{1111}   *A*   Symphony No.2 ("Little Russian"), Op.17, in c --
            see entries Nos.{814} and {1106}.

{1112}   *B*   Symphony No.3 ("Polish"), Op.29, in D
            Oslo Philharmonic Orchestra; Mariss Jansons,
            conductor; Chandos CD-8463 [DDD] (TT=47.12).

{1113}   *A*   Symphony No.4, Op.36, in f
a   Cleveland Orchestra; Lorin Maazel, conductor; Telarc
            CD-80047 [DDD] (TT=41.38).
b   Pittsburgh Symphony Orchestra; André Previn,
            conductor; Philips 400 090-2 [DDD] (TT=43.44).

{1114}   *A*   Symphony No.5, Op.64, in e
            Cleveland Orchestra; Lorin Maazel, conductor; CBS
            MK 36700 [DDD] (TT=46.47).
            Also -- see entries Nos.{404}, {810} and {1109}.

{1115}   *A*   Symphony No.6 ("Pathétique"), Op.74, in b
            Philharmonia Orchestra; Vladimir Ashkenazy,
            conductor; London 411 515-2 [DDD] (TT=46.44).
            Also -- see entry No.{1102}.

TELEMANN, GEORG PHILIPP
1681-1767

Orchestral

{1116}   *B*   Overture in C ("Hamburg's Tides")
            Musica Antiqua Köln; Reinhard Goebel, conductor;
            Archiv 413 788-2 [DDD] (TT=49.10). Includes Telemann's

Concerti in a, B flat and F for Two Recorders, Bassoon and Strings.

VAUGHAN WILLIAMS, RALPH
1872-1958

Concerted
{1117}   B   The Lark Ascending (Romance for Violin and Orchestra) (1914)
   Barry Griffiths, violin; Royal Philharmonic Orchestra; André Previn, conductor; Telarc CD-80138 [DDD] (TT=63.22). Includes Vaughan Williams' Symphony No.2 ("A London Symphony") (1914, 1920), rated A.

Orchestral
{1118}   A   English Folk Song Suite (1923) -- see entry No.{9}.

{1119}   A   Fantasia on Greensleeves for String Orchestra, Harp and Two Flutes (1934)
   London Philharmonic Orchestra; Sir Adrian Boult, conductor; Angel CDC 47213 [AAD] (TT=59.51). Includes Vaughan Williams' Symphony No.2 ("A London Symphony") (1914, 1920), rated A.
   Also -- see entries Nos.{370}a-b.

{1120}   C   Fantasia on a Theme by Thomas Tallis for String Quartet and Double String Orchestra (1910, 1919) -- see entries Nos.{370}a-b.

Symphonic
{1121}   B   Symphony No.1 ("A Sea Symphony") (1910)
   Sheila Armstrong, soprano; John Carol Case, baritone; London Philharmonic Choir and Orchestra; Sir Adrian Boult, conductor; Angel CDC 47212 [ADD] (TT=65.28).

{1122}   *A*   Symphony No.2 ("A London Symphony") (1914, 1920) -- see entries Nos.{1117} and {1119}.

{1123}   *B*   Symphony No.3 ("Pastoral") (1922)
Margaret Price, soprano; New Philharmonia Orchestra; Sir Adrian Boult, conductor; Angel CDC 47214 [ADD] (TT=72.04). Includes Vaughan Williams' Symphony No.5 (1943), in D, rated B.

{1124}   *A*   Symphony No.4 (1934), in f
New Philharmonia Orchestra; Sir Adrian Boult, conductor; Angel CDC 47215 [ADD] (TT=68.46). Includes Vaughan Williams' Symphony No.6 (1944-1946, 1950).

{1125}   *B*   Symphony No.5 (1943), in D -- see entry No.{1123}.

{1126}   *B*   Symphony No.7 ("Sinfonia Antartica") (1953)
Sheila Armstrong, soprano; London Philharmonic Choir and Orchestra; Bernard Haitink, conductor; Angel CDC 47516 [DDD] (TT=41.39).

{1127}   *B*   Symphony No.8 (1956), in d
London Philharmonic Orchestra; Sir Adrian Boult, conductor; Angel CDC 47217 [ADD] (TT=63.37). Includes Vaughan Williams' Symphony No.9 (1958), in e, rated C.

{1128}   *C*   Symphony No.9 (1958), in e -- see entry No.{1127}.

VERDI, GIUSEPPE
1813-1901

Choral
{1129}   *A*   Requiem Mass (In Memory of Manzoni) (1874)

a   Katia Ricciarelli, soprano; Shirley Verrett, mezzo-soprano; Plácido Domingo, tenor; Nicolai Ghiaurov, bass; Chorus and Orchestra of La Scala, Milan; Claudio Abbado, conductor; DG 415 976-2 (2 discs) [ADD] (TT = 89.16).

b   Elisabeth Schwarzkopf, soprano; Christa Ludwig, mezzo-soprano; Nicolaï Gedda, tenor; Nicolai Ghiaurov, bass; Philharmonia Chorus and Orchestra; Carlo Maria Giulini, conductor; Angel CDS 47257 (2 discs) [ADD] (TT = 128.34). Includes Verdi's Pezzi Sacrum <"Sacred Pieces">) (4) Nos.1-4 (1898) (with soloist Dame Janet Baker, mezzo-soprano).

Despite Abbado's recording being newer and being possessed of better sound, the Giulini performance is in a class with the seraphim.

Operatic

{1130}   *A*   Aïda (1871)

a   Montserrat Caballé, soprano; Esther Casas, soprano; Fiorenza Cossotto, mezzo-soprano; Plácido Domingo, tenor; Nicola Martinucci, tenor; Piero Cappuccilli, baritone; Nicolai Ghiaurov, bass; Luigi Roni, bass; Chorus of the Royal Opera House, Covent Garden; New Philharmonia Orchestra; Riccardo Muti, conductor; Angel CDCC 47271 (3 discs) [AAD] (TT = 146.22).

b   Leontyne Price, soprano; Mietta Sighele, soprano; Rita Gorr, mezzo-soprano; Franco Ricciardi, tenor; Jon Vickers, tenor; Robert Merrill, baritone; Pinio Clabassi, bass; Giorgio Tozzi, bass; Rome Opera Chorus and Orchestra; Sir Georg Solti, conductor; London 417 416-2 (3 discs) [ADD] (TT = 152.34).

c   Katia Ricciarelli, soprano; Elena Obraztsova, mezzo-soprano; Lucia Valentini-Terrani, mezzo-soprano; Plácido Domingo, tenor; Leo Nucci, baritone; Nicolai Ghiaurov, bass; Ruggero Raimondi, bass; Chorus and Orchestra of La Scala, Milan; Claudio Abbado, conductor; DG 410 092-2 (3 discs) [DDD] (TT = 140.38).

Of the three Aïdas above, Abbado's is the weakest (it is, however, the newest). The other two are very good, with strong tenors and exceptionally fine Aïdas in Caballé and Price (both at the top of their forms). I lean towards Solti, both for the cast and the brilliance of his conducting.

{1131}   Un Ballo in maschera ("A Masked Ball") (1859)

a   Reri Grist, soprano; Leontyne Price, soprano; Carlo Bergonzi, tenor; Piero De Palma, tenor; Shirley Verrett, mezzo-soprano; Mario Basiola Jr., baritone; Robert Merrill, baritone; Ezio Flagello, bass; Ferrucio Mazzoli, bass; RCA Italian Opera Chorus and Orchestra; Erich Leinsdorf, conductor; RCA GD 86645 (2 discs) (must be specially ordered) [ADD] (TT = 128.13).

b   Edita Gruberova, soprano; Katia Ricciarelli, soprano; Elena Obraztsova, mezzo-soprano; Plácido Domingo, tenor; Renato Bruson, baritone; Luigi de Corato, baritone; Giovanni Foiani, bass; Ruggero Raimondi, bass; Chorus and Orchestra of La Scala, Milan; Claudio Abbado, conductor; DG 415 685-2 (2 discs) [ADD] (TT = 127.05).

{1132}   C   Don Carlos (1867, 1884)

Montserrat Caballé, soprano; Maria-Rosa del Campo, soprano; Delia Wallis, soprano; Shirley Verrett, mezzo-soprano; Ryland Davies, tenor; Plácido Domingo, tenor; Sherrill Milnes, baritone; John Noble, baritone; Simon Estes, bass; Giovanni Foiani, bass; Ruggero Raimondi, bass; Ambrosian Opera Chorus; Orchestra of the Royal Opera House, Covent Garden; Carlo Maria Giulini, conductor; Angel CDCC 47701 (3 discs) [ADD] (TT = 233.18).

{1133}   A   Falstaff (1893)

a   Anna Moffo, soprano; Elisabeth Schwarzkopf, soprano; Fedora Barbieri, mezzo-soprano; Nan Merriman, mezzo-soprano; Luigi Alva, tenor; Renato Ercolano, tenor; Tomaso Spataro, tenor; Tito Gobbi, baritone; Nicola Zaccaria, bass;

Philharmonia Chorus and Orchestra; Herbert von Karajan, conductor; Angel CDCB 49668 (2 discs) [ADD] (TT = 120.30).

b   Barbara Hendricks, soprano; Katia Ricciarelli, soprano; Brenda Boozer, mezzo-soprano; Lucia Valentini-Terrani, mezzo-soprano; Francis Egerton, tenor; Dalmacio Gonzalez, tenor; Michael Sells, tenor; Renato Bruson, baritone; Leo Nucci, baritone; William Wildermann, bass; Los Angeles Master Chorale; Los Angeles Philharmonic Orchestra; Carlo Maria Giulini, conductor; DG 410 503-2 (2 discs) [DDD] (TT = 122.44).

{1134}   *B*   La Forza del destino ("The Force of Destiny") (1862)

Mirella Freni, soprano; Dolora Zajic, mezzo-soprano; Plácido Domingo, tenor; Sesto Bruscantini, bass-baritone; Paul Plishka, bass; Chorus and Orchestra of La Scala, Milan; Riccardo Muti, conductor; Angel CDCC 47485 (3 discs) [DDD] (TT = 164.03).

{1135}   *A*   Macbeth (1865)

a   Shirley Verrett, soprano; Stefania Malagú, mezzo-soprano; Plácido Domingo, tenor; Piero Capuccilli, baritone; Nicolai Ghiaurov, bass; Chorus and Orchestra of La Scala, Milan; Claudio Abbado, conductor; DG 415 688-2 (3 discs) [ADD] (TT = 153.45).

b   Maria Zampieri, soprano; Neil Shicoff, tenor; Renato Bruson, baritone; Robert Lloyd, bass; German Opera Chorus and Orchestra, Berlin; Giuseppe Sinopoli, conductor; Philips 413 133-2 (3 discs) [DDD] (TT = 162.27).

{1136}   *B*   Nabucco (1842)

Renata Scotto, soprano; Elena Obraztsova, mezzo-soprano; Kenneth Collins, tenor; Veriano Luchetti, tenor; Matteo Manuguerra, baritone; Nicolai Ghiaurov, bass; Robert Lloyd, bass; Ambrosian Opera Chorus; Philharmonia

Orchestra; Riccardo Muti, conductor; Angel CDS 47488 (2 discs) [ADD] (TT = 123.37).

{1137}   *A*   <u>Otello</u> ("Othello") (1839)
a   Katia Ricciarelli, soprano; Petra Malakova, mezzo-soprano; Plácido Domingo, tenor; Justino Diaz, bass; John Macurdy, bass; Chorus and Orchestra of La Scala, Milan; Lorin Maazel, conductor; Angel CDS 47450 (2 discs) [DDD] (TT = 140.58).
b   Renata Scotto, soprano; Jean Kraft, contralto; Plácido Domingo, tenor; Sherrill Milnes, baritone; Paul Plishka, bass; Ambrosian Boys' Choir; Ambrosian Opera Chorus; National Philharmonic Orchestra, London; James Levine, conductor; RCA RCD2-2951 (2 discs) [DDD] (TT = 133.45).
c   Renata Tebaldi, soprano; Ana Raquel Satre, mezzo-soprano; Mario del Monaco, tenor; Aldo Protti, baritone; Fernando Corena, bass; Vienna State Opera Chorus; Vienna Children's Chorus; Vienna Philharmonic Orchestra; Herbert von Karajan, conductor; London 411 618-2 (2 discs) [ADD] (TT = 138.10).

{1138}   *A*   <u>Rigoletto</u> (1851)
           Dame Joan Sutherland, soprano; Huguette Tourangeau, mezzo-soprano; Luciano Pavarotti, tenor; Matteo Manuguerra, baritone; Martti Talvela, bass; Ambrosian Opera Chorus; London Symphony Orchestra; Sir Richard Bonynge, conductor; London 414 269-2 (2 discs) [AAD?] (TT = 118.38).

{1139}   *A*   <u>La Traviata</u> ("The Fallen Lady") (1853)
           Renata Scotto, soprano; Alfredo Kraus, tenor; Renato Bruson, baritone; Ambrosian Opera Chorus; Philharmonia Orchestra; Riccardo Muti, conductor; Angel CDC 47538 (3 discs) [DDD] (TT = 128.51).

{1140}   *A*   Il Trovatore ("The Troubador") (1853)
a   Rosalind Plowright, soprano; Brigitte Fassbaender, mezzo-soprano; Plácido Domingo, tenor; Giorgio Zancanaro, baritone; Santa Cecilia Academy Chorus and Orchestra; Carlo Maria Giulini, conductor; DG 413 355-2 (3 discs) [DDD] (TT=139.35).
b   Leontyne Price, soprano; Florenza Cossotto, mezzo-soprano; Plácido Domingo, tenor; Sherrill Milnes, baritone; Bonaldo Gialotti, bass; Ambrosian Opera Chorus; New Philharmonia Orchestra; Zubin Mehta, conductor; RCA 6194-2 (2 discs) [ADD] (TT=137.27).

Orchestral
{1141}   *A*   Overture: Aïda (1871)
         Vienna Philharmonic Orchestra; Giuseppe Sinopoli, conductor; Philips 411 469-2 [DDD] (TT=51.50). Includes Verdi's Overtures: Attila (1846); Un Ballo in maschera ("A Masked Ball") (1859), rated B; La Forza del destino ("The Force of Destiny") (1862), rated B; Luisa Miller (1849); Nabucco (1842), rated B; La Traviata ("The Fallen Lady") (1853), rated A and I Vespri siciliani ("Sicilian Vespers") (1855).

{1142}   *B*   Un Ballo in maschera ("A Masked Ball") (1859) -- see entry No.{1141}.

{1143}   *B*   La Forza del destino ("The Force of Destiny") (1862) -- see entry No.{1141}.

{1144}   *B*   Nabucco (1842) -- see entry No.{1141}.

{1145}   *A*   La Traviata ("The Fallen Lady") (1853) -- see entry No.{1141}.

VIEUXTEMPS, HENRI
1820-1881

Concerted
{1146}   *C*   Concerto for Violin No.5, Op.37, in a
Itzhak Perlman, violin; Orchestre de Paris; Daniel Barenboim, conductor; Angel CDC 47165 [ADD?] (TT=50.59). Includes Vieuxtemps' Concerto for Violin No.4, Op.31, in d.
Also -- see entry No.{256}a.

VILLA-LOBOS, HEITOR
1887-1959

Orchestral
{1147}   *B*   Bachiana Brasileira No.2 for Orchestra (4) Nos.1-4: La Chanson du campagnard ("The Song of the Peasant"); Le Chant de notre terre ("The Song of Our Earth"); Souvenir du désert ("Remembrance of the Desert") and Le Petit train du paysan brésilien ("The Little Train of the Caipiri") (1930)
Orchestre de Paris; Paul Capolongo, conductor; Angel CDC 47357 [ADD] (TT=54.25). Includes Villa-Lobos' Bachiana Brasileira No.5 for Soprano and 8 'Celli (1938-1945) (with soprano Mady Mesplé), rated B; Bachiana Brasileira No.6 for Flute and Bassoon (1938) (with Michel Debost, flute and André Sennedat, bassoon) and Bachiana Brasileira No.9 for String Orchestra (1945).

Vocal
{1148}   *B*   Bachiana Brasileira No.5 for Soprano and 8 'Celli (1938-1945) -- see entry No.{1147}.

VIVALDI, ANTONIO
1678-1741

Chamber

{1149}   *B*   Chamber Concerto for Recorder, Oboe and Bassoon (<u>La Pastorella</u> <"The Shepherdess">), RV 95, in D
Musical Offering; Nonesuch 79067-2 [DDD] (TT=47.13). Includes Vivaldi's Chamber Concerto for Flute, Oboe, Bassoon and Violin, RV 107, in g; Chamber Concerto for Recorder, Oboe, Violin and Bassoon, RV 94, in D; Sonata for Oboe and Basso Continuo, RV 53, in c and Sonata for Violin, 'Cello and Basso Continuo, RV 83, in c, rated C.

{1150}   *C*   Sonata for Violin, 'Cello and Basso Continuo, RV 83, in c -- see entry No.{1149}.

Choral

{1151}   *A*   Gloria, RV 589 in D -- see entry No.{41}.

Concerted

{1152}   *A*   Il Cimento dell' armonia e dell' invenzione ("The Contest Between Harmony and Invention"), Op.8 (12) Nos.1-4 Are Four Violin Concerti Known Collectively as <u>Le Quattro stagioni</u> ("The Four Seasons") and Comprise Four Concerti for Violin and Orchestra

a   Simon Standage, baroque violin; English Concert; Trevor Pinnock, conductor; MHS 11084F [ADD] (TT=40.20).

b   Felix Ayo, violin; I Musici; Philips 416 611-2 [ADD] (TT=61.00). Includes Vivaldi's Concerto for Violin (<u>L'Amoroso</u> <"The Amorous">),RV 271, in E, rated B.

c   Michala Petri, recorder; George Malcolm, harpsichord; Guildhall String Ensemble; RCA 6656-2 RC [DDD] (TT=47.57). Includes Vivaldi's Concerto for Soprano Recorder, RV 443, in C, rated A.

{1153}   *A*   Il Cimento dell' armonia e dell' invenzione ("The Contest Between Harmony and Invention"), Op.8 (12) Nos.5-12 Are Eight Violin Concerti (No.5 <u>La Tempesta di mare</u> ["The Raging of the Sea"], in E flat; No.6 <u>Il Piacere</u> ["The

333

Pleasure"], in C; No.7, in d; No.8, in g; No.9, in d; No.10 <u>La Caccia</u>> ["The Hunt"], in B flat; No.11, in D and No.12, in C)

Simon Standage, baroque violin; English Concert; Trevor Pinnock, conductor; MHS 11085Z (2 discs) [AAD] (TT=91.42). Includes Vivaldi's Concerto for Transverse Flute and Strings, RV 429, in D (with Stephen Preston, baroque flute), rated A and Concert for 'Cello and Strings, RV 424, in b (with Anthony Pleeth, baroque 'cello), rated B.

{1154}   *B*   Concerto for 'Cello and Strings, RV 424, in b -- see entries Nos.{11} and {1153}.

{1155}   *A*   Concerto for Transverse Flute and Strings, RV 429, in d -- see entries Nos.{11} and {1153}.

{1156}   *B*   Concerto for Oboe, RV 446, in C
Heinz Holliger, oboe; I Musici; Philips 411 480-2 [ADD] (TT=58.54). Includes Vivaldi's Concerti for Oboe, RV 447, in C, rated B; RV 452, in C, rated B; RV 454, in d, rated A; RV 463, in a, rated A and Concerto for Oboe and Bassoon, RV 545 in G, rated A (the bassoon soloist is Klaus Thunemann). All works other than the RV 446 are [DDD].

{1157}   *B*   Concerto for Oboe, RV 447, in C -- see entry No.{1156}.

{1158}   *B*   Concerto for Oboe, RV 452, in C -- see entry No.{1156}.

{1159}   *A*   Concerto for Oboe, RV 454, in d -- see entry No.{1156}.

{1160}   *A*   Concerto for Oboe, RV 463, in a -- see entry No.{1156}.

{1161}   *A*   Concerto for Oboe and Bassoon, RV 545 in G --
see entry No.{1156}.

{1162}   *B*   Concerto for Two Mandolins and Strings, RV 532,
in G -- see entry No.{60}.

{1163}   *A*   Concerto for Soprano Recorder, RV 443, in C --
see entry No.{1152}c.

{1164}   *B*   Concerto for Strings, RV 151, in G ("Alla
Rustica") -- see entry No.{60}.

{1165}   *B*   Concerto for Violin and String Orchestra,
(Concerti for Violin and String Orchestra, Op.8) ("Il Cimento
dell' armonia e dell' invenzione") ("The Contest Between
Harmony and Invention"), Op.8 (12) No.11, in D -- see entry
No.{11}.

{1166}   *B*   Concerto for Violin and String Orchestra,
(Concerti for Violin and String Orchestra, Op.8) ("Il Cimento
dell' armonia e dell' invenzione") ("The Contest Between
Harmony and Invention"), Op.8 (12) No.12, in C -- see entry
No.{11}.

{1167}   *B*   Concerto for Violin (L'Amoroso <"The
Amorous">),RV 271, in E -- see entry No.{1152}b.

{1168}   *A*   L'Estro armonico ("Harmonic Inspiration"), Op.3
(12) Nos.1-12
        I Musici; Philips 412 128-2 (2 discs) [DDD]
(TT=106.31).

WAGNER, RICHARD
1813-1883

335

Operatic

{1169}   *A*   Der fliegende Holländer ("The Flying Dutchman")
(1843)
Dunja Vejzovic, mezzo-soprano; Peter Hoffmann,
tenor; Thomas Moser, tenor; José van Dam, bass; Kurt Moll,
bass; Vienna State Opera Chorus; Berlin Philharmonic
Orchestra; Herbert von Karajan, conductor; Angel CDC 47053
(3 discs) [DDD] (TT = 146.10).

{1170}   *A*   Die Götterdämmerung ("The Twilight of the
Gods") (1876) (Number Four of Der Ring des Nibelungen
<"The Ring of the Nibelungs">)
Gwyneth Jones, soprano; Birgit Nilsson, soprano; Lucia
Popp, soprano; Claire Watson, soprano; Anita Välkki,
soprano; Grace Hoffmann, mezzo-soprano; Christa Ludwig,
mezzo-soprano; Helen Watts, contralto; Wolfgang
Windgassen, tenor; Dietrich Fischer-Dieskau, baritone; Gustav
Neidlinger, bass-baritone; Vienna State Opera Chorus; Vienna
Philharmonic Orchestra; Sir Georg Solti, conductor; London
414 115-2 (4 discs) [ADD] (TT = 265.42).

{1171}   *B*   Lohengrin (1850)
Jessye Norman, soprano; Eva Randová, mezzo-soprano;
Plácido Domingo, tenor; Dietrich Fischer-Dieskau, baritone;
Siegmund Nimsgern, bass; Hans Sotin, bass; Vienna State
Opera Chorus; Vienna Philharmonic Orchestra; Sir Georg
Solti, conductor; London 421 053-2 (4 discs) [DDD]
(TT = 223.24).

{1172}   *A*   Die Meistersinger von Nürenberg ("The Master
Singers of Nuremberg") (1868)
Caterina Ligendza, soprano; Christa Ludwig, mezzo-
soprano; Plácido Domingo, tenor; Dietrich Fischer Dieskau,
baritone; Roland Herrmann, baritone; Peter Lagger, bass;
German Opera Chorus and Orchestra, Berlin; Eugen Jochum,
conductor; DG 415 278-2 (4 discs) [ADD] (TT = 264.16)

{1173}   *B*   Parsifal (1882)
Christa Ludwig, mezzo-soprano; René Kollo, tenor; Dietrich Fischer-Dieskau, baritone; Hans Hotter, bass-baritone; Zoltan Kélémen, bass-baritone; Gottlob Frick, bass; Vienna State Opera Chorus; Vienna Philharmonic Orchestra; Sir Georg Solti, conductor; London 417 143-2 (4 discs) [ADD] (TT=259.50).

{1174}   *A*   Das Rheingold ("The Rhine Gold") (1869) (Number One of Der Ring des Nibelungen <"The Ring of the Nibelungs">)
Kirsten Flagstad, soprano; Claire Watson, soprano; Jean Madeira, mezzo-soprano; Ira Malaniuk, contralto; Hetty Plümacher, contralto; Paul Kuen, tenor; Set Svanholm, tenor; Eberhard Wächter, baritone; George London, bass-baritone; Gustav Neidlinger, bass-baritone; Kurt Böhme, bass; Walter Kreppel, bass; Vienna Philharmonic Orchestra; Sir Georg Solti, conductor; London 414 101-2 (3 discs) [ADD] (TT=145.53).

{1175}   *A*   Siegfried (1876) (Number Three of Der Ring des Nibelungen <"The Ring of the Nibelungs">)
Birgit Nilsson, soprano; Dame Joan Sutherland, soprano; Marga Höffgen, contralto; Gerhard Stolze, tenor; Wolfgang Windgassen, tenor; Hans Hotter, bass-baritone; Gustav Neidlinger, bass-baritone; Kurt Böhme, bass; Vienna Philharmonic Orchestra; Sir Georg Solti, conductor; London 414 110-2 (4 discs) [AAD] (TT=237.26).

{1176}   *B*   Tannhäuser (1865)
Anja Silja, soprano; Grace Bumbry, mezzo-soprano; Else-Margrete Gardelli, mezzo-soprano; Georg Paskuda, tenor; Gerhard Stolze, tenor; Wolfgang Windgassen, tenor; Eberhard Wächter, baritone; Franz Crass, bass; Josef Greindl, bass; Gerd Nienstedt, bass; Bayreuth Festival Chorus and

Orchestra (1962); Wolfgang Sawallisch, conductor; Philips 420 122-2 (3 discs) [ADD] (TT=170.22).

{1177}   *A*   Tristan und Isolde (1865)
Margaret Price, soprano; Brigitte Fassbaender, mezzo-soprano; Anton Dermota, tenor; Werner Götz, tenor; René Kollo, tenor; Dietrich Fischer-Dieskau, baritone; Kurt Moll, bass; Leipzig Radio Choir; Dresden State Orchestra; Carlos Kleiber, conductor; DG 413 315-2 (4 discs) [DDD] (TT=233.33).

{1178}   *A*   Love Death from Tristan und Isolde (1865)
Jessye Norman, soprano; London Symphony Orchestra; Sir Colin Davis, conductor; Philips 412 655-2 [ADD] (TT=41.03). Includes Wagner's Prelude to Tristan und Isolde (1865), rated A and Wesendonck Lieder ("Wesendonck Songs") (1857-1858), rated B.

{1179}   *A*   Die Walküre ("The Valkyries") (1870) (Number Two of Der Ring des Nibelungen <"The Ring of the Nibelungs">)
Régine Crespin, soprano; Birgit Nilsson, soprano; Christa Ludwig, mezzo-soprano; James King, tenor; Hans Hotter, bass-baritone; Gottlob Frick, bass; Vienna Philharmonic Orchestra; Sir Georg Solti, conductor; 414 105-2 (4 discs) [ADD] (TT=229.11).

Orchestral
{1180}   *A*   Siegfried's Rhine Journey and Siegfried's Funeral March from Die Götterdämmerung ("The Twilight of the Gods") (1876)
Philharmonia Orchestra; Otto Klemperer, conductor; Angel 47255 [AAD] (TT=64.35). Includes Wagner's Overture and Dance of the Apprentices to Die Meistersinger von Nürenberg ("The Master Singers of Nuremberg") (1868), rated A; Prelude to Parsifal (1882), rated B; Entry of the Gods into

Valhalla from <u>Das Rheingold</u> ("The Rhine Gold") (1869), rated A; Forest Murmurs from <u>Siegfried</u> (1876), rated A and Ride of the Valkyries from <u>Die Walküre</u> ("The Valkyries") (1870), rated A.

{1181}   *A*   Overture: <u>Der fliegende Holländer</u> ("The Flying Dutchman") (1843)

a   Chicago Symphony Orchestra; Sir Georg Solti, conductor; London 411 951-2 [ADD?] (TT=54.50). Includes Wagner's Overture: <u>Tannhäuser</u> (1865) and Prelude and Venusberg Music from <u>Tannhäuser</u>, rated A and Prelude to Act I of <u>Die Meistersinger von Nürenberg</u> ("The Master Singers of Nuremberg") (1868), rated A.

b   Philharmonia Orchestra; Otto Klemperer, conductor; Angel 47254 [AAD] (TT=65.59). Includes Wagner's Prelude to Act I of <u>Lohengrin</u> (1850), rated A; Overture: <u>Tannhäuser</u> (1865), rated A and Prelude and Love Death from <u>Tristan und Isolde</u> (1865), rated A.

{1182}   *A*   Prelude to Act I of <u>Lohengrin</u> (1850) -- see entry No.{1181}b.

{1183}   *A*   Overture and Dance of the Apprentices to <u>Die Meistersinger von Nürenberg</u> ("The Master Singers of Nuremberg") (1868) -- see entry No.{1180}.

{1184}   *A*   Prelude to Act I of <u>Die Meistersinger von Nürenberg</u> ("The Master Singers of Nuremberg") (1868) -- see entry No.{1181}a.

{1185}   *A*   Prelude to Act III of <u>Die Meistersinger von Nürenberg</u> ("The Master Singers of Nuremberg") (1868)
           Berlin Philharmonic Orchestra; Herbert von Karajan, conductor; DG 413 754-2 [DDD] (TT=50.04). Includes Wagner's Overture and Venusberg Music from <u>Tannhäuser</u>

339

(1865), rated A; Prelude and Love Death from <u>Tristan und Isolde</u> (1865), rated A.

{1186}   B   Prelude to <u>Parsifal</u> (1882) -- see entry No.{1180}.

{1187}   A   "Wedding March" from <u>Parsifal</u> (1882) -- see entry No.{290}.

{1188}   A   Entry of the Gods into Valhalla from <u>Das Rheingold</u> ("The Rhine Gold") (1869) -- see entry No.{1180}.

{1189}   A   Forest Murmurs from <u>Siegfried</u> (1876) -- see entry No.{1180}.

{1190}   A   Overture and Venusberg Music from <u>Tannhäuser</u> (1865) see entry No.{1185}.

{1191}   A   Prelude and Venusberg Music from <u>Tannhäuser</u> (1865) -- see entry No.{1181}a.

{1192}   A   Overture: <u>Tannhäuser</u> (1865) -- see entries Nos.{1181}a-b.

{1193}   A   Prelude to <u>Tristan und Isolde</u> (1865) -- see entry No.{1178}.

{1194}   A   Prelude and Love Death from <u>Tristan und Isolde</u> (1865) -- see entries Nos.{1181}b and {1185}.

{1195}   A   Ride of the Valkyries from <u>Die Walküre</u> ("The Valkyries") (1870) -- see entry No.{1180}.

Vocal
{1196}   B   <u>Wesendonck Lieder</u> ("Wesendonck Songs") (1857-1858) -- see entry No.{1178}.

WALDTEUFEL, CHARLES EMILE
1837-1915

Orchestral
{1197}   *A*   España Waltz, Op.263
Cincinnati Pops Orchestra; Erich Kunzel, conductor;
Vox Cum Laude MCD-10025 [DDD] (TT=40.37). Includes
Waldteufel's À Toi Waltz, Op.150; Bella Bocca Polka, Op.163;
Bella Mazurka, Op.113; Estudiantina Waltz, Op.191, rated A;
Grande Vitesse Galop, Op.146; Nuée d'Oiseaux Polka (1878?)
and Les Sirènes Waltz, Op.154.

{1198}   *A*   Estudiantina Waltz, Op.191 -- see entry
No.{1197}.

WALTON, SIR WILLIAM
1902-1983

Orchestral
{1199}   *B*   Crown Imperial Coronation March (1927)
Royal Philharmonic Orchestra; André Previn,
conductor; Telarc CD-80125 [DDD] (TT=59.04). Includes
Walton's Orb and Sceptre Coronation March (1953), rated B
and Symphony No.1 (1932-1935), in b flat, rated B.

{1200}   *B*   Orb and Sceptre Coronation March (1953) -- see
entry No.{1199}.

Symphonic
{1201}   *B*   Symphony No.1 (1932-1935), in b flat -- see entry
No.{1199}.

WEBER, CARL MARIA VON
1786-1826

Operatic

{1202}   *A*   Der Freischütz ("The Marksman") (1821)
Hildegard Behrens, soprano; Helen Donath, soprano;
René Kollo, tenor; Hermann Sapell, baritone; Raimund
Grumbach, bass; Peter Meven, bass; Kurt Moll, bass; Bavarian
Radio Chorus and Symphony Orchestra; Rafael Kubelik,
conductor; London 417 119-2 (2 discs) [ADD] (TT=134.09).

Orchestral

{1203}   *A*   Invitation to the Dance (Orchestrated by Berlioz),
Op.65 -- see entry No.{537}b.

WEINBERGER, JAROMIR
1896-1957

Orchestral

{1204}   *B*   Polka and Fugue from Schwanda the Bagpiper
(1927) -- see entries Nos.{348} and {362}a.

WIDOR, CHARLES-MARIE
1845-1937

Instrumental

{1205}   *C*   Toccata from the Organ Symphony No.5, Op.42
No.1, in f
Marie-Claire Alain, organ; Erato ECD-88111 [AAD]
(TT=65.06). Includes Widor's Symphonie gothique (1897) and
Organ Symphony No.6, Op.42 No.2, in g.

WOLF, HUGO
1860-1903

Vocal

{1206}   *B*   Goethe Lieder ("Goethe Songs") (1888-1889)
Dietrich Fischer-Dieskau, baritone; Gerald Moore,
piano; DG 415 192-2 [AAD] (TT = 63.14). Includes Wolf's
Mörike Lieder ("Mörike Songs") (1888), rated B.

{1207}   *B*   Mörike Lieder ("Mörike Songs") (1888) -- see
entry No.{1206}.

ZIMMERMANN, CHARLES
1861-1916

Orchestral

{1208}   *A*   Anchors Aweigh (1907) -- see entry No.{9}.

343

A

Q

INDEX

371

Y

Z